My Life among the Savage Nations
of New Spain

MY LIFE AMONG THE SAVAGE NATIONS OF NEW SPAIN

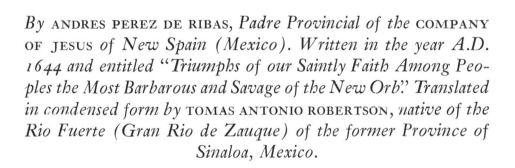

By ANDRES PEREZ DE RIBAS, *Padre Provincial of the* COMPANY OF JESUS *of New Spain (Mexico). Written in the year A.D. 1644 and entitled "Triumphs of our Saintly Faith Among Peoples the Most Barbarous and Savage of the New Orb". Translated in condensed form by* TOMAS ANTONIO ROBERTSON, *native of the Rio Fuerte (Gran Rio de Zauque) of the former Province of Sinaloa, Mexico.*

THE WARD RITCHIE PRESS
Los Angeles, California

Table of Contents

BOOK ONE

The Province of Sinaloa

BOOK TWO

Indian Nations of the Sierras of Topia

BOOK THREE

Missions of the Central Plateau of Mexico

Illustrations

Following pages 64, 128 and 192

Contemporary
MEXICO
with
Major Highways

Rio

Eagle Pass

vo Laredo • Laredo

85

VO LEON

★Monterrey

Brownsville
Matamoros

Linares

101

85

57

Ciudad
Victoria

TAMAULIPAS

80

S

C. Mante

OTOSI

85

n Luis
otosi

Valles

Tampico

an Luis
de la Paz

Tamazunchale

QTO.

ato

eretaro

Zimapán

45

HIDALGO

Pachuca

Mexico
City

85

Toluca FED. DIST.
MEXICO
Cuernavaca

Tlaxcala
TLAX.
Puebla

140 Jalapa

Cordoba

Tuxpan

VERACRUZ

Golfo

de

Mexico

Golfo de Compeche

Progreso

★ Merida

YUCATAN

Campeche

260

QUINTANA
ROO
(TER.)

Chetumal

261

Veracruz

Taxco

MOR.

190

PUEBLA

Orizaba

Lago
Catemaco

San Andres
Tuxtla

Coatzacoalcos

Escárcega

CAMPECHE

RO

95

lpancingo

OAXACA

180

Acayucan

Villa Hermosa

TABASCO

BR.
HOND.

apulco

Oaxaca

185

CHIAPAS

Tuxtla Gutiérrez

190 ★ San Cristóbal las Casas

Tehuantepec

190

Tonalá

Comitán

GUATAMALA

HONDURAS

200

Golfo
de Tehuantepec

Tapachula

EL SALVADOR

Introductory Chapter by Tomás A. Robertson, Translator of this History

THE PAST THREE YEARS of my life have been much enriched by association, even though across a span of well over three hundred years, with the personalities who still live, in the pages of this fascinating history of Padre Andrés Pérez de Ribas.

It was my good fortune to have been born and to have spent my boyhood, and some of the years since, among the Indians of the area called by Pérez de Ribas the Province of Sinaloa. During the period of which he writes, many Tribes or Nations, of diverse languages, populated the northwest coastal area of Mexico, principally along the borders of the Sonora, Yaqui, Mayo, Fuerte and Mocorito Rivers, from the Sierras to the Sea of Californias, as the Gulf of California is described in his writings.

I have in my possession a treasured volume, *Arte de la Lengua Cahita (Art of the Cahita Tongue)*, said to have been written by Padre Juan Bautista de Velasco about 1600, left in manuscript form until it was printed on a wooden press in 1737, being reprinted in 1890 from torn parts of three old volumes. This work is now unobtainable. Cahita is even today the language most common to the Indians of the Plains of Northwestern Mexico. However, I have not found one of those Indians who knew that this language had once upon a time been committed to writing.

During my boyhood, in the early years of this century, the Indians of the Fuerte River, by now called Mayos, still lived a life quite apart from their Mexican neighbors. I often sat with them at their campfires, listening to their songs, perhaps better described as chants, that were apt to be accompanied by the music of harps, violins or other stringed instruments of their own manufacture.

Religious days were very strictly observed by the Indians. Those who labored on our plantation always asked permission to go to their Mission villages of San Miguel or Mochicahui for their religious festivals. Their celebrations still include the dances of their ancient days, such as the famous Baile del Venado.

Celebrations leading up to Easter include many weeks of traveling about the countryside garbed in their hideous masks and costumes purporting to be those of the people who persecuted Jesus Christ.

In 1923, together with two companions, I traveled with a mule pack train from the old Mission pueblo of Sinaloa, so important in this story, upward day after day through those rugged Sierras which the good Padre so well describes, to one of the principal sources of the Petatlán (Sinaloa) River, the 11,000 foot peak of the Cerro de Mohinora in the State of Chihuahua. We found that mountain wilderness much as Pérez de Ribas describes it. We hunted wild turkey and deer, and had need to keep our animals near us at our campfire for several nights because of the approach of timber wolves. At one isolated rancho a jaguar came to disturb our slumber, fortunately in search of nothing other than the sheep and goats huddled in a stone corral.

In those high Sierras we found the Tepeguane Indians who figure so prominently in the second book of Pérez de Ribas. Their campfires burned in caves that had been formed by nature in cliffs across the gorges of the river. Many Tepeguanes still lived there, isolated from the world, descending to their caves by means of ladders, which they could remove to prevent others from intruding upon them.

This trail the Padres, including Pérez de Ribas, had used when journeying from the City of Mexico to Sinaloa via the Sierras of Durango, some of them even before the year 1600.

In 1943 I packed with some friends from near Parral, mining center in the foothills of the State of Chihuahua, riding westward into the great Mexican Sierra Madre, in search of a lost lake, not known even to the Forestry Service of Mexico. Our Tarahumara Indian guide had been to this lost Laguna de Juanota with his parents when eight years of age.

We rode our animals in the footsteps of this little Indian for five days, became lost on a great timbered plateau dotted with little lakes, saw deer and timber wolves, and finally came upon this place, wondrous to behold, some two miles of deep blue water nestled into a circle of peaks and promontories, with a great castle rock standing above an island in the center of the lake.

This was the sacred land of the Tarahumaras. Little José Pastrano, our guide, warned us that we must not remain here overnight so we lingered but a few hours to drink in the beautiful scene, then rode away through a flurry of snow into the forest.

From our guide we heard many interesting tales. The Tarahumaras were still governed by a council composed of the Chiefs of their various little villages. Their code of honesty is strict, especially relating to theft. One punishment is to be put into stocks, reminiscent of the stories of the Pilgrim fathers in New England, except that the Tarahumaras accustomed placing the culprit on his back on the cold hard ground, his ankles enclosed in the stocks, where he was kept without food or shelter for the time corresponding to his crime, even though this punishment might result in death.

In 1952 I traveled first by plane and then by back of mule, to the abandoned mining center of Guadalupe y Calvo, in the State of Chihuahua, once so rich in silver that a Federal Mint had been established there, even though the area is many days pack from nearest rail or highway transportation. This was a thrilling adventure, for we were in search of buried treasure. Traveling down a stream which is a principal source of the Fuerte River (*Gran Rio de Zuaque*) we came upon the lovely Mission of Nabogame, said to date back to the 1600's. Here too we found Tepeguane Indians, who although not favored by regular visits of a Padre, were very faithful in their worship at the old Mission.

The story of the Indian Nations of the Gulf of Mexico, the Isthmus of Te-huantepec and the central and southern highlands has been well told by numerous writers of the era following the conquest of Mexico by Hernan Cortéz; this despite the destruction of so many of their artifacts and records by the conquering Spaniards.

However, except for this conscientuous and comprehensive writing of Pérez de Ribas, there was little recorded, during that early period, relating to the Indian Nations of the northwestern mountainous and coastal areas, nor of the desert eastward towards the Great Laguna de San Pedro (*present State of Coahuila*).

In a previous work, *A Southwestern Utopia;* The Ward Ritchie Press, Los Angeles, California, I have pointed out that the Indians of the areas now comprising the United States were largely hunters, traveling with the seasons, so did not easily adjust to the new civilization and have practically disappeared. In contrast, the Indians of Mexico in greater part were settled into permanent villages, were engaged in agriculture and advanced in handicrafts and were generally more peaceful in nature. Although often enslaved by the Spaniards, and though many were killed, or died from hardship or disease, they have survived to become the dominant race of Mexico today.

The Indians of the Northwestern area principally referred to in this history were a rugged, savage people. It fell to the lot of the Jesuit Padres to change them into "rational human beings," as Pérez de Ribas expresses it, and often to defend them from the impositions of the Spanish Conquistadores.

I do not happen to be of the same faith as the author, yet through the pages of his remarkable memoirs, for such in reality they are, I have come to hold a great admiration, respect and affection for this fine Padre and those others who so greatly labored among the Indians there, and only hope that through this translation I may, paraphrasing the words of his friendly critics of long ago, help to again bring him and his dedicated fellow workers back from the verge of oblivion.

In the course of the history there appear some fantastic characters; Captain General don Diego Martinez de Hurdaide; the Indian woman Luisa; the Cacique don Batista; the great Chief Sisibotari; the Indian Padre Lorenzo, and not least of all the many Jesuit Padres who dedicated their lives so cheerfully to the perilous task of civilizing such multitudes of Indians.

Perhaps the most outstanding of all the characters who are mentioned was the author, Padre Andrés Pérez de Ribas, yet his modesty was such that it has been necessary to picture his adventurous life largely from stories of the lives of others with whom he was associated.

In reference to Pérez de Ribas, as well as to other persons and events, I have taken the liberty of relocating phrases, paragraphs or whole chapters where indicated, for the purpose of giving easier continuity in reading. However, the reader may be assured that all that appears in this briefed translation may be found in the substance of the text in Spanish.

In conclusion, I must apologize in spirit to the author for the necessity of reducing his beautiful and scholarly work to one volume, in the interest of saving time for the reader, that time which is considered of so much value here, and of so little in eternity.

TOMÁS ANTONIO ROBERTSON
Villa de San Miguel
Ensenada, Baja California
Mexico
January 1967

Biographical Sketch of The Author
Andres Perez de Ribas

THE PROLOGUE to the 1944 printing of this History has been written by my very esteemed friend Raul Cervantes Ahumada, President of the National Bar Association of Mexico, distinguished jurist, educator and historian, who terms it the most authentic history written of the Indian Nations of the Northwest of Mexico, and of their conquest and subsequent civilization by the Spanish Crown and the Church of Spain.

Cervantes Ahumada is himself a native of the area of the Petatlán (*Sinaloa*) River, scene of much of the action described in this History. He provides this interesting biographical data regarding Andrés Pérez de Ribas:

He was born an Andalucian, in Córdoba, Spain, of a distinguished family. Ordained to the priesthood in the Company of Jesus at an unusually early age, after a few years in the ministry in Spain, he was designated for Missionary service in Mexico in 1603, at twenty seven years of age.

After a brief period of preparation, Pérez de Ribas departed for the Northwestern frontier, the distant Province of Sinaloa, in 1604.

He traveled in the company of the famous frontiersman, Captain General don Diego Martinez de Hurdaide. The adventures, adversities and triumphs of this Captain and Padre form a very principal part of this History.

Pérez de Ribas labored for sixteen years, from 1604 to 1620, in the Missions of Sinaloa, on the Petatlán (*Sinaloa*), the Gran Rio de Zuaque (*Fuerte*), and the Yaqui Rivers, returning then to posts of successively higher importance in the City of Mexico, until becoming Padre Provincial, in charge of all the activities of the Jesuit Order in New Spain.

It is known that Pérez de Ribas once journeyed from Mexico to Rome as the representative to the Eighth World Congregation of Catholic Churches.

His later life was to a great extent dedicated to the writing of numerous valuable histories, dealing largely with the activities of the Catholic Church and the Spanish Crown in the New World.

In the History which is here translated he writes principally of his years among, (quoting from his title page), "peoples the most barbarous and savage of the New Orb."

His death came in 1655, at 79 years of age.

Cervantes Ahumada describes this History as "fundamental to the study of the early History of Sinaloa and Sonora," stating that "Pérez de Ribas writes with brilliance of style, clearly and truthfully; a singular master among historians."

Among the approvals required in 1645 for publication of such a History may be found these laudatory phrases:

By Fray Alonzo de la Corte, Representative of the Crown in Spain: "All must enjoy this pleasing story of so many and varied events of which are told. To this author it is owed by those dedicated workers of Church and Crown of whom he writes, that they have been brought back, through the pages of his History, from the verge of oblivion."

From the Most Reverend Ivan Ponce de Leon, Judge of the Council of His Majesty for the Sainted and General Inquisition: "This is a work most worthy of its distinguished author. In it he shows throughout the charity of thought and deed which are so much a part of his character . . ."

Padre Pérez de Ribas himself fixes the theme for his story, by declaring that, ". . . in the History of these Missions, the motives of Divine Providence are so enlaced with those human and political in nature that I should not, and could not disunite them, and do not doubt that it will be more pleasing to the reader to have them treated together . . ."

The interesting manner in which these matters of humanity and divinity are treated in this story, which relates to the Indian Nations of Mexico, will be disclosed in the pages to follow.

BOOK I

THE PROVINCE OF SINALOA

BOOK I

The Province of Sinaloa

NEW SPAIN
(MEXICO)

16th and 17th Centuries

(Imuris)
HUMERIS

(Nacozari)
NACOSURAS

(Cumpas)
CUMUPAS

(Guasabas)
BUASDABAS

(Ures)
HURES
BATUCOS
Batuc • Suaqui
SUAQUIS
(PIMAS)
UPPER NEBOMES
• Sahuaripa
SISIBOTARIS

SONORAS

HERIS
(SERIS)

Rio

Sonora

Rio

• Teeoripa

(PIMAS)
LOWER NEBOMES

• Onavas

CABEZA DE VACA RANGE

(Chihuahua)

• Movas

Cumuripa • • Cabeza
de Vaca

GUAYAMAS

YAQUIS

NURES

Yaqui

Rio

Mayo

Rio

CHINIPAS
GUASAPARIS
TEMORIS
HUITES
ZOES

Quiriego
TEPAGUES
Tepahui
MAYOS
Rio
Baeabachi

• Conicari

CONICARIS

TARAHUMARAS

Parral

Santa Barbara

BACABACHIS
MONTARASES

BACOREGUIS

(Choix)

• Toro

SINALOAS
• Fuerte
• Tegueco
TEGUECOS
OCORONIS

Rio Fuerte

ZAQUES
San Miguel
AHOMES
Ahome

• Moehieahui

Sinaloa
Petatlan

Rio
• Bacubirito

• Bamoa

Guasave •
GUASAVES

• Mocorito

Bahia
San Ignacio

Badiraguato •

Rio Humaya

ACAXEES
Topia

Isla
San José

Rio Culiacan

XIXIMES

• Santiago
Papasqui

Culiacan

TEPEGUANES

Bahia
de
La Paz

Otatitlan

GUAICURAS

San Pedro

San Ignaeio
San Javier •

Santa Apolonia

Gu
(I

HINAS

HUMIS

Yamoriba

Quelite •

• San Sebastián
(Concordia)

Mazatlán •

• Chiametla
(Chametla)

Acaponeta

MAR DEL SUR

OCEANO PACIFICO

CHAPTER 1

Location, Climate, Rivers, Forests and Animal Life

THE PROVINCE OF SINALOA lies 900 miles northwestward of the City of Mexico, Capital of the very extended Empire of New Spain (*Mexico*). From its southern border on the Petatlán (*Sinaloa*) River it extends northward some 500 miles to the fortieth parallel. Still north of here live innumerable savage Nations, without knowledge now of the end of them. Eastward lie the extremely high Sierras of Topia, for distances of one to two hundred miles, until descending to the great Central Plateau of Mexico. Westward the Province of Sinaloa is limited by the arm of the Sea of Californias, which continues in a generally northerly direction.

To the south of the headquarters Mission of Sinaloa on the Petatlán River lies the very ancient pueblo of San Miguel de Culiacán, now capital of the Province of Culiacán. [*Pérez de Ribas gives distances in leagues which, for convenience of the reader have been transposed into miles, in the ratio of three miles to one league.*]

The temperature of this land is torrid, despite the fact that in mid-winter it may be very cold. In summer the heat is so great that riding animals may have their grease melted within them and fall dead, or become so exhausted that it is necessary to bleed them.

Rains are short, particularly along the seacoast, where it may rain only three or four times yearly. These rains usually come in summer, God thus disposing it that the heat may be tolerated.

The land is healthful, because of the dryness of its soil and climate.

Were it not for the great rivers which flow from its Sierras across the plains to the Sea of Californias, it would be uninhabitable for man, as there are scarcely any other sources of water.

The greater part of this Province is a vast plain, covered with brambles and forests of such trees as rosewood, brazil and ebony. This forest is so dense for many miles that even birds cannot fly through it, and it serves only as a shelter for wild beasts.

However, in the areas of the rivers there are many agreeable valleys, with open land, shaded by great cottonwood trees.

In the dense forests there are many jabalí (*peccary*), deer, lions and leopards. These leopards are not so large as those of Africa. There are tigers (*jaguars*), immensely strong creatures, but fortunately not accustomed to eating human flesh, as within the woods they easily find their food.

There are several varieties of wild cats, foxes and many other vermin, as well as poisonous snakes.

In the river valleys there are great flights of birds such as quail, doves and pheasants (*chachalacas*) and at certain times of the year many sand hill cranes (*grullas*). There are parrots in great variety, including the papagallos and the larger guacamayas, whose plumes are esteemed by the Indians in their dress. There are many other smaller birds.

Some of the rivers are large. All have their source in the great mountain ranges of Topia. In times of great rains or snows, their waters flood over the fields and plains, to a width of several miles.

It is difficult to find, along these rivers, secure locations for habitations or churches. The Indians, in time of floods, which may last for several days, assure their safety and that of their families in a fashion uniquely accomodated to their manner of living. They place several poles horizontally through the upper branches of the larger trees, upon these laying straw, and finally earth. Here they build their fires and make their habitation until the waters have receded.

When the churches, even those on highest ground, have been flooded, the Christian Indians have sometimes carried us Padres on their shoulders for as far as five miles to the safety of these trees.

Along the rivers there are many kinds of duck and geese. At the river entrances to the sea there abound alligators, which inhabit there in droves, capturing fish for their food. Even man they sometimes capture, so that the Indians dare not cross the rivers at such places except in great numbers, all making noise to frighten these fierce animals.

The grip of their jaws and teeth is so strong that, once taken, they cannot be loosed, except by the loss of the limb; and so not few Indians have died in their grip.

The Sea of the Californias is of great benefit to the Indians, especially those who inhabit near the entrances of rivers to the sea, as here there is fish in such abundance, especially mullet (*lisa*) and snook (*robalo*), that Indians sent to fish have returned in two hours with a catch of over 1,000 pounds (*50 arrobas*).

They use sisal nets which they draw through the water, sometimes in the open sea, at others in lagoons or estuaries (*esteros*) of which there are many along these shores. Others kill fish with bow and arrow, especially in estuaries with little water.

Another manner of catching fish in large quantities by the Indians, as recently as this century, was to build extensive brush walls across tidal flats, leaving open spaces for the fish to enter at high tide. As the tide receded, the fish would follow along the inside of the brush wall, seeking an outlet, and soon would become trapped in a cleverly built interior wall in which they became confused and remained until the tide had left them stranded]

Here, too, are found quantities of oysters, clams and other shellfish, which the Indians use for food.

The coastal Indians have numerous salt deposits, from water accumulated in pools. This salt must be freed by beating it with clubs. It is used for trading with Indians farther inland, receiving in exchange woven cloth and other articles.

The terminus of this arm of the Sea of the Californias has not yet been discovered (*1645*) nor is it known if it communicates with the Northern Sea (*Atlantic Ocean*) or if it ends in land.

Certainly it is well known, because of reports of pearls growing there, for at times these have been taken up to the 32nd parallel.

In this year past Admiral don Pedro Porter de Cassanate has come, by order of our King Felipe Cuarto, to explore and populate those opposite shores.

In the Sierras of this Province there are rich deposits of silver. They have not yet been greatly exploited because of the poor means for doing so.

CHAPTER 2

Nations of Sinaloa

I CALL NATIONS the various groups of Indians of this Province, not because they are so populous as the Nations of Europe but because they live so separate, one group from another.

Some of these Nations speak in a different language than others, although there is a similarity running through all their languages.

There is a definite division of boundaries of the land occupied by each. Anyone daring to enter the land of another Nation is in peril of leaving his head in the hands of his enemies, and his flesh in their cooking ollas.

The habitations of these people are ordinarily along the borders of the rivers for there is little water elsewhere. In the time of their paganism their habitations were small villages or rancherias, rarely as much as a few miles apart, depending on where they should find water and lands for planting.

Their houses are constructed of poles buried at intervals in the ground. About these poles is woven brush to form walls. These brush walls are bound together with reeds, after which they are plastered with mud to keep out rain, wind and sun. The roofs are made of poles, then straw, over which is placed a layer of earth, and with this shelter they are apt to be content. [*Many of these houses with roofs of earth are still to be seen in the countryside of Sinaloa and Sonora.*]

Others make their houses of mats of bamboo, sewn together to form a wall and roof which is supported over poles formed into arches. These roofs somewhat resemble in form the covered carts of Spain.

Facing their houses they build brush covered sheds to provide shelter from the sun. On these sheds they are apt to store the products of their fields. Under these sheds they sleep in warm weather, upon mattresses made of a series of bamboo poles lashed side by side to each other.

They have neither door nor key to their houses, nor have any fear of thieves.

In their absence, they content themselves by placing tree branches before their entrances.

The principal crop which these people cultivate is maiz, which in Spain is called wheat of the Indies. It bears in such multiplicity that it is apt to yield a hundred fanegas for one fanega seeded. Between the hills of corn they plant pumpkins of several varieties, all tasty and sweet. Of some of these they make slices (*tasajo*) which when dried may last for the greater part of a year. They also plant beans, which are a seed similar to the horse bean (*haba*) of Castile, only more well flavored. They also harvest many wild seeds from their fields and woods.

A principal form of sustenance in its season (*May-June*) is the pod of a tree which is called mesquite. These pods, when ground, they drink with water and this drink, being somewhat sweet, is to these people what chocolate is to the Spaniards. The woods abound with these trees and many others which bear edible pods or fruit. They also use as food the plant of the *mescal* (*agave family*). This plant is celebrated in their histories. After its spike-shaped leaves are removed, it is roasted in a pit, then pounded to release its juice and hasten fermentation. From this juice is made a wine (*tequila*), or a syrup, or vinegar. From its leaves is extracted the sisal fiber, which has many uses. The head, being very sweet when roasted, is a principal source of food. This plant only do they cultivate near their houses, and no other. There are many prickly pears in the woods. These cacti in Castile are called "figs of the Indies."

Plants from Castile which do particularly well in these lands include oranges, figs, watermelons and other melons, all of which are extremely delicious.

I have first told of the Nations which inhabit the borders of the rivers. There are many others of the most barbarous ever known, who neither till the soil, nor plant, nor have any abode, nor defense against the inclemencies of the weather. The mode of living of these is the most strange of any of the human race, and is well to know of, to comprehend to what misery people may arrive.

Some of these people live in the denseness of the forest. Others live near salt water lagoons and among the dunes of the sea. The first support themselves by hunting, or eating roots and fruits from the woods, drinking water from little pools collected from rains. The others live by fishing from the sea. For lack of fish, they may gather locusts, snakes or other insects and animals for food.

At certain seasons the Indians who live along the seashore go up country to assist in the harvesting of corn, for which they may receive a portion of the harvest; or they may exchange corn for dried fish.

At other times these Indians harvest the seed of a plant which grows under the sea. This they use for bread. Incredible as it may seem to people of the nations of Europe, these people sustain themselves the greater part of the year without bread, eating instead either fish, or little seeds, or fruits of the woods.

The fruit which they enjoy for the longest period is of the pitahaya, a tree unknown to Europe. Its branches are several inches in diameter, and of the nature of thorny green striated wax tapers extending as much as thirty feet in height.

6

The fruit grows from these thorny striated branches and is, itself, covered with thorns. It is similar in appearance to a chestnut, or to a prickly pear. Its interior consistency is much like that of a fig, although softer and more delicate. Its color is at times white, at others red, or yellow. It is very savory, particularly when harvested before the rains which come in summer. The abundance of these pitahayas is such that one may often travel among them for a distance of 10 or 20 miles.

The foods mentioned are the principal sustenance of all these pilgrim Nations. It is worthy of note that, despite their having so little food, and that little so difficult to acquire, they are the most muscular people, and of the largest stature, of any of the Nations of New Spain; in fact, comparing favorably in size with people of Europe. They are very agile and swift and, though existing on such short rations, live until a decrepit age.

I shall now describe their manner of securing themselves from the inclemencies of the weather. When it rains, they make use of a bundle of straw taken from the fields or woods, tying it together at one end, then turning it over their heads in the way of a cape, spreading it to cover the body on all sides. By seating themselves under this covering, they are secure from the rain, although it should last all through the day and night.

Against the hot sun they have no better defense than to place some branches of trees upright in the earth and sit, live and sleep under their shade. Against the winds they have no defense; they must be suffered on their bare skin. During the more rigorous nights they build fires, lying on the earth near them. This protection from cold they are apt to use also when traveling at night. In such case they build a series of fires some distance apart, and on arriving at a fire, lie down to rest and sleep before continuing their journey. If an Indian wishes to travel several miles in the night his practice is to carry a lighted faggot, holding it before the middle of his body, leaving the rest of the body exposed to the wind. These wandering people are many less in numbers than the tillers of the soil. It may be truthfully said that with this manner of life they seem more content than if they had all the possessions and palaces of the world.

CHAPTER 3

Customs of the Indians of Sinaloa

THE INDIANS OF SINALOA had the vice of drunkeness to an exaggerated degree. They spent days and nights drinking, not just alone, nor in their homes, but in public, with constant invitation one to another.

They made wine in large pottery ollas, inviting people of the nearby rancherias to drink with them. As there were so many people who made wine, there never was a lack of invitation to drink.

Their intoxicating drinks they made of various plants and fruits, such as tunas, pitayas, or the pod of the mesquite tree. We have already mentioned that heads of the mescal plants, after roasting, are also commonly used. Placed in water for two or three days, these products become fermented, and they quickly affect the sensibilities of people so that they are no longer rational souls.

Of all the wines, the most esteemed was that of the honey bee, taken in its season.

No women took part in this drunkeness, nor did workers of the lower classes nor people newly arrived in a village.

Drunken orgies were held especially when they were assembling for war or in celebration of a victory. The beheading of an enemy was motive for a general dance, with much drinking. At such dances, the beating of their war drums could be heard three miles away. Women entered into these dances also. The head or scalp, or perhaps a limb of the victim, would be hoisted on a pole in the central plaza and the dance would be celebrated around it. There would be much barbarous clamor, including insults to the dead enemy, and there would be songs of victory. These scenes took on altogether the appearance of a real hell, with Devils leading them in their orgy.

At such feasts an important ritual was the offering of tobacco, which was much used by all those barbarous peoples. Should one Nation invite another to join with them in making war, the form of invitation was to send bamboo canes filled with tobacco, which was smoked in these canes. If the canes were accepted this signified an alliance for war.

Wars were carried on continuously, by one neighbor group against another, killing one or another in open combat or in ambush while in their fields, or in surprise attacks at dawn (*Albazos, derived from "alba" — the dawn*). In these battles there was no pardon for age or sex; rather there was much boasting over the killing even of women and children. The names of the warriors often were taken from some particularly horrible murder they had committed. Rarely did they take captives. When they did, these were made slaves. Because of these continuous wars, the people of a Nation had little communication nor commerce with more distant Nations.

The arms generally used by the Indians are bow and arrow. The arrows they carry in quivers suspended over their shoulders. In the use of these weapons they are dextrous in the extreme, for having exercised their use since childhood. As soon as a child can walk a small bow is placed in his hands and he is taught to shoot lizards, which move so rapidly that the child soon becomes swift and accurate in his shooting. In the time that a Spanish soldier may shoot an arquebus, an Indian will shoot ten or a dozen arrows.

Most of their arrows are smeared with an herb so poisonous that if it has been recently applied to the arrow, with the least penetration of the flesh there is no means of the wounded person escaping with his life. Another of their barbarous customs is to plant, in the trails of their enemies, pointed hardwood spikes covered with this same poison, with only the bare point protruding. As they usually walk barefooted, many lose their lives from the poison of these pointed barbs. A wound from an arquebus, if it falls on an arm or leg, is not apt to be mortal, but from the wounds of poisoned barbs and arrows, there is no salvation.

In open combat, at close range, they use a macana, which is a great club of hardwood, which at one blow can crack a skull. Others use a long spear (*chuzo*) of pointed brazil wood. These weapons are apt to be used by their captains or leaders.

For defense, the principal leaders carry small shields covered with alligator hide which resists arrows, except at very close range. They wrap the fur of the marten about the left wrist and forearm, as protection from the terrific blow of the bow string after the arrow has been fired. In firing, their bows are drawn with such force that the ends almost touch; and their speed and accuracy is surprising. When they fight, their movement of body is so rapid, now prostrate, now elevated, or swiftly shifting, that they make a difficult target.

When going to war their principal captains wear capes of tightly woven cotton, which are dyed deep blue. [*This dye was from the indigo plant which grows along the rivers of Sinaloa.*] These capes are often adorned with shells of mother of pearl, which make a bright show. They also wear charms of these same shells about their necks.

There had to be the vice of immorality where there was so much drunkeness and they were so possessed by Devils. However, only the chiefs usually accustomed having several wives. Their weddings ordinarily were insoluble. Weddings of maidens were celebrated with solemnity. Marriage usually was with consent of the parents. During the ceremony there was removed from the neck of the bride the mother of pearl necklace that attested to her maindenhood.

I was pleased to observe the security with which women and maidens traveled their trails alone, without offense from anyone. Nor are these Indians so barbarous that they fail to admire the purity of the life of Evangelical Ministers.

The vice of cannibalism, instituted by the Devil, was practiced generally among these Nations. Among the Acaxees and other mountain tribes this practice was as common as the eating of wild animals. As they went forth hunting for deer, so did they for human flesh. They searched out their enemies in the fields and woods and, if taken, they were cut into pieces and cooked in the large earthen pots (*ollas*) or roasted. Some of the Nations practiced cannibalism only on their bravest enemies, whose flesh when eaten was supposed to multiply the strength of those who ate it. However, since the doctrine of Christianity has been accepted, this savage and barbarous custom has been eradicated.

They had no written laws, nor rulers with sufficient authority to enforce them. They did recognize the authority of certain principal chiefs (*Caciques*) who served as heads of family groups, or of rancherias, but their sole privilege was to determine whether they should wage war or make peace. In these cases

9

no decision was made except through them. Before going to war there were celebrated great dances, with much drunkeness. A privilege of a Cacique was to have a somewhat larger field, and the help of others in its cultivation. The Caciques acquired their authority not so much by inheritance as by valor in war, or by being the head of a large family clan. On occasion they acquired their office by being great orators and prophets, in their own opinion.

These primitive Nations had no knowledge of letters, painting or art. Their knowledge of agriculture was limited to their own fields. For planting and cultivating these, they made use of some wide and long blades of wood with which they turned the soil. In this occupation they were assisted by their women.

Women practiced the art of spinning and weaving, not only cotton, but other fibers such as those used for ropes in Castile. From these various fibers they made sheets of cloth, not on looms, of which they had no knowledge, but in a more laborious manner, by driving two rows of stakes opposite to each other, from which they stretched strands which were then cross-woven in the opposite direction.

The dress of these people was usually very scant. The men wore almost nothing. The women were covered from the waist down with the cloths which they wove. The women who did not weave were apt to cover themselves with a skirt of buckskin. On these buckskin garments the women sometimes painted colors of ochre or Indian Red; this was especially a practice of the better looking women. These also painted their faces and suspended little stone pendants from their ears. Children from birth are covered with a garment of cotton. Of the males it could be said that they went naked, for although some among them wore garments of cotton or fiber, these they would put on or throw off at will.

The people of whom we now speak were those who lived in the more populated places. There were other poorer and more isolated Nations who used even less dress, although the women always wore some covering, even though of leaves of plants. In this they proved themselves to be true daughters of Adam and Eve, who covered themselves with leaves, in shame of their sin, until God chose to clothe them in the skins of animals.

Men as well as women wear their hair long. Some women carry it falling from their shoulders; others wear it braided about their heads. The women much esteem their hair. The men usually carry their hair gathered together, encircled by an attractive band or crown plaited from palm leaves and adorned with bright colored plumes. Upon entering the woods for hunting they bind their hair in a covering of buckskin, that it may not be caught in the branches of the trees.

There was peace and concord among the families of each Nation, and freedom from deceit, fraud or trickery which is still so common in the more enlightened countries of the world. What they possessed they shared with liberality, even with strangers, so long as they were not enemies. Strangers who appeared at time of meals were invited and served as though in their own homes.

Such were the customs of these people in the time of their paganism, before the coming of the Law of Christ, which is the Law of Peace, and which joins and binds even savage peoples in Christian charity and clemency toward each other.

CHAPTER 4

Hunting Practices, Games and Diversions

HUNTING was a very principal occupation. The forests abounded with deer, wild peccary, jack rabbits, cotton tail rabbits, and other animals useful for food. Sometimes the Indians killed tigers, lions, wolves or foxes; although these were sought more for their skins, which served many useful purposes. Hunting also was helpful to them for maintaining their skill with bow and arrow for time of war.

Some of their hunts were general, participated in by all the people of a rancheria. They also hunted individually, the smaller boys beginning with shooting quail and doves. In a general hunt, a circle was cleared around a brushy thicket, and fenced in with broken trees and branches to contain the game within the circle. If the hunt were in the dry season, the woods within the circle were set on fire. The hunters surrounded the area, bow and arrow in hand. Fire caused all the animals, even serpents, to flee. Few escaped the hunters arrows and, these arrows being poisoned, any wounded animals that did escape would be found dead not later than the day following.

It should be noted that the poison from the arrow does not affect the meat of the animal poisoned.

The manner of locating the dead animals is by watching the buzzards circling overhead. The whole animal is roasted when found, and all partake of the feast.

The Indians are avid hunters of Iguanas, a lizard of the appearance of an alligator, which in this land grows to two palms in length. These are to be found in the trunks of hollow trees, also around places where there is water, and so are deemed as fish and may be eaten on the days when meat is forbidden. They are savory and healthful. In some of them are found small stones which are medicinal, being effective for urinal trouble. The Indians are most clever in extracting these Iguanas from the trunks of the trees, and at once break their jaws to prevent their biting, after which they are carried in bundles, secured one Iguana to the other, to be kept for several days if desired.

Indians do not hunt on the day a child is born; considering this would bring misfortune to the child.

One of their favorite occupations is hunting for wild honey. The little native bees, although they do not make wax, do provide a honey that is sweet and fragrant, comparing favorably with the finest of Castile. Bee hives are circular in form, and if large may measure a vara (33 inches) in diameter. The entrance to the hive is only large enough to admit one bee. Hives are formed around a forked branch, usually high in the tree.

An Indian looking for honey goes to an open clearing, preferably a lagoon where bees come for water. Here he observes the course of flight of the bees, following them to the location of the hive, which is then removed by severing the branches. The Indians not only enjoy the honey, but the small bees, which in their worm-like stage, are eaten after being toasted over a fire.

Of their games, that called patoli is very common. It corresponds closely to the playing of dice in Europe. However, instead of dice they use short pieces of split bamboo, on which are carved figures to indicate the points to be made. These are shaken in a leather cup, then cast upon a flat stone that they may scatter well. The points scored are marked upon the ground until a game is finished. In this game they wager little strings of sea shells, which are highly prized for their adornment. They may also wager bows and arrows, knives or axes.

Another celebrated game is called "running the ball," and is much practiced to help to condition them for war. For this game they gather in large numbers, one pueblo often challenging another. Each side has its own ball, which is round, made of heavy wood, and only a short span in diameter. Its center is hollowed to admit the toes of a player. The balls of the competing teams are let drop simultaneously to begin the game, the players kicking the ball, with toes inserted, with such force that a ball thrown with the arm could carry no further. No person may touch the ball except with the feet, but may use a stick to move the ball into a position to be kicked. Players are posted ahead to play the ball from where it lands, and so the game continues to a given point, perhaps five or more miles distant, from where it is returned to the starting point; the side to first return the ball winning the game. After this violent exercise all the participants plunge into the river, to bathe in great contentment. [*This game is still played in Sinaloa, only using a hard rubber ball. In 1943 I saw it being played by the Tarahumara Indians, who kicked the ball while circling the shores of Laguna de Juanota, in Chihuahua.*]

These Nations play another game, ule, with a ball of compressed rubber. It is played on a court prepared for the purpose, often in the plaza of the pueblo. The playing field is called Batei. [*This game, now called pelota, is still being played in Sinaloa.*] Teams may be of four, six or eight Indians, each team confronting the other. The ball is bounced from the nearest player on one team to a player on the other, and from there the game continues until a score is made, usually by bouncing it high over the heads of the opponents to cross their goal line. The unusual feature of this game is that the ball must not be touched by the hand, but can only be played on with shoulder or hip. It is a dangerous game, in which players have been known to lose their lives by permitting the ball to strike them in the stomach. After each game players, and spectators as well, refresh themselves by diving into the river. In bathing they take great joy and all swim like fish. With this I pass on to other matters, but it is well to tell of some of their customs and diversions, although they may seem less important than other matters.

CHAPTER 5

Idolatry and Witchcraft

THESE PEOPLE without doubt are atheists. They have lived with minds closed to all divine light, which is fundamental to eternal salvation. There were among them some evidences of idolatry. They had no knowledge of any Diety, even though a false one, nor concept of a God who should rule the Universe.

They did have certain barbarous superstititions. Witchcraft was practiced by persons who were influenced by the Devil. These persons, called Hechiceros, would usually, before their death, pass on their arts to their descendents, such arts being for the purpose of healing or deceiving, or even murdering, in order to maintain their authority. The Hechiceros, being much in league with the Devil, are those most opposed to acceptance of the Evangelical doctrine by the Indians. They apply all their intelligence to persuading the pueblos to rise, burn the Christian churches, and return to the woods.

A method of healing by these doctors of the Devil is to blow on the afflicted part of the body, which they do with such force that they may be heard many paces away. Others suck the afflicted area, trying to make sick persons believe that they are, by this procedure, removing from their bodies little sticks, thorns or pebbles which are purported to be the cause of their pain. These articles the Hechiceros have concealed in their mouths, or in their hands, very cleverly producing them at the proper time to impress their victim. They will also suck poison from a wound, a practice which is beneficial and could be condoned, were these healers not so much in league with the Devil.

They carry, wrapped carefully in the hide of some small animal such as a ferret, a collection of small, brightly colored stones. These they guard jealously. If at time of baptism an Indian gives up such a treasure, it is a very good indication that he is truly receiving the Faith of Christ.

The image of Christ they are apt to call "Grandfather." The Devil they are apt to envision as an animal or a serpent. Sometimes they depicted these animals in drawings. They also might erect a stone, or a piece of wood, to represent the figures so drawn, and worship before it. To this extent they could be said to practice idolatry.

One of the important offices of the Hechiceros was to preach sermons to the pueblos. The Caciques also preached sermons. The most probable occasions for the sermons were to plan for war, or to discuss terms of peace with other

Nations, or with the Spaniards. On such occasion there gathered in the evening, in the Plaza of the pueblo, the principal Caciques and Hechiceros. In the center of the Plaza they would build a fire, seating themselves in a circle about it, all lighting their pipes of bamboo. Then there would arise the Indian of greatest authority among them to deliver an oration. Presently, leaving the circle, he would pace slowly about the Plaza, continuing his sermon in a high voice, finally shouting so that he might be heard by all the pueblo. In this turn of the Plaza he might pass a half hour before returning to the fire where he would be acclaimed by his companions. Were the man old, as he usually was, the acclaim was apt to be in this manner: "You have enlightened us well, oh my grandfather. My heart is with yours." If the compliment were from an older person, he would be apt to say: "My younger brother, my heart agrees with what you have spoken," after which he might invite the speaker to another cane of tobacco.

One after another those in the circle would go through this performance, so that councils were apt to last all through the night. If the theme of the council was to incite to war, the orator would tell of his valor with bow and arrow, and the need to defend his land, women and children. He would remind the others of the valor of their other leaders and warriors and talk of the fruits of the victory that should be theirs in the coming battle.

If, on the other hand, the subject under discussion were a proposal for peace with the Spaniards, the orator might speak with as much conviction of the desirability of living quietly on their lands, perhaps dwelling on the pleasure there would be in building a lasting friendship with the Spaniards, and in having the services of the Padres for the purpose of insuring their spiritual redemption.

At the conclusion of such sermons they would exhort their people, calling on them individually to be all of the same heart and purpose. These sermons were, in truth, a great force in moving these people for the purpose intended, whether for good or evil. It should be mentioned that these sermons were permitted to them after their conversion, that they might thus more easily become adapted to the practices of Christianity.

CHAPTER 6

Origin of These People and Their Diversity of Languages

IT IS DIFFICULT to comprehend by what route or means these savage people came to populate the New World, which lies so apart from the ancient world, and was so unknown to historians of centuries past, who held that the Pillars of Hercules in Cadiz were near the end of the world.

These Nations of the New World, although savages in their manner of living, must be admitted to be descendants of the lineage of Adam. The most probable opinion is that they have passed this way from the Continent of Asia, by way of the north, or across a narrow arm of sea which, until now, has not been discovered. There was no art of navigation in antiquity, nor needle nor compass nor chart to show the way, as now, over the extended seas.

I often questioned those people of Sinaloa, especially the oldest and most understanding of them, from whence they came, and in what period they had populated these lands. They responded as one that they had come from the north, having been disposessed of their lands there. They told me that only the Spaniards had come out of the south and east. [*Licenciado Raul Cervantes Ahumada, who wrote the prologue of the existing edition of this History, in the year 1944, emphasizes the high importance that may properly be placed on the direct testimony of the Indians, as told by Pérez de Ribas, in regard to their origin being from the north. He further reflects on how from these ancient tales of the Indians Pérez de Ribas speculates upon the existence of a narrow strip of sea between Asia and North America, a century before the discovery of such a Strait by the Scandanavian Behring.*]

The name "Yori" given by them to a Spaniard signifies valiant, and is also used when referring to wild beasts, such as lions and jaguars.

I am further convinced that the Mexican (Aztec) Nation, as well as the Nations of Sinaloa, come from the north, because of the similarity of the roots of their words. So peradventure God has hidden this arm of sea or strip of land over whence they came; to be revealed when, in His inscrutable providence, it shall be willed.

The number of languages of the Tribes or Nations of which we write are very many. Several of these Nations may speak the same language, then again distinct languages may be spoken among villages of the same Nation.

Although these are barbarous languages, it is to be remarked that being so, they all observe certain rules in common as to the formation of their tenses, their derivation of names, and other rules of languages that are of greater elegance. It is difficult to understand how, in each of these Nations, where so many languages have developed separately one from another, they should all be so similar in form and construction. Evidently, this is required in the art of language.

Our Evangelical ministers laboring among these people have not only learned many of their languages, but have left them recorded for others who are to follow. They have also written, in the Indian languages, treatises on the mysteries and practices of the Christian Faith.

There is certainly no medium so powerful for the subjection to the faith of these people as to preach to them in their own language. From personal experience I can say also that a knowledge of their languages can serve to liberate Evangelists from the danger of death in moments of crisis. Speaking to them in their own language is an effective means of quieting and subduing them when they are disturbed.

Now I shall turn to the story of the discovery of the Province of Sinaloa.

CHAPTER 7

The Saga of Cabeza de Vaca

[In the Spanish text of this first volume there is published, at its very beginning, the original account written by Alvar Nuñez Cabeza de Vaca, of the ill-fated Expedition of Captain Pánfilo de Narvaez, for the purpose of conquering and colonizing Florida for the Spanish Crown. Cabeza de Vaca was a Captain, and second in command of this expedition. As a story of stark adventure, enduring courage, and steadfast faith, it is unsurpassed in history.

The last and most inspiring part of this story has its locale in Sinaloa. I have chosen to place it here, in its proper sequence in the History of Padre Andrés Pérez de Ribas, albeit in much condensed form, rather than at the beginning.

The Expedition of Captain Pánfilo Narvaez left Spain for the conquest of Florida on the 17th day of June, 1527. It was composed of five ships, which carried 600 men and 80 horses.

After an incredible series of misadventures, including a period for re-outfitting in Cuba, the flotilla of ships anchored off the coast of Florida, in an area believed to be Tampa Bay, this being on Good Friday of Easter Week of 1528. Three hundred men were disembarked to explore the shores for a place to form a permanent base and harbor. The rest sailed away in the ships, planning to rendezvous at a later date. Of those who landed, only four survived the cold, hunger, disease, and attacks of the Indians. These were Captains Alvar Nuñez Cabeza de Vaca, Andrés Dorantes and Alonzo de Castillo, and a Moorish or Negro slave of Captain Dorantes named Estebanico. These four were separated, and enslaved by Indian Tribes. After eight years of privation, they were able to meet and plan an escape, traveling always into the setting sun, with the constant dream of reuniting themselves with their countrymen.

They knew some rudiments of healing, and acquired more knowledge from the Indians among whom they traveled. Being devout Christians, their healing was accompanied by prayer, which very much impressed the Indians. Eventually they acquired, as companions in their travels, sometimes as many as 2,000 Indians.

They first had notice of the Spaniards in the vicinity of the Yaqui River, in the present State of Sonora, Mexico. At this time they were accompanied by some 600 Indians, the greater number of them Nebomes, now called Pimas, from the upper reaches of that river.

They heard most disturbing news. Their Spanish countrymen were raiding villages, capturing Indians for slaves. Very much saddened, and concerned too for their own safety, the wanderers hurried onward, telling their followers and other Indians whom they met that they went to tell the Spaniards not to molest the Indians.

Everywhere they found the villages burned, and the crops destroyed. After

16

doing this to discourage their enemies, the Indians had fled to the Sierras east-
ward, preferring starvation to enslavement.

From here we shall quote from the story of Pérez de Ribas.]

A Spanish Captain of that period (*Diego de Alcaráz*), acting on his own account, and ignoring both Law and King, had, together with some companions,
entered into that unknown country, populated by many peoples, with the intention of enslaving and selling them.

Embarked upon this hunting of men for slaves, they became witness to one
of the most rare adventures in the history of the world. On their journey (*near
the Fuerte River.*) they met four men, sole survivors of those who had gone in
the year 1527 with Governor Pánfilo de Narvaez for the discovery of Florida.
All others had perished, from war, hunger or sickness. God reserving life to
these four, they had for a period of ten years traveled through barbarous Nations, performing miracles of healing, and preaching the Gospel, the worship
of the Holy Cross, and the value of prayer.

Among the Indian Nations they had gained great respect and reverence, being termed Men of the Sky, and Sons of the Sun. Everywhere as they journeyed
they were accompanied by Indians who guarded them, and everywhere they
were begged to remain.

When Captain Alcaráz first saw Alvar Nuñez Cabeza de Vaca and his companions in the habits of Indians he thought they were of those he had come to
capture and, blowing his horn, he rode upon them. Then Alvar Nuñez, un-
recognizable as a Spaniard, came forward to defend his Indian companions,
placing himself upon his knees and speaking in such Spanish as he could recall
after so many years absence from his own people.

Although his plea sufficed to save him and his three companions, it did not
deter the Captain from continuing in search of the Indians who had followed
the wandering pilgrims.

The four continued to the Petatlán River, where they met Captain Lázaro
de Cebreros, who accompanied them to San Miguel de Culiacán. Here they
were warmly received by Captain General Melchor Diaz, Military Governor
of that Province, who plead for their intercession with the Indians, to persuade these to return to their lands and to accept the Christian Faith, and the
rule of the Spanish Kings.

This Cabeza de Vaca did, in due time returning those Indians who had fled
to the cultivation of their fields.

The 600 Indians, principally Nebomes, who had accompanied the four
Spaniards on this last part of their pilgrimage, learning that their four friends
planned to continue on to the City of Mexico, plead that before leaving their
benefactors should place them securely on lands which they might cultivate
and to make sure their liberty was assured.

This was done. They were given lands at Bamoa, on the Petatlán River,
twelve miles below the area where was later situated the Villa of Sinaloa. This
pueblo exists today (*1645*). [*It exists as a prosperous farming community now,
over 300 years after.*]

These strangers from 300 miles northward have, because of these peculiar circumstances of their locating there, been always of particular faith and devotion to the Spaniards. Upon parting with the four companions, these Nebome Indians had requested of Cabeza de Vaca that he counsel them as to how they might live with greater security among his people. He answered that they should always identify themselves by greeting the Spaniards with the sign of the cross, which they must carry in their hands. This they have done; and, in addition, often wear little crosses, of pieces of mother-of-pearl, secured about their foreheads.

Thus it may be seen that the great pilgrimage of these four companions was the medium of Divine Providence for bringing the first notice of these far away peoples, who inhabit places so distant that their limits are not yet known.

From here Cabeza de Vaca and his three companions continued their journey to the City of Mexico. Everywhere along the way they were received with interest and admiration. They recounted that after sleeping for so many years on the bare earth, beds felt most uncomfortable to them.

Arrived in Mexico City, the four were received most graciously by the Viceroy, don Antonio de Mendoza. They gave a lengthy narration of their experiences, some of which had been pleasant, others very sad.

Their story created a great fervor for the discovery of new places. The viceroy soon made a levy of 400 men, including mounted and foot soldiers, as there were yet too few horses in New Spain for all to be mounted. As Captain General of this Expedition he named Francisco Vásquez de Coronado; as Royal Councilor, don Pedro de Továr, who was then a prominent resident of the Villa de San Miguel de Culiacán. The Viceroy himself accompanied these forces as far as Compostela [*Former Capital of the State of Nayarit.*] to insure their proper outfitting. For sustenance they drove a herd of cattle before them.

They were accompanied by four priests of the Seraphic Order of San Francisco.

This Expedition followed generally the route taken by Cabeza de Vaca, continuing their explorations for two years. They searched especially for a city of seven stories in height, said to be named Quivira. They arrived finally at 40 degrees north latitude, where in winter it was so cold that the rivers were frozen over. They crossed a country called by the Indians, "of the cows," where people passed their days hunting Cíbolas (*Buffaloes*).

Most unfortunately, Captain General Vásquez de Coronado was killed by a fall from his horse. Following his death there developed dissention among his followers. Finally, not finding the riches they had been seeking, they turned back. Arriving at the Villa de San Miguel de Culiacań, they dispersed, many remaining to partake in mining and other enterprises. Don Pedro de Továr, who had been second in command of the Expedition, eventually stocked large areas of the Petatlán River with cattle.

Still later there came, by order of the Viceroy, an expedition led by a Franciscan Friar named Marcos de Niza, guided by the Negro Estebanico. The purpose of this Expedition was to win the friendship of the Indians as Cabeza de

Vaca and his companions had done, without recourse to arms. In some places they were successful, but many Indians remained hostile. Estebanico was murdered, whereupon the other members of the group returned to Culiacán. The time was not yet ripe for the conversion of the savage Nations of the Province of Sinaloa.

CHAPTER 8

Expedition of Don Francisco de Ibarra

SINALOA for many years remained under the jurisdiction of the Province of Nueva Vizcaya, whose seat of government was Guadiana. (*Durango*) In 1563 don Francisco de Ibarra, the Governor of Nueva Vizcaya, with a goodly number of soldiers, crossed the Sierras by the route of the Valley of Topia, coming out at Culiacán.

From there he continued northward through the Province of Sinaloa. He was everywhere received in peace, and in turn offered peace to the Indian Nations through which he traveled.

He crossed many rivers, and found great numbers of people. Ibarra observed that the Indians painted themselves with minerals that gave evidence of being rich in value. Hoping to find the source of these minerals, he founded a Villa on the Rio Grande de Zuaque. (*Fuerte River*) This Villa was located at a place called Carapoa, and was named San Juan Bautista.

Here he settled 60 persons. Among them were several families. He divided the lands and the watering places among these colonists, placing under their rule the pueblos along the river.

As Captain and Chief Justice he named a soldier of great valor, Esteban Martin Vohorques.

This group of colonists was of but poor resources. However, they built a small church in which is said to have officiated a Priest named Hernando de Pedrosa. There was said also to have been three Franciscan Friars among the settlers.

Having heard of a rich strike in minerals at a pueblo of his jurisdiction, named Chiametla, Ibarra soon hurried southward. Near Chiametla he founded a village which was named San Sebastián (*now Concordia*). Although very rich in ore in the beginning, these mines were soon depleted.

The founders of Carapoa discovered rich minerals also and took some ore, but the hostility of the Indians did not permit them to continue mining.

There were charges of injustices on the part of both Spaniards and Indians. Such charges are not uncommon in such interprises. The soldiers sometimes are harsh in their treatment of the Indians. Neither is it strange for the Indi-

19

ans to flee from the Spaniards, to escape laboring in the mines. Liberty means much to these primitive people who have always enjoyed liberty.

The Zuaque Indians of this area were a fierce and independent people, of whom much shall be written later.

A company of Spaniards from Carapoa journeyed on an occasion to the land of these Zuaques to gather corn, against the wishes of the Indians. The Spaniards were later invited by the Indians to a great feast at which was served the meat of wild game taken from their forests, and fruits which they grow. While seated at the feast, the Spaniards were fallen upon and beheaded.

One Spaniard they kept to be dismembered at one of their orgies in celebration of this massacre. Only one Spaniard escaped to carry the sad news to Carapoa. Those remaining there barricaded themselves in a small fort, which they reinforced with a stockade of poles set upright in the earth and padded with straw.

They at once sent notice to their countrymen at Culiacán, who quickly organized an expedition for their rescue. However, the refugees soon decided to abandon the fort. They set out for Culiacań, on the way meeting the force that was coming to their assistance.

After much deliberation it was resolved not to abandon the Province to the ferocious Zauques, but to establish a Villa on the Petatlán (*Sinaloa*) River, lying 40 miles southward, where the Indians had shown themselves to be more friendly.

This place was named Villa de San Felipe y Santiago. [*The present pueblo of Sinaloa.*]

CHAPTER 9

Expedition of Governor Hernando de Bazán

A GENTLEMAN by the name of Hernando de Bazán succeeded don Francisco de Ibarra as Governor of Nueva Vizcaya.

Having had notices of the excesses of the belligerent Zuaques, he determined to chastize them, in order to redeem the reputation of the Spanish soldiers among those savage peoples. Gathering more than one hundred soldiers, he placed a brave leader, don Gonzalo Martín, at their head and they marched upon the Zuaques. After several skirmishes with other Indians they arrived at the land of their enemies.

An advance guard of twenty Spanish soldiers fell into an ambush. A dense wall of brush had been built and cleverly concealed along the two sides of a path upon which the soldiers must enter. There followed a terrific battle; the Spaniards fighting with arquebuses, swords and daggers, while the Zuaques used arrows and great war clubs. In the end, all but two of the soldiers were killed.

Such was the fierce pride of those savage Zuaques in their victory that they engraved, upon some great mesquite trees, the figures of their victims with their heads removed. These figures they showed to me many years later, after I had been occupied in their conversion. The heads of the soldiers they took to display at the time of their dancing and feasting in celebration of their victory.

The same Indians told with admiration of the valor of Captain don Gonzalo Martín. Seeing himself surrounded by the dead bodies of his companions and the Indians, he placed his back against a large tree to protect himself from their arrows. Here he remained fighting for many hours, the Indians attacking him in large numbers, and he cutting them down as they came. Finally, because of the extreme heat, they resorted to attacking him in groups, in order to rest one another, while he alone fought on, slaying them in great numbers until finally felled by an arrow fired from a distance.

Such was their admiration for his great bravery that they dismembered him completely, dividing his flesh among their many warriors, that these might gain strength for battle.

Governor Bazán, in great anger, united all available forces to avenge this massacre. However, the Indians by now were securely hidden in their woods, and he could only destroy their fields. He marched up the Zuaque river to Carapoa, site of the abondoned fort. From there he continued northward twenty leagues to the Mayo River. He was received in peace by the Mayos. However, he arrested some Mayos he believed to be accomplices of the Zuaques. These were sent to the City of Mexico for trial, but were soon given their liberty.

It was left to another valiant Captain, of whom honorable mention shall later be made, to restore the reputation of the Spaniards in Sinaloa.

[I would feel guilty should I not digress here for a moment to pay tribute to the extreme bravery of the Zuaque Indians during their participation in the Mexican Revolution beginning in 1910.

The Spanish overlords and, later, the wealthier class of Mexicans, had encroached increasingly upon the lands of the Indians on the Fuerte River (formerly Rio de Zuaque). The Mexican Revolution had, as one of its principal goals, a more equitable distribution of lands and these Indians (by now called Mayos) were easily persuaded to join in this Revolution.

From our area there were recruited some 800 Mayos, their first objective being the capture of the walled and fortified pueblo of Navojoa, Sonora, 100 miles northward, garrisoned by 3,000 Federal soldiers. These soldiers were well equipped with modern rifles, small cannon and machine guns.

Our Indian foreman, Rosario Leyva, son of a Mayo Chief, Domingo Leyva, was made a Captain of the Indians. Lined up to entrain at our town of Los Mochis, they made an interesting picture.

Each Indian wore a blue denim shirt and trousers. None wore shoes, only guarachis. In the straw sombrero of each had been inserted a red parrot feather.

21

Their arms were a hooked machete each, and a heavy bow supplied with arrows from two quivers, these crisscrossed on the backs of their shoulders.

To complete their equipment they carried an ixtle fiber provision bag (morral) hung below the left shoulder, with a red blanket folded over it.

They were accompanied by four adventurous Americans from our community. Three of the Americans operated machine guns. The fourth carried crude bombs made of a black powder which the Indians long ago learned to manufacture. The containers for the bombs were small, empty cans.

Building scaling ladders, these brave men attacked at break of dawn as had been their custom for hundreds of years. Within a few hours they had taken the pueblo, after a terrific battle in which many Indians were killed and the Federal soldiers well-nigh exterminated.

Their fate deserved a greater reward. When the first wave of revolution was over, in 1915, they were disbanded to return to their homes without the promise of return of their lands having been fulfilled. In their anger, some 3,000 of them gathered at Jaguara, opposite the ancient Zuaque pueblo of Mochicahui, much referred to later in this story.

From this base, under the direction of a much esteemed leader, Bachomo, they terrorized the Fuerte River Valley over a period of a year (1915) until Bachomo was captured and executed. He is revered by the Indians there today, some believing that he will be reincarnated and return as their leader.

Their practice of rolling heads was not lost in the 17th Century. I have a picture, taken in 1915, of the head of Lic. Dionisio Torres of the pueblo of El Fuerte, impaled upon a pitaya pole. This gory trophy the Mayos carried about for days in protest of his representing the wealthy hacendados who robbed them of their lands.

Eventually, within the pattern of the Agrarian Reform Laws of Mexico, many of the Mayo Indians were given land and became farmers. These lands are under an irrigation project developed by the Mexican Government in the fertile Fuerte River Valley. This system will irrigate nearly a million acres of land with the waters of several rivers originating in the mountainous areas of the four states which comprise the principal area referred to in this history.]

CHAPTER 10

The First Mission of Sinaloa

IN THIS CHAPTER there shall be written of the events, temporal and spiritual, which took place during the first years of labor in conversion to the Saintly Faith of the Nations of Sinaloa.

The first people to be converted were those of the three rivers named Sebastián de Ébora (*Mocorito*), Petatlán (*Sinaloa*), and Ocoroni. This latter river is only some 50 miles in length, but is populated by many people, these being of several languages.

The pacification of the people of these rivers cost great effort but, once accomplished, those people came to be of great assistance in the conversion of much greater numbers of people who inhabited the valleys of the larger rivers northward.

Divine Providence decreed that in 1590 there should be named Governor of Nueva Vizcaya a gentleman of great valor, prudence and Christian faith.

This gentleman, don Rodrigo del Rio y Loza, had served His Majesty with distinction in the pacification of the fierce Chichimeca Indians of the central plateau north of the City of Mexico. He had also acquired valuable experience as a member of the expedition of Governor don Francisco de Ibarra to the Province of Sinaloa.

As a reward for his valorous assistance, King Felipe Cuarto granted to him vast tracts of land, which came to produce a crop of 24,000 calves annually.

Of this wealth he shared most generously with the poor, who could always find refuge on his lands. These extended from the City of Zacatecas to Guadiana (*Durango*).

In the year 1604 I passed through these lands on my first journey, with Captain Martinez de Hurdaide, to assist in the Mission of Sinaloa. Seeing the magnificence and liberality of this gentleman, and learning of his Christian virtues, I was brought to compare him in my mind with the Patriarch Abraham, whom God placed on those broad plains in ancient days, for the refuge of pilgrims.

This gentleman wrote to the Provincial of our Company in the City of Mexico, begging that some priests be sent to the dominions which he governed. The Padre Provincial acquiesed in his request, selecting for this arduous and hazardous undertaking two outstanding Missionaries. As Director of the new Mission of Sinaloa, he chose Padre Gonzalo de Tapia. As Co-Founder he chose Padre Martín Pérez. Padre Gonzalo de Tapia, although young in years, was mature in experience. He was born in the City of Leon, in Castile. The youngest son of a very illustrious family, he was destined, as another David to be a warrior and Captain for Christ in many evangelistic enterprises. He was admitted to the College of the Company at Leon at so early an age that upon graduation he was too young to enter the priesthood. Padre don Antonio de Mendoza, who was shortly to become Viceroy of New Spain, was gathering recruits for employment in the extended Missions of the Indies. The young Gonzalo, together with other advanced disciples, returned with him to New Spain.

This was in the year 1584. Although so young, he was soon teaching in the College of the Company in the City of Mexico.

Three Padres teaching at the Jesuit College of Pátzcuaro, Province of Michoacan, fell gravely ill, and the young Padre Gonzalo was dispatched to assist the spiritual workers there. So great was his facility for learning languages that within fifteen days he was preaching to the Tarascans in their own tongue. He preached with such grace and fervor that soon Indians from the Sierras of Michoacan were coming in great numbers to hear him.

At this time the Padre Rector at Pátzcuaro had great need of a Padre of special ability to go among the Chichimeca Indians, perhaps the most savage of all those of New Spain. Padre Gonzalo de Tapia, with great enthusiasm, and intrepid spirit for divine service, entered among those fierce Chichimecas, who were simply amazed, exclaiming, "Who is this one who seems to have no fear of us?"

They were quickly attracted to him, and with his facility for languages, in seventeen days he was speaking to the Chichimecas in their language. He induced many groups of them to gather together for easier indoctrination.

The Chichimecas had been making frequent raids on convoys and passengers journeying from Mexico City to Zacatecas, menacing constantly all the country between. It suited the Padre Provincial next to transfer Padre Gonzalo to our College at Zacatecas. At this fabulously rich Real of Mines Padre Gonzalo found a multitude in need of his Christian zeal and ardent spirit. Many Tarascans had come from Michoacán to work in the mines. Some of these were fugitives from their old pueblos. Soon there were great concourses of Indians coming to hear his sermons. He did much for the rehabilitation of these Indians, so changing their manner of life that it was commonly said among the people of Michoacán, that Padre Gonzalo de Tapia had brought their pueblos back to life by sending home their men to their families.

A vicious custom of the people of various Nations employed in the mines was to challange each other to combat, as a form of sport, on the feast days when they were otherwise idle. Leaving the city, they would go out into the country nearby, where they would engage in furious battles, in which combatants were often wounded, and sometimes killed, from their use of fists, arrows, spears and stones. In order to face their opponents with greater fury, they would first go into an orgy of drunkeness.

The authorities had attempted to uproot this practice, but without success. Rather, the combatants made a common front against them. However, Padre Gonzalo de Tapia soon gained such favor and authority among these unbridled and fiery people that whenever they saw him climbing, with staff in hand, to their battle ground, they would abandon the field, and even surrender their arms to him.

So was the voice of this great evangelist heeded in the desert, and such were the ministries in which his saintly zeal was employed before going to found the Mission of Sinaloa, where God had reserved for him the triumphs and final reward for his saintly labors.

Padre Martín Pérez, Co-founder, with Padre Gonzalo de Tapia, of the Mission of Sinaloa, was of great assistance in establishing this Mission, living to see its churches extended 300 miles northward and far eastward into the great Sierras.

Padre Martín was born at San Martín, in the Province of Nueva Vizcaya in New Spain, an area rich in silver. He was the only son of a very principal family, but chose to enter the church, completing his studies in the College of the City of Mexico, under the renowned Padre Pedro Ortigosa, recognized in New Spain as a Master Teacher.

He was admitted to the Company in June, 1577, at twenty one years of age. He soon became Director of the College of San Idelfonso, in Mexico City, then served as a minister in the city of Puebla. After going as a missionary to various places on the central plateau, including the lands of the savage Chichimecas, he was designated to the Mission of Sinaloa, where he journeyed with Padre Tapia in the year 1590.

Because the route through the mountains of Topia was controlled by rebellious Indian tribes, these two Padres were forced to travel the longer route through the barrancas. [*Present states of Jalisco and Nayarit.*], then continuing through the jungles to San Miguel de Culiacán, nearest point of Spanish occupation to their new Mission.

Although they were received here with much rejoicing by their own people, they were restless to begin their labors and at once sent word of their coming to five Spaniards who lived at the Villa, these being the only countrymen they were to see for a long while. Two of these, together with a few Christian Indians and numerous unconverted Indians, came to escort them to their new Mission.

All traveled happily together to the Mocorito River, where the Christian son of a Cacique gave them a warm welcome. Here they performed their first baptisms of children in Sinaloa. They then continued thirty-three miles to the Villa of Sinaloa, on the Petatlán River.

On approaching, they found their path strewn with flowers. The trees under which they rode were bent into ceremonial arches, and other arches of green branches had been placed about the Plaza of the pueblo.

The Padres gave the assembled people a loving greeting. They described the places they had traveled from, and their purpose in coming, and there was much rejoicing. Finally they repaired to a little house of poles and straw that had been constructed for them, feeling more content than had they been received in a royal palace.

They soon made a division of their labor. Padre Martín Pérez attended the pueblos of Cubiri, Bamoa, (*where had settled the followers of Cabeza de Vaca*), and several others. Padre Gonzalo de Tapia attended the pueblos among the foothills up river, including Baboría, Deboropa, Lepochi, Matapán and Ocoroni, this latter pueblo being on the river of the same name, 15 miles northward.

Soon they began construction of churches which, at first, were only brush sheds. The houses of the Padres, too, were made of poles and straw with roofs of earth. Their tables and beds were of bamboo poles lashed in parallel fashion together. In the beginning, they had no experience of better construction, nor facilities for undertaking it.

The food of the Padres, as of the Indians, was usually corn, beans and pumpkins, these latter either boiled or broiled over a fire. Rarely did they have fish from the river, or game from the woods, or perhaps some grasshoppers (locusts)

25

roasted. When I arrived in Sinaloa some years later, I was served a plate of these same locusts roasted, which were most revolting to my stomach, until I observed with what gusto my companion Padre ate them, after which, recalling their having been the food of that great penitent, Saint John the Baptist, while in the desert, I too ate them, and came to relish them.

They immediately applied themselves to learning the Indian languages, including the catechism, which they prepared with the help of the five Spaniards living there. The first labor of the Padres was the indoctrination of the Indian men, women and children, in preparation for their baptism. At time of baptism the men and women were married in the Christian manner, the five Spaniards serving as Godfathers for this occasion.

CHAPTER 11

Ceremony of Adoption of Orphaned Children

NOT ONLY BECAUSE OF SICKNESS, but due to constant wars, many Indian children were left orphans. The remaining Indians of the Nation received these orphans into their families with pleasure; in fact, their adoption was made an occasion for feasting and rejoicing.

One of these celebrations took place in the year of the arrival of the Padres. There were first built, about one hundred paces apart, two sheds or enramadas. Into one of these were taken all the orphans, being kept here for a period of eight days. During this time they were served atole, which is corn ground and cooked into a gruel, which served with the honey from wild bees, is considered one of their greatest delicacies.

In the second and larger of the two enramadas, there was spread a circle of sand. The Indian men, their faces and bodies gaudily decorated in paint of various colors, entered into this circle dancing and singing.

Presently, certain ones of them seated themselves in the sand and, with canes, drew various figures which when finished they brought into clearer outline by filling in the lines of their drawings with various bright colors of sand. The figures they painted appeared to be human. One they called Viriseva, another Vairubi. This latter they said was the mother of the first. Of what these figures represented they talked to the Padres in some confusion, as do blind people who do not know the light. At times they seemed to consider these figures to be God and His Mother, and that from them all people had descended.

In the sand surrounding the two figures they drew pictures of ears of corn, beans and pumpkins. They made other drawings, as of serpents, birds and smaller animals. Each morning and evening the men entered this place with much solemnity, to continue their dancing. No woman was permitted there during these eight days of ceremonies.

When the eight days of dancing had been concluded the men went, still dancing, to the enramada sheltering the children. Here they underwent certain ceremonies such as opening the eyes of the children, in this manner emphasizing that they should be vigilant in their own protection. The children were then conducted to the enramada where the figures had been drawn in the sand. With this sand they were rubbed and sprinkled, evidentally to express the hope that of these birds, plants and animals, the children should enjoy feasting during their later life. They were also presented with weapons for use in hunting. After this, they were given to eat abundantly, with which the feast terminated, children and foster parents then all going joyfully to bathe together in the river.

The Padres had some notice of this ceremony. Guided by a Cacique, they went to the place where it had been held. While there the Cacique, with a cane, drew the figures of various animals which their ancestors had held in reverence, such as snakes, toads and others. These animals they accustomed to propitiate, by picturing them in such manner hoping to save their fields from harm. The Padres disillusioned them of these superstitions, giving them to understand that little or no benefit was to be derived from them. The Feast of the Nativity was celebrated soon after. The Indians constructed another enramada similar to that used for the orphaned children. They here drew a picture of a river, with figures of lions, tigers, serpents and other animals. However, in the place of their gods Viriseva and Vairubi, there were now drawn in sand, figures representing God, the Holy Mother and the Christ Child, to whom they now prayed for protection. To the Padres, whom they had invited to see their handiwork, they said: "Of these figures we are now teaching our children, and shall hereafter."

The Padres praised their good intent, although it seemed to them that this new ceremony resembled rather too closely that celebrated in their gentility. In order to better remove this ancient practice from their minds, the Padres arranged with them that at the next ceremonies of Easter, the Indians should enter the church dancing, and there pray to God and the Virgin, whose images they would there behold, that they might be helped in saving their crops. And to this they became educated, and were content.

CHAPTER 12

Expedition to Sierras of Topia

OUR GLORIOUS PADRE SAN IGNACIO, Founder of the Company of Jesus, instituted his ministers as though they were a company of soldiers who, like swift running horses, must be ever in readiness to fly to where necessity calls, for the saving of souls.

This spirit was well exemplified in the Padre Gonzalo de Tapia. Four months after his arrival in Sinaloa, he answered an urgent invitation to visit the rich mining area of Topia, 150 miles eastward into the high Sierras. The Spanish miners of Topia rode many miles down the mountain passes to welcome him. Arriving, he spent several days in preaching and receiving confessions. He found here a group of Tarascan Indian laborers, to whom he was able to preach in their own language.

Also while at Topia he was told that in a nearby forest, under a tree of notable size, the Indians had built an idol, to which they took offerings of corn in time of harvest and bows, arrows, and other weapons in time of war. Padre Gonzalo ordered built a beautiful cross and, accompanied by many people, went to this place. They uprooted the tree, and on the spot where it had stood, planted this precious cross, blessing the place, in order to remove any memory or taint of superstition.

This being done, the Padre returned to Sinaloa, by way of the Villa of Culiacán.

Meanwhile, Padre Martín Pérez was kept busy visiting down river at the pueblos of Bamoa, Guasave, Sisinicari and Ures.

CHAPTER 13

First Christmas in Sinaloa

PADRE GONZALO DE TAPIA, returning from Topia by way of the Villa of Culiacán in the days just before the Nativity, brought back with him a chorus of singers and musicians to assist in celebrating Christmas.

This first Christmas celebration was held at the pueblo of Lopochi, 3 miles up river from the Villa of Sinaloa. There were in attendance over 1,000 baptized Indians, besides many not baptized. The chorus with special music was most gratifying to the Indians. There was also a procession outside the church, in which Indian dancers took part, this making them very happy.

The response of the Indians to these efforts of the Padres was so great that by the year 1593 there were sent two more Padres to Sinaloa; Alonso de Santiago and Juan Bautista de Velasco. [*Padre Velasco is said by historian Lic. Eustaquio Buelna (1890) to have written the manuscript of "Art of the Cahita Tongue" in 1600. It was first published in 1737, then re-published in 1890, at the instance of Buelna, a former Governor of Sinaloa, and in 1890 Minister of Education of Mexico.*]

To Padre Juan Bautista de Velasco were assigned the churches of Mocorito, Bacubirito and Orabato.

Padre Gonzalo de Tapia in 1593 paid a visit to his Superiors and to the Viceroy in Mexico City. With Padre Tapia traveled several principal Indians, who were presented to the Viceroy. He treated them with affection, that they should comprehend the interest of the Crown of Spain in their spiritual and temporal welfare. To Padre Tapia the Viceroy presented numerous gifts for the Mission, including ornaments, church bells and musical instruments.

Such was the affection of the Christian Indians for Padre Gonzalo that several of their leaders journeyed 300 miles to meet and welcome him on his return. The Indians who had accompanied him returned bearing many gifts, and had much to relate of their kindly reception and of what they had seen on their journey.

CHAPTER 14

Pestilence and Earthquakes

THERE CAME upon the land a terrible pestilance of small pox, and at the same time an epidemic of measles of a virulence never before known. It was painful to see the houses so filled with suffering. Often there remained no one well enough to feed the sick. The Padres, with untiring charity, gave what assistance they could, furnishing of the little food that they had, and administering the blessed sacrament. Day and night they traveled among the pueblos and rancherias, and even to the fields, where some sick had fallen.

At the same time there came a great earthquake, which was most frightening to the people. There is a rocky hill next to Mochicahui, principal pueblo of the Zuaque Nation. This hill was split open by the quake, and from the opening came flowing a stream of water. The Zuaques, in their superstitious fear, sought to stop this flow by throwing into the stream, to appease the evil spirits, such valuable possessions as mantles of cloth, beads, aquamarines, and other objects they most esteemed. In their concern they came to Padre Tapia at Sinaloa, bearing gifts of fruits, beans, pheasants and green corn, hoping by these gifts to assuage the wrath of the God of the Christians. The Padre enlightened them as to the great works of God, exhorting them to become Christians and be baptized. This they promised to do, although for the time they forgot their promises.

Indians of the Sinaloa Nation who lived above the Zuaques on the Gran Rio de Zuaque, also frightened by the quake, were moved to visit Padre Tapia bearing gifts. They earnestly invited him to pay them a visit. This the Padre decided to do. They first passed a pueblo named Cacalotlan, (*Valle de Cuervo*) then arrived at the land of the Sinalas, 60 miles north of the Villa of Sinaloa, where he counted twenty-four villages and rancherias. Here he preached and baptized many children before returning to his principal headquarters at the pueblo of Ocoroni.

The Sinaloas, although receptive at the time of his visit, proved to be a rebellious and difficult people; and remained for ten years thereafter without indoctrination.

CHAPTER 15

Martyrdom of Padre de Tapia

EVANGELICAL DOCTRINE made great progress in Sinaloa in the first four years, from 1590 to 1594. However, it can well be understood that the forces of the Devil, in the form of the Hechiceros, were always at work attempting to impede the progress of Christianity.

In the pueblo of Deboropa, only one and a half miles from the Villa, there lived a bedeviled old Indian named Nacabeba. He never attended church. He and his companions were continuously holding drunken brawls in their fields. They held great resentment against the Padre for his influence over the people, and decided to murder him in order to feel more free to return to their licentious manner of living.

The Padre knew of the opposition of Nacabeba. At first he tried with kindness to persuade this Indian to change his ways. Finally, after a year, he gave account to the Alcalde and Captain of the Villa, Miguel Maldonado, who, after investigation, ordered that the Indian be given some lashes.

Far from proving a remedy, this spurred Nacabeba to vengeance against Padre Tapia. To this end, he persuaded nine other Indians to accompany him. They arrived at the little house of the Padre at dusk, finding him at his prayers. Nacabeba engaged the Padre in an argument, while two accomplices clubbed him from behind. Sorely wounded, Padre Gonzalo staggered outside to kneel before the cross of the little church cemetery, where he was killed by further blows of his assailants. In a rage of fury, these savages severed his head and an arm from his body, drinking of his blood as was a custom of their savagery, before leaving him to celebrate their barbarous triumph.

Advised of the murder, the Alcalde, then Miguel Ortiz, called together the few Spaniards of the Villa and sent three soldiers on horseback to the scene of the murder. They wrapped the poor mutilated body in sheets to be removed to the Villa.

Amid sorrow and tears of all the people, Padre Gonzalo de Tapia was buried in the cemetery of the church of the Villa de Sinaloa on July 11, 1594.

The other Padres remained some days at the Villa. The Ocoroni Indians, in their anger, not finding Nacabeba and his accomplices, killed two other Indians of Deboropa. Twenty soldiers were sent from the Villa of Culiacán to insure maintaining peace.

Two Padres, Hernando de Santarén and Pedro Méndez, whose assistance had been requested by the deceased Padre Gonzalo de Tapia, had arrived as far as Culiacán on their way to assist in the Mission of Sinaloa. They were detained there; working instead for some months among the thirty pueblos of the Valley of Culiacán. Here they learned the Tave language native to the Culiacán area.

No sooner had the tempest subsided than Padre Martín Pérez and his three companions returned to their tasks, and through diligence and perseverance eventually overcame the difficulties created by the murder of Padre Tapia.

The friendly Ocoronis were found celebrating a dance over the scalps of the two Indians killed at Deboropa. They were reproved, accepting the reproof in good grace. It is not easy for these people to change the habits of their barbarous past. However, it is quite something to now see groups of these Indians so recently converted, entering the Villa, from up or down the river, carrying their tall crosses adorned with bright plumes, and carrying flowers. As they march they chant their prayers, until arriving at the church to hear Mass.

The life of Padre Gonzalo de Tapia was ended at thirty three years, the same span of life allotted to our Blessed Savior. Of his brilliant career before coming to Sinaloa there has already been told. In his relatively brief years in the Company, he had mastered six Indian languages and had left countless numbers of converts in the Nations where he had labored. As the closing tribute to this venerable Padre there will be copied a letter, written in their own language and style, by the Tarascan Indians who were working in the mines of Topia at the time of his death. The letter is directed on its covering to the Governors, Alcaldes, Regidores and other principal persons of the Province of Michoacán.

It reads as follows:

"Very honorable Senores, residents of Pátzcuaro, Sivinia, Nauatzín, Charán, Arantzán and all other pueblos of the Province of Mechoacan: to all these we make known, that they may advise all the smaller pueblos, how now has died our very Reverend Padre Gonzalo de Tapia, who had come to Sinaloa to preach the Faith of Christ to these peoples. They killed and made of him a great martyr, cutting off his head and left arm, only his right arm remaining to form a cross, and as if crossing himself he was left lying on the ground — and so he lay outside his house until he was buried. The pueblo where he was martyred is named Deboropa. We advise you of his death, that all may recite for him a Padre Nuestro. God and the Virgin Mary be with you."

This letter, after having gone to all the pueblos of the Tarascan Indians of Michoacán, was given to Padre Francisco Ramirez, beloved friend of Padre Gonzalo de Tapia, to be read in the church of Arantzán. In tears he began reading and there was so much sobbing and mourning that neither could he finish, nor they hear the letter, for some while. He sought to console these loyal friends by saying that he who had been so much their Padre in life, would not be less their Padre in heaven, having passed to there in such a glorious death.

A picture of Padre Tapia hangs in the Chapel of Santa Maria, in Leon of Castile. A part of his remains were sent there also and services were held, attended by the most distinguished people of the city, as well as the people of Quintana de Raneros, who were proud to have been vassals on the estate of his family.

And we can well believe that God has crowned this Padre in the greatest heights of glory, which he will enjoy for eternity.

CHAPTER 16

Capture and Hanging of Nacabeba

THE INDIAN NACABEBA, murderer of the Padre Gonzalo de Tapia, together with his nine companions, continued in attempts to harm the Spaniards. Finally, one of his group was recognized and arrested. This man agreed to lead his captors to Nacabeba. Instead, he guided them along a high cliff, from which he attempted to leap to his death. Failing in this, a little later he found a poisonous weed along the trail, which he ate, and perished before twenty four hours.

Feeling insecure in the woods near Sinaloa, Nacabeba and his accomplices took refuge with the warlike Zauque Nation. For some time these made common cause with him against the Spaniards and their Christian allies, constantly threatening attacks on their pueblos. Eventually, some Indians friendly to the Spaniards captured two of the group, including a son of Nacabeba, and beheaded them.

A relative of Nacabeba one day met on a trail an Indian of the Tegueco Nation, who were mortal enemies of the Zuaques, and beheaded him. In revenge, the Teguecos, lead by their principal Cacique Lanzarote, raided the Zuaques, killing many of them. This same Lanzarote later became a Christian leader of much distinction in the church.

Nacabeba, by now fearing treachery from the Zuaques, made terms with the Teguecos, and entered with his followers into their territory. No sooner were they among the Teguecos than they were captured, bound to trees, and word of their capture sent to the Spaniards at the Villa. In the absence of Lieutenant General Alonzo Diaz, his second in command, don Diego Martinez de Hurdaide, ordered twelve soldiers outfitted with horses and rode in all haste to the pueblo of the Teguecos. Nacabeba, upon seeing his new captors, exclaimed in a rage, "O, Teguecos, did I not beg of you to kill me yourselves, rather than deliver me over to the Spaniards!"

Taken to the Presidio, he and a nephew were sentenced to be killed and quartered. The Padres at once went to prepare the two men for death. To Nacabeba they gave instruction in the catechism, as he had refused in former times to enter a church. The nephew, who had been baptized, was confessed, and they died at the gallows, with great remorse of their sins.

CHAPTER 17

Rule of the Spanish Crown

THERE WAS MUCH UNREST among the Indian Nations following the death of Padre Tapia. The Mission pueblos were threatened. Horses of the Spaniards were stolen, or killed with arrows. An urgent request for soldiers was sent to the Viceroy, the Conde de Monterrey. This request was heeded; there being established by 1596 a garrison of forty-six Spanish soldiers at the Villa of Sinaloa under command of Captain General Alonzo Diaz. It might seem strange that such a small number should hope to maintain order among savage peoples who could assemble not less than 20,000 warriors to oppose them. However, many of the principal Indians recognized the advantages of being under a government of the Spaniards. Before the coming of the Spaniards they had no government common to their numerous Nations, and were constantly warring with one another.

The Alcaldes Mayores and Captains of the Presidios entered into agreements with the Indian Nations under which the Indians agreed to keep the peace, in exchange for the support of the Spaniards in case of an unjust agression by another Nation.

Indian Governors were named to administer to the temporal needs of the various Nations. In the event of war, the Indians agreed to take part as allies of the Spaniards. With this assurance the position of the Spanish soldiers was greatly strengthened.

A soldier, well armored and mounted on an armored horse, is like a moving fortress. Spaniards have become most dextrous in making armor for their horses, using a thickness of two bull hides, through which arrows may not penetrate, except at extremely close range. Because of the weight of this armor the horse is not used until the moment of battle. The point of danger lies in the possibility of an Indian throwing himself under the horse, to sever its tendons, so rendering it useless. A soldier heavily laden with armor, once fallen from his horse, is apt to be at the mercy of a horde of savages who carry war clubs, lances, bows and arrows.

The cost to the Royal Treasury for maintaining garrisons is great, but it is to be considered that the conversion of millions of souls is a glorious undertaking. Also, without the protection of soldiers it would be impossible to operate the many mines of New Spain which are now producing so richly.

It should be explained that although the security given by the soldiers is of immeasurable benefit to the labor of the Missionaries, these are rarely accompanied in their travels by soldiers, often attending pueblos 100 or 150 miles from any possible assistance, where they could easily be killed and eaten by the savages. Neither are their homes nor churches ordinarily guarded by soldiers.

The piety of the Spanish soldiers makes a profound impression on the Indians, who marvel when finding hardy soldiers in the churches, bending to their knees in adoration of God. They held extreme admiration for the piety of the great and valorous don Diego Martinez de Hurdaide, for many years Captain General of the Spanish garrisons of the Province of Sinaloa. In the same manner they had before been impressed by the action of the valorous Hernán Cortéz, in kneeling in prayer before the Franciscan Friars who accompanied his expedition for the conquest of New Spain.

CHAPTER 18

Labor of Padres Among the Indians

AFTER THE BUILDING of the Presidio at the Villa of Sinaloa, the Padres went about their task of conversion with renewed fervor. Nations among whom they labored were the Nios and Vocayoes, 15 miles down river from the Villa, these being about 500 families. Continuing down river were the Guasaves, of about 2,000 families, then the Vacaues, a Nation numbering 4,000 warriors, who lived along the shores of the sea, north and south of the Petatlán River.

Among the Guasave Nation there lived a very able Christian woman, who had many years before been a slave of a family of Spaniards at the Villa of Culiacán. While there she had adopted the Christian faith, and so diligently did she work among the Guasaves that she soon had them attending church twice daily.

One of the Padres, traveling one day with some companions along a trail near Guasave, observed an Indian suddenly depart into the woods. In curiosity they followed this Indian, presently coming upon him in the act of making reverences before a stone. This stone was about a vara (*33 inches*) in height, shaped in the form of a pyramid, and had some crude inscriptions carved upon it.

The Padre ordered this false idol destroyed. The Indian, horrified at the thought, declared that he dare not destroy it, for fear of death.

Although the idol was heavy, the Padre had it carried to the Plaza of the

Villa. Here, in order to prove that nothing was to be feared from it, he and others rolled it about the Plaza.

The Indians witnessing this act were horrified, predicting dire consequences. They told that in times past they had carried this idol with them for several days at a time, when wishing for good weather for their crops, or when on their way to make war.

The Padre assembled all the people in the church to talk to them of the absurdity of their superstitions regarding this stone idol. However, it was something for the Padre to be confronted with, that at the very moment of his preaching, there arose a tempest of dust and wind so fierce that it threatened destruction of the church and all the people.

From the Villa this storm passed on to frighten the people of Guasave and these, led by their witch doctors, fled into the woods.

Despite such reverses the work of conversion continued. Padre Martín Pérez wrote of going with some faithful Indians 40 miles distant into the Sierras, to the Valle de Cuervo, finding many Indians living there. The Padre related that their children resembled deer more than people, fleeing upon his arrival. However, he finally indoctrinated and baptized between 300 and 400 of them.

By the year 1600 there were upwards of 7,000 Indians converted and baptized in the pueblos of the Mission of Sinaloa.

CHAPTER 19

Captain General don Diego Martinez de Hurdaide

AN OUTSTANDING PERSONALITY in the history of Sinaloa was Captain General don Diego Martinez de Hurdaide, for thirty years in charge of the Province of Sinaloa, with responsibility for the temporal welfare of the Indian Nations who inhabited its rivers, mountains and seashores.

Captain Martinez de Hurdaide was born in Zacatecas, a very rich mining center of New Spain. His father was a Spaniard of good birth and his mother Mexican (*Aztec*), both being very respected and honorable people. He inherited richly from both Spanish and Indian parents those qualities of daring, astuteness and perseverance which marked him as one of the truly great leaders of the frontier.

At an early age he enlisted in the Spanish Militia. As a soldier he labored tirelessly at whatever task he was assigned, especially when it involved the honor of God and King, or the extension of the Christian faith among barbarous peoples.

Against an enemy he was like lightning in action, moving before the opposition should gather strength, often falling upon them when they supposed him to be scarcely preparing his men. From this swiftness in action he gained among the Indians the reputation of being able to read the minds of his adversaries.

Previous to taking service in Sinaloa, he had served in His Majesty's militia on the frontiers of Nueva Galicia, Nueva Vizcaya and Zacatecas. He had also seen service in the protection of the mines of Guanaceví, Santa Barbara and Masapil, during the wars of pacification of the fierce tribes of those areas. However, his most outstanding service was in the pacification of some twenty Indian Nations of the Province of Sinaloa.

The great authority and dominion he achieved over those people, not only Christian Indians but the savages who lived distant and apart, was a matter for much wonder and admiration. Incredible as it may seem, in the thirty years that he commanded the Spanish forces in Sinaloa, he did not lose one soldier on the battlefield, although he and others often were sorely wounded. His authority was so complete that his messengers were permitted to move freely among the Nations, even though these should be at war with each other. His messengers carried always a paper upon which had been impressed his seal. This paper, rolled in a small cane of bamboo, was placed in the head band of the messenger.

A threat was held over all the Nations, that they must be responsible for the safety of these messengers, and should any be missing, the Captain would come personally to search for the messenger and, if not found, his captors would pay with their heads. And he carried out these threats, with the result that he sent messages for a distance of 300 miles from the Presidio with all security.

His obligations as a soldier were no more important to him than those of a Christian leader. All his earnings were spent in assistance to the Indians. Never did he use the Indians for labor in his personal interest, as others have done. On the contrary, as he was able, he gave them from his own savings gifts of clothing and many young horses, these especially to the chiefs among the Indians. The Indians were very proud of owning a horse. Their favorite pastime was to indulge in horse races, riding bareback, with only a cord fastened to the jawbone.

The best proof of this extreme liberality was that after having held this post for over thirty years, at his death he left more debts than wealth, because of his unselfish deeds while in the service of his God and King. A favorite saying of this valiant Captain was, "Now we must give another push against the Devil in Sinaloa."

A complete book might be written of his adventurous life and extraordinary accomplishments. By order of the Real Audencia of Mexico, the history of this great man was recorded for Spain and for the King. However, his death intervened before his merits were rewarded by the special recognition from the Crown that he so well deserved.

CHAPTER 20

Captain Hurdaide Moves Against the Zuaques

THE INSOLENCE of the Zuaque Nation was a matter of much preoccupation to Captain Martinez de Hurdaide. These Indians prided themselves for being murderers of Spaniards, and their land served as a place of refuge for rebellious Indians of the Province.

They even went so far as to send a messenger to the garrison at the Villa defying the Spaniards to enter into their lands. The Lieutenant General, having orders to avoid war if possible, did not take this challenge to an issue at this time. However, the impatient soul of Hurdaide, then subordinate in command, could not be so restrained. Throwing the messenger to the ground at his feet, he exclaimed, "Run, Indian, to the Zuaques, and tell them that they shall one day see me in their lands, and shall then curb their audacity." Then, to the Lieutenant General he said, "As long as these people have so little respect for our valor at arms, we shall have no peace nor security in this province."

One of his first preoccupations, upon becoming Captain General, was how to deal with the savage Zuaques.

Without letting even his soldiers know his intention he ordered made numerous heavy iron collars with chains attached. These he concealed in some sacks in his house. Next, he ordered his soldiers to prepare for a journey, in search of steers that had gone wild, that they might be slaughtered for making dried beef. These steers had remained in the area of Carapoa at the time the fort had been abandoned. Taking only half his garrison, twenty-four soldiers, together with some Indian allies, the Captain traveled to the border of the Zuaque Nation.

The soldiers had been ordered to take along their armored horses in order to be prepared for any emergency.

After arriving at the place mentioned he confided to his soldiers his plan for taking prisoner the Zuaque leaders who had been inciting their people against the Spaniards. He asked his soldiers to undertake to bind two Zuaques each with cords which he had prepared.

The coming of the Spaniards had taken the Zuaques completely by surprise. Soon there came the principal Zuaque leaders, to inquire of the Captain why they had come. He answered that they had come to kill the wild cattle, and would share them with the Indians.

The Indians then asked why the hunting of the wild cattle did not begin. The captain replied that they needed to first gather wood for the fires on which to roast the beef. The Indians then offerred to bring the wood; an offer which the Captain accepted.

The Captain then invited the principal Caciques to remain with him. This they did, while the others went to gather wood in happy anticipation of the feast of roast beef. As they were leaving, an Indian ally reported to the Captain that one Indian had said to another, "We go in search of wood with which to roast the Captain." The Captain chose to ignore the remark, continuing to entertain the attention of the leaders, showing them spurs, bridles, and some trinkets he had brought for the purpose.

The Caciques soon were well scattered among the Spanish soldiers, feeling complete security in the nearness of their multitude of followers. At this instant the Captain gave the word, at the same time grasping by the hair of their heads the two Caciques nearest him. One of these was a principal chief, Toa, an Indian of such stature that he towered high above the stocky Captain. The struggle ended with 42 prisoners being taken, and iron collars being placed about their necks.

There had been some women present at this meeting with the Zuaques, among them one very principal one named Luisa, who had frequently visited the Mission, and whose confidence had been gained by the Captain. The Captain sent a messenger to bring her back from among the women, who had meanwhile fled to the nearby woods.

He explained to her that these men had been taken prisoners because they were the ringleaders of the rebellious ones among the Zuaques and, therefore, must be punished. He offered to Luisa that if among these prisoners she had a relative, this one he would release.

The Indian she indicated was set free. He was thereafter named by the Spaniards, Buena Ventura (*Good Fortune*) for his having so happily secured his freedom. This man afterwards became a Christian, and was of much assistance in bringing others to a peaceful existence with the Spaniards.

Two leaders who had escaped carried the word, on the instant, to their companions who were gathering wood. These quickly assembled, threatening attack on the Spaniards with their bows and arrows. However, they were without leadership, their captains prisoners, and in grave danger from their own arrows. For all their cholera over the stratagem into which they had fallen, they did not venture to attack.

The Captain, talking again through the well-known Zuaque woman, Luisa, counseled them not to begin a battle, under penalty of having their homes and fields destroyed. He told them that he would be content with punishing these Caciques who were to blame for their troubles, offering not to harm any other Indian men, nor their women nor children. In proof of his good will, the women of the prisoners were permitted to bring them food and drink, the other Indians being told to return to their homes and fields. In the food brought were concealed some stones, with which the prisoners attacked their guards, but none were permitted to escape.

The Captain was filled with pious desire that the souls of these rebellious Chieftains should not be lost to heaven. Despite the grave menace of the 1,000 or more warriors in the woods surrounding them, he kept his troop here for four days and nights, until the Padres had received word and had come in all haste to the salvation of these souls. Those who came were the Padres Pedro Méndez, and Juan Bautista de Velasco, the latter of whom understood the language of the Zuaques.

They took much pains that these souls should be well prepared for death and ready to secure salvation. They were told of the necessity of Saintly Baptism for eternal well being, it being explained to them that with the loss of life in their bodies, they would not lose the life of their souls. Of them all, only two remained hardened and obstinate during the two days required for their preparation for death.

Meanwhile, the Captain had ordered two large trees well prepared for their hanging. At the base of these trees the prisoners were baptized, and consoled during their last moments. During this time they were well surrounded by a guard in armor. And so there were left hanging from these trees forty-two chiefs, who had made to tremble in fear the Christians of the Province of Sinaloa.

Through the able and friendly Luisa the Captain sent word that the Zuaques should now remain at peace in their pueblos and their fields; that there they would be protected by the forces of the Spanish King.

It should be said that this Indian, Luisa, was a woman of much worth and valor. In the passing of time, when I had the good fortune to live among the Zuaques for eleven years, this same Luisa was of great assistance in securing the conversion and baptism of the people of this Nation.

At the time of the events related, there were five Padres in the Province of Sinaloa serving the Nations of Mocorito and Petatlán Rivers and in the Valle de Cuervo, in the Sierras. Indians continued coming in ever increasing numbers to hear the doctrine and to be baptized.

These pagan peoples had various superstitions as to the burial of their dead, of which I will tell here. The bodies were placed in caves dug into the earth. Sometimes they were placed sitting, sometimes lying, but always free from the earth itself, this in the event the body should wish to travel. There were placed in the cave with the body, articles to eat and drink, to serve the dead until arriving to where they should be going.

In these practices they seemed to recognize that there exists another world. This feeling on their part served us well in teaching them the immortality of the soul.

Our Evangelical ministers soon learned to preach with much freedom in the languages of these peoples, and to write their rules and precepts for the benefit of others to follow. Much study is required to comprehend their exquisite manner of expressing themselves.

CHAPTER 21

The Captain Explores the Sierras

THE CONDE DE MONTERREY, Viceroy of New Spain, had notice of great riches in minerals in the Sierras of the Province of Sinaloa, which would be most satisfying to the King to have discovered. He therefore gave orders to Captain Hurdaide that he should penetrate the Sierras, especially those of Chínipas, which were reported to be the most rich in minerals. The Sierras of Chínipas lie distant [*northeast 200 miles*] from the Villa. To arrive there it was required to pass through Nations not yet at peace with the Spaniards including, in this respect, the Chínipas themselves.

On this journey the Captain took some men of experience in mining. Besides the soldiers, he took some Indian allies, including some warriors of the Sinaloa Nation, through whose lands they must travel.

In the land of the Chínipas the expedition had, at one point, to pass through a defile in the mountains so narrow they could proceed only in single file. Here the Chínipas, with the aid of some treacherous Sinaloas, rolled great boulders down upon the Spaniards from the cliffs above, until they were split into two parties. The Captain, who was with the advance guard, ordered them to take shelter under the steep cliffs where the rocks must bound harmlessly over their heads into the canyon.

The little army was separated for two days, with no communication, nor opportunity for securing water or food. Finally the enemy, themselves in want of food, dispersed, and the Spaniards were able to unite their forces, by great good fortune, without the loss of a soldier.

Freed from this predicament, the Captain continued resolutely on to Chínipas, finding this pueblo deserted. The silver ore discovered did not assay to expectations. [*Chínipas later became a rich mining area.*] The Captain took with him on the return trip a Chínipa Indian mother and child, whom he kept in his household for many years, where they were converted and baptized and served well as interpreters in the later Christianization of that Nation.

Returning through the lands of the traitorous Sinaloas, he laid waste to their homes and fields, hanging several of their Caciques. He then returned to the Villa of Sinaloa, to await a more opportune time for their civilization.

CHAPTER 22

Government and Christianity Come to Sinaloa

THE PADRES labored continuously to persuade the Indian men to cover their barbarous nudity. They were persuaded also to plant more cotton and the women were interested in weaving cotton mantles with which to clothe themselves.

This advice as to dress the women accepted with pleasure, soon liking so much to dress that they brought grain from their fields and fruits from their trees to trade for cotton cloth from which to make more ample dresses. Not infrequently they passed a part of the season eating roots from the woods, in order to trade the crops of their fields for clothing. At other times they went to labor in distant places, in order to earn the means for buying more attractive garments for themselves.

The Captain, on his part, continued to establish political government in the pueblos, naming Indian Governors and Alcaldes to rule in somewhat the manner of a republic. The Indians accomodated themselves readily to this form of government.

The Padre Hernando de Villafañe had in his charge the three pueblos of the great Guasave Nation. He soon began the construction of churches of solid material, large enough to accomodate all the people. This Nation was of a more amiable nature and more disposed to work than some of the others. In great numbers they put themselves to making adobes. From these they began to erect walls and, the pride of their labor growing in them, they went into the woods to cut and hew hardwood timbers for ceilings. These heavy timbers they carried among many of them, on their shoulders. The work continued with enthusiasm, and soon there were erected three fine churches. The Padres had the walls painted with what colors could be found there; and to these people their churches apeared as splendid as those called miracles of architecture in Europe.

However, by the inscrutable judgment of God, there came presently a rainstorm lasting five successive days and nights, and with such fury that it destroyed the pueblos, together with their churches. The people were forced to flee to the tops of the larger trees for safety. One of the Padres remained for two days and nights perched in a tree, without food, and should he have fallen asleep, was in grave danger of drowning. Another took shelter for five days in a corner of his chapel, with the torrent constantly threatening to engulf him, until some Indians swam with him to safety. The Indians stayed by the Padres most steadfastly in these emergencies.

Such was the faith and strength of will of these Guasaves that they soon set about rebuilding their homes and churches. Taking their example, the people of the Sebastían de Ébora (*Mocorito*) River and of other places were animated to build churches also; and all these resulted attractive and pleasing.

All writers, whether modern or of antiquity, agree that the basis for the development of a successful community or Nation lies in rearing their youth in doctrine and in the practice of good customs. Youth is the age for the laying of the foundation for the life of a man. If this be true in the established republics of the world, then how much more it is true in regard to peoples totally destitute of doctrine and human government.

Our Padres gave most particular attention to the development and preservation of faith in the young people of these Indian Nations. They selected from among them the most alert of each Nation to become students in a College that was soon established at the Villa of Sinaloa.

Here they learned reading, writing, singing and the practice of good customs.

Later they came to be of great help to the Padres in the Missions. These young people are like a yeast for leavening Christianity among their own race.

Their faith and constancy is well exemplified in this story: On a certain occasion a group of rebellious Indians took flight into the woods. On the day previous a chorus of young singers from the College had been sent to hold services at a church of a neighboring pueblo. On the way they received messages from various of their parents who were in rebellion, telling them to leave the Spaniards and join in the revolt. This the young Indians refused to do saying they must, in this case, desert the side of their carnal fathers. This firmness on the part of the children proved to be the effective means of bringing their rebellious parents to their senses, and they returned in peace to their pueblos.

Some of the young people who grow up in the Seminary become so devoted, and so adept in their speech that the Padres permit them to stand at the altars of the churches, properly robed, to make a talk to their own people.

Hearing the word of God from the lips of their own sons and relations and in their own language is most effective, and brings special pleasure to the hearts of the listeners.

CHAPTER 23

Second War Against the Zuaques

ON THIS FRONTIER of restless savages there never were lacking incidents which obligated Captain Hurdaide to take up arms. Soon after the end of the expedition to the country of the Chínipas Nation, there came to the Captain two messengers from the Ahome Nation, which populates the lower part of the great River of Zuaque.

The Ahomes complained that the fierce and belicose Tegueco Nation, which populates the borders of the river up stream from the Zuaques, had descended to the land of the Ahomes, driving them away and taking possession of their fields and, not content with this, had stolen several of their women. This report disturbed the Captain exceedingly. Although both Teguecos and Ahomes were still in their gentility, the latter had always remained at peace with the Spaniards having, in fact, by agreement placed themselves under their protection. Deeming no other measure sufficient, the Captain found himself obligated to go to the support of the Ahomes.

With his force of soldiers, armored horses and friendly Indians, he first arrived at the land of the Zuaques, which is on the way to the land of the Ahomes. These latter Indians live in a valley named Mathaoa, down river toward the sea. The Zuaques were not yet well subdued, despite their former chastisement. On this occasion they called on their companions in arms, the Sinaloas, who had also been chastized by the Spaniards, to come to their assistance.

Arrived at the Zuaque, the Captain made headquarters at a pueblo of some 500 families, named Mochicaui (*Mochicahui*), which is situated on a plain above the river. The Zuaques and their allies did not choose to begin battle upon arrival of the Spaniards, hoping for a better occasion, when the soldiers should be dismounted from their armored horses. It may be said, however, that the Captain always kept some soldiers mounted in readiness for battle.

The Captain was seated in the camp of the Spaniards at Mochicahui, conversing with the principal Indian woman Luisa, before referred to, when there came marching a band of the Sinaloas, with bows and arrows in readiness, these being led by a belligerant and renowned Hechicero, who was much looked up to by the Indian Nations of the Province of Sinaloa. Such was his fame, that it was said that when mounted on a horse, both he and horse would rise into the sky. This man would boastfully say, "When the Padres that preach to you can do this, as I do, you may then believe what they tell you." With such stories and arts of the Devil he had kept the Indian Nations in a state of restlessness.

The Captain had very especially desired to come face to face with this Indian. Now the Indian woman, Luisa, exclaimed to him, "Here comes Taxícora with his warriors." The Captain well knew that these people do not at once disclose what they are planning, but he felt certain that behind this apparent coming to give him greeting there was a plan to take him prisoner by treason. In that brief moment, the Captain deliberated on whether to lay hands on this famous witch doctor or to leave this for another occasion when the whole Zuaque Nation, as well as the Sinaloas under Taxícora, should not be involved.

Then there flashed through his mind a vision of his Vizcaino father, who had taught him to be alert and brave to face any danger. He exclaimed to himself, "Oh! Vizcaya, where are you now?" and resolved to act at once. He quietly ordered the soldiers nearest him to bring close their armored horses, and so awaited the approach of the famous Indian and his followers.

43

Pretending not to know Taxícora, the Captain casually asked his name and, as he asked, he quickly pulled the Indian's bow from his hands, catching a leg of the Indian with the cord of the bow, at the same time grasping the long hair of his head with the other hand. Thus holding him prisoner, he ordered Taxícora to be well tied and guarded, and gave orders to prepare for battle.

To the woman Luisa the Captain said, "Tell your people to remain quiet in their pueblo. Tell them that with the capture of Taxícora we will leave content. If they do not act as I tell them, they will answer for the consequences."

Taxícora was bound upon a mule and a soldier assigned to guard over him. Placing their prisoner in the center of their troops, the Spaniards again began their march down river toward the land of the Ahomes.

They presently came to a place where they were forced to proceed in single file. Here they were attacked with great showers of arrows. The Spanish troops never had been in such grave danger, for it was impossible to bring their arquebuses and swords into play, nor to charge the enemy with their armored horses.

The soldier who guarded the rebel chief was ordered to threaten him with his dagger if the attacking Indians did not desist, but by now the fury of the attackers was such that, despite the pleading of their own captive chief, arrows continued to rain upon the Spanish troops. Next to the Captain an armored horse had fallen with its rider. It is most difficult in such cases for a soldier to remount, because of the weight of his armor.

The Captain, spurring his horse, captured a nearby Indian, with a rope hanging him from the limb of a tree. This action diverted the attention of the other Indians until the soldier could be again set upon his horse.

Finally extricating themselves, the Spanish troops and Indian allies continued to the Valle de Mathaoa. Here they caught the marauding Teguecos unprepared, scattering them over the valley, and making prisoners of their women and children.

The Spaniards and their allies established a camp here. Captain Hurdaide sent word to those Teguecos who had fled to the nearby woods, that they must leave the Ahomes in peace and return at once to their own homes and fields. He sent word also that they should come for their women and children that these might return with them to their own lands.

Confiding in his promise which they knew, from past experience, would be kept, the Teguecos gathered their families and departed; leaving the Ahomes once more in possession of their lands. For this help the Ahomes were most grateful, and soon requested that Padres be sent to teach them Christianity.

There is now told of the return through the land of the Zuaques, which is one of the most adventurous stories in the life of Captain Hurdaide. Keeping the Hechicero Taxícora in their midst, the troops returned to the pueblo of Mochicahui, where the Zauques, not daring to do battle, had retired to the surrounding woods, here feeling safe from the armored horses of the Spaniards.

Through the woman Luisa, the Zuaques plead to be excused for their attack from ambush, saying they had been incited to do so by the Sinaloas, because of Taxícora being prisoner.

The Captain meanwhile had placed his soldiers in order of battle. Through the interpreter Luisa, he explained to the Zuaques that he had no wish to shed their blood, nor to burn their pueblos, nor destroy the crops they had just harvested. He said, however, that he would not go leaving them unpunished, and this punishment would be that all the Zuaque warriors must come to him, one by one, and have their hair cut short. Their hair is a matter of extreme pride to these people. He further stipulated that to reward his Indian allies, the Zuaques warriors must give to them the beads with which they adorned themselves. He pointed out to them, too, the pleasure and advantage they could in the future enjoy, by maintaining a firm friendship with the Spaniards.

To many this punishment, especially losing their long hair, seemed so severe that they chose for the moment to remain at the borders of the woods, to see what should next happen. Others, seeing the peril of resistance, and knowing the Captain was a man who made good his threats and promises, came to accept their punishment. Their hair was not cropped close, but only to their shoulders, that they might still have protection from the sun. They also gave up their beads, and bows and arrows, after which each was sent to remain at his own home.

In order to persuade the Indians who still remained watching from the edge of the woods, the Captain sent soldiers to set fire to each house where there was no Indian warrior beside it. The woman Luisa, at the same time, shouted loudly that they must come to take their punishment, if they wished to save their homes from burning. This threat soon brought them all running to be sheared.

This task finished, the Captain lifted his camp and marched onward to the Villa with his Hechicero prisoner. Arrived there, the prisoner was sentenced to be hung, as he well deserved.

The Padres assisted him in preparing for the hour of his death. He proved to be well disposed to receive baptism, leaving hope for his salvation. And in the manner we have written there was removed a great barrier to the teaching of Evangelism in Sinaloa.

CHAPTER 24

The Captain Reports to the Viceroy

ONCE THE CAPTAIN and his soldiers and Indian allies had conquered the savage Nations of the Gran Rio de Zuaque, these, through their Caciques, came to request of the Padres and the Captain that they should enter into their lands to govern them and to bring Christian doctrine. To this purpose they offered to build churches, and to bring their people into larger pueblos. This was happy news to the Captain and the Padres.

However, in order to extend the labor of evangelism to these new places, there was need for more Padres, also there was required a permission from the Viceroy of New Spain. It was decided that the Captain himself should journey to the City of Mexico to advise the Viceroy of the state of affairs in the Province, and of the desirability of acquiescing in the request of the Indians for Padres.

Several Caciques accompanied him, that they might see the Viceroy, and personally plead their cause. The Captain, four soldiers and the Caciques made this long journey, a Lieutenant being left in charge of the Garrison at the Villa.

The Viceroy received them well and, after consultation with the Provincial Father of the Company, it was decided to send two more Padres to Sinaloa to assist the five already there, with further Padres to be sent as needed.

An order was given on the Royal Treasury for two complete sets of vestments for the priests, and adornment for the altars. The order included also church bells and musical instruments.

For the Indians accompanying the Captain, there were ordered clothing and swords, with which they departed from Mexico City contented. For the expenses of their return journey they were given alms by the Viceroy, don Fray Garcia Mendoza y Zúñiga.

The Padres who returned with Captain Martinez de Hurdaide were the writer (*Andrés Pérez de Ribas*) and Pedro de Velasco.

On this journey it was that we passed through the vast territory granted by the King of Spain to don Rodrigo del Rio y Loza, where we were entertained by this distinguished gentleman.

After arriving at Zacatecas, 240 miles from Mexico City, we were deserted in the night by four of our Cacique companions, with no apparent reason other than their inconstancy of nature. The Captain was much disturbed at this, fearing their thought in deserting was to stir up rebellion in their pueblos before his return to the Province.

It is worthy of comment here, that these Indians, who had only once traveled this route, were able to return over 600 miles of deserts and mountains, most of them uninhabited, to their homes, living only on herbs or roots found along the way.

The Captain made long marches to Topia, but was unable to catch up with them. At Topia he heard the disquieting news that the four deserters had murdered three Culiacán Indians they had found sleeping, taking their scalps with which to celebrate a war dance with their Tegueco neighbors, upon their return to their pueblos. It was soon learned, however, that the Teguecos had refused to join in plans for war, because of their fear of the Captain, and that the four rebellious chiefs had thereupon fled with some followers to the mountain tribes called Tepagues.

Further bad news was that the Indians of two supposedly Christian pueblos, Ocoroni and Bacubirito, had revolted, and burned their churches, although they had been followed by only a few people.

With the Captain traveling while ill, we descended through the cold mountain passes from Topia, finally arriving at the Villa of Sinaloa, to the relief and rejoicing of the inhabitants there.

The Captain at once began to put matters in order. He sent assurances of support to those Nations who had remained quiet. He sent offers of peace to those in revolt. Some took advantage of his offer, others continued in revolt and eventually paid with their heads. Those he did not hang, he forced to labor in rebuilding the churches.

He soon called together the Tegueco Indians, telling them of the good treatment in Mexico City of the four Teguecos who had revolted and of their murder of the Culiacán Indians, explaining that he must pursue these rebels even into the most inaccessible Sierras.

The friendly Teguecos offered to send a group of their warriors to capture the fugitives, which was done. Most of them were eventually delivered into the hands of the Captain, who ordered justice to be executed upon them on the exact spot where they had murdered the Culiacán Indians, that the relatives of these might be assured of their having been punished.

Another Indian Tribe, named Toroacas, lived near the Guasaves toward the sea. After some of them had been converted, they arose in revolt under a Cacique, creating much unrest. They soon fled to an island separated from the mainland by almost six miles (*probably San Ignacio Island*). Here they had lived before, and felt secure from the Spaniards, as the Indians had passed to the Island by swimming. The Indians had no boats, using only small rafts built from poles tied together with reeds. However, the Captain was determined that no one who became delinquent from his authority should escape. With his soldiers and some Indian allies he built rafts much larger than any before used, crossed over the six miles of sea, hunted down the refugees, and returned them to the mainland. Seven of the principal offenders he caused to be hanged. The others he pardoned, distributing them among the pueblos of the Guasaves, where they were watched over and, in good time, when they had become satisfied with this manner of living, they were accomodated on lands of the Guasave Nation.

CHAPTER 25

Indians of the Lower Sierras

THERE WERE two mountain tribes, the Chicoratos and Cavametos, in total some 1,500 persons, living not far eastward of the Villa of Sinaloa. In order to accomplish their conversion, the Captain brought them down from their peaks and crags to be settled in an area where he had purchased land from some

Christian Indians. These latter were charged with teaching the strangers the cultivation of crops and fruit trees, and the building of adobe houses. That they should take deeper root, their former places of habitation were burned, and so they chose to be content.

These mountain Indians are of less stature, but are very swift in running over rocks and peaks, and most dextrous in the use of bow and arrow.

The arrow points they make of stone. These stone points do not penetrate as easily as the points of burnt wood of the plains Indians, neither are they so apt to use poison on the tips of their stone arrows. Nevertheless, wounds from these stone arrow points are difficult to heal, because at the extraction of the cleft of the arrow, the stone point may remain embedded in the flesh and, if deep, may only be extracted with much pain and danger. The Spainards fear these arrows less, as they are not apt to penetrate their armor, but the Indians fear them more, as they wage war while almost naked, and have no protection from the stone arrows.

The women and children of these mountains are diligent at their tasks. They are great packers, carrying these packs on their shoulders, suspended by a broad sash (*faja*) across their foreheads. In this manner they climb those high slopes and peaks, bearing heavy loads of corn, pottery ollas or other things which they use, aiding themselves by the use of a staff in their hands. They use meshed bags for carrying. In this same manner they may carry one or two of their children.

As the fathers place a bow and arrow in the hands of their little sons, so the mothers place loads on the backs of their little girls. As the entire family is well trained in packing, they can move their household with little trouble.

The Padre Pedro de Velasco, who attended to the spiritual needs of these people, taught them, when meeting on their mountain trails, to give the greeting of "Jesus, Maria," and so they continue to give greeting to each other to this day.

The Devil was most rabid at losing these Indians whom he had kept hidden among their rugged peaks, and continued to create unrest among them. On an occasion when these Indians were gathered to play the game of ball that we have described, there arose a dispute so fierce that some of the players were disposed to take recourse to bow and arrow. The Padre, who was present, with kindly reproof persuaded them to desist from attacking each other. However, the rancor in their hearts remained, and one group later ambushed the other in the woods, after which they fled to take refuge with some Indian friends.

From here they plotted the killing of the Padre. He was saved only through the kindness of some gentile Indians to whom he had done some favors. These Indians, happening to meet those of evil intention on the trail, learned of their plans and persuaded them to desist. However the group, still angry, felt they must have vengeance on someone and, finding two Christian Indians fishing by a stream, these were beheaded, and their bodies taken for the celebration of an orgy of drunkeness.

Soon after Padre Velasco had quieted these pueblos there occurred the uprising of the Indians of the great Sierras so much heard of throughout New Spain (*1616*). These rebels sought to enlist the aid of the Christian Chicoratos and Cavametos. First they tried promises, then threats, but all to no avail; the Christian Indians remained firm in their loyalty to their Padres. The rebels then determined to destroy them. On a Sunday morning, at the time when services were being held, 600 Tepeguane rebels came to attack. A boy saw them and rang the bell violently, causing the congregation to pour out of the church. In the fierce battle that followed, several of the invaders lost their heads, and peace was restored to the village.

The Tubari Nation populated various rancherias in the upper reaches of the Gran Rio de Zuaque. They were always of good heart toward the Spaniards. Sometimes they traded for salt with the Indians of the plains. In the year 1620 they came down from their Sierras to the Villa to ask to be taught the Christian faith. They brought several children to study in the College of the Mission and these, in the course of the years, returned to teach their own people. It is interesting to note that these Tubaris spoke two languages, evidently having descended from two separate tribes.

Among the Indians of these Sierras the good Padre Pedro de Velasco labored for many years, moved by his great zeal for the salvation of those poor, impoverished souls. Padre Pedro was of a prominent family, the son of don Diego de Velasco, who had once been Governor of the Province of Nueva Viscaya. Because of his ample preparation, he had opportunity to become a man very distinguished in the Jesuit Order in the City of Mexico, but he loved the rugged service of the frontier and could not be persuaded to exchange it for the easier life of the City.

CHAPTER 26

Mass Migration of Nebomes to Sinaloa

THERE HAS BEEN TOLD of the 600 Nebome (*Pima*) Indians who accompanied Cabeza de Vaca to Sinaloa in the year 1536, and who were settled by him on the Petatlán (*Sinaloa*) River at a place called Bamoa. In the passing of the years, and the land being now at peace, the thoughts of these Nebomes turned to the lands of their ancestors, which lie high up in the Sierras between the Mayo and Hiaqui Rivers. Some Nebomes returned to visit this land of their fathers and were well received. They in turn told of their good treatment at the hands of the Spaniards, and how they lived in contentment on their fertile lands, after having been converted to Christianity.

Their story so moved the mountain Nebomes that many of their principal people returned with their relatives to the Villa, to ask the Padres to go into their mountains to baptize their children. They were received with much pleasure, but at that time it was not deemed advisable to make the journey of 240 miles, until peace could be made with other savage Nations whose lands lie in between.

Seeing this delay, God moved the hearts of the Nebomes to migrate, in a group of 350 persons, to the lands of their people at Bamoa. They carried with them their children and their few belongings and, because of a drouth that had come upon the land, suffered many hardships on their journey. Except for fear of the Captain, other Indian Nations would have attacked them along the way.

These Nebomes arrived at the Villa of Sinaloa on the first day of February of 1615 [*79 years after the migration of the first Nebomes with Cabeza de Vaca*]. After a warm reception, they continued on to the land of their people at Bamoa, 12 miles below the Villa.

A procession of the relatives received the pilgrims at Bamoa. The church bells rang in welcome. There was singing from the chapel choir, accompanied by numerous instruments. They passed under arches formed from green boughs, while a choir sang the Te Deum Laudamus, composed for the great doctor of the Church, Saint Augustine.

They marched together; the new arrivals with their hosts and relatives, men with men and women with women, as though they had known each other for all those years.

In this order they entered the church, where the Padre offered a prayer and orations were sung, with the people kneeling before the altar.

The Padre then told the pilgrims of the joy that was felt by all in receiving them, and so must they too be joyful for God having led them to a land where they should be received as brothers and that, in token of their new faith, they should now worship the Saintly Cross.

Each Indian family of Bamoa took to their home the number of pilgrims they could provide with food, which was shared liberally, and all were most content.

On the day following, the 114 children of the newly arrived were baptized. A week later the Padres distributed corn to them for seeding; dividing some lands into parcels for this purpose.

I close this story by saying that none of this pilgrim group returned to the land of their birth, as these people are wont to do. They now have built a church and are continuing its adornment. They plant annually a plot of land, the product of which is sold to maintain their Church.

CHAPTER 27

The Rio Grande de Zuaque (Fuerte River)

THE GRAN RIO DE ZUAQUE (*Fuerte River*) flows from out of the Sierras of Topia, from so far away that no one knows its source. It is more copious than the Guadalquivir of Spain. It is given the names of the various Tribes or Nations in the area where each Nation populates its borders; and for these the river is variously called.

The Zuaque flows across the coastal plains for a distance of 90 miles. In time of flood it fertilizes beautiful valleys on its way to the sea. These floods are apt to come twice yearly, in summer, and in winter. The floods which result from winter snows in the Sierras spread across the coastal plain for five or ten miles, irrigating the soil as does the Nile in Egypt.

These floods leave moisture for planting two and, sometimes even three, crops annually; the third crop growing in good seasons without further flooding from the river. On occasional years when the rains fail, these Nations suffer severely the lack of crops.

The Sinaloa Nation populates the upper river where it emerges from the Sierras. They were more than 1,000 families, and a larger number of warriors of bow and arrow. Twenty miles down river lies the land of the Teguecos, a Nation valiant and greatly feared, who could field in battle 1,500 men of bow and arrow. Five leagues farther down river lived the ferocious Zuaques, numbering about 1,000 families. They occupied an area of some thirty miles on the borders of the river.

Finally, for a like distance of thirty miles to the sea, lived the Ahomes, and various adjoining tribes. The Ahomes were the most peaceful of the pueblos. With their adjoining groups, including the fishers of the sea, they numbered about 1,000 families. Of these hunters and fishers who lived near the sea I have already told that they were the most savage and barbarous found in all the Indies.

Of the sweet and healthful waters of the Rio Grande de Zuaque, the Indians preached in the sermons of their antiquity. The Indians living along the river caught great numbers of fish. These, as we have told, come in greatest numbers at the period of laying their eggs, at which time they swim up river from the sea.

When the river recedes, leaving pools, the Indians come together for a general fishing. They take large amounts of the barbasco plant, with its branches threshing the surface of the pools. The fish, intoxicated by its poison, come to the surface and are easily taken. It is to be noted that the effect of the poison is not present when the fish is eaten.

In the time of their barbarity, the rituals, games and other customs of these people were much the same as those of whom we have written.

No sooner had Captain Hurdaide returned with the two Padres from Mexico City, than there came Indians to learn in what places they were to be employed. From the Zuaque Nation came the distinguished woman Luisa, and her kinsman, the Cacique Ventura, who had, by her intercession, been saved from hanging by the Captain. From the Tegueco Nation there came, among other Caciques, their great leader Lanzarote, now a convert to the Christian faith. From the Sinaloas came their principal chiefs, to talk with the Captain and the Padres. The Ahome Nation had been the very first requesting to receive the faith.

The Indians of all these Nations offered to form their smaller villages and rancherias into larger pueblos, and to build churches. In the beginning these were to be only huts with brush walls.

The Padre Martín Pérez, now Superior of the Mission of Sinaloa, assigned to the Tegueco Nation Padre Pedro Mendéz, who lived at the Mission of Ocoroni. To the Padre Cristobal de Villalta were assigned the Sinaloas, and to the author (*Andrés Pérez de Ribas*), the Zuaques and Ahomes. In the Villa there was great rejoicing over the proposal for conversion of these people.

CHAPTER 28

Padre Pérez de Ribas Civilizes the Ahomes

THE PRINCIPAL PUEBLO of the Ahome Nation, consisting of 300 to 400 families, is situated on a fertile plain along the River Zuaque, and is surrounded by woods. It has nearby, many cultivated fields. It lies distant only twelve miles from the Sea of Californias. There was a legend among the Indians that the Valley of Ahome was the Paradise of the Indian peoples, and that here lived the souls of their ancestors. There was another tradition, of the Ahomes having come from the north in a perigrination together with the Zoe (*Choix*) Nation, which is now living 90 miles up river.

[*Lic. Eustaquio Buelna, in the introduction to "Arte de la Lengua Cahita" describes the perigrination of the Toltec Nation, after a habitation of 800 years on the Gila River of Arizona. According to Buelna, one group of the Toltecs moved down the West Coast mainland, crossing the Sierras at Culiacán, Sinaloa, and finally settling at Tula, later their historic capital in the present State of Hidalgo, near the Valley of Mexico. This journey is said to have been made in stages, over a period of some 215 years, so that they could have spent some years in Sinaloa, and some of them might well have remained there.*]

The Ahomes maintained friendship with the Guasaves; they are said to be related in their recent ancestry, and speak the same language. The Ahomes are, by nature, docile and learn quickly, as do their children. These latter were soon able to read, write, sing and play musical instruments.

During the eleven years I lived among these people I felt perfect security. I enjoyed the further assurance of knowing that if I were endangered among the other tribes, I could take safe refuge among the Ahomes.

They were of better appearance than most other Indians of the Province. They indulged less in drunkeness, and were not so inclined to war. They rarely had more than one wife. They guarded their doncellitas (*maidens*) very carefully. These wore suspended about their necks a pretty collar of sea shells, until the day of their marriage.

The dress of their women was more modest than that of the women of other Nations. They wove their own cotton fabrics, some with curious figures, and of attractive colors.

Of witch doctors, either men or women, there were few. However, they persisted in one custom, which was their lamentation for the dead, wailing so loudly that it was almost intolerable to listen to. This was the more trying because, in the home of the deceased, the lamentations continued for a full year, with such great howling that it sounded like shouts from the condemned. Every morning, at break of day and, again at evening, for the space of an hour, these shouts continued, with variations of tone, and would be answered from other houses, until the entire pueblo was in an uproar. This custom was so imbued in them that it was most difficult to moderate or correct it.

On the occasion of my first entry into the land of the Ahomes, I was accompanied by a number of their people, who had come 60 miles to the Villa of Sinaloa to escort me to their pueblo. It was necessary to take a route near the sea, through the lands of the Caribes (*cannibals*). Of these, various ones came to meet me. I took care to make little gifts to them of food and other items that they treasure.

While I was seated among a group of these Caribe Indians in a field, talking to them of God the Creator, there suddenly came a great earthquake. The startled Indians leapt quickly to their feet, but I soon seated them, continuing to explain to them the power of God, and the need to know and have faith in the divine word. They were calmed, took heed to my words, and later came to join the other Indians in their Christian pueblos.

Upon nearing the pueblo of the Ahomes, I was received by their principal Cacique, don Miguel. He was mounted on a horse that had been presented to him by the Captain. He was an Indian of excellent disposition and of much capability, being later most useful in the work of the Mission.

With him came other Indians, whom he referred to as his children. After exchanging greetings, we all went forward together to the pueblo. Upon arriving, we were escorted under a series of green arches formed from the branches of trees. At the village plaza I was greeted by many people, of all ages, who came marching in procession, carrying a cross before them. This cross had been adorned as brightly as possible with colored plumes, and many flowers.

53

Greatly to my surprise, I was then greeted by a chorus of voices, singing the chants of the service. I soon discovered who had prepared this fine surprise. An old man who was blinded had attended services at Guasave, had memorized the chants and music, and even the sermons, and it was his joy to travel among the peoples of the pueblos to teach them from his knowledge.

Soon I entered the brush enramada which was to serve as a church in the beginning, and sat among these people. I discussed and answered questions, after which I held service and began the baptism of the children.

The Godparents of the children later took them, and their Padre with them, to their homes, regaling all with their favorite foods, which were tortillas and tamales.

On this first visit I remained among them for eight days. During this time they took me to see their beautiful river, bordered by large cottonwood trees.

Here they had sometimes been attacked by the Zuaques and Teguecos. The men, armed with bow and arrow, had always to accompany their women when these came with their ollas for water.

After a visit among the Zuaques, I returned to Ahome, to find timbers ready hewn for the construction of a church, in which task I must assist, as they had little knowledge of building.

Soon came the baptisms of the men and women. In baptism, the Indians usually were given a Christian name, their former name being preserved as a surname. A careful record was kept of all these names.

One day the Ahomes came to request permission to celebrate a dance in their ancient manner. I assented, on condition that the boys and girls should not dance together. They explained that, although they did partake in the same dance, I should find that it was in a manner pleasing to see.

And so it was, for, although they dance near to each other, the girls do not lift their eyes to the boys, nor touch their clothing, not even looking directly at the youth they know their parents have selected for them to marry.

To a group of Caciques who came to visit me, I gave some small articles which mean much to them, such as colored beads, a knife, an old horse shoe from which to make an ax, or a needle for sewing fish nets; and with such presents they were contented.

Soon there came a group of Indians of those who lived along the seashore, to discuss uniting their people, although under their own leader, with the Ahome Nation, that they might all worship together. A most serious problem was that they were accustomed to living on fish, and the sea lies twelve miles distant. Taking this into consideration, there was selected a beautiful site for worship, ten miles down river toward the sea.

The Cacique of this group was a man of such gigantic proportions that he dared to attack an alligator in the water alone, and carry it to the shore.

For teaching in this new and lovely little pueblo we secured the services of the old blind Christian Indian. With this arrangement the Bacoreguis, for so they were named, were much comforted.

At Ahome, the people came morning and evening to study in preparation for baptism. Those who had married according to the custom of their gentility, when baptized were married with the sacrament of the Mother Church.

The Batucari Nation had their habitation, although without houses, on the borders of a little lagoon which was about twelve miles from Ahome [*probably Laguna San Pablo*]. They came sometimes to glean from the harvest of corn, or to exchange labor for corn. For the rest of their food they had to be content with what they found to eat in the woods. These people, following the good example of the Ahomes, soon accepted the doctrine, but their woods continued to call them. Also, they wished to continue their drinking, seeking their ancient solitude for this purpose. God chastized them by bringing upon them a sickness, which obligated their Padre to take the Blessed Sacrament to them in the place of their isolation.

There was also indoctrinated a group of fisher Indians, including a hundred children, and this increased the population of Ahome to about 500 families.

Being in the pueblo of the fisher Indians, Bacoreguis, I was told that twenty miles farther, on a lonely peninsula formed of sand dunes and trees [*probably Bahia de Agiabampo*], there lived the Comopori Indians, who were of the same tongue as the Ahomes, but regarded themselves as their enemies, killing Ahomes as they found opportunity to do so. These Comporis were so savage and fierce that not even the Zuaques, of whose fierceness and arrogance we have written, dared to confront them in open battle. Once, upon doing so, they had left many dead, and those who escaped remained scarred with the memory for many years.

I learned that occasionally a Christian Indian was permitted entrance among them, as may happen, through ties of kinship or for other reason. With one of these Christian Indians I sent an invitation for them to come to see me at Ahome. One and another, including some of their Caciques, did eventually come to visit. I gave them small gifts which they esteem, and arranged for them to be permitted to come to glean at the next harvest. As they gained confidence, they began to move about the pueblo as they pleased.

I was next given an invitation to visit them. For this I had need to secure permission from the Padre Rector of the College at the Villa.

This permission was given me, on condition that I be accompanied by at least two dozen friendly Ahomes. The Cacique don Miguel, with great good will, agreed to gather men for the journey. However, the wife of don Miguel became very disturbed and grieved, saying that the Comoporis were not of good heart, and only wished us to go to their lands in order to take our lives. This gave me some preoccupation, but having learned from experience that it is unwise to show fear, I tried to comfort her so that she should not dissuade her husband. Commending the matter to God, I began the journey with the others.

Greatly to my surprise, upon crossing the river to the opposite bank from where lies the pueblo, we found waiting to join us a hundred Ahome warriors, well equipped with bows and quivers of arrows. I asked don Miguel what was meant by this, as I feared the impression that would be made upon the Comoporis. To my question don Miguel replied, "Padre, I called only those you asked for, but these men, your sons, distrust the Comoporis, and do not wish you to risk your life. They go to protect you, and I cannot forbid them."

In order to calm the fears of the Comoporis as well as possible, I sent ahead a youth of eighteen years, of the Ahomes, who had accompanied us, riding a good horse. Having no armor for the horse, he had painted on it with ochre the appearance of armor such as the Spanish soldiers used. This youth rode with all the dexterity of a horseman of Spain.

We traveled principally along the seashore, where my Indian companions entertained themselves by shooting arrows at the great numbers of fish. Finally we arrived at the camp of the Comoporis. They had no village, nor house, but lived as savages. On the sand dunes they had made an enramada of poles and leafy branches, to provide me with shelter from the warm sun. We were met at the camp by their very renowned leader, Cohari, and a number of his followers. However, there were no women nor children in the group, which caused me some concern, for their absence might be an indication of bad intentions on the part of our hosts. The day passed, and only a few of the women and children came to our camp. This fact was disturbing to my Indian escort.

When evening had come, and we were all gathered together, the Cacique Cohari began to speak, saying, "Father, on this site we wish to build a church, that you may come to teach us the ways of God, and baptize us. We feel that we cannot leave our land and our places of fishing to live in a pueblo, as some other Indians have done." And so I came to understand what was troubling them, and keeping so many from coming to greet us. They were fearful that I would insist on their going to live away from their beloved sand dunes by the sea.

Perceiving that these people could be won only with time and patience, I explained to them that I had not come to lead them away from their land, but that a church could not be built here because of the distance from fresh water, and lack of land for cultivation of corn and other crops. I expressed content-ment with my visit, and urged them to continue coming to visit me as they could, and also to make friends with the Christian Indians in the pueblos, for they were now all friends and brothers. I further told them that should some of them wish to go to the land of the Ahomes to prepare lands and plant crops they would be made welcome. They seemed well pleased with what I told them, and presently went to sleep in the area surrounding my quarters. Still fearing possible treachery, don Miguel and my companions the Ahomes dis-tributed themselves carefully; a number by me, the rest scattered among the sleeping Comoporis.

The morning following, the entire tribe came to visit, bringing the women and children, and thereafter they came friquently to call on me at Ahome. Some among them began to cultivate crops, and to attend church, and in the end most of them moved to the vicinity of the pueblo, although they made fre-quent trips to fish in the sea.

I found among these Comoporis an odd form of superstition. On the high dunes overlooking the sea, at intervals they had raised some poles. At the base of these they had piled numbers of human skeletons and bones and, together with them, some bundles of ixtle fiber, of the material used for making their nets for fishing. Asking the Cacique Cohari what was meant by this piling of bones and nets, he explained that the bones were of Indians who had perished from the teeth of tiger sharks, while crossing that branch of ocean to the mainland. There are many in these waters. The bones and ixtle were placed there as an offering, to insure their safe crossing.

I quickly disillusioned them, pointing out that only God should be prayed to for the sparing of these people who were in such peril, he being the author of life, and who concedes it to us. I asked that these bones be removed and buried.

At this request the great Cacique Cohari went into an agony of fear and trembling, so deeply was he affected by the thought of changing a custom and belief so impressed upon him and his people. I then asked one of my Ahome companions to bury the bones, which he did; and as no harm came to this Indian they became undeceived of what they had formerly believed.

The men, women and children of the Ahomes soon became so dedicated to Christian doctrine that they resolved to discontinue their savage dances and drunken orgies. In the first year, 2,000 people were baptized.

A chorus of singers was trained to present music for the Easter services. To the usual services they were permitted to add dances that were decorous. This was most pleasing to them, and they invited people from their own and other Nations living along the great river.

Just before these feasts the fisher Indians had a great fishing, sometimes providing fish for 2,000 or 3,000 persons, which gave much pleasure to all.

To the penitences of the Lenten season they applied themselves with diligence, making their disciplines of blood with devotion, in concert of great numbers, following in the processions singing the litanies.

It truly seemed a miracle to see this devotion in people who had until so recently been as free as the stags of the field, as fierce and belligerent as lions and tigers, as wild as the jabalíes, and as hidden in their forests as are the fish in the sea.

Their interest soon led them to the construction of permanent churches. There were brought persons who could teach them to make adobes, and to hew in the right proportions the great hardwood timbers for the church ceilings. They entered into this labor with great enthusiasm. Sometimes a hundred men could be seen carrying one great timber. The women took an active part in all these enterprises, helping, together with their children, in carrying materials and in construction. Finally there was completed, whitewashed and painted, a church capable of holding 2,000 persons. It was dedicated with much feasting, to which were invited the Indians of the neighboring pueblos. These Indian visitors gazed upon this fine building with admiration; and in their hearts was born a desire to see similar churches in their own pueblos.

CHAPTER 29

The San Miguel Mission

THE PEOPLE left from the groups we have mentioned as living along the sea, the Bacoreguis, Batucaris, Comoporis and others, were presently gathered together to form a large new pueblo ten miles up river from the Ahomes. To this pueblo was given the name of the Archangel, San Miguel, whose favor was seen in achieving such noteworthy changes in these remote tribes.

Changing the habitation and manner of living of these Indians from the shores of the sea cost great effort to their good Padre, Vicente del Águila. However, in the end they took such great pride in their new lands that they built another church as handsome as that of Ahome, and here they persevere most faithfully, being outstanding in their signal Christianity.

[It is perhaps significant that the Indians of San Miguel are now (1967) those who persist most faithfully in the worship of Catholic Christianity, albeit accompanied by their formal rituals, feasts and dances. They are also the Indians who maintain the closest relationship with the Carrizo Indians, who still live along the sea on the shore of San Ignacio Bay.]

CHAPTER 30

The House on Water

IN THE YEAR 1615 there sailed into the Sea of Californias two Spanish ships, under command of Captain Juan Iturbi. They came by permission of King Felipe III, under commission to Tomás Cardona of Seville, to search for pearls, of which many reports had been sent to Spain.

In this same year the Dutch (*Pechilingues*) entered with some ships into the Sea of the South (Pacific Ocean) through the Straits of Magellan. Sailing along the shores of New Spain, near the entrance to the Sea of Californias, off a Cape called San Lucas, these Dutchmen captured one of the two Spanish ships, Captain Juan Iturbi escaping with the other.

Following this branch of the Californias along the shore opposite to Sinaloa, they explored pearl oyster beds, finding them in abundance, and taking some as far northward as 30 degrees.

At this point they ran low of provision, and there being no port to which to repair in that country so new to navigation, they set sail southward along the shores of the Province of Sinaloa. This, I recall, was in the springtime of the year. One day there came numerous Indians to me at Ahome, with the exciting report of seeing, at a distance from the land, something resembling a great bird, or a house (*teopa*), moving over the water.

I hoped that this might be a Spanish ship of those come in search of pearls. At the same time I knew there was danger of it being a Dutch ship of those pirating the Spanish galleons.

Nonetheless, I resolved to risk communicating with the ship. I prepared a brief note, advising the Captain that if they should be in need of supplies, they would find the coast here populated by Christian Indians. This note I dispatched with an Indian who was a great swimmer, telling him that should he see one of these houses approaching from the sea, he should place the note in his head band (*guirnaldina*) and swim to meet it.

Before he had opportunity to deliver this note, there appeared at Ahome two Spanish sailors from the ship. They arrived faint from hunger and, when they saw me, raised their voices to heaven in thankfulness. After partaking of some food, they told me that the Captain had dispatched them in a small boat to search for a place to which the crew of the ship could repair to keep from starving. They had, in truth, been fortunate in coming to the pueblo of Ahome, for had the ship approached land a little further northward, their emmisaries would no doubt have been captured and eaten by the Indians.

I called don Miguel and the other Caciques, who prepared as much corn and other provisions as they could carry, in readiness to depart before dawn the next day to the shore where the little boat had landed. They were in great haste to go, in their desire to see this house of wood that traveled over the sea.

The Spaniards had difficulty in locating the spot where they had left their boat, finally become lost in trying to cross some estuaries. Some Indians continued ahead with the Spaniards. Others stayed with me. The next day, the boat having been located, the Indians guided me to where Captain Iturbi awaited us on the shore.

The ship lay a league out to sea, but so ardent was the desire of the Indians to see it, that I begged the Captain to allow them to do so. They filled the small boat nearly to capsizing, making numerous trips to gaze upon the ship, as if at a miracle.

After having rested, I made plans with the Captain to meet the ship later at a point southward near the entrance of the Rio Zuaque to the sea. I then departed with the Indians, who were still filled with wonder at what they had seen. The ship remained near the mouth of the river for several days taking on provision and water, while ceaseless numbers of Indians traveled to see it, and to trade provision for clothing of the Spaniards.

Later the ship sailed to the entrance of the Petatlán River. From there they sent word of their arrival to Captain Hurdaide, who gave them what assistance they required for again outfitting themselves.

The Dutch were still cruising the waters of the Sea of the South, hoping to raid the Spanish ships arriving at Acapulco from the Phillipines.

Captain Iturbi turned northward from the mouth of the Petatlán River, entering a good port which he named San Ignacio, not far from the mouth of the river. Here he constructed a long boat (*barcon*) and being now well provisioned, returned northward in search of pearls, arriving as far as the 32 parallel.

Other ships have returned to these waters since. Their crews have made friends with the Indians of the coast, and have been permitted to take some pearls. If this taking of pearls is continued, the provisioning of these ships will provide some commerce for the province of Sinaloa.

CHAPTER 31

Labors Among the Savage Zuaques

THERE ARRIVED the time planned by Divine Providence to subject to the tender yoke of evangelical law the rebellious Zauque Nation. This, by my good fortune, it fell to my lot to do. In the year 1605, accompanied by the able Christian woman, Luisa, her kinsman, don Ventura, and numerous other Caciques, I traveled into the land of the Zuaques, visiting three of their pueblos containing a total of some 1,000 persons.

The principal pueblo of the Zuaques, Mochicahui, was located on a beautiful plain overlooking their Gran Rio de Zuaque, and was considered to have surrounding it the most fertile lands of all that river valley.

On arriving, there came to greet me great numbers of men, women and children, kissing my hand and placing it on their heads, which in them is a sign of reverence. I talked with them, among other things pointing out that I came without arms nor soldiers for company, and that my only purpose in coming was to assist them, to be as a father to them, and to show them the way to their spiritual salvation.

The woman Luisa had assembled many mothers with their children. I baptized these, to the number of 300, there serving as Godparents the few Christians present. The little girls who were baptized with the name of Maria were given especial acclaim by the others, who would exclaim, "Iaut teua," which in their language means "Great Woman."

So, in each pueblo, the Indian woman Luisa served as the instrument of God to encourage all these people in becoming Christians. There were baptized over 800 children and, with this, ended the asperity of this Nation, which has never since been in rebellion. The Caciques, formerly leaders in their drunkeness, now preach sermons in the village Plazas against their former vices.

One of the great problems that arose at the time of baptism of the adults, was that of the men often having several women. The Indian Cacique, Ventura, who had been saved from hanging by the intercession of Luisa, was one of these. He had great influence among the Zuaques, having often led their attacks in war during their gentility. He was finally baptized under the name of don Cristobal Anamei, and governed the Zuaque Nation for many years.

He was of great assistance in directing the people in the building of their churches. With the help of as many as one hundred persons, in carrying water, in the making of adobes, in securing timbers and building, their two churches were finally finished. They were white-washed, and pictures painted on the walls. Great crosses were erected in the spaces before the churches, where were enclosed their cemeteries.

So happy were they in the results of their labor that they next erected a little shrine on the crest of a small hill overlooking their river. This was the hill from the base of which the water had flowed following the earthquake.

On the night before dedication of their new places of worship, there was placed on the roof tops of each of the two churches a trumpeter. These played in turn, each being answered by the other. They were replaced at periods during the night with other musicians playing oboes (*chirimias*). The buildings were illuminated throughout the night by torches.

There were hoisted over the churches standards of Chinese silk that measured three heights of a man.

In the central Plaza there burned other fires, and around these they held their native dances, accompanied by their great drums which had once called them to war; these now being played in celebration of feasts in honor of Christ and his holy Mother. To this feast came the people of many other Nations.

On the day following there was held a procession. In anticipation of this, there had been erected at each of the four corners of the Plaza a small enramada. The processional moved from one of these stations to another while singing mass. A Padre who spoke their language most perfectly, [*Probably Padre Juan Batista de Velasco, who committed it to writing*] came from a distance for the purpose of preaching the sermon at these inauguration services.

The services over, the Zuaques invited their visitors to a great feast, where all were regaled of the very best the land could offer; beef furnished by the Padres, and fish brought from the sea by their neighbors the Ahomes. This feast being terminated, the Indians all returned to their homes very much contented.

Soon the Zuaques were planting a common plot of ground from which to sell corn to the Spaniards and the soldiers of Captain Diego Martinez de Hurdaide, using the proceeds to obtain ornaments for their churches.

Their three villages were finally reduced to two, in which lived some 800 persons, these pueblos being located about seven miles one from the other. [*The first pueblo was Mochicahui, the second probably Charáy.*]

This made it easier for the Padre to attend to these two pueblos, while at the same time attending to the Ahomes.

61

CHAPTER 32

Repentance of a Cacique

DON CRISTOBAL ANAMEI, at the time of his baptism, had given up his passion for many wives, in favor of one. However, at a time when he was in another pueblo, being disturbed by the Devil, he took an Indian woman away from her husband.

The head man of this pueblo, much disturbed, came to advise me of this happening. I wrote at once to the Captain suggesting he decide upon, and execute, a proper punishment for this crime. When the Captain received this notice he was much aggrieved, and also very troubled, because of the great influence this Cacique had over his people, to the point that should he take to the woods, great numbers would follow him, and could then become a menace to the peace of all the Christian Zuaques. The Captain recommended to me that first I study further what remedy I, as a Padre, could apply to this perplexing problem. Matters stood in this state when, at midnight of the fourth day after commiting this act of violence, Anamei came to my house, requesting to speak to me. I bade him enter, although with some misgiving as to the purpose of his visit.

He entered very gentled and humbled, throwing himself at my feet to beg pardon for this sin into which he had been led by the Devil. I received him with kindness, yet at the same time pointing out to him with some sterness the bad example he, as Governor, had set for his people, and insisted that to restore himself in his authority he should suffer some punishment.

The thought of punishment was, without doubt, most difficult for this proud Cacique to accept. However, he agreed to punish himself, in the presence of two witnesses who were people of importance. Removing his jacket, shirt and sword, all these being badges of his office as Governor, with a discipline such as were used at Easter services he inflicted the most severe blows on his own back and shoulders, causing such lacerations that I restrained him from continuing. Following this self-punishment he underwent confession. He continued to show penitence in the manner in which he thereafter fulfilled his obligations as a Christian, and a leader of his people. The pueblo heard of the measures taken and were satisfied. The Captain, too, was much pleased over the happy outcome of this difficult problem.

It has become the practice of these Zuaque people to defer any difficult matters to their Padre for decision. In the eleven years I attended them, there was no major disturbance in their Nation. Many Zuaques bought horses for riding and for carrying their loads, and in other ways began adjusting themselves to a civilized manner of living.

The story of their conversion and pacification carried into other distant Nations. The Mayo Indians, one hundred twenty miles distant northward, who previously had held no amity for, nor communication with, the Zuaques, now sent numerous Caciques to see our new churches and houses, and to witness our services. They were much impressed and invited me to go to their country, to teach them of these matters, in the meanwhile asking permission to send certain of their principal people to live with the Zuaques in order to learn Christian doctrine. They soon were coming in groups to visit our churches, and in this manner began the conversion of the great Mayo Nation.

CHAPTER 33

Padre Pedro Mendéz Undertakes Conversion of the Tegueco Nation

UP RIVER, 12 miles from the farthest border of the Zuaque Nation, were the pueblos of the Tegueco Nation. These lay on beautiful and fertile plains bordering the river. The pueblos had been built at higher elevations to insure their safety from floods. They were surrounded by high and dense woods, which abounded in game, and the Teguecos were great hunters of bow and arrow. These pueblos are fifty miles from the Villa of Sinaloa and not more than ten down river from the old fort (*Curapoa*) that had been destroyed by the Zuaques. In the course of the years, these Teguecos traveled to the Villa to ask for indoctrination into the Christian faith.

In these people there had predominated, more than in many others, the vices of their gentility, particularly that of sensuality, it being customary for their men to have three, four or five wives, often members of their own families. This vice was so strong in them that it was feared that it would interfere exceedingly with the introduction of Christianity. Taking these matters into account, it was resolved to assign to the Teguecos the venerable Pedro Mendéz, a minister of much experience in the Mission of Sinaloa.

Several of the principal Teguecos came to guide the Padre on his first journey into their lands. He went without escort of soldiers, happy to have the opportunity to labor for Christ among these people whose sole occupation seemed to be to make war against other Nations.

Quoting from a letter of Padre Mendéz· "I was received with demonstrations of joy; there coming to meet me many more people than we had anticipated. The river being in flood, many crossed it by swimming.

"Following the baptisms, there was much feasting, people coming throughout the day to visit the parents of the baptized children. Since I have arrived, no Indian has been in my presence carrying a bow and arrow, nor is there now any evidence of their former drunkeness.

"On Sundays the Indian families come from five or ten miles to services, the men and women carrying their little children. At the hour of their coming it seems that the fields are filled with people.

"They make me many gifts, not only of food, but of cotton cloth which they weave, and with which some of them now dress their children. They also bring wax for the tapers of the altar. They ask many questions, among others, in what manner there should be buried a child that had been baptized.

"Two groups of Indians living across the river, who spoke another language, swam the river one day, bringing their children to be baptized. They brought parched ground corn (*pinole*) to feed the children, and gifts for the Christians who should serve as Godparents.

"I baptized, during the time of which I write, some 700 children. . . ." here ends the quotation from Padre Mendéz.

These baptisms concluded, the Tegueco Indians set themselves to the building of churches in their pueblos, and a well constructed house in which the Padre should live. They laid out streets, and a square was reserved for a Plaza. Don Diego Lazarote, their principal Cacique, was of great assistance in all these undertakings. Padre Mendéz again writes: "During the Lenten season, I have not seen even those who are not yet Christians eat meat. One day a group of them had gathered for a hunt, then recalling it was Friday, they returned to their houses. They confessed, with more feeling than could have been expected from people so new in the faith. . . . when I told, in my sermon on Easter Day, of the lashes given to Christ our Father, they, taking their disciplines, lashed themselves with a fervor that caused in me new wonder and admiration of them.

"On this day four Indian men whose women continued to be infidels abandoned them. These women then took baptism, and in time were married to Christian husbands. One Cacique had five wives, two of whom were his sisters. He, relieved of the four, very cheerfully became a Christian, and married the fifth.

"An old blind Indian and his wife were baptized, and came often to catechism. Going to another church to hold services, I found this old couple awaiting me. To reach the place, they had to swim across a river that was two heights of a man in depth in flood and which I had crossed on a raft.

"Another Christian Indian persisted in coming to church painted, face and body, as they accustom in their barbarity. I explained to him that this was not a Christian practice, and sent him to the river to bathe. . . . This custom of painting is as difficult to change as it would be to persuade the women of Europe to abandon the colorings with which they so happily adorn themselves.

"At this same period there came also to learn doctrine some Indians called Bacabachis Montarases, who were known as the people who ate the rats of the woods." Here ends the letter of Padre Pedro Mendéz, in which he relates interesting incidents of his labors among the Tegueco Indians.

View of old pueblo of Sinaloa, with tower of original Mission (right center of picture) and Petatlán River and Sierras in distance.

solitary tower is all that remains of the head- ters Mission at Sinaloa, founded by Padres Gon- le Tapia and Martín Pérez in 1590.

"One of their favorite occupations is hunting for wild honey . . . bee hives are circular in form, and may measure a vara (33 inches) in diameter . . ."

". . . in bathing they take great joy, and all swim like fish." View of Petatlán (Sinaloa River) opposite old Mission Pueblo of Bamoa.

"Padre Hernando de Villafañe had in his charge the three pueblos of the great Guasave Nation." Belfry tower and bells of old Mission of Guasave.

"Nations among whom the Padres labored were the Nios . . ." Ruins of Mission at Nio. Fifteen miles down-river from Sinaloa.

Stone axes, flute and clay idols found in Sinaloa.

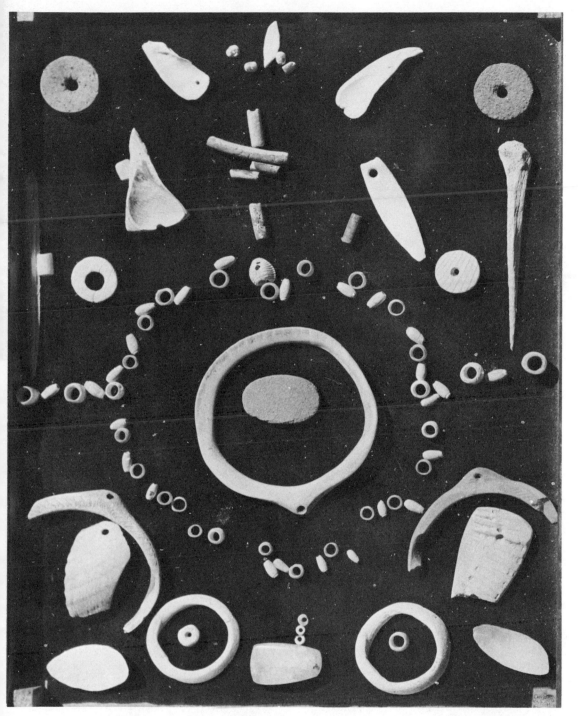

"These mountain tribes are very swift in running over rocks and peaks, and most dextrous in the use of bow and arrow. The arrow points they make of stone . . ." Three plates showing stone arrowheads.

Stone arrow heads and spear heads found in Sonora and Sinaloa.

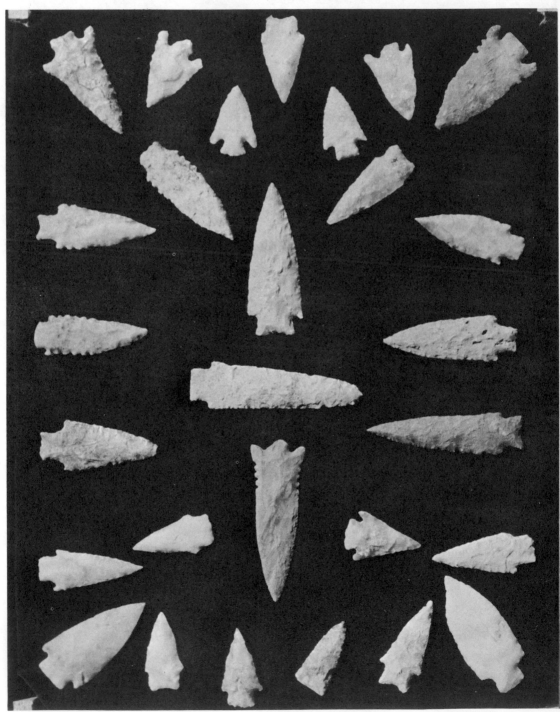

Arrow heads, spear heads, shell bracelet and shell and bone necklace pieces found in Sonora and Sinaloa.

"The Ahomes guarded their doncellitas very carefully. These wore suspended about their necks a pretty collar of sea shells until the day of their marriage."

CHAPTER 34

The Bishop Pays a Visit

IN THEIR POLITICAL LIFE these Nations were all governed by Caciques named to their offices by the Spanish Captain General don Diego Martinez de Hurdaide. Their spiritual lives were guided by the Padres of the Mission of Sinaloa. Pleased that the work of conversion was progressing so well, the Bishop of the Diocese of Guadalajara, in the Province of Neuva Galicia, decided to pay a visit to the Province of Sinaloa, which lay within his jurisdiction, although in land so remote that no Bishop had ever before undertaken this journey. This venerable man, don Juan del Valle, was a person of great letters and high example.

The distance from Guadalajara was 600 miles, and there were difficult trails to travel, over mountain passes and through lowland jungles. There were also many large rivers to be crossed. Pausing from time to time to administer the sacrament to the people of the pueblos along his route, the Bishop finally arrived at San Miguel de Culiacán. From there, he sent notice to the Villa of Sinaloa, of his arrival.

The only Padre present, on the arrival of the messenger to the Villa, at once set off on his mule to receive the Bishop at Culiacán, and to express the gratitude of all for his coming to a region so poor and isolated, to give encouragement to the Padres and to these Indians so new in Christianity.

At a little distance from the Villa the cavalcade of the Bishop was met by Captain Hurdaide with a troop of soldiers. Close behind followed a large group of Indians, who came adorned with head plumes of bright feathers, gaudily painted on face and body. They carried bows and arrows, and made a great pretense of attacking the visitors, causing the Bishop true alarm until, comprehending that it was their manner of welcome, he gave them his blessing, which they received kneeling on the earth before him.

Soon they came to a lane built of arches of green branches. Down this lane the distinguished visitor rode to the Villa. Alighting, he entered the church, to find congregated there great numbers of Indians from all the villages.

The "Principal Padre," as the Indians termed him, was occupied five days in their confirmation. They were filled with admiration of his evident authority, and of his pontifical investitures, all this serving to instill reverence in them for divine matters. Such evidences of authority weigh much with these people.

The Padres had taken care to have prepared clean and respectable clothes for the covering of many Indians who came without clothing, that they might appear with decency. The pious Prelate received them all with singular benignity, even an occasional one who in his haste to see the great man had come to kneel before him only in his bare body. To the soldiers who assisted in placing the visitors in their proper turn, he insisted that no one must be turned away, nor spoken to in an unkindly manner.

With the Padres who spoke their various languages assisting, there were confirmed 8,000 souls. The Señor Bishop was most happy to find the seeds of evangelism so well sown, in a land once destitute of Christian peoples, and returned with a glowing report to don Rodrigo de Cabredo, then Padre Provincial of the Company, in the City of Mexico.

Some years later the Fray don Gonzalo de Hermosillo, newly named Bishop of the Diocese of Guadiana, undertook the trip through the rugged Sierras of Topia to Sinaloa. The Christian Indians of the Province gathered to greet him at Macori, the principal pueblo of the Teguecos. Here he confirmed 11,000 Christian Indians.

This trip ended in a great tragedy. Returning on a mule toward the Villa, the Bishop suffered a fall from the animal. He was carried in a chair to the Villa where, despite the little medical assistance that could be given him, he passed away, surrounded by our ministers of the faith who had gathered there.

Other Bishops later visited the Province: don Alonzo Franco y Luna and the Benedictine Monk, Frey Diego de Evia, who gave glowing reports of the flowering of Christianity in this distant country. Of the Padres who labored in Sinaloa he wrote, "I seemed to have found here hermit saints retired from the world."

CHAPTER 35

The Fort of Montesclaros

As the Indian Nations accepting Christianity increased in number, the Presidio of the Villa was seen to be too far removed from some of these Nations to insure against the dangers of unrest that are apt to occur among such primitive peoples. A site for a new Presidio was chosen, where the soldiers would find convenience of living, a good location for a fort, water, firewood, and pasture for cattle and horses. The King sent orders to Captain Hurdaide that this Fort should be built. This place was named the Fuerte de Montesclaros, in honor of the Conde de Montesclaros, then Viceroy of New Spain.

It was located on a small hill six miles up river from the principal pueblo of the Teguecos, near the site of the abandoned Fort of Carapoa. Below the Fort ran the Gran Rio de Zuaque, with fertile plains lying between, where could be grazed livestock without fear of ambuscade by the Indians.

The Fort, although of adobe bricks, was of such capacity that in time of war all the horses could be stabled inside its walls, so keeping them safe from enemy arrows. Horses are prime targets of an Indian enemy, for they know that if the

Spanish soldier loses his horse, he is in much greater danger of losing his life also.

At the four corners of the Fort were built towers (*torreones*) which served as lookouts and which, because of their massive construction, were impressive to the Indians.

Soon after the Fort was finished, there came to visit the Captain, four Caciques from the mountain country eastward. They said they came in peace; in proof of this bringing a gift of a thousand arrows, and furs of wildcat and marten. They especially came to see the Fort and the churches. The Captain received these people with courtesy, and made them gifts which they esteem. They then expressed the wish that churches be built on their lands also.

The building of this Fort also put fear into the hearts of the savage Chínipas, with whom the Captain had been at war on the occasion of his going to search for mines.

The principal Cacique of these Chínipas sent a son to negotiate for peace, and to ask for indoctrination of their people.

Some restless Indians, including several Christians, made plans to attack the Fort. The Captain, being advised of this, ordered some daggers to be coated with the blood of a steer, and sent by messenger to the plotters, warning them that their blood would soon be spilled on the daggers of the Spanish soldiers in this same manner. Disturbed to find that the Captain knew of their plans, these restless Indians curbed their belligerence.

The Fort of Montesclaros thus served a very useful purpose in curbing the savage impulses of the Indians of the adjacent plains and Sierras.

CHAPTER 36

War Against Teguecos and Tepágues

IT IS NO EASY TASK to change the customs of savage peoples, even after their conversion to Christianity. Padre Pedro Mendéz discovered that among his Christian Teguecos there were some who continued the worship of certain stone idols. Upon learning this, the Padre had these idols destroyed.

This aroused great feeling among the Teguecos. They insisted that this rash action would bring misfortune and sicknesses to them. Their Hechiceros began to convoke gatherings at which were celebrated wild dances in their former pagan manner. At the conclusion of these dances the Hechiceros would deposit certain articles of their profession in a cotton sheet, which was then held at the four corners while they pronounced visions over it. Then, carrying this sheet from house to house, they gathered in it certain objects which were, in this manner, supposedly ridding them of the evil that caused the sickness.

A faithful Christian Indian gave notice of these pagan rituals to the Padre who decided, for the time, not to let the Indians suspect his knowledge.

Captain Hurdaide was also given notice of the unrest; but it involved so many Caciques of high authority that he decided not to move against them without first attempting to pacify them.

The Teguecos who had deserted the Captain on his return trip from Mexico City had gone into hiding with the mountain tribe of Tepágues who were friendly to the Teguecos. Accompanied by some Tepágues, they came down from their Sierras by night, attempting to set fire to the church, but were repulsed.

During the Lenten season, while the Padre was asleep, there came four Indians to awaken him, urging him to leave the pueblo at once, saying that he had been sentenced to die as had, also, the Captain. They said that the Indians in revolt were divided into four bands, each holding a route of escape. They proposed to lead him to freedom by yet another trail. One of the Indians said he had been held prisoner by the marauders but had escaped.

Padre Mendéz, of long experience in dealing with Indians, suspected this news to be false. He chose instead to retire to the church, under the protection of the Christian Indians who remained faithful to him. He ordered great bonfires to be built, to reveal any approaching enemy. Knowing their plot had been discovered, the enemy retired to the Sierra of the Tepágues, fearful of the wrath of the Captain and his soldiers.

Upon hearing of these events, Captain Hurdaide first sent word to those that had remained faithful, to stay quietly on guard over their Padre and their pueblo, assuring them that they could count on his protection. Next he undertook the punishment of those who had fled.

It was a difficult country into which he proposed to follow these savages. In the Sierras horses and armor could be of little use. There were also other hostile Indians to be confronted before arriving at the rugged country where lived the Tepágues. This expedition must be successful; for upon its outcome rested the fate of Christianity in the Province of Sinaloa. It must be undertaken. To ignore the actions of these restless savages was to invite constant trouble in the future from them, and from others.

The Captain and the Padres conferred, invoking the counsel of God. They decided to first send some loyal Teguecos with offers of peace. The rebels scorned these offers, the messengers barely escaping with their lives. Seeing that no other recourse remained, Captain Hurdaide prepared his forces. Of this expedition I can tell as an eye witness, as I accompanied it as spiritual counselor to both the Spanish soldiers and their Indian allies.

The Captain marched with forty armored soldiers of horse, some Spaniards who lived in the Province and 2,000 Indian allies. The allies imposed, as a condition, that they be permitted to take the scalps (*cabelleras*) of any of the enemy captured and be allowed to put on a war dance with them. With this, they considered they would be well repaid.

The Captain, in keeping with his feelings as a Christian, imposed as a counter-condition that for all women and children spared he would present a gift of a horse. This offer was accepted, although probably not from the same motive for which it was proposed.

The Captain next prepared provision for a long journey. The enemy felt sure of victory, boasting that the attacking forces could not sustain themselves for more than five or six days, for lack of supplies. Sage and prudent in such matters, the Captain saw to it that the enemy was advised that he would not retire from their lands without punishing them, though it took all of that winter, as he planned to drive with him a great herd of cattle.

That they should know he spoke the truth, he caused to be gathered some 500 cattle, placing them in a pasture convenient to their being taken on the expedition.

He gathered his troops and cattle into a camp at the base of the Sierras, at a pueblo of the Sinaloa Indians. Here he also gathered a great supply of corn. For some days he remained here, drilling his forces, they being now only some four or five days march from their enemies.

These enemies had already gathered their forces, ready for combat with those of the Captain. The army of the Captain each day would ask, "When do we march?" The Captain would reply, "Be patient; we are not losing time." Spies he had sent reported the enemy to be awaiting them in the heights of their peaks. "Well, we shall let them wait," said the Captain. "I know they will finally finish their store of corn, and will be forced from their fastnesses by hunger."

Spies reported that the Conicari Indians, a Nation living along their route into the land of the Tepágues, were stationed in ambush in a very narrow pass, intending to finish off the Spaniards and their allies by hurling rocks upon them from the cliffs above.

A Cacique of the Conicaris came to the Captain offering the assistance of his people in their passage through his country. The Captain received this Cacique in his tent. When the Indian had finished speaking the Captain suddenly discharged a double barreled pistol, frightening the Indian extremely. He then told the Cacique that he knew all about their plans for ambush. This so disturbed the Indian that he agreed to order his warriors to disperse. When the Captain arrived in their country the Cacique met him, to plead that their rancherias should not be molested. This the Captain agreed to, so ordering his troops.

The march was continued; the great herd of cattle being driven in advance of the forces. After two days travel there were seen coming down the trail toward them, a large group of people, many women among them. The Captain, turning to me, said, "These are the Christians who have fled and are now returning in fear to their pueblos, as we have ordered them to do. The men must be given some punishment. When I propose to punish the women, Your Reverence please to intervene on their behalf. With the women, the threat of punishment will be sufficient."

There first came forward the Indian warriors with their bows, arrows and warclubs. They plead that they had been deceived by the boasting of the Te-págues; but now wished to return to their homes.

The Captain first ordered a bonfire made of all their bows, arrows, quivers and clubs, which had been gaily decorated for war. Next he ordered some lashes, although few, to be given to the men, with the ends of some bridle reins. Turning then to the women, he reprimanded them most severely, telling them they could have prevented their husbands from joining this rebellion which had forced them all to go wandering like dogs, tired and hungry, among those mountains. He threatened them with lashing, whereupon I came out of the tent where I had been keeping apart, and interceded for them. They were then let go free and given an order which insured their safe conduct to return to their pueblos.

The day following we met a similar group, which also surrendered to us and were treated in the same manner.

However, the greater forces of the enemy remained before us. They were now burning the country ahead, to destroy the pasture for our cattle and horses. Only along the borders of the streams where the grass was green, had it escaped burning.

We finally made camp in the heart of enemy territory, in a beautiful valley through which ran the river of the Tepágues. Here they had built their principal pueblo. The rebels had fled into the peaks of the surrounding Sierras, from where they could observe our movements.

The Captain ordered his soldiers, while on patrol, not to engage in any battle, nor kill any Indians, but only to bring them into headquarters for questioning. The Indian allies he permitted to explore among the crags in search of the enemy. They also found corn that had been hidden, with which they helped to feed themselves. At the abandoned rancherias they found mescal plants, the heads of which they enjoyed roasted on the coals. However, the principal food supply was the six to eight steers slaughtered daily and roasted; their meat being eaten despite it being the Lenten season.

Here we remained for a week, the Captain sending messages to the enemy Indians perched upon their crags. He stated he did not wish to wage war against them, requiring only that they should surrender the Tegueco Caciques who had stirred the others to revolt.

These messages being of no avail, we decided to give battle. Permission was given to the Indian allies to fight any Indians they encountered. Camp was raised and our forces again moved upwards into the Sierras. All the trails over which they now moved had been sown with stakes and barbs hidden upright in the weeds and covered with juice of the poisonous plant (*hierba de la flecha*) so well known to these lands. The Spaniards, who wore shoes, went ahead to clear the paths for the Indian allies who traveled either barefoot or with poor sandals.

The expedition finally arrived at a great deep canyon, whose walls extended sheer toward the sky, and through which the river disappeared into thick underbrush to a depth unknown. The Indian allies were dispatched to search for an ascent. None was found, the expedition facing the task of forcing their way through this formidable canyon with troops and cattle. A Mass was held, commending our forces to the mercy of the most Saintly Virgin, offering suitable recognition of her Saintly favor should we return safely to the Villa. We then undertook the passage, which took two hours and was made without mishap.

At the far end of the canyon the enemy awaited us. From sheltered places they opened fire on the Indian allies who were in the lead. The Captain, by whose side I rode, put spurs to his mule without waiting for his armored horse which was led by a servant and, calling to the soldiers nearest him, began the battle, firing with the arquebus which he always carried on his saddle. The enemy Indians, frightened by the arquebuses exploding so near to them, fled up the canyon, pursued hotly by our own Indian allies. These returned presently, bearing numerous enemy heads suspended on thongs. I must confess that it caused horror in me to see how they were carried. The skins and scalps of the heads had been removed to be displayed in their dances. The heads were carried suspended from their nostrils, which had been perforated, and cords run through them, these cords being made from fiber found in the woods. Pity it caused to see them, but this is a part of war.

The night following, when the Royal forces made camp, there was such feasting and dancing over these scalps and heads that it seemed that a roar from Hell itself had reached to the encampment. There danced hordes of our warriors, in the light made by a thousand torches, howling and shouting of their triumph, and their inharmonious chants and noises reverberated throughout those canyons all through the night.

The Christian Indians who accompanied us accustomed to make their camp next to the tents of the Captain and mine, and here I practiced holding Mass in the evenings. On the night of this barbaric feast I was able to detain the Christian Indians from taking part; but their participation was not needed to make enough noise for an Inferno.

With the savages who were allies it was prudent to be as careful as with the enemy, for had they united with treasonable intent, they could easily have destroyed us. The Captain found the solution to this problem by not having with him a preponderance of warriors of any Nation. Those of each Nation he separated into their own groups and, as an additional precaution, saw to it that there was a constant guard of Spanish soldiers, fully equipped with armor for themselves, and for their horses.

Among the Indians captured, there were seven principal leaders, whom the Captain sentenced to be hanged. Some of these were Christians who had allowed themselves to be deceived by the witch doctors. I took care that the seven should be well prepared for death, confessing the Christians, and baptizing the others, all but two who preferred in their stubborness to die like dogs. They were buried at the very spot in the Sierras where they had plotted so much trouble for the Christian pueblos of Sinaloa.

By this time hunger was upon us. We were reduced to beef, without salt, and began to fall ill. The Captain decided to return to the plains, first destroying the fields of the Tepágues to give them to understand that they could not revolt without suffering serious consequences. They soon saw the desirability of keeping the peace and came to the Villa to request it. The Teguecos also returned to the quiet of their pueblos.

One Indian ally, a giant of a man who had received a small wound from the poisonous plant, died in a delirium within twenty-four hours. His relatives who accompanied us burned his body, that their enemies should not triumph over it.

The few Tepágues who continued in rebellion were finally captured by their own tribe, were beheaded, and the heads sent to the Captain as proof of their determination to now remain at peace.

This expedition was of one and a half months duration. Upon our return, the Captain gave liberally of the remaining cattle to our Indian allies, so that there were only some twenty head of these when we arrived at the Villa.

The Tegueco Nation, for better government and learning of doctrine, reduced themselves to two pueblos with a total of about 1,000 families. In these pueblos were built beautiful churches of ample capacity, which were dedicated with great solemnity in the same manner as those of the Zuaques. A marvelous change has now come to this Nation, a harmony and peace worthy of pueblos much older in the practice of Christianity and civil government.

CHAPTER 37

Witchcraft Among the Teguecos

AMONG THE TEGUECOS who adopted Christianity were some who had been Hechiceros, practicing their witchcraft in close collusion with the Devil. One of these, whose heart had been touched by a sermon of his Padre, came to make confession; and told him of some of their diabolical superstitions and practices. He explained that the Devil presented himself to the witch doctors in numerous ways. To those he wished to lead to war he represented himself as being very ferocious. In this case, the Devil required the Indians to make presents to him, through the Hechiceros, of bows, shields, arrows and other arms. To those whose carnal appetite he wished to arouse the Devil would appear in a manner gentle and delightful. In such cases, the Indians were required to make presents of plumes, woven cotton cloths and other attractive items.

Sometimes the Devil would appear as a streak of lightning which made the sky tremble, and might kill people if the Devil so wished. He was then described as the God of Life, or the God of Death. He also might appear as God of Knowledge, in which guise he could recall to people things of their past, or tell them of things to come. In this form, he might also be termed the God of Light.

Not all Hechiceros were endowed with the same ability to see visions, nor could these visions be communicated to all people, but only to those susceptible to believing them.

Of the figures or idols which these Hechiceros at times consulted some were of stone, some of wood, and all apt to be very malformed. These idols they kept well hidden in the woods. The Padre of the Teguecos discovered some of them, broke them into pieces and buried them deep in a cave, erecting in their place a cross, that the Devil might not be able to abide in that place.

Thereupon the Devil appeared before the former Hechicero we have mentioned, as well as before others, shouting and howling, saying that should they continue to deny him in favor of Christ, he would kill them and destroy their church. However, this converted Indian now refused to be intimidated.

As when the day breaks, the night departs; so the evil spirits and wild beasts flee to their places of hiding away from the light. Thus also, when evangelism comes to a people, the Princes of Darkness flee to the lands of barbarism, where alone their delusions and falsehoods may be believed.

For many years our Padres have lived in the same villages as these Hechiceros, while serving the thirty five Missions of Sinaloa. During all these years Divine Providence has so strengthened their hands in their labors, that no witch doctor has been able to bewitch nor harm an evangelical minister, nor even to poison his food or drink, as might well be expected. Much to the contrary, they have lived to see the fruits of their labor ripen in the great new faith of these people. Each day at dawn the Indians are in their churches singing, praying and confessing themselves; sometimes with such manifest feeling that their Padres are moved to tears.

Those who have learned to read and write are apt to record their sins on paper for confession. Those who have not, may often be seen tying knots at intervals on a little piece of cord, in order to better recall them.

They now live as do the Spaniards, in homes located in pueblos, with streets laid out in good order, and all maintained in cleanliness. In their dress they cover all their bodies, as do the Spaniards. At their festivals, they sit at tables, men with men and women with women, and serve themselves with modesty and composure.

The men are learning various arts such as reading, writing and painting. There are carvers of wood of such dexterity that with a knife they can carve a candelabra or a flower vase for an altar, as though it had been made on a lathe.

And here we shall leave the Tegueco Nation and pass on to their neighbors, the Sinaloas.

CHAPTER 38

Civilization Comes to the Sinaloas

THE SINALOA NATION lived along the highest part of the Rio de Zuaque, beginning some twenty miles above the Fuerte de Montesclaros. Their name was given also to the Villa of Sinaloa, where the Mission and College were located, this being on the Petatlán River some sixty miles southward.

[*The Petatlán is now (1967) called the Sinaloa River, and the Zuaque the Fuerte River, a name taken from the Fuerte de Montesclaros.*]

The Sinaloas were by nature more restless and less constant than other Nations. However, following the example of others, they made a request for Padres to bring them the evangelical doctrine. Permission to do this was secured by Captain Hurdaide while on a visit to Mexico City.

For this undertaking there was selected Padre Cristobal de Villalta who had, a few months previously, arrived to work in the Missions:

The principal Caciques of the Sinaloas came to escort the Padre to their lands, where he was received with the same manifestations of pleasure as have been described in other Nations. He very quickly mastered their language. His manner of treatment of the Indians was most agreeable and he quickly gained their confidence.

In a letter he states that these people had moved in from several rancherias to build a pueblo, where they were soon settled. The men directed themselves to planting corn, cotton and other crops. The women were attentive to the care of their homes and found time to weave cotton cloth, and to make baskets and mats of bamboo.

They gave ready obedience to their appointed leaders and to their Padre. They seemed never to tire of hearing the word of God and were very quick in learning. Conversions and baptisms progressed rapidly. The men who had many women began to leave some of them, selecting one among them to have baptized and to marry.

The clamors of the abandoned ones were something to hear. It tore out the hearts of these people, and of their children, to be separated from those of their own flesh. However, within a year all these changes were made and 1,000 families baptized.

Not long after the indoctrination of the Sinaloas was begun there occurred an eclipse of the moon. The Sinaloas quickly gathered in the Plaza of their pueblos, shooting arrows into the sky. They also beat their clubs with great fury against the mats of their houses. These actions, they said, were intended to protect the moon, which they considered to be a live being, now engaged in a fierce battle against an antagonist up in the sky.

They insisted that this eclipse was most evil and would bring sickness and death to their people. To secure themselves against this they set to building fences of thorns about their homes. The Padre explained to them, with patience, that only God gave health and life; and persuaded them to burn these fences. A delegation of Sinaloas came to plead with the Padre to do something to insure them against the coming of cocolitzle (*small pox*). They had made such petitions to him formerly, when in need of rain. To these requests the Padre acceded, taking the supplicants into the church to pray to God that He grant their desires. He also persuaded them to discard the implements of their witchcraft such as bones, human hair, skins of human beings, various seeds and certain figures carved in wood or stone. All these were delivered to the Padre, who burned them in the presence of the people of the pueblo.

However, smallpox did eventually come to the Sinaloas, causing great numbers of deaths, as in all the Nations of the Province. There were days when there were 300 ill, and the deaths among the Nations altogether totaled many thousands.

It is impossible to describe the great labors of the Padres in their ministry to these afflicted. Their suffering was greatly increased by the lack of human succor, even for the feeding of the sick. The Padres toiled ceaselessly, traveling from one village to another, to give what comfort and aid was possible.

In their despair, they could only reconcile themselves by reflecting that sometimes there are hidden from us the meaning of such calamities.

One fruit of the labor of the Padres in this terrible time was the conversion of sixty three old men and women who had, theretofore, remained hardened in their refusal to accept the doctrine. They were baptized, and within three days all had been taken by God in their new state of salvation.

There having passed, by divine grace, the difficulties related, the minds of the Padres and the Sinaloas turned to the erection of permanent churches. They took care that these should be in no way inferior to those of their neighbors the Teguecos and Zuaques. They were dedicated with the same solemnity as the others. For its dedication services there were placed in the new church two carvings made by Christian Sinaloas: one of the Annunciation and the other of Saint Christopher. Although these were not rich nor sumptuous, they were so attractive that they were later sent to the City of Mexico.

The Sinaloas were the first of the Indian Nations of the Province to introduce the wearing of rosaries. From a little fruit of the right proportion they made beautiful beads. Also, they made beads for rosaries from bits of woods of various bright colors. These were very gay (galán) and gave the wearers, both men and women, much pleasure to wear.

On the roads the Sinaloas may be seen traveling in groups, chanting the Rosary. On Saturdays, in the afternoons, they sing in church in choruses of men, and other choruses of women. Captain Hurdaide related that when the Sinaloas were on the march during a campaign, at the end of the day they would retire into an area away from the others to sing and pray. Another practice of the Sinaloas is to toll their church bells at a certain hour of the night, to call the people to pray for the souls of their deceased.

One custom of the Sinaloas which the Padre found difficult to eradicate was their so readily committing suicide by the use of the leaves of the poisonous plant we have before referred to. This plant they had easily at hand in the woods, often even in the patios of their houses. It took little to cause them to partake of this fatal plant; only such an action as the wife complaining against the husband, or the husband against the wife. Fortunately, in the course of the years, Padre Cristobal Villalta was able to uproot this tragic practice of their savage days.

It is the opinion of the Padres that the Sinaloas are the Christians in whom have been most deeply implanted, and have more richly yielded the fruits of Christianity, moreso than in any of the other Indian Nations.

They have easily learned the customs that are necessary to community living. In manual arts they are so dextrous that some even make flutes and other musical instruments, as well as altar pieces, sacred cups and other vessels. So it may be seen that there is no soil, no matter how difficult it may be, but will yield to preparation and cultivation, and thus it was with these savage Sinaloas.

CHAPTER 39

Story of the Zoe (Choix) *Nation*

THE ZOE (*Choix*) NATION had their habitations up river and into the Sierras, beginning twenty miles above the land of the Sinaloas. With soft syllables God called these people from their mountain peaks, to seek Padre Cristobal de Villalta, among the Sinaloas. Guided by a Cacique of the Zoes, Padre Cristobal went to visit them. He explained that in order to properly minister to them, they would need to congregate into a pueblo. This raised such a violent discussion among them that the followers of the Padre feared for his life and secretly sent a messenger, in all haste, for a group of his faithful Sinaloas to come with bow and arrow to his defense.

On this journey he found a man of such age that he had only skin clinging to his bones; he was very deaf and, altogether, more dead than alive. Padre Cristobal made an ear trumpet of a piece of bamboo cane with a mouthpiece fashioned from a piece of paper, through which he attempted to communicate with the ancient one. For a half hour he spoke into this trumpet, asking whether the old man would like to ascend to Heaven, to enjoy happiness and see his God. The old man finally began to show signs of understanding and presently could hear without the aid of the trumpet. He received enough instruction to take baptism, was taken to the church and received extreme unction before passing away.

A part of the Zoe Nation lived across the great river where, especially in times of flood, it was impossible for the Padre to attend them. He finally persuaded them to populate a fine plain down the river, moving to this place (*Choix*) 500 families.

Satanas, who never sleeps, attempted several times to disturb these people by recalling to them the memory of their mountains, the trees and the fruits from these, and their greater liberties; and some of these Zoes returned to the lands of their paganism. During these times the life of the Padre was endangered; but with suffering, patience, rewards and compliments, he finally returned those lost sheep to the fold.

The Zoes eventually were inspired to build a church, and so beautiful it turned out to be that they continued to enter it with admiration and wonder. It had required the carrying of forty great cedar logs from the mountains for its ceiling. It was dedicated in a solemn celebration, with the presence of people from many other Nations.

The Zoes next set to building adobe houses for themselves, with roofs of earth, placing these in well ordered streets, with a Plaza in the center. After building the church and houses, they never again attempted to move, but continued to live in their new homes in contentment and peace.

CHAPTER 40

Story of the Huites Nation

THE NATION OF HUITES, whose name signifies the use of bow and arrow, at which they are extremely dextrous, lived in huts and caves among the highest of peaks and precipices. Their places of habitation were so remote that if one were not a deer, or a bird, he could scarce penetrate there.

For men to enter, they must assist each other in climbing.

These places were so dry that the only water available was that gathered in the crevases between rocks during rains.

Their main rancheria was in a small valley, which was encircled by mountains so high that they prevented the rays of the sun from penetrating, during a long period of each day.

In this isolated place lived 300 families, only 20 miles distant, in direct line, from the Sinaloas. However, these Nations had never seen nor dealt with each other, except to engage in battle. These Huites ate human flesh. The Huite who could hang the most enemy skulls before his cave or hut was deemed the most valiant of his Nation.

The first notice by Padre Cristobal de Villalta of the existence of these remote people was when a boy of the Huites was captured by the Sinaloas and offered to the Padre for upbringing. The Padre soon sent some of the Christian Sinaloas to treat with the Huites of amity and peace, taking care to send with the emissaries some small presents of the sort which Indians all esteem. There soon came to be a friendly exchange of visits, and trading of such items as salt and knives of the Sinaloas for the Huites' bows and arrows. Next they began to send their children to school to the Padres at the Villa.

Finally there came down from out of these peaks some 3,000 persons. They were warmly welcomed by the Sinaloas, and given lands among them for planting.

Others who chose not to come down sent their children to be taught Christian doctrine and these, in turn, returned to teach their parents and others of their people. Eventually, a treaty was signed with the Captain under which they agreed to live in friendship with the Spaniards and with their neighbors.

Padre Cristobal Villalta made a journey into their Sierras, where he was warmly received by not only the Huites, but many other people who lived in the mountains that lay still higher eastward.

He held services in a brush enramada prepared for the purpose, after which all partook of a feast of corn, beans and pumpkins. He remained here for several days in order to become better acquainted with these isolated people; returning, very contented, to his home among the Sinaloas.

At the request of Padre Cristobal, some Christian Sinaloas who knew the river area located a place with land and water on which to relocate the Huites. Here were built some enramadas to serve as a church, and for houses.

The Huites came down from the mountains in good numbers, cleared land, opened a road, built homes and a church of hardwood timbers. Others could not bring themselves to leave their rugged Sierras, and still remain there today.

CHAPTER 41

The Great Cacique don Batista

IN A BATTLE between the Chínipas and the Huites, a number of Huite women and children had been carried captive to the land of the Chínipas. These Chínipas now having become Christians, Padre Cristobal plead for the release of these prisoners, and they were removed to the land of the Sinaloas to begin a new life there. This created a good feeling on the part of the Huites.

Among the Sinaloas there ruled a very able Indian of exemplary habits and Christianity, named don Batista. Don Batista became a widower and the Padre, in good time, persuaded him to take as his wife a bright and honorable maiden from among the Huites who had been enslaved by the Chinipas and now lived among the Sinaloas. The Huites were most content that this great and just Cacique of the powerful Sinaloa Nation should wed this maiden of their people.

Don Batista was very much esteemed by the Spaniards, and by his own people, and his reputation as a leader and a Christian had spread to other Nations. After his marriage to the Huite maiden, a trip was made to visit her people in the Sierras. They were accompanied by a number of her relatives who were secure in their loyalty.

Notice of their coming having been given to Indian tribes farther into the Sierras, these sent envoys to don Batista with invitations to visit them. Accepting these invitations, the party of don Batista traveled for six days, further into the higher Sierras, to the lands of the Guazaparis, Chinipas, Hios, Temoris and others of whom shall later be written.

At each village they were received with fiestas attended by great concourse of Indians, many of these seeing strangers in their lands for the first time. These Indians rarely, if ever, had left their habitations among their precipices. They were especially impressed with seeing this girl who had once been a slave of the Chinipas, now returning as the Governor's lady, married in the formal Christian manner to a leader of so much fame among the Nations.

Everyone brought them gifts of such poor little things as they possessed. Crowds of people would remain until midnight around the campfires listening to their visitors' stories of their new lives, now spent in peace and harmony between themselves and other Indian Nations, as well as with the Padres and Spaniards.

In the mornings the people observed in wonder and admiration the gathering of their Christian visitors into a group, to kneel in prayer. At dusk they again gathered to sing the rosary in chorus, a little rosary being suspended from the shoulders of each of them. After singing, prayers were said for the dead, they never failing in all these devotions.

These Christian travelers found among one of the most distant Nations of those Sierras something that brought them much comfort and renewal of faith. In a great cave in these mountains there had been painted three large crosses, indicating that some Christians had passed this way before them. This could have been a trace left of the journey through these mountains of the party of Cabeza de Vaca, on their way from Florida to Sinaloa. The crosses also might possibly have been left by Christians exploring these Sierras from the region of the mines of Santa Barbara, on the eastern slope of the great Sierras.

On the return to Sinaloa of don Batista and his party, they were accompanied by ten prominent Caciques of the several tribes visited, and numerous of their followers. Their homecoming was such as they never could have dreamed. They were first met by a cavalcade of Sinaloas on horseback. Horses had never before been seen by Indians from those distant Sierras. Arriving at the Christian pueblos, the travelers and their visitors passed under a series of green arches formed of boughs of trees, while the church bells rang in welcome and

79

music was played on trumpets and chirimias. The women all embraced in greeting. Meals were served; and there was much dancing, although now in an orderly and Christian manner.

Padre Cristobal de Villalta was richly rewarded in his labors, at seeing his people return so happily, accompanied by these strangers whom God had willed should come to him from out of these distant Sierras. At the door of his little house he awaited the procession. Upon seeing him, all ran shouting to him and, on their knees before him, repeated the word, "Nono," which means "Father," then remained to talk to him of their journey. The Padre visited with them with affection, inviting the men among the visitors to eat with him, while the women visitors sat under an enramada to share their food with the women of the pueblo. This visiting over, the principal families of the pueblo took the visitors to their homes, treating them with singular kindness, and almost all that night there could be heard talk of one to another.

This happy pilgrimage of don Bautista and his bride resulted in many new friendships being formed among the Nations, and safe communication being established for visiting and trading in such matters as cotton cloth, necklaces of beads and other little ornaments.

Guided by don Batista, the party continued onward, being acclaimed at one pueblo after another, until arriving at the Villa of Sinaloa, where they were warmly received by Captain Martinez de Hurdiade and the Padres of the College.

To each of the ten Caciques the Captain made a handsome gift of a young horse. He also gave to each a Rod of Justice, to signify their authority to govern their people, in cooperation with the Captain, and with these presents they were very pleased.

They finally continued to the Villa of Culiácan, where they were given a very special greeting by the Padre Visitador of the Missions, don Diego de Guzmán, who by good fortune had come to Culiacán to meet with the Padres there. A promise was given them that Padres would one day be sent into their Sierras. They returned happily to their mountains, laden with gifts of horses, Rods of Justice and other articles, such as salt, which they value highly.

The Governor don Batista it was, who labored together with Padre Cristobal de Villalta to bring down the Huites from their high Sierras, to populate the good lands prepared for them, as has been told.

A sub-tribe of the Sinaloas, named Calimonas, had formerly been at war with the Huites. To insure their friendship, the Padre procured that these Calimonas should become the Godparents of Huite children, thus insuring the future friendship of their families. At the new location the Huites built a church, with roof timbers of cedar, and of three naves. It was adorned with images and ornaments, the walls being richly painted. It resulted altogether one of the most beautiful and spacious churches of the entire Province. Here they came most faithfully to worship, nor ever after caused a disturbance, as has sometimes happened in other Nations new in the faith.

I here wish to give a eulogy to this great Cacique don Batista. Even in his earlier life as a savage he had been of great capacity and excellent disposition, and was loved and esteemed by all who knew him.

Captain Hurdaide, recognizing his great talent, designated him Governor of the Sinaloas, a post which he held for thirty years, with great fidelity to the Spanish Crown and to the ministers of evangelical faith, even though this often had placed him in peril of death.

There shone in Don Batista a great zeal for the extension of the Christian faith among the Indian Nations. At the age of twenty seven years he had been baptized; and for all the years thereafter he was a bulwark to the Padres, accompanying them in the face of danger, to assist and protect them on their journeys into lands of the Guazaparis, Chinipas, Temoris and others.

In acts of piety, charity and virtue he was of the greatest. Through his sermons and his good example he brought many into the church. In worship he was constant and faithful. In the corporal labor of building churches and houses he stirred others by his example. Like the good Captain Hurdaide, he shared with others with such liberality that he had little left for himself.

The valorous Captain paid much heed to his counsel, whether in war or in peace, and so did the Padres in their guiding of his people. Their deference to him in such matters don Batista accepted with the gratitude worthy of a fine and noble Christian. Upon his death there attended upon him all the people of his native village of Toro, where he died. Before his death, weakened as he was, he made his people a very excellent talk in which he enjoined on them to continue in their Christianity. His testament was written for him in the last days of his illness by the village school teacher. In it he said, "My sword I will to the Padre, that he shall keep it, and provide that the Captain shall permit it to be used only by someone of the same good heart and faith that I have tried to show in my years of service."

At his burial there was a great concourse of Caciques and people from the neighboring Nations. Their distinguished men bore him on their shoulders to the church, where he was given their manner of burial, with music on the one hand and tears on the other, in honor of this great man who had been at once their counselor and protector. Mass was held and a sermon given, in which his life was upheld as an example that should remain a living memory to his people.

CHAPTER 42

Journey to the Land of the Chínipas

IT WILL BE RECALLED that Captain Diego Martinez de Hurdaide made a perilous journey into the land of the Chínipas, by order of the Viceroy of New Spain, in search of deposits of silver. Their country lies in rugged mountains three days travel still beyond the Huites, the route being over mountains and into canyons (*barrancas*) of the greatest asperity. One rise continues steeply for ten miles, followed then by a descent of extreme danger.

After the building of the Fort of Montesclaros, the Chínipas, as already told, came to the Captain asking for peace and for Padres to indoctrinate their people. Unfortunately, just before the time set for the entry of the Padre into their lands, a goodly number of the Chínipas, led by a principal Cacique, decided to have one last orgy of drunkeness. During this drunkeness, the Cacique referred to discharged an arrow which wounded one of his woman relatives.

Feeling himself very much in disgrace, and fearful that news of these events might cause the Padre to delay his coming, the Cacique sped over those rugged Sierras to make his apologies, making the usual three day journey in one long day. Throwing himself at the feet of the Padre, he told his story and begged forgiveness.

The Padre Cristobal, withal that he felt much kindliness towards this transgressor, felt he must set a penance for such a transgression. This was that he should return to his pueblo, gather the other Caciques at the enramada they had just prepared for their first church services, and tell them of his repentance, asking that they should give him two disciplinary lashes each, upon his shoulders.

Although disciplinary measures are most foreign to these haughty and belicose savages, this Indian accepted his punishment. Afterwards he addressed his people, urging that they all set drunkeness aside upon becoming Christians, himself assuming the resonsibility of imposing punishment on any who should become transgressors.

With Padre Cristobal on his journey into the Sierras of the Chínipas traveled a hundred Indians, clearing the way of rocks and limbs of trees. There had been built little brush enramadas to shelter him along the way.

At their first pueblo there had gathered all the Chínipa Nation, about 500 families. Here they had built a church of brush and timbers. To celebrate in greater measure this occasion, the Padre entered into the church dressed in a cape of gold which he used for baptisms, and the children carried before them a beautiful image of Our Lady of Populo, that she should be moved to receive this pueblo under her protection.

The church services were followed by much feasting and dancing. There were baptized 400 young children.

The houses of the pueblo were of adobe construction, these making altogether a most agreeable impression.

There was scarce a family that in their barbarism had not stored skulls and bones of their victims of past wars. They also had put away in their houses little idols and other instruments of their superstitions.

Under instruction from the Padre, the principal Indians gathered forty eight large baskets of skulls and bones, as well as other articles of their witchcraft, delivering them to the Padre, who asked that two great bonfires should be made and all these objects of their paganism put into the flames.

Twenty four Chínipas children were selected to return with the Padre to the Villa, to be reared among the Christians and to be taught reading, writing, singing and the Christian doctrine.

CHAPTER 43

The Guazaparis and Temoris Indians

THE GUAZAPARIS and Temoris Nations, living twenty five miles further into the mountains, were mortal enemies of the Chínipas. A short time before the trip of the Padre Cristobal, they had cut off the heads of several Chínipas and celebrated a barbarous orgy, with feasting and dancing. This news came to the Padre soon after his return to his home among the Sinaloas. Much distressed, he went into his church and made a most earnest supplication to the guardian angels of these poor souls for help in bringing these barbarous peoples together.

His oration finished the Padre stepped to the doorway of his little home, to be met by a Chínipa Indian who told him that there was hiding nearby in the forest, a Guazapari Indian, brother of one of their principal Caciques, who desired to see him, but was much in fear of being killed by the Chínipas.

The Padre sent some faithful Indians to conduct this Guazapari safely to him. This man had come to treat of peace between the tribes, and of the acceptance of the Christian faith. The Padre urged the Chínipas that they accept these overtures of peace and take the Guazaparis now as friends and brothers. This the Chínipas willingly agreed to do; and soon a hundred Guazaparis, men, women and children, came with joy to meet the Padre, together with the Chínipas. Presents were exchanged, and an agreement of peace was reaffirmed.

The new friends were feasted, and then loaded with corn for their return to their higher mountains. A new era of peace began, with all moving freely to and from their rancherias.

A delegation of Chínipas, Guazaparis and Temoris came together to the Villa, 240 miles distant, to plead for a minister to be sent again to their pueblos. Padre Cristobal de Villalta was once more assigned by the Padre Superior to this service.

The Padre left in charge of these people, one of his Christian disciples of the Sinaloas whom he had persuaded to marry a Chínipa maiden. The maiden selected was so modest that she had horror of the company of a man; and only by the persuasion of the Padre did she agree to the marriage.

Their wedding was the motive for much feasting and rejoicing, and the young woman became the inseparable consort of her husband, going from one rancheria to another with him in his ministry, the couple now and again making the three days journey to take counsel of the Padre. This Christian Indian soon extended his visits to include the Guazaparis and Temoris. Among the Guazapari Indians there was a much renowned Cacique named Cobameai. He was a man about 50 years of age, of great stature, and of fierce countenance and frightening manner.

Although this Indian had not before been to any Christian pueblo, Padre Cristobal sent an invitation to him to be present on the occasion of his first visit to the Chínipas. Chief Cobameai had arrived to meet the Padre dressed in a fine cloth of blue color, that extended to his ankles. His ears had been perforated in the form of a circle and decorated with pieces of mother of pearl, which had been fastened into the holes of the ear with a series of bright blue strands, making a most striking picture.

Cobameai accompanied the Padre to the central Plaza of the village. Here he climbed to the roof of a house, from where he delivered a fiery oration, with great energy and loud voice, urging the desirability for peace and amity between the Nations. He concluded by inviting the Christian Indians and the Padre to visit his lands.

At the conclusion of his stay among the Chínipas, Padre Cristobal enjoined on Cobameai that his people should open a trail to his country, that he might be able to come to visit there. This was done, and Cobameai and his sons built little enramadas for the Padre and his companions to use for shelter during their journey.

In these groups, Guazaparis and Temoris, there were 500 families. There was so little land that their corn was planted on steep hillsides among the rocks [*And still is, today*]. The climate was cold and the area was subject to snows.

Following this visit, the Christian disciple of the Padre, accompanied by his wife, made frequent trips to see these people.

There had come to see the Padre during his visits to the Chínipas, yet other tribes of the Sierras, named Thios and Varohios. These people began coming freely to visit the Padre and the Christian Indians in the lower pueblos, and at the Villa. Thus, by all the means we have related, the Nations of these Sierras came to an understanding and acceptance of the Christian faith and, of a measure of civil government, and learned to live in peace among themselves.

CHAPTER 44

The Story of Padre Juan Bautista de Velasco

MANY APOSTOLIC MINISTERS gave their lives, during the years of which I am writing, to the glory of God in these Missions; if not to the blade of a sword, or to clubs or arrows, then in a great and enduring struggle with primitive man and with nature, in these remotest places of the earth. The story of their lives are as proper material for history as writings of conquests of a temporal nature, such as those of the Spanish Captains and soldiers who distinguished themselves among these savage peoples with memorable actions and heroic deeds.

I shall write here of the signal virtues and saintly death of the Padre Juan Bautista de Velasco, one of the earliest evangelical workers of Sinaloa. He was born in the City of Oaxaca, in the southern part of New Spain, of honorable parents, and was received into our Company at the age of 16 years. He went to the ministry of Sinaloa at 29 years of age, serving there for 22 years, during the most difficult early period, when all the people were savage, barbarous and free, with fear of no one and reckless in their vices, especially in their drunkeness.

In the midst of these people he moved with zealous dedication, transforming them from savagery to the peaceful way of life they now enjoy.

In this endeavor he had to endure the lack of almost all ordinary means of living. Being of a delicate complexion he suffered unusually from the rigors of the sun. He spent much time in personal conversation with his disciples, as a better means to their education. He was quick to come to their defense against the abuses of others. In their sicknesses he was their physician as well as spiritual counselor. He went to much effort to secure medicines for them from the Mother Church in Mexico City.

Padre Juan Bautista de Velasco knew very perfectly the two principal languages of the Province. He reduced them to writing, and preached in them in such an eloquent manner that the Indians were charmed at hearing him. He it was who became the teacher of the Indian languages to other Padres and Spaniards who arrived in Sinaloa.

[*It has already been told that the book "Arte de la Lengua Cahita, por un Padre de la Compania de Jesus," containing the grammar and vocabulary of the Yaqui-Mayo language has been attributed to Padre Velasco.*]

He gave of everything that he had to his disciples, even the little alms sent to him from Mexico City, remaining in such poverty that after twenty years he wore some of the same clothing in which he had come to Sinaloa.

His was a great serenity of spirit, nor was he ever seen by anyone to alter his kindly expression under provocation. With patience in every adversity, he persevered in his labors, hidden and forgotten in this land so remote and apart, applying talents such as would have distinguished him in higher posts, he actually having refused these in order to work among these savages.

He had the virtue of being of wise counsel in important matters. The Captain Diego Martinez de Hurdaide often consulted with him, and he was spiritual confessor to this famous Captain.

His death came on the 29th of June of 1613, at 57 years of age, 22 years after founding his first church in Sinaloa. The end came while he was returning with his principal Indian disciples from the Annual Conference of the Padres. Calling his friends to his side, he asked that they remember his teachings and love and reverence the Padre who should succeed him.

Padre Juan Bautista de Velasco was buried in the church yard of the Villa of Sinaloa, his funeral services being attended by eleven other Padres of the Province and Christian Indians from all the Nations. His fine example carried on for long years in the hearts and memories of his people.

CHAPTER 45

Francisco Castro, Coajutor of the Mission of Sinaloa

AMONG SUCH PRIMITIVE PEOPLES, and in such far away places, there is ever a lack of physical resources, as also of men who are skilled in securing them.

On a trip to Mexico City, the Director of the Mission of Sinaloa, Gonzalo de Tapia, secured the services of Francisco de Castro as temporal Coadjutor for the churches of the Province. Francisco was a native of the Village of Guines, near Seville, in Spain, and a member of a very honorable family, his father having had under his care the Haciendas of the Marquis de Villamanrique.

Upon this Marquis becoming Viceroy of New Spain, young Francisco was invited to accompany him to that distant country.

Don Antonio de Mendoza, who was at that time Provincial of the Company of Jesus in New Spain, accepted Francisco into the Company, he being at that time twenty five years of age. From here he was assigned to the difficult task of providing for the physical needs of his fellow workers in Sinaloa.

Upon his arrival there were no churches, nor even dwellings for the Padres, except very temporary brush enramadas whose manner of construction was known to the Indians. He at once directed the building of a house and two churches of solid wall construction at the Villa; from there continuing similar labors for a period of thirty three years.

At the season when the sun's rays were strongest, this Padre would be out at daylight laying adobes, or moving timbers together with his Indian helpers. There never was in Padre Francisco any thought of conserving his strength.

For all those 33 years he was a counselor to the Padres in their temporal problems. He ever held great respect and reverence for them, speaking before them with head uncovered.

It is difficult to describe the charity and affection he held for the children who came from the many Indian Nations to study at the College. He was their counselor and, too, their physician when they were ill.

The Indians of the Province greeted his arrival in their villages with sincere pleasure. He moved freely and safely among them all, whether trading for corn and other supplies for the Mission, or instructing them in such matters as laying out their pueblos and building churches and houses.

Padre Francisco never slept in a bed, only reclining in a chair at intervals between his never ending labors. While traveling, he would sleep while reclining against the trunk of a tree.

No occupation was too low or humble for this man. He hoped only that he might exchange temporal poverty here on earth for spiritual wealth in eternity.

His end came while working in a field belonging to the College, some six miles from the Villa. He was placed on a bed but could not rest there, preferring to be placed in a chair. He then asked for a crucifix and a lighted candle and, holding them in his hands, he commended himself to God before expiring.

All the life of this worthy man had been spent in preparation for death. Had our great Patron San Ignacio known Padre Francisco, he surely would have embraced him and said, "Here is a proper son of the Company of Jesus, such as I seek for my service."

CHAPTER 46

The Mayo River—Its Land and People

THE STORY of the Indians of the Mayo River follows in proper order of time, that of the Nations which we have heretofore described.

The Mayos were the most populous Nation of those of whom we have written. The Mayo River, which they populated, lies some 120 miles north of the Villa of Sinaloa and 75 miles north of the Gran Rio de Zuaque.

The word Mayo, in their language means "end" or "terminus," perhaps because so many of them lived at the lower end of their river, towards the Sea of Californias. The Mayo is not as large as the Petatlán nor the Gran Rio de Zuaque but it, too, has its beginning far into the Sierras of Topia, and floods a vast plain in times of heavy rain, or of the melting of snow in the mountains.

ted lands were extensive enough to support a population of 30,000
e Mayos were able, when occasion required, to put into battle
o 10,000 warriors of bow and arrow.

nguage is essentially the same as that of the Yaqui and Zuaque

ure of the Mayos is less warlike than that of most of the Nations surrounding them. They are tillers of the soil, except for a very few who are deni-
zens of the forest. There are among them many who spend a part of their time
fishing from the sea and from the river, especially where this river empties into the sea. Both river and sea are abundant in fish.

Because of their being so surrounded by hostile Nations the Mayos had little communication with the Spaniards and Padres during the early years of
the Mission of Sinaloa. However, after Captain Diego Martinez de Hurdaide
opened the way through the savage Nations living along the borders of the
Rio Zuaque, Mayos began to come in numbers to the Villa of Sinaloa. They
were much impressed with the appearance of the churches of the Christian
pueblos through which they passed; and pleased to note how happily the people now lived, at peace one with another.

Soon they became friendly enough that in times of war by the Spaniards
against other Indian Nations, the Mayos became their allies, furnishing large
contingents of warriors for the expeditions which were required to quell the
unrest among other Nations.

The unusual fidelity of the Mayos was recognized by Captain Hurdaide,
who made them gifts, as he was able, of young horses for their Caciques, and
other presents which they most treasure. Eventually a treaty was entered into
between the Captain and the Mayos, placing them under the protection of
the Spanish Crown; and there was thus cemented a strong friendship between
Mayos and Spaniards.

These were the conditions prevailing when the principal Cacique leaders
of the Mayos came to ask with insistence for Padres to come into their country.

According to Royal Decree, in order to undertake such a project it was
necessary to procure permission from the Viceroy of the Crown in New Spain.

The Viceroy at this time was the Marquez de Guadalcazar. This gentleman,
upon receiving the request of the Captain and Padres, approved the action of
Captain Hurdaide and communicated with the Padre Provincial of the Jesuit
Order in Mexico City, asking the Company to assume charge of the conversion
of the Mayos.

This project was no easy one, for there were some 30,000 Indians to be visited and indoctrinated; these living scattered along many miles of river, or in
the woods and in a land only 40 miles away from the country of the very belicose Yaqui Nation. The nearest protection available from Spanish forces was
the small garrison maintained by Captain Hurdaide at the Fuerte de Montesclaros, southward 75 miles, on the Rio de Zuaque.

Such considerations led the Padre Provencial to select for this undertaking
the veteran Padre Pedro Méndez, of seasoned experience in the Province of

Sinaloa, and very well versed in the language of the Mayos. Padre Mendéz was then seventy years of age, and had retired, after twenty four years of service on this frontier, to Mexico City to enjoy a well earned rest. However, he happily undertook this new post of so much labor and responsibility and promptly set out on muleback for the journey of 1,000 miles to assume his new charge.

Arriving at the Villa of Sinaloa, head of the Missions of the Province of Sinaloa, so impatient was he to begin his new labors that he did not even wait to receive the greetings of the Padres who attended the Missions of the Petatlán River, who so much loved and venerated him; but pushed forward on his journey.

From Sinaloa he was accompanied by his old friend, Captain Martinez de Hurdaide, together with an escort of twenty Spanish soldiers equipped with their armored horses. This force was deemed necessary, in case there might have been planned an ambush by warriors of the belligerent Yaquis.

CHAPTER 47

Felicitous Labor Among the Mayos

PADRE MÉNDEZ wrote his Superiors in Mexico City of his joyful welcome and his felicitous labor among the Mayos:

"Our entry into the land of the Mayos was, by the glory of God, most promising, our endeavours in the beginning being much lightened by the good offices of Captain Hurdaide.

"Thirty miles before arriving at the Mayo River we were met by a delegation led by a very principal Cacique. Upon nearing the first pueblo, there came to greet us a group of perhaps 400 people, among men, women and children. Everyone was adorned in a very gala manner, as for a holiday, most of them in bright plumed head dresses.

"From where these people received us, we proceeded under a series of arches, formed by green tree branches. There had also been high crosses erected at intervals. So great were the manifestations of joy of these people that we were moved to tears.

"Nearer the pueblo there had formed two columns of people, some on foot, others on horseback, the men on one side of the lane through which we passed, the women and maidens on the other, to a total number of several thousands.

"In this pueblo, as in all the others we visited along the Mayo River, the people had taken pains to erect large brush enramadas under which to hold our services.

"We continued from one to another of seven pueblos of the Mayos, until reaching the sea; in this journey meeting perhaps 20,000 people. Even more were not present because of a famine that was distressing the land. Supplies of food had been so reduced that many were out in the woods, digging roots, or hunting animals for food.

"During the first two weeks I baptized 1,300 children and 500 adults, and married 72 couples after their having been baptized, and the man having selected a woman to be his wife, from among the several they accustomed having. To this new arrangement they have all agreed in good faith.

"It is pleasing to see these people, in evidence of their now having become civilized, men and women alike, removing their mother of pearl ear pieces which they carry suspended by a series of loops from their ears, many doing this in church upon instruction of their Padre. Many others have shortened their long hair, leaving only a que, as do Christians of other more civilized countries.

"I have by this time indoctrinated and baptized seventeen of their principal Caciques, and believe them to be altogether the most promising leaders of any I have encountered among the Indian Nations."

Here ends the letter of the venerable Padre Pedro Méndez.

Captain Hurdaide also wrote of this momentous journey. I quote from his letter:

"It was in a time of great hunger that I accompanied Padre Pedro Méndez, to participate in his conversion of the Indians of the Rio Mayo. I used all the provision I had carried for myself, the Padre and the soldiers, giving it as it lasted to the many Indian friends we found along our route. Finally I found myself obliged to dispach some of my packers with mules into the Sierras eastward, where lie the lands of the Nebomes and Nures, in search of corn.

"The muleteers, finding little corn in the lower Sierras, continued 150 miles farther into those Sierras than I had instructed them to do. There eventually arrived a messenger from them to advise me that they found themselves in a tight place, being surrounded and attacked by enemies.

"Although it seemed to me that perhaps we were in a yet tighter place, being reduced to digging roots from the woods to keep from starving, I felt obligated to go to the rescue of my companions. Taking twenty soldiers with armored horses, I entered into the high mountains of the pagan Nebomes, who had heretofore been friendly.

"We were again received among them with every sign of affection. Crosses had been erected for us at intervals along our trail. Their elderly women carried water in clay ollas for us to drink, as we passed near their rancherias. Of this water they sprinkled on our heads as we drank, saying such words as "May there come as many of your people to live among us as these drops of water which we scatter over you."

"The packers had by now escaped from their peril, and had returned as far as the land of the Lower Nebomes. However, not deeming it wise to let the matter of their being attacked go without chastisement, I pushed on to where lived the Upper Nebomes, who had started the trouble. They had, by now, repented, coming to us to beg for peace, bringing with them large gifts of food for us to take back with us.

"They had also taken pains to erect a series of crosses along the route we must take before arriving at their village, and at the village entrance had placed a series of arches under which we should be received. At this village we found a great multitude of Indians.

"They had also gone to the trouble of building brush enramadas for our comfort. As I went forward to meet them, the women and children begged that I should place my hand upon their heads, some of them saying that now that they had been privileged to meet the great Captain, an important wish of their lives had been fulfilled.

"These Upper Nebomes are generally tractable and good natured, and much domesticated in their manner of living. They are little disturbed by wars, generally being left in peace to cultivate their lands, which lie in the upper areas of both the Yaqui and Mayo rivers. Some of their habitations lie still northward of the Yaqui River.

"They have mastered the art of irrigation by the use of little canals taken at angles from the rivers, as successfully as have the farmers of Spain. They have acquired by this time chickens of the same that grow in Castile, and these they raise commonly about their houses.

"Their pueblos are well ordered. Their houses are made of blocks of earth, packed together in the manner of adobes. In the building of these houses they are much advanced over the Indians of the plains westward, who are apt to be satisfied with houses made of mats of bamboo. Altogether the Nebomes are a very civilized people, even though they are not yet Christians.

"Their women are exceedingly modest in their dress. They cover themselves to their ankles with garments of tanned deerskin, these garments being well and artistically made, and kept by their owners with much pride. For no price would a woman sell such a garment for me to take back to the Villa.

[Here we find our most detailed description of the Nebome (Pima) Indians, who have formed such an interesting part of our story since we first read of them accompanying Cabeza de Vaca, in a number of 600, in his exploration of the Province of Sinaloa.]

"There came here to the land of the Upper Nebomes to visit me, two Caciques from tribes living much higher into the Sierras, for the purpose of offering me allegiance. I visited with them and gave them some gifts, after which they departed. Although I questioned them, none could by now remember the Spaniards (*Cabeza de Vaca and his companions*) who had passed through here on their way from the lands of Nuevo Mexico. They did, however, give me notice of having seen buffalo (cíbolas) farther northward and eastward. They also told me of other and larger pueblos that lie in that direction.

"I sensed a true docility and good faith in these people, and found them most willing to accept the Holy Faith. The Nebomes plead that we send Padres to minister to them, they fearing that many may die before receiving baptism.

"Their conversion is doubly desirable, as it will serve as a curb for the barbarous Iachimes (*Yaquis*), who are their neighbors and enemies. The coming of the Padres may well lead to the conversion of the Iachimes as well, so bringing peace to both Nations.

"While I was on this journey another Nation, the Nures, also traveled down from their mountain fastnesses to greet me, in keeping with a pledge of friendship made six years before, in this pledge there having been given mutual assurances of protection. Their friendship is continuing to be cultivated, in the hope of finally sending Padres into their country to carry to them the Divine Word.

"Of you, good Padre Rector, I ask that you plead to God for his divine assistance in our efforts at conversion of these savage peoples, and to appeal to the Padre Provincial to send more laborers to this vast field, which promises such abundant yield."

Here ends the letter of this most dedicated Christian and valorous soldier, Captain don Diego Martinez de Hurdaide, who for so many years upheld us most staunchly in our interminable labor in behalf of the Indians of Sinaloa. Happily, I may add that those Indians referred to in this chapter were all converted within a few years of the time of which is written.

CHAPTER 48

Breaking Lances with the Devil Among the Mayos

IN THE FIRST YEARS after the conversion of the Mayos God favored them with much rainfall and abundant harvests. There was much contentment in the land, Christianity prospered and there were converted some 12,000 souls.

The Indians came to regard the Padres as their arbiters in both temporal and spiritual matters and the Padres worked diligently to uproot the evil practices of these people, that had been inspired by the Devil.

On an occasion a witch doctor came to ask for baptism. Padre Méndez required that he should first give up the implements of his witchcraft. The man returned with various little objects which he said he had used to attain certain purposes; one to bring water from rains to crops when dry, another to insure the crops against floods of the river, and other similar superstitions. The Padre destroyed these relics of Devil worship, indoctrinating and baptizing this Hechicero, time proving that he had truly been converted to the law of God.

Another abuse, found among the Mayo women, was the practice of abortion. They were apt to excuse this practice by pointing to a child in their arms, saying that they felt it was more important to nurse and rear this child then to carry another to birth.

There was an old woman among them who practiced this diabolical art, giving remedies to pregnant women, which she accompanied by incantations. God finally felt pity for this poor misguided soul, moving her to ask for baptism. She was duly prepared and baptized and on the day following death brought her salvation.

It was most gratifying to Padre Méndez to witness the diligence of these new Christians in the confession of their sins. During the first period of Lent they would make special confessions. They found various means of recalling their sins. Some kept count of these by using little bundles of twigs of varying colors; others tied knots in little cords, to remember the number of sins committed. Yet others kept count by the use of their fingers, this being their ordinary manner of counting.

[*Counting in the Yaqui-Mayo* (Cahita) *language is by units of twenty, in a somewhat primitive fashion, as follows: Beginning with one: Senu, goy, baji, naiqui, mamni, busani, gojbusani* (six and one), *gojnaiqui* (twice four), *batani, gojmamni* (twice five), *gojmamni ama senu* (twice five and one) *and so continuing, gojmamni ama mamni ama senu* (twice five and five and one), *being sixteen. The unit for twenty is tacagua; as, senu tacagua, goy tacagua, baji tacagua. After the coming of the Spanish peso, of five tacaguas each, the Indians adopted the term "senu pesota," in referring to a peso.*

In a previous work "A Southwestern Utopia" The Ward Ritchie Press, I have described the unique manner in which our Mayo Indian laborers, although illiterate, could figure their accounts, which we kept for them on a sheet of paper termed a "vale" (voucher). This account was kept with debits and credits on opposite sides of the paper, in Roman numerals; X for ten pesos, V for five pesos, O for one peso, a half circle for fifty centavos, a perpendicular line for one real (twelve and a half centavos), *a half line for a half real, and a dot for a centavo. By placing in separate piles, grains of corn, beans, pebbles or other units to the amount of the total debits and, in another pile, the total credits, then tossing away from each pile like kinds of grain or other counters used, they finally were left with only the debit pile, to determine what their debt might be.*]

I shall now tell of a problem that confronted Padre Méndez in the early days of his ministry, and the manner in which he came to resolve it. There was in the land of the Mayos a maiden to whom, because of an external beauty rare to see among these people, the venerable Padre Méndez had given the name of Magdalena. Her natural beauty this woman adorned with all manner of paints and colors, as is sometimes their custom.

Eventually the beautiful Magdalena, who was much sought after, became a lost woman, creating much scandal in the pueblos of the Mayos, and causing to be as lost as she was, numerous Indian men, some already married. Her occupation, or entertainment, came to be the stealing of husbands, she usually keeping two or three men blinded and entangled in their stupidity, while she entertained herself with them.

During this period of her life she had avoided, in every manner possible, meeting Padre Méndez. God willed that finally they should meet along a road she was traveling in the company of some other Mayo women. She attempted to avoid being seen, but the good Padre greeted her, asking gently why she had not come to be baptized. Magdalena responded lightly and with much disdain that it was because she had no man with whom to marry. Well could the good Padre have replied as did Christ to the Samaritan woman, that she had five men or more; but rather he answered her that as they were going towards the same pueblo, he would there find her a husband to marry.

At the time of this remark the Padre seemed to make no impression on the woman Magdalena. Later, coming to the pueblo where she lived, for the purpose of hearing some confessions, the Padre sent some Christian Indians to request her to come to him.

She came, with no less adornment of her countenance than before, and with such a display of anger that it seemed that her heart could scarce be contained in her body. The Padre, with his accustomed patience, began to plead with her to change her way of life, to select a husband, and live thereafter in the service of God. In her fury this woman shouted in answer, "Three days ago I had one husband, and today another, and shall continue to change husbands as I have in the past."

This gentle Padre was so moved by this blasphemy that his anger rose within him, and raising his voice with much authority, he ordered the poor woman to place herself on her knees before him to ask for forgiveness, and to discard all the gaudy ornaments which she wore. Here was manifested the strength of divine grace as it shone resplendent in this fine old man, for this woman who had come roaring to the Padre as a lioness, now changed meekly into a lamb, knelt before him, removed her baubles, and asked in all humility for baptism.

The Padre at once gave diligence to finding her a husband. God offered a youth who desired to marry her and whom she was pleased to marry. The Padre discussed carefully with them this serious step which they proposed taking, and the importance of their maintaining fidelity toward each other. He instructed them in the catechism, they were baptized and married; and their souls found great joy in their new state, in this setting others of their pueblo a virtuous example.

In the following letter to his Padre Provincial in Mexico City, Padre Méndez writes of the Mayos:

"Never have I indoctrinated people so eager to learn. They are tireless in their devotions. Each night there may be heard the voices of groups gathered in houses saying their orations. From the day of their baptism they come, large and small, to give a morning greeting to their Padre, and again bid him good night, after saying their evening prayers.

"Groups of children come to church, saying their orations together as they come. It has been a source of joy to the Padre Rector, who has just come from the Villa for a visit, to witness the happiness and peacefulness which now reigns among all the people of the Mayo River.

"I must confess that my one great dread upon returning here was of having to listen so continuously to the pounding of their great war drums, and to the shouts accompanying their drunken orgies, which had seemed to me in other years to be comparable to the noises of the infernal regions. However, I now find no trace of these excesses, but rather am charmed with the sound of their prayers at evening.

"Of the two most important Caciques of all the Mayo River, one had three women, two of them his sisters, and the other Cacique had six women. They desired to be baptized, but were most loath to give up their women. Finally, the first found husbands for two of his women, and married the third. On the occasion of my coming to the pueblo of the other Cacique, he sent away all of his women but one, later helping to find them husbands; meanwhile, he married the one he had selected. Only through infinite patience has this practice of having several women been changed in these people."

As assistant, Padre Méndez was given Padre Diego de la Cruz. By the year 1620 there were 30,000 baptized Indians inhabiting the lands of the Mayo River.

As many as 1,000 Indians, men and women, labored at erecting churches at their three principal pueblos. From their own alms the Padres have adorned these with becoming murals and have bought musical instruments, and proper ornaments for the altars.

Regretfully, I must refer to the fact of the great reduction in the numbers of the Indian population throughout the Occidental Indies, while at the same time the number of Spaniards has been increasing. There are several causes, one of the principal ones being the prevalence of the epidemic sickness called cocolitzle (*small pox*). Due to the inroads of this disease and other causes, there are not now (*in 1645*) probably more than half the number of Indians that there were when the Spaniards came to these lands.

It is commonly said that their employment by Spaniards in farming, mining and other enterprises has also greatly reduced their numbers, but this is not altogether true, for in populous Nations far removed from the places where live the most Spaniards, as in the Province of Sinaloa, their numbers have been as much decreased.

Many Indians have deserted their native pueblos to labor elsewhere, sometimes in quite distant places, on cattle ranches, in farming communities, in mines, or in sugar factories. Living on estáncias seems to suit the Indian manner of living very well. Here they are given land to plant on shares, and commodities are rationed out to them for living while the crop is maturing. Their employers are usually careful as to the health of their laborers, more so than the Indians could be while living in more isolated places.

Although it is undoubtedly true that some Spaniards are extreme in their treatment of the Indian laborers, this is very much the exception, rather than the rule. The conservation of the health of the Indians of New Spain has been of singular interest and concern to their Catholic Majesties, who have issued many decrees designed for their greater protection.

The Mayos are much inclined to travel to far places, largely from a curiosity to see other lands than their own. Wherever they go, they are diligent in their labors, are everywhere well accepted, and are apt to remain. Those still remaining in their pueblos and on their farms of the Mayo River are now a prosperous, civilized and Christian people.

CHAPTER 49

Revolt of the Mountain Tribes

THE TEPÁGUE NATION, as before related, came down from their peaks to populate a fertile plain lying some fifteen miles north of the Mayo River, on a tributary of that stream. Here they formed a pueblo of 600 families. They studied Christian doctrine and constructed a church for themselves.

The Conicaris likewise came down from their Sierras, some 200 families, to live along the same arroyo that flowed from the lands of the Tepágues into the Rio Mayo. These Conicaris were of good disposition, and advanced rapidly in their learning.

Of other savage tribes living on rancherias between the Mayo and Zuaque Rivers, I have mentioned the Chínipas, Guazaparis, Temoris, Ihios and Varohios.

To indoctrinate these tribes, there was designated Padre Julio Pascual. It was my privelege to have met Padre Julio when he first arrived at the Mission of Sinaloa. He was a tall, kindly man of gentle appearance.

Beginning his labors with the Chínipas, Padre Julio quickly mastered their language. At Chínipa he built a sightly church, about which congregated some 500 people.

From here he traveled to the other mountain tribes, until he had united into one pueblo 1,400 families. For four years, in constant peril of his life, he traveled from one mountain fastness to another, in search of souls to wrest from the clutches of the Devil.

Some of those infidels were most unhappy with the new order. For his instrument through which to incite these savages against their Padre, the Devil chose the great and fierce Indian Cacique, Cobameai; Satan recalling to him memories of the days of his licentiousness and barbarism.

The fierce old man began calling meetings in secret, of those Indians least imbued with the Christian faith.

Some faithful followers gave notice of these meetings to Padre Julio, but this saintly young man, with a heart incapable of harboring suspicion, gave little heed to their warnings. Other Padres, too, had heard the rumor and communicated it to the Captain, who promptly sent an escort of six soldiers to guard over Padre Julio. However, rumors of uprising subsided, and the soldiers returned to the Presidio on the Rio Zuaque.

The pueblo of the Varohios was selected by Cobameai and his accomplices as the place to murder Padre Julio. Their first plan miscarried when the Padre returned rapidly to Chínipas to greet a fellow Padre, Manuel Martinez, the first Padre to come to assist him in the work of these Missions during his four years there.

After saying Mass at the pueblo of Chínipas on the morning of Sunday,

January 25, 1632, the two Padres, so recently met, departed for the land of the Varohios.

Here they were met with many false manifestations of pleasure. However, on the day following, there came two faithful Varohios, their eyes filled with tears, to warn them of a plot to kill them that night.

Padre Julio sent word with all speed to his faithful followers among the Chínipas to come to their rescue. Tragically, there were but few Chínipas gathered at the pueblo to hear this message. These few traveled swiftly towards the land of the Varohios, but soon found that they were hopelessly outnumbered and returned to Chínipas.

On Saturday morning, the house in which the Padres were staying was set on fire, as was the church. The Padres confessed themselves to each other, and gave confession to nine craftsmen who had been planning with them the construction of a new church, as well as to eight juvenile choir singers who had gathered in the church.

Padre Julio, well versed in the language of these savages, still tried to calm them with kindly words, but to no avail. To further torture them, the apostate Cobameai ordered them to be left alive until Sunday morning, that more of his accomplices in the revolt might be present at their destruction.

On that morning great hordes of Indians surrounded the house, climbing its roof and forcing in its walls, at the same time discharging showers of arrows. One arrow pierced the body of Padre Julio Pascual. Upon seeing his fellow Padre wounded, Padre Manuel Martinez exclaimed, "Let us not remain to die here as cowards, rather let us go forth to die bravely for Christ," and so saying, came forth from the house, where his arm was soon pinned to his body by an arrow.

Wounded as he was, Padre Julio followed, and the two, with rosaries upraised in their hands, knelt to receive showers of thousands of arrows in their bodies.

An apostate Indian named Diego Notimeai dragged the bodies of the dead Padres to a nearby log, where their heads were crushed by blows from Indian macanas, and their bodies further mutilated with thrusts from enemy knives. Two choir boys who were present and escaped being murdered, were the witnesses to the events we have described.

A faithful Indian of the Varohios, Nicolas Caviori, had warned the Padres of their danger. At the hour of their being attacked, he made a fervent appeal to the savages and, when this failed, he fired upon them until he too was overwhelmed and murdered. Another faithful Indian, Crisanto Simemeai, who had accompanied the Padres on their journey to this place, now burning with anger against the attackers, placed himself with his back against the wall of a house, firing arrows until he had killed five of the assailants. By a miracle he escaped, and continued to fire arrows at those about the dead bodies of the Padres, until they were forced to flee. A large group of Chínipas gathered and marched rapidly to the scene of the murder, but arrived too late to save their Padres.

The bodies were removed to the pueblo of Chínipas, and buried in front of the main altar of the Church there, although there was no minister present to perform a burial service. Later they were removed to Conicari, fifty miles distant from Chínipas, where Padres from all the nearer Missions gathered to hold services for these young men who had glorified God by their example of bravery in the face of death.

The constant threats of the rebel Guazaparis and their consorts decided the Chínipas to move their pueblo to a more secure place, in the lands of their friendly neighbors, the Sinaloas, and here they remain today (*1645*).

Don Pedro Perea, now Captain of the Presidio at the Villa, gathered a force of soldiers with armored horses and, supported by Indian allies, marched into the lands of the rebellious Guazaparis and Varohios, defeating them in several encounters and killing about eighty of their number.

Padre Francisco Torices, then in charge of the Mission to the Sinaloa Nation, finally persuaded most of those who had taken part in the rebellion to come to live in the land of the Sinaloas, on the upper Zuaque River, and to become Christians. Some few, however, remained hidden in their remote forests and mountains for many years.

CHAPTER 50

Story of Padres Julio Pascual and Manuel Martinez

IT IS MERITED to record the deeds of men brave in heart and strong in spirit in the service of God, that their memory shall not be buried in oblivion.

I wish to tell here of the heroic virtues of the two martyred Padres, Julio Pascual and Manuel Martinez.

Padre Julio was born in the city of Bresa, of the Señorio of Venecia in Italy. His parents were very honorable people, of ample temporal resources, and yet richer in Christianity. These parents, being devoted followers of the Company of Jesus, despite the prohibitions of their country against such devotion, resolved to send their son to study at Parma, and later at Mantua, in preparation for taking vows in the Company.

In his studies the young Julio was a signal example of modesty, serenity, honesty and devotion. Completing his training, he was received into the Company in 1611.

The Padre Procurator of the Company for New Spain, don Nicolas Amaya, arrived in Rome shortly thereafter in search of volunteers who should return with him to the Indies. Brother Julio had long held a desire for missionary service, although preferring to be designated to Japan or the Orient. However, he cheerfully took ship with others bound for New Spain, devoting himself for three years thereafter to studying, and growing in knowledge of the work of the Missions. After this period of preparation, he was sent to the frontier Mission of the Province of Sinaloa.

It seemed to be ordained from Heaven that it should fall to the lot of Padre Julio to relieve other Padres in their labors among several Nations, including the Zuaques, Teguecos, Sinaloas and Yaquis, giving him opportunity to learn those languages. Finally he was assigned to the Chinipas Nation, where he labored until his untimely death.

An outstanding characteristic of Padre Julio was his great humility. While traveling with others, he was apt to take over such duties as the saddling of their mounts and the loading of the alforjas in which were carried their necessities for traveling.

It is told that on his first journey on muleback, from the Port of Vera Cruz to Mexico City, he camped with his brother priests in a dense jungle, next to a stream infested with alligators and, a companion having lost his saddle mule, Padre Julio ran after the animal into that perilous jungle, following it all through that afternoon and night. His brother Padres had given him up for lost when he returned leading the mule at dawn on the day following.

Padre Julio desired nothing for himself; all his little alms provided by the King went for purchase of musical instruments and other articles needed for the services of the church.

In the Chinipas Nation his energy and fervor brought a flowering of Christianity that was marvelous to behold.

His ministry was to the physically ill, as well as to the spirits of those barbarians, this ministry too, giving him opportunity to discuss with them matters of Heaven.

It was his custom to have his church bells rung for anyone of his congregation at time of illness, through this means appealing to fellow Christians to offer their prayers for the person afflicted.

While at the Fuerte de Montescalros he had trained the sentries there to this duty, and in all the many years since his death this practice has been continued by the soldiers there, in memory of their deceased companion, Padre Julio. His death came, as we have described, on February 1st, 1632, at 42 years of age, 22 of these being in the service of the Company.

Of the virtues of Padre Manuel Martinez, who accompanied Padre Julio in his Martyrdom, I can attest to from personal witness, as by good fortune, after my return from the ministry to the Yaqui Nation, I had Padre Manuel in my classes in the College of the Company in Mexico City.

He was Portugese, a native of the city of Tariva in Algarve. His father was Jorge Martinez, his mother Maria Farela, of the lineage of the Bullones, related to the glorious San Antonio de Padua. Padre Manuel was born in the year 1600.

As a youth he suffered great and terrible temptations of the Devil, intended

99

to rob him of his chastity, but from this danger he was liberated through the intercession of the Saintly Virgin, for whom he held a great adoration.

He was full of industry, arising at the very first peal of the bells in early morning. His worship was profound, his penitences severe. These included sleeping on rough bare boards, abstinence from food, and mortification of the flesh. On the occasion of his telling me of his desire for going to Sinaloa, his eyes filled with tears. To the people of Tepotztlan, where he studied, he insisted that he was going, with much happiness and resolution, to his death, which he knew would occur while preaching to the savage peoples of Sinaloa.

His very first assignment, to assist Padre Julio in the service of the Chínipas and other Nations, was also his last. He had first been welcomed by several of the Padres, who had gathered at the Mission of Tegueco. Later he was received with much feasting and rejoicing by the Chínipas Nation, where he met Padre Julio, with whom he was so soon to be martyred.

As those two brave young men have died, so have many others, in the most exquisite torment, for the glory of Christ, because of their zeal to make known His word to the peoples of the world.

CHAPTER 51

The Yaqui River—Its Land and People

FROM THE MISSIONS of the Ahomes and the Zuaques, on the Gran Rio de Zuaque, where I labored from 1606 to 1617, it was my good fortune to be ordered to undertake the conversion of the very belicose Yaqui Nation, who were the greatest in number of any of the Indian Nations of whom I have until now written.

The Yaquis lived along the borders of a large river of that same name. It, like the other rivers of which have been written, has its source in the great Sierras of Topia, flowing for a hundred miles, after leaving the high mountains, across a beautiful fertile plain before emptying into the Sea of Californias. This river lies some forty miles northward of the Rio Mayo, and 150 miles from the principal Presidio and Head of the Missions of the Province of Sinaloa, which is the Villa of Sinaloa, lying at the base of the Sierras on the Petatlán River.

From the Sea of Californias into the lower ranges of the Sierras lies the land of the Yaquis. In time of floods their lands are covered with water, bringing bountiful moisture for crops. Many large groves of cottonwood trees border this fine stream.

Crops most commonly planted are corn, beans, pumpkins and cotton. Winter floods may come from the melting of snow in the far Sierras, giving another irrigation sufficient for harvesting a second crop.

There are extensive areas of mesquite trees in the land of the Yaquis. The bean pod which they produce, when dried, is crushed in a bowl of hardwood to make a flour, which being somewhat sweet and rather tasty, serves them as food. This mesquite pod flour is commonly mixed with a little water and molded into cakes, which are then baked in an earthen vessel over the fire. This same flour mixed with a larger amount of water produces a drink which is palatable to the taste.

The Yaquis had little contact nor commerce with the Mayos, nor any other Nation, their ferocity making them much feared and leaving them isolated from the other savage Nations.

When the Spaniards first arrived, the Yaquis were already tillers of the soil, although much of their sustenance came from hunting the game so abundant in the forests, or from fish from the river and the sea. Of fish they caught vast quantities, especially in the traps which they set across the entrances to the estuaries, the river, or the shallow bays of the seashore. These fish they ate broiled over the coals, or dried it with salt, to be eaten later.

[*When my father, Louis Robertson, explored the mouth of the Yaqui River in the year 1894, he found many fish traps still in use by the Yaqui Indians. These were in the form of brush fences similar to those used by the Indians of the Mayo and Fuerte Rivers. As did the Mayos and Zuaques, the Yaquis barricaded with brush the outlets of little estuaries into the sea, placing the last barricade across the stream at high tide. As the tide receded, the fish were left stranded.*]

At the time of my entry into the land of the Yaquis in 1617, this Nation lived dispersed along one and another borders of their river, in some eighty rancherias, besides eight large pueblos, altogether in the number of 30,000 people.

They were considered by the Spaniards to be the most valiant, belligerent and independent of all the numerous Indian Nations of New Spain. That great Chronicler of the Indies, don Antonio de Herrera, states that Captain Nuño de Guzmán, one of the first explorers into this country, claimed them to be the most savage of all the Indian Nations. That most famous of all Indian fighters of the northern frontier, Captain Diego Martinez de Hurdaide, told me that he had never found in another Indian Nation a courage in battle equal to that of the Yaquis. Rather than losing heart at seeing the bodies of their dead comrades piled before them, they would use the dead for barricades, placing their feet upon the bodies to take better aim with their arrows, and shout in defiance to the enemy to continue the slaughter.

When I entered their lands, I scarce found a Yaqui warrior whose name was not taken from some act of extreme violence, usually related to war. Although this was true to a lesser degree among the other Indian Nations, these would usually consent to their name being changed to a more pacific surname upon their being baptized. Not so the Yaquis, who, although given Christian first names, insisted on keeping as surnames those descriptive of the savage deeds of their barbarism.

It must be said in their defense that, although they were so savage in war, I found many among them of good disposition, and capable of loyalty and gratitude, as shall be seen later in this story.

The customs of the days of their savagery were much the same as those of other Indian Nations. There was much drunkeness, accompanied by dancing and shouting and beating of their great war drums, often while carrying the head of an enemy impaled upon a pole as a symbol of victory.

The Yaquis are of greater stature than most of the other Indians of the New World.

They are accustomed to talking very loudly, almost shouting, in order to give greater emphasis to their words. Upon my first meeting with them I was much surprised at this seeming rudeness of manner, so different from the moderation of the other Indian Nations. When I at first sought to suppress this manner of speech, they would protest, "You must understand, Padre, that we are Yaquis, and the very word Yaqui signifies HE WHO TALKS BY SHOUTING."

Except for an occasional Cacique among them, the men of the Yaqui Nation went naked. The Caciques wore a costume of buckskin, or of the skins of lions or jaguars, or otherwise of cotton cloth dyed blue, which their women had learned to weave skillfully and attractively.

Unlike the men, the Yaqui women covered themselves with skirts which came to their knees. These skirts were, for the greater part, woven of tiny willow twigs drawn so closely together that they made a more complete covering than that commonly worn by women of other Nations, who pleated their dresses from fiber of cotton, or of the mescal plants common to this region. Only now and again a very principal woman among the Yaquis would wear a garment very neatly woven of cotton. Now the Yaqui women have become great spinners, being able to dress themselves quite neatly in cotton garments.

Yaquis, both men and women, stain their faces and arms with the juice of the wild mulberry tree, which makes a dye of orange color. [*In the earlier years of the twentieth century the dye of the wild mulberry (mora) was so esteemed that hundreds of carloads of mora wood were shipped into the United States to be transformed into dyes.*] Their ears they adorned with loops of cotton strands which were dyed bright blue with the wild indigo plant that grows in their country. These strands were tied into loops which hung suspended from a series of holes perforated around the circle of their ears. From each loop hung little ornaments, as of bright sea shells. They also place ornaments in the center cartilage of their noses, which, from childhood, are punctured for this purpose. For these nose ornaments they often use small green stones resembling emeralds, which stones they particularly esteem.

CHAPTER 52

Wars Between Spaniards and Yaquis

I MUST FIRST WRITE of the events that led up to the conversion of the Great Yaqui Nation.

The Spaniards had far more severe encounters with the Yaquis than with any of the other savage Nations. The first of these came as a consequence of the flight of the rebellious Ocoroni Indians, to which we have before referred, to the land of the Yaquis.

Captain Hurdaide sought to secure the subjugation of these Ocoronis through peaceful measures, that they might not pervert other Nations, but was not able to do so. The rebels were led by a very astute, clever and deceitful Indian named Juan Láutaro, who had originally been of the Sinaloa Nation. He had, some years before the period of which we write, crossed over the great Sierras to work in the mines of San Andrés, where he had associated with Christian Indians, but he had no liking for either church or doctrine.

His first attempt to stir other Nations to revolt was among the Mayos. However, they would not join in his plans; whereupon he returned to the land of the Ocoronis, gathering from among them some forty families, with whom he traveled to the land of the Yaquis, where he dedicated himself to spreading a feeling of hatred for the Spaniards. In order to ingratiate himself with the Yaquis, he gave some of the daughters of his Ocoroni followers to certain ones of the Yaqui Caciques, as well as making them presents of cotton cloth and clothing.

Captain Hurdaide, not being successful in securing the capture of the rebellious Ocoronis through negotiation, found himself obligated to go in search of them. Not finding them among the people of the Ocoroni, Zuaque nor Mayo Rivers, he continued on with his company of Spanish soldiers, accompanied by some Indian allies.

They made camp by the Yaqui River, where great numbers of Yaquis were gathered. From here the Captain sent messengers to the Yaquis, with offers of friendship and peace, asking only that the leaders of the rebellious Ocoronis be delivered to him for punishment.

The Cacique Láutaro had, however, so poisoned the minds of the Yaquis that they refused to accede to his request. The position of the Captain and his forces, especially because of being very short of supplies, was precarious; and besides, the Captain had not given up hope of negotiation. Therefore, he concluded to break camp at this time and return to the Villa.

Not long after, a principal Yaqui Cacique named Anabailutei came to the Villa with an offer to return the recalcitrant Indians, and to enter into a treaty of peace with the Spaniards. The Captain received this Indian with all kindness and, in evidence of his good faith, dispached with him on his return journey, some Christian Teguecos, as well as two Yaqui women who had some years before been captured and were now converted to Christianity. However, this offer of the Yaquis was one of premeditated treason; for the Tegueco Christians were murdered, their horses stolen and the Yaqui women were made slaves by their own people.

This act so aroused the Tegueco Nation that they came to the Captain to demand that vengeance be taken upon the Yaqui Nation. Although without sufficient soldiers, arms or supplies, the Captain found himself obligated to take action, in order to sustain the reputation of the Spanish arms, for this counted for much in dealing with such savage peoples. He soon equipped forty soldiers of horse and some Spanish foot soldiers clad in armor of leather. Next he made a levy of 2,000 Indian warriors from the friendly Nations, especially the Mayos, even though these had not yet been converted to the faith.

With these forces the Captain marched to the Yaqui River, capturing several Yaqui spies along their route. Arrived there, he sent messengers with suggested terms of peace. These terms were rejected and, at daybreak of the morning following, the camp of the Spaniards and their allies was attacked by some 6,000 to 8,000 Yaquis.

The battle was joined for almost that whole day, many of the Yaquis being killed, and large numbers of their women and children taken prisoners. Many of the Indian allies also were killed in this battle. Although no Spanish soldier was killed, many were sorely wounded. Neither side was able to defeat the other. Finally, the Captain was forced to withdraw his troops, for lack of water and provision, and in order to care for the wounded. All returned to the Villa to await a more opportune time for the subjugation of the fierce Yaquis.

The Yaqui prisoners were returned with the Spanish forces to the Villa, where they were well treated. The Captain thought that the prisoners might well serve as hostages of a future occasion and perhaps also be a medium for opening new negotiations for peace.

The Spaniards and their friendly Indian allies, well realizing that there could be no security to any of them so long as the renegade Caciques remained free to disturb the Yaqui Nation, resolved upon another expedition into the land of the Yaquis, this time with the largest possible number of forces. Captain Hurdaide secured fifty armored soldiers with armored horses, some of these being brought from the Villa of Culiacán. From the confederated Nations he recruited 4,000 warriors, among Christians and non-Christians.

Leaving a smaller number of soldiers, together with some Spaniards who lived in the vicinity, to guard the Villa, this force once more marched into the land of the Yaquis. Before departing, a Mass was held at the Villa for the members of the expedition.

The Yaquis, meanwhile, had prepared a very large supply of arrows, and maintained a constant guard to prevent a surprise attack by the Spanish forces.

Upon arriving once more at the Yaqui River, Captain Hurdaide set up his encampment, after which he sent another messenger, with the requirement that the rebel Láutaro and his companions should be delivered to the Spaniards. This request was again refused.

All through that night there could be heard the beating of the great war drums of the Yaquis, and the drunken shouting of their warriors. There had by now gathered Yaquis from all their eighty rancherias, not less than 8,000 warriors. The Indian Láutaro had continuously bragged that he would, himself, capture the Captain and deliver his head to the Yaquis for a victory dance.

As the first rays of dawn appeared, this great mass of enemy warriors assaulted our forces, firing endless clouds of arrows among us. A fierce combat ensued, continuing for many hours, with heavy losses among the Yaquis, as well as among our Indian allies. Many of our Spanish soldiers were sorely wounded.

The Spanish soldiers on their armored horses could give little support to the Indian allies defending our camp on the side nearest the river, nor were they sufficient in number to form a perimeter about these friendly Indians for their better protection. For hour after hour both the Indian allies and the Yaquis engaged each other with great courage, but finally our allies, who were only half the number of the Yaquis, began to lose heart.

Seeing this, the Captain gave order to raise the encampment and retire in good order. The Caudillo, second in command of the Spanish forces, marched first with over half of the Spanish soldiers on their armored horses, followed next by men with the baggage, on other horses; then by the Indian allies. The Captain remained to defend the rear of the column with a force of twenty two of our armored cavalrymen.

The Yaquis pressed upon our forces most furiously. The course of retreat was through a forest where many trees had been felled, giving little opportunity for charging the enemy with our armored horses, which were our strongest force. Comprehending this, the Yaquis charged with renewed vigor, raining multitudes of arrows upon us from behind the shelter of the fallen trees.

Finally, our Indian allies turned and fled. The Caudillo, upon seeing the flight of our allies, and the Captain with his cavalry being lost from sight, concluded that the Spanish soldiers had all been killed and gave orders to the soldiers under his command to strip their horses of their armor, for faster travel; and soon all were retreating in full flight.

There now remained on the scene of battle only the Captain with his twenty two soldiers on their armored horses, with some extra led horses, plus one Indian Cacique who had refused to flee with the others. The savage Yaquis charged this group repeatedly. Most of the soldiers had already been wounded. The Captain had received five arrow wounds on his hands and face, fortunately from arrows that had not been poisoned. The arrows used by the Yaquis were of points of hardwood further hardened in fire. One of these arrows had penetrated the visor of the steel head casket of the Captain.

However, not even in such dire straits did this great soldier lose heart, but with a courage that showed at its greatest when hardest pressed, he rallied his little troop, shouting to them with animation to fight on. He instructed them to make the greatest use of their arquebuses by firing in unison into the enemy masses. He soon led them, in repeated charges, to a small mound or hill where they could make more effective use of their horses.

The enemy meantime had captured all the baggage, including the powder loaded on some mules, leaving the little forces with only what powder remained in their cannisters.

The little hill upon which they stood lay a half league from the river, leaving them without hope of securing water. The summer sun bore down upon them mercilessly. They suffered sorely too, from wounds and weariness. Nevertheless, these brave men fought on throughout that day against a horde of ruthless savages not less than 7,000 in number. In droves the Yaquis charged, and so they struggled on. The volleys fired in unison from the arquebuses stopped their fiercest onslaughts. Under orders of the Captain, the one Indian ally gathered the arrows that dropped among the Spaniards, breaking them into pieces, that they should be of no further use to the enemy.

The sun bore down so fiercely on the Spanish coats of armor that they were all but intolerable to wear. Tortured too by thirst, they witnessed their enemies leaving by turns to rest in the shade of the nearby forest, while their women carried water to them in their pottery ollas. The only poor comfort the soldiers found was to place the ball of a musket in their mouths, as is their custom when thirsty in hot weather.

Finally, as the day waned, the Yaquis, failing to overcome our brave little force by frontal attack, conceived a plan sometimes used by these Indian Nations, of routing their enemy by fire. On the windward side of the little hill they set themseles to starting a fire, by rubbing some sticks together, as is their practice. The fire caught quickly in the dense underbrush and would have soon suffocated the Spaniards, had not the Captain been most wise in the ways of Indian fighting. Quickly he moved his men as close to the fire as they dared, meanwhile using the flint and powder from an arquebus to start another fire down wind, moving his force to the burned over ground in time to escape being caught in the flames from the fire started by the enemy.

In the course of the day the numbers of their attackers diminished, as many left to share in the pillage of the baggage of the Spaniards. This baggage included spare clothing and the silver plate upon which the soldiers ate, and their spare horses, and some mules with pack saddles. Many horses and mules had been killed.

Night approaching, the enemy retired to the bank of the river, leaving only a guard considered to be sufficient to keep the Spaniards pinned down to their desperate position. Captain Hurdaide again showed his sagacity. Once night had fallen, he ordered a number of the horses they had kept within their circle, some of them wounded, to be loosened and started at a run toward the river. The Indians on guard, hearing the animals running through the darkness, believed the Captain to be leading his men toward the water and ran to give notice to the main body of the Yaquis. Once the guards had departed, the Captain and his forces mounted on the freshest of the remaining horses, with what arms they could carry, and began a return march to the Villa, 150 miles away.

Meanwhile, the advance guard which had fled the field of battle was safely on its way to the Villa also, accompanied by the greater number of their Indian allies.

The report of the defeat of the Spanish and allied forces, and the supposed massacre of the troop led by the Captain, spread consternation among the Christian peoples, both Spanish and Indians. The venerable Padre Martín Pérez, Co-founder of the Mission of Sinaloa, and for many years its Padre Superior, shed tears of emotion, in contemplation of what had happened and the probable consequences. His life, and that of many others had been dedicated to these Missions.

Recognizing the grave danger in which they were now placed, he quickly dispached messengers to those of us Padres who were scattered among the Missions, advising us to repair in all haste to the Villa of Sinaloa. This order reached me at Mochicahui, the principal pueblo of the Zuaques. I departed at once for the Villa, where soon eight brother Priests were assembled.

We were now left without the governing authority of the Captain, and must consider what precarious means might be taken in attempting to preserve Christianity in Sinaloa. On the second day after our arrival we said a Mass for the Captain and the other Christians who had died in battle. We were truly stunned, for it seemed impossible that this just and brave man who had so valiantly upheld our cause for so many years, should now be lost to us.

One of the soldiers among those who had fled, but of the last to leave, had described the tremendous action of the Captain and his soldiers on the scene of battle. He told that when last seen, the Captain had abandoned his arquebus, and was fighting his way on horseback, wielding only his sword, through a vast horde of Yaquis, and must certainly have been killed.

Matters being in this state, on the late afternoon of the second day, into the midst of all the suspense, confusion and sadness, there came riding at great haste toward the Villa, shouting with joy, a soldier, to tell us that our Captain was yet alive, and was even now marching toward the Villa with the remainder of his forces.

With this notice all broke into great rejoicing, and the spirits of all were much restored. This soldier carried a note to Padre Martín Pérez, which had been written on a ragged bit of paper obtained from the wad used in loading an arquebus. It said, "God forgive those who abandoned us, causing so much danger to our entire Province. I and all those who remained with me, although wounded, are yet alive. We travel slowly, because of the fatigue of our horses. I am dispaching by post this faithful soldier."

So happy was the Padre Superior at this news that he resolved to go at once to meet the Captain, and I accompanied him. Upon our meeting, the Captain and his troops described to us the great struggle which they had undergone, all being much rejoiced, as were we, that they had escaped from such danger with their lives, and without having lost even a single Spanish soldier who might serve as a victim to the Yaquis for their barbaric dances that follow such occasions.

The Padre, with the pity befitting his position, supplicated the Captain that a pardon should be granted to those soldiers who had faltered, and deserted him on the field of battle. I was witness to the generous response of the Captain that his wish should be granted. This word he steadfastly honored, even when the Governor of Vizcaya, within whose jurisdiction lay the Province of Sinaloa, ordered an investigation of the conduct of these soldiers. The Captain sent a messenger to this Governor, asking him to pass over the matter, reasoning that as the Indian allies had also fled, a punishment meted out to the Spanish soldiers would alarm these friendly Indians, creating in them a state of uncertainty as to their own future. The Captain pointed out also that the problem overshadowing all others was the matter of making peace with the Yaqui Nation and, for this purpose, he had need of every soldier at his command. Viewing these considerations, the Governor carried the matter no further.

Having driven back the greatest force the Spaniards and their allies could muster against them, the Yaquis now became more arrogant than ever. However, their pride still suffered from one great mortification, which was that they had been unable to capture the famous Captain, nor even one Spanish soldier whom they could carry in triumph before their people. In fact, Captain Hurdaide from his great feat of arms gained yet greater fame among the Yaquis, as well as among the people of the other Indian Nations. He came to be regarded, more than ever, as a great Hechicero, and there grew a superstitious fear among the Yaquis in regard to him, and a conviction that one day he would come to gain a great victory over the Yaquis.

The Captain had sources of communication which kept him informed in all these matters, and which served as a means of fomenting this belief on the part of the Yaquis. Knowing well that he could not raise the funds nor forces necessary for another expedition, he determined to exert other means for their subjection, of which shall be told here.

By great good fortune, it was at just this time (*1615*) that there appeared off the coast of Ahome the Spanish ship of Captain Iturbi which we have described. This event, to be sure, caused much comment, and brought added respect for the Spaniards among the Indian Nations of Sinaloa. With this advantage as a beginning, the Captain called together various prominent Indians of his confidence, of those who lived near the borders of the Yaqui Nation, and whom he knew could find means of communication with them. To them he confided that he was even then preparing a campaign for the chastisement of the Yaquis such as they could never dream of. He gave them to understand that during this campaign the homes and crops of the Yaquis would be destroyed, and their women and children taken prisoners and carried away. This undertaking he said he was placing in charge of three Captains, each with his separate army, all to enter Yaqui territory simultaneously, at separate points along their river, so that the Yaqui forces would have to be divided for their defense. The attack on the lower pueblos, he explained, was to be made from Spanish ships that would gather at the entrance to the river, and disembark great numbers of

108

soldiers and horses. He confided that this time their Indian allies would be permitted to take full vengeance as they chose, on the Yaquis, and even their families, in revenge for their own people who had been lost in previous raids by the Yaquis upon other Indian Nations. All these discussions, of course, came to the ears of the Yaquis, causing them much concern; in fact, so much so that they took to holding councils among themselves, and finally came to the surprising resolution of which will be told in the chapter following.

CHAPTER 53

Captain Hurdaide Negotiates Peace With the Yaquis

THERE WERE, as may easily be supposed, those who from afar and without proper understanding, criticized the determination of Captain General Hurdaide to move against the Yaquis. They could not easily comprehend that matters had arrived at such a crisis that to submit to the Yaquis, and to the rebels to whom they had given refuge, would have made impossible any further advances of either Christianity, or the authority of the Spanish Crown, in the Province of Sinaloa. Neither could they judge the extraordinary qualities of leadership of this astute and brave man, that could enable him to keep in relative peace perhaps a hundred thousand savage Indians with a force of forty six Spanish soldiers. Nor could they appreciate the manner in which, after failing to win success with arms against such hordes of Yaquis, he was able, in his wisdom, to wrest victory and peace from apparent defeat.

The manner of final subjection of the proud Yaquis coming so near to being miraculous, and being so much more inspired by the grace of God than by force of arms, I have thought to describe it here, as it fell to my lot to witness it from personal observation, and also as it is recorded in writings which I have in my possession.

As a result of the discussions of the Captain and the Indians of highest authority of Nations bordering the Yaquis, which discussions reached the ears of the Yaquis, a group of their Caciques resolved to treat of peace with the Spaniards and the Padres. A principal difficulty in negotiating for peace lay in the fact that the route of communication between Spaniards and Yaquis was through the land of the Mayos and, after these, the Teguecos. The Teguecos were particularly incensed by the treacherous murder of their Caciques who had been sent as envoys to the Yaqui Nation.

However, a principal Yaqui Cacique, named Conibomeai, enlisted the services of an outstanding woman Cacique of the Yaquis, even though placing her life in grave jeopardy, to carry a message of good will to two principal Mayo

Caciques, whose names were Osameai and Boothisuame. Conibomeai particularly desired to know from the Mayo Caciques the real intent of the Captain toward the Yaqui people.

This brave and spirited woman departed alone from the Yaqui River. Upon her leaving it had been agreed that should she not return in four days, she should be given up for dead at the hands of the Mayos.

God willed that after traveling alone through the woods for thirty miles, she should come into the hands of some friendly Mayos, who guided her to the two Caciques.

These men, who had over the years developed a strong friendship and a firm alliance with the Captain, heard her words with pleasure, agreeing to forward the messages at once to the Captain at the Villa. They asked this woman, as evidence of the good faith of the Yaquis, that these should now send further envoys to confirm the message she had carried. It can be understood, after these people having been at war against each other for so many generations, that they had little reason to have faith in each other. The Yaqui woman messenger was given an escort of Mayo warriors to accompany her on her return journey, until reaching the border of the Yaqui Nation.

Upon her return, a conference was held between her, the Chief Conibomeai and other Yaqui leaders. It was resolved that this woman ambassador, whose mission had proven so successful, should next return to the land of the Mayos accompanied by two other women, one of these being of the Mayo Nation, although married to a well known Yaqui Cacique named Otatavo. They carried a request that the two Mayo Caciques should take a message to the Captain, telling of the desire of the Yaquis for peace. Acquiesing willingly, the two Mayo Caciques quickly departed for the Villa, leaving the three Yaqui women ambassadors to rest among the Mayo families.

It can well be imagined with what deep pleasure the message was received by the Captain and the Padres. The Captain dispached a message in reply, which included a request that more of their principal Yaqui leaders come to confer with him.

Meanwhile, the Yaqui women, in their haste to hear the results of the message had, accompanied by some forty Mayo warriors and women, continued toward the Villa. Upon meeting the Mayo Caciques, all returned to hear the distinguished Yaqui woman and her sister envoys deliver their message personally to the Captain.

After the communication had been graciously received, the Captain asked whether it came from all the people of the Yaqui Nation. At this question the three women envoys were embarrased, explaining that some of their people, especially their more fiery young braves, had during their council meetings, denounced this move toward peace, but that their greatest and wisest Caciques, including Conibomeai and Hinsumei, had reprimanded the restless young men, telling them sternly to guard silence in the presence of their elders when such vital matters were under consideration.

The Yaqui women remained several days at the Villa, during which time they became familiar with the surroundings and friendly with the people there. For their return to their own people, there was presented to each a horse to ride, as well as some very nice gifts of clothing.

The Captain arranged that the Mayos and Teguecos should give safe escort to the Yaqui representatives who might come to discuss terms of peace. He added that those who did not attend to the request of their Caciques in respect to making peace, he must proceed against with reinforcements being made ready by the Spanish Crown. This latter statement might seem a menace not indicated at this time; but the experienced Captain knew that it was necessary to talk in strong terms in dealing with those hardened people. Finally, at parting, he assured the women envoys that should the Yaqui representatives not agree with the Captain on terms of peace, they would still be given safe conduct for return to their lands.

The messages carried by the women were well received by the Yaquis. However, being so little used to dealings in good faith, they at first ventured to send only two of their principal Caciques to continue negotiations.

After long discussions with the Captain, the two Yaqui Caciques were given gifts of horses, blankets and other items which were veritable treasures to them. They returned in the company of the Mayos to the borders of their own country. The terms of peace which they carried back with them were: First; that they should agree to maintain peace with the Mayos and other allied Nations; Second; that they should capture and send for judgment and punishment, should this be required, all those persons who had caused or should later cause disturbances among the Indian people; Third; that the horses and baggage taken from the Spaniards should be returned. The Captain on his part agreed that the Spanish authorities would assist in defending the Yaqui Nation against any other Nation who should be an aggressor. Finally, he stipulated that for the conclusion of a treaty of peace, there must be present a good representation of their Yaqui leaders.

Upon the return of the two Caciques to the Yaqui River, there was held a great council at which were heard the messages brought from the Captain. A very favorable impression was made by the two Caciques, who had returned in fine attire, mounted on spirited horses. The women ambassadors were also present at this council, attired in fine native Mexican dresses, with bright skirts and blouses, and huipiles (shawls) of attractive colors, that had been presented to them by the Captain.

The emissaries talked, most of all, of the feeling of contentment of the Indian peoples of the Christian Nations, of their dedication to their new religion and of their friendly reverence for the Padres who ministered to them as their spiritual advisers.

This meeting moved to friendliness even some of those Yaquis who had been most rebellious, although many remained restless; especially the witch doctors who saw their power waning. The counsels of the more pacific having prevailed, there were named a large group of their principal leaders, altogether some 150 Yaquis, to return with the former envoys to confirm a treaty of friendship with the Captain, representing the authority of the Spanish Crown.

These leaders brought with them, in evidence of their good faith, a substantial number of Yaqui children to be educated and indoctrinated in the College of the Villa, that they should, in their turn, return to perform this service of teaching among their own people.

With them this delegation brought the baggage they had captured in battle, but not many of the horses, as these had since become fat and grown wild, and were impossible to capture. These 150 Yaquis remained for many friendly visits with Captain Hurdaide and with the Padres. They visited often at the College, with its schools, went to the churches and to the homes of the Padres who were in residence at the Villa. They eventually went for visits to several nearby pueblos, where they were well received. They were shown the churches, and met the Padres who ministered to each of these pueblos. They were pleased and impressed to find so many Christian Indian families living in such harmony and peace with each other.

It was agreed that the Yaquis should reduce their rancherias to larger pueblos, as had the other Indian Nations, where there could be built substantial churches and where there could be a more stable authority, to be administered by their own leaders under the guidance of the Captain. At the conclusion of the conferences a treaty was prepared and signed, to be sent to the Viceroy in the City of Mexico for his approval.

At the conclusion of this historic visit, Captain Hurdaide made gifts to the principal Caciques of some fine young horses, which greatly pleased them. He also gave all the visitors some clothing, and ample provision for their return journey. Upon departing, the visitors agreed that they and others of their Nations should return frequently to visit, now that the way had been opened to them.

Upon arrival at the Yaqui, they gave a most felicitous account of their warm reception by their former enemies. More councils were held, and sermons were preached by the Yaqui leaders who had made the journey, proclaiming the desirability of peace with the Spanish authorities. From these councils also came a request for Padres to be sent into their lands.

Soon the Yaquis, men, women and children, were coming in large numbers to visit the Villa. Upon the initiative of the Yaqui Caciques, the rebel Teguecos, Láutaro and Babilonio were captured and sent under strong guard to the Captain. His judgment was that they should be hanged for their sins.

It pleased God to cause these savages to see the light, to acknowledge their sins and to ask for baptism in the hour of their execution. All the other rebel leaders were pardoned, returning with much gratitude to their pueblos to become good Christians. Thus was the Devil frustrated in his plan to conquer and win for himself the great Yaqui Nation of the Province of Sinaloa.

CHAPTER 54

Padre Pérez de Ribas Reports to the Viceroy: Is Chosen to Head the Mission to the Yaqui River

IT BECAME IMPERATIVE that someone should make the journey from the Province of Sinaloa to the City of Mexico, who could, in a personal interview, inform the Viceroy and Captain General of New Spain of the true situation; especially of the motives and purpose of the expeditions into the country of the Yaquis that had turned out so badly but which, in the end, had persuaded the Yaquis of the desirability of making peace with the Spaniards. Captain Diego Martinez de Hurdaide had, as a result of the failure of those expeditions, received much unfair criticism from persons not familiar with conditions in Sinaloa, which conditions required a show of force being made, even though with the tragically few soldiers with whom the brave and sagacious Captain had been provided.

The present good disposition of many of the Yaquis required also that their invitation to the Padres to go into their country should be acted upon without unnecessary delay.

At a conference held at the Villa by the Padres of the Province, I was chosen to undertake this mission to inform the Viceroy of conditions prevailing in Sinaloa, as well as to report to our Padre Provincial in the Capitol.

I first traveled upwards through the great Sierras of Topia to Guadiana (Durango), the seat of government of the Province of Nueva Vizcaya, from where the direction of the Province of Sinaloa depended. Here I rendered an account of events in Sinaloa to the Governor, don Gaspar de Albear, Knight of the Order of Saint James.

This Governor was but new in his charge, and of little experience in ways of the Indians, nor of other matters of the frontier. He neither heard my story with any pleasure, nor approved the actions of Captain Hurdaide which had led to the final pacification of the Yaquis, nor was he interested that the Yaquis should be given Christian teaching at this time. This indifference was soon to be a contributing cause to the sacrifice of eight of our missionaries and some 300 Spaniards, besides much greater numbers of Christian Indian allies, in a bloody war with the savage Nations of the Sierras through which I had just traveled.

For all his displeasure, I resolved to continue to the City of Mexico to treat of this matter, which was of such importance, and of so much service to God and King. In Mexico I told my story to the Marquis of Guadalcazar, the Viceroy, to whom its resolution properly belonged.

His Excellency listened to my account with most commendable patience and piety, showing evident comprehension, as well as proper appreciation of the efforts and sacrifices made to bring about such a favorable state of affairs in Sinaloa. He expressed great admiration for the valor and prudence of

Captain Hurdaide, and wonder that this wise man could have induced the savage Yaquis to seek peace, after the apparent defeat of the Spanish arms. At the close of the interview he requested that I should present in writing my opinion of what was now needed to further the project of civilization and Christianization of the Yaqui Nation.

God so moved the spirit of this distinguished Viceroy that, after having studied my report, and having consulted with his advisors of the Chancellery, he issued a decree that Captain General Martinez de Hurdaide, acting directly under orders of the Viceroy, should be authorized to maintain peace and order in the Yaqui Nation, as well as in the other Nations of the Province of Sinaloa, and that for the present there should be sent two Padres of our Company into the land of the Yaquis, to undertake their indoctrination.

These men, it was agreed, should be selected by our Padre Provincial for New Spain, then don Rodrigo de Cabredo. The Viceroy gave further orders to the officials of the Royal Treasury that the two Padres to be named should be well provided with such articles as altar ornaments, church bells and musical instruments, all this being in conformity with orders previously given by the Catholic Kings of Spain, in respect to those of us who served as vicars in the areas to where Catholic Christianity was being extended in the New World.

The Viceroy refrained from sending more than two Padres on this occasion to the land of the Yaquis, even though they were so great in numbers; in the first place, because he felt he could more easily require the support of Governor Albear of Nueva Vizcaya in such a modest undertaking and, secondly, because of the uncertainty of this Mission being successful, as it still faced the opposition of strong forces among the Yaquis.

It was insisted that I should undertake to lead this Mission, because of my years of experience in the Mission of Sinaloa and my knowledge of the language of the Nations of the Gran Rio de Zuaque and the Mayo River, which is basically the same language as that of the Yaquis.

As my companion I was assigned Padre Tomás Basilio, a young priest just arrived from Italy, he being of those Padres who, by orders of the King of Spain, come from time to time to serve in the scattered Missions to the Indies.

We departed with a pack train of mules loaded with the goods mentioned, as well as other articles needed on the frontier, and with an escort of three soldiers. We had traveled about 400 miles of our return journey when, upon arriving at an estancia just south of the city of Guadiana (*Durango*), we received the tragic news of the revolt of the Tepeguane Nation only a week previously. These savages had already cruelly murdered eight ministers in various places, and were burning pueblos, churches and rancherias along our usual route of travel, which led through the Sierras to our Mission Headquarters at the Villa of Sinaloa.

This grievous news, as may well be imagined, caused us much apprehension as to the possibility of this rebellion extending into the Christian Nations of Sinaloa, whose lands lay westward just beyond the mountainous country of the Tepeguanes. Had we not been detained at a previous stopping place, we would have had the good fortune of sharing the glorious fate of martyrdom of our eight brother priests.

We concluded that it were best to return some distance upon our trail, in order to continue to Sinaloa by a southerly and much more circuitous route, which added 300 miles to our usual 1,000 mile journey.

Captain Hurdaide had thoughtfully dispached six soldiers southward with armored horses, to accompany us for the most perilous part of our return journey. After some adventures which will be related in another chapter, we finally arrived safely at the Villa, grateful to find all quiet among the Christian Nations of the Province.

Most fortunately, this rebellion had begun after terms of peace had been successfully negotiated with the great Yaqui Nation. Meanwhile the Captain had continued most diligent and watchful to see that the emissaries from the rebel Nations should not be permitted to circulate among the Christian Nations of Sinaloa to incite them to war.

CHAPTER 55

Mission to the Yaqui Nation

DESPITE THE SITUATION upon our return to Sinaloa being so unsettled, and our Mission to the Yaqui being by this circumstance so much more dangerous and possible of failure, we resolved to attempt, without further delay, the conversion of the Yaquis. Word was first sent to the Yaqui Caciques who had been most friendly, that two Padres had arrived from Mexico City and were awaiting them at the Villa.

Many Yaquis leaders came to greet us. There were renewed consultations with these Indians and, between the Captain and the Padres, in which were weighed the added problems created by the revolt of the Tepeguanes and the other Nations of the Sierras who had followed their example.

However, considering that the invitation given us, and the opportunity made possible through the generosity of the Viceroy and the Padre Provincial, once forfeited, might not easily be conceded to us again, and that the Rebellion in the Sierras might be of long duration, we decided to undertake our Mission without further delay.

We were instructed to first remain for some days in the land of the Mayos, among Christian Indians, from whence we might receive the latest advice as to the disposition of the Yaquis. My companion, the young Padre Tomás Basilio, new to such projects, nevertheless entered with much zeal and enthusiasm into this undertaking, his first since leaving his native Italy for these distant lands of the Indies.

From the Mayo River we sent word of our arrival to certain of the Yaqui leaders who had been conspicuous in negotiations for peace with the Spaniards. These men came at once to the land of the Mayos to give us welcome. Accompanying them were large numbers of their ordinary people, who had never before seen a Padre, and wished to form their own separate judgment of us.

Among these ordinary people had been spread the fear, originating from the Yaqui Hechiceros who opposed our coming, that the Padres, being of the same blood as the Spaniards, did not come in reality in the true spirit of peace. In fact, the hope of these Hechiceros and their many followers was to persuade the Yaquis to engage the Spaniards in another war.

After word of our kindly reception by the Yaqui leaders reached the Villa, we received permission to proceed with our venture. Placing our glorious enterprise in the hands of God, we departed; accompanied by two very principal Yaquis and some of their followers, on our adventurous Mission into the land of the Yaquis.

[*This seems to me to be perhaps the most dramatic moment in this moving story that is so much centered around the life of the venerable Padre Andrés Pérez de Ribas; when these two youthful priests, supported only by their religious faith, went forth virtually alone to the spiritual, and at once the civil conquest of 30,000 proud and arrogant Yaqui Indians, who had been steeped in their own superstitions and beliefs for centuries past.*]

It was on the Day of Ascension of our Lord, in the year 1617, that we two Padres departed for our Mission to the Yaqui. We were without soldier escort, nor company of any other Spaniard. My companion Padre Tomás Basilio did not speak the Yaqui language. Our only Christian followers were four faithful Zuaques who had the courage to accompany me, this giving proof of their fidelity and affection. They went to assist in the offices of the church, such as administration of the sacrament, and to serve as Christian Godfathers to the Yaquis who should be baptized.

Our friends commonly expressed the opinion that we were giving ourselves up to being murdered. Our brother Padre who ministered to the Mayos, and who accompanied us for a little distance on our journey, afterwards confessed to me that he returned with the feeling that we had deliberately placed our heads upon the block, to be sacrificed to the bloody ceremonies of the wild Yaquis.

By agreement with our Yaqui counselors, our little cavalcade first followed a trail leading from the Mayo River to some of the Yaqui villages farthest up their river, whose inhabitants had manifested the greatest interest in having us come to teach them the ways of God. Our two Caciques were chiefs in these villages.

We came first to a small pueblo of perhaps 200 people. There came here to greet us many groups of Indians, including women and children. In their hands they carried little crosses which they had made from bamboo which grows so luxuriantly along the Yaqui River. We were escorted to a newly constructed enramada which had been placed in the plaza for the holding of services.

Many Yaquis had come to the pueblo from the surrounding areas. Upon our arrival they all placed their crosses in rows along the brush walls of the enramada.

After placing my hand upon the head of each of the congregation in blessing, as is accustomed, I caused all the people to be seated, either under the enramada or nearby in the little Plaza. I then told them, in their own language, our motive in coming to this place so far away.

I explained that we felt this effort well employed, in our desire to assist in the salvation of their souls, which were immortal.

I added that they should know that after this life, there would come another and that God, who had created us, would one day require from us an accounting of our deeds in this present world. I further told of how God, in his desire to make our lives more full on earth, and richer in heaven, had sent his only Son as the Redeemer of our souls.

These matters I treated with them, as well as others that are necessary, in order to prepare them for the beginning of their study of religion.

What these savage Yaquis heard of our Mission made a deep impression upon them: the two fundamental articles of our faith, which are that our one God and Father is Creator of all things, and that the soul is immortal, have much appeal to these people.

These first fundamentals of our religion being understood, I next explained to them the need for the sacrament of holy baptism for the salvation of their souls. I told them of the innumerable Nations of the earth who had received the Christian faith.

It will be recalled that my companion, Padre Tomás Basilio, was newly arrived from Italy, and was not yet prepared to take part in these discussions, although later he became a great minister, and still perseveres in his labors among these people.

I presently undertook the baptism of the smaller children, as is accustomed. Dressed in a surplice, stole and robe of white damask, I requested the mothers to stand in order with their babies, who were altogether more than two hundred, under seven years of age.

This brought much pleasure to their parents, and as much to me, and so was concluded that blessed first day of our entry into the land of the Yaquis.

That night, after we had retired to our enramada, many groups of Indians came to visit us, bringing of their food, which is pumpkins and maiz.

Following this meal, they began their form of fiesta, with invitations to smoke tobacco together in the homes of the Caciques. There followed loud sermons by various of their principal leaders, delivered from the Plaza of the pueblo. These speakers preached of the benefits of peace, and of receiving the blessings of religion.

Their preaching continued with great shouting all through the night, so that although we were in much need of repose, it was not possible for us.

Nor is it well to discourage these fiestas, for they serve as a means for these people to express their emotions.

It must not be supposed that the Devil remained indifferent to this invasion of his stronghold. He instituted a vicious persecution of the Christian movement in its very beginning; on that first night, a witch doctor who had come along uninvited and without our knowledge, went also among the Yaqui mothers, telling them that the baptism by the Padres would take the lives of their children, as well as of the others who were so baptized.

Upon the following day, when I spoke to their principal leaders about continuing the baptisms, they were obliged to explain that the mothers had fled with their children into the fields and woods. The Hechicero (*witch doctor*) had meanwhile disappeared. They assured me, however, that upon my return to the village they would have the mothers and children ready to receive me. I felt deeply this persecution coming at the very inception of our Mission, but I knew that I must continue to carry the word of God to the other pueblos, where there were groups awaiting my arrival.

In the next three of these pueblos there were assembled a thousand families. Multitudes of people came through the fields to greet us, all with bamboo crosses carried in their hands.

The rumors of the harm of baptism still persisted, however. These Indian women, though barbarians, love their children extremely, and it took much persuasion for them to submit their children to me for baptism. But it did give them much pleasure to come to hear a Padre who spoke to them in their own language, and of such matters as the salvation of their souls and those of their children.

I observed that in many cases, at the point in baptism where the holy salt is placed upon the tongue of the child, that the mother would take care to wipe it thoroughly from their lips.

In such manner we traveled from pueblo to pueblo, people coming in droves to sit and visit with us under the shade of our enramadas.

Their curiosity was so importunate that they must even gather in numbers watching us eat our portions of calabazas (*pumpkins*) and maiz; and all this must be tolerated, for these were a proud and sensitive people.

Visiting with the Caciques, these recounted to me their wars against the Spaniards and their Indian allies, expressing their disillusionment of those who had incited them to war, and their joy at now being at peace and receiving us in their lands.

Withal, during these discussions it became evident that the hearts of many were not altogether quieted. Yet they came to see me when I visited their pueblos, and I strove to send them to their homes with a feeling of kindliness in their hearts.

It was necessary to spend much time recalling to the mothers the names given to their children at time of baptism, as the Christian names were so new to their language.

The children being so many, there were apt to be perhaps twenty Juanas and as many Pedros and other names, and it was necessary to go among the mothers, baptismal records in hand, to find the children's names, by reference to those of their parents.

Older persons who were ill to the point of danger, were also baptized. Including both children and these elderly ones, a total of 1,000 persons were baptized in the first four villages.

As we passed on to the fifth of the eleven pueblos to be visited in this journey, our faithful Caciques warned us that from here onward we would travel with little or no security. However, on arriving at this fifth pueblo, named Abasorin, we found gathered there many hundreds of persons from each of the other six villages that lay between us and the sea.

At the moment of dismounting from our mules there took place a very disturbing incident. I was given a message that an Indian lay ill, at the point of death, in a field some two miles distant.

There were already awaiting us here great numbers of mothers with children to be baptized. This put us in a perplexing situation. I wished to see this Indian so gravely ill, yet I knew that should I abandon these many mothers gathered here, they would scatter, and perhaps many souls be lost, and some die in their paganism before I could get them together again. Also, there were many Indians gathered to hear the talk which I accustomed making upon arrival at a pueblo.

We finally resolved that Padre Tomás Basilio should go to visit the sick man, accompanied by one of our Christian Zuaques who was adept at indoctrination. The Padre departed with the Christian Zuaque and several of the Yaquis. Among these was the Indian who had brought the message.

Soon after their departure, some friendly Yaquis came to the principal Cacique who had accompanied us, to apprise him that the message concerning the sick Indian had been given with treacherous intent, it being planned to separate the Padre from our protectors in order to murder him, confident that once one of us was killed, the populace would turn against the other.

This principal Cacique, however, immediately went flying from our midst, to find the threatened party. On overtaking them, he told the Padre and the Christian Indians that word had come that the sick man was much improved, and that they should return at once. As he spoke, he took the bridle of the mule on which the Padre was riding, returning him forcibly to where I was talking with the others.

Later, as he found opportunity, the good Cacique drew me aside to relate what had happened. This Indian continued thereafter to be most faithful, proving his fidelity on other occasions as shall be told. In baptism, he was given the name of don Ignacio.

In this pueblo we remained for some days, in order to get to know well these people who, although they demonstrated friendliness, needed much to gain confidence in us.

We were advised by our Yaqui friends that the people in the pueblos down the river, who were much greater in number, were not yet kindly disposed toward us, and that we should, for the present, confine our labors to the pueblos already visited.

These counsels disturbed us not a little, yet we were very loath to interrupt this Mission in which God had until now so favored us; also we felt that our delay might lead to feelings of distrust between the upper and lower pueblos. Therefore, confiding in God, we resolved to proceed with our Mission.

I had by now become friendly with those Caciques of the lower pueblos who had come to greet us, and many of them chose to accompany us on this, our first visit to their villages.

We first traveled to Torim, the sixth pueblo down the river. Here lived more than 1,000 families of the most belicose Indians of the Yaqui River. However, our Cacique friends had so well prepared the way that we found many people awaiting us, with demonstrations of joy.

I talked to them with very particular care to create a friendly feeling on the part of those who had been opposed to our coming. These talks met with such success that, from the pueblo onward, we were accompanied by various speakers from pueblos previously visited. In each Plaza these speakers, in their own manner, with great fervor, spoke in favor of peace, and of hearing the Word of God that had been so well received and accepted by so many of the other Indian Nations.

What is most worthy to relate is that leaders among these speakers were gentiles whom I knew to have been their most famous Hechiceros, and these now spoke in favor of the Law of God. I marveled to see them moving the hearts of their people, advising them to receive in peace this Rule of God which had newly come to their lands.

Upon our departure from one of these pueblos to another such great numbers of the people would follow us that they surrounded our troop of riding animals, being in such multitudes that they covered the plains about us. If I protested to them that they were tiring themselves unduly, they would respond that they took great pleasure in traveling in our company and seeing how well we were received in the other pueblos.

Although many still carried their bows and arrows, which robbed me of some of my assurance in their presence, we found them all of good disposition toward us; and in these lower pueblos we baptized, on our first journey, some 3,000 children.

I left in these pueblos a few gifts, which, although poor, they much esteem; and in addition to these gifts I invited the people to come often to visit me in the upper pueblos where I would be, for a time, living.

My return to the Caciques of the upper pueblos was an occasion for demonstrations of pleasure on their part. They were both surprised and gratified that our visit to the lower villages had been completed without disturbance.

The Indian women who had previously fled from us now came from their fields, their children in their arms, to give us greeting, and to offer them for baptism. Upon our return from this first journey we sent word to the Padres of the Villa, and to Captain Hurdaide, of the felicitous result of our Mission and they were singularly pleased and happy.

It was not long before the mothers of the baptized children began to come to Mass and receive indoctrination, as did the older people. Teaching continued, morning and evening. The Zuaque Indian temachtianos (*teachers*) gave classes, as did some Yaquis who had studied during the months past at the Villa.

Led by their Caciques, many Yaqui men also came to study, and took baptism, choosing one from among their wives to whom they should now be married.

The two principal Caciques, upon receiving baptism, took the names of don Pablo Hymsimeai and don Geronimo Conibomeai. These, being among the first Christians of their people, became Godfathers to many of those that were to follow.

These new Christian Caciques preached with great fervor in favor of the saintly Law they had accepted, and preached with equal fervor against their former vices, such as drunkeness and other practices of their barbarism.

The angels themselves would have rejoiced at hearing these new converts to the faith threatening punishment to any who should henceforth make wine, or use it in their celebrations.

The newly baptized Christian Caciques, as well as many of their followers journeyed to the Villa to visit with the Captain and Padres there, to apprise them of the happy state of affairs among the people of the Yaqui Nation.

The Padres entertained these visitors at the College, and the Captain presented them with young horses, and clothing. They all returned to their homes in great contentment.

When I prepared to make another trip to the lower pueblos of the Yaqui, my Cacique friends again attempted to dissuade me but, finding I was determined, they agreed to accompany me.

On this journey these friends were so attentive to my safety that when night fell, they would come, armed with bow and arrows, to sleep in a circle about me.

On this second trip there came to be baptized some 4,000 more children.

Up to this time we had held meetings, services and classes under the brush enramadas and nearby trees; now the newly made Christians set themselves to building churches of timber, until more substantial ones could be provided.

Many desired to hear Mass not only on Sunday, but during the days of the week. They were particularly pleased to hear sermons on the life of Christ our Savior. Also, they came for confession when ill, and took care that we should be told of others who were ill, even though these had not yet been indoctrinated.

Significant of their sincerity in taking the Christian faith was that they were willing to give up their long braids of hair, which they so much esteemed as a sign of manliness or bravery. Their hair was now cut to fall no lower than their shoulders, as is the custom with civilized people.

It must be understood, however, that not all the Yaqui Nation quickly became subject to Christ.

A small rancheria of people called Guayamas (*Guaymas*) had requested to learn the doctrine at the same time as the Yaquis. Being brought together for these teachings, a woman of the Guayamas Nation took a principal Yaqui for a husband, although their peoples were enemies.

Hearing of this marriage, a group of Yaquis sought out and found this poor woman, and severed her body into pieces.

Being at a rancheria three miles distant, I was at once advised of this dreadful outrage. Calling upon several of the Christian Indians to accompany me, not knowing at that time if the woman was yet dead, we went to her aid.

The pueblo where this deed had been committed, the last of the Yaqui Nation, was in a drunken uproar. Upon arriving, I was met by a Christian Cacique, who informed me that the woman was dead, and that I should not appear there. In truth, those savages were even then engaged in cutting the body into pieces, these to be taken to the various rancherias, impaled upon poles, to be displayed in their savage dances.

Taking the friendly Indian's advice and that of others who joined him, I returned to the pueblo from whence I had come. In this place there were some Christian Yaquis, but many more were gentiles.

After darkness had fallen that same night I heard, from the shelter of the house that was provided me, the chanting which accompanied their barbarous dances.

Going to investigate, I found that the savages had obtained a part of the poor murdered woman, and that the pole upon which it had been impaled served as the center of their celebration. I required of them that they lower it from the pole, and bury it.

Another incident worthy of relating took place at about this same time: A group from the Nebome Nation, who lived some thirty miles into the Sierras, and who were by tradition enemies of the Yaquis, came to ask for Padres to enter into their lands. Despite the fact that it was known that they came in peace, a Yaqui fired upon them as they entered Yaqui territory. They all turned and fled back to their own country, except one principal Nebome who, being cut off from the others, resolved to continue on his mission alone.

God willed that this determined Nebome should meet up with two faithful Yaquis, who rescued him and brought him to me. I received him with the pleasure merited by his good intentions and, fearing a further disturbance by those who had fired upon his group, I guarded him in my house.

Soon there gathered many of my Yaqui Caciques to inquire what had happened. On hearing the story, they expressed their regrets and volunteered to learn who had been so bold as to defy their authority by such an action. They then spoke with kindliness to the Nebome Indian, and promised to return him in safety to his own people.

I questioned their ability to guarantee the Nebome a safe return. However, one of the Caciques, being quite resourceful, placed the Nebome on a horse, himself riding in the saddle behind him, in such a manner that an arrow fired was apt to wound the Cacique. In this fashion, accompanied by other loyal

Yaquis, the Nebome was conducted safely to the border of that Nation.

Thereafter the Caciques made diligence to learn who had fired the offending arrow. The man discovered excused himself, saying that he had been influenced by recalling the death of one of his brothers at the hands of the Nebomes, and felt he must follow their custom of taking revenge upon an enemy.

Later, when time permitted, I undertook to bring peace between these Nations, God willing that it should come about in this manner: At their common boundary the Nebomes erected a large cross, sending a message to the Yaquis that if they had the desire to meet them there in peace, the Nebomes would be waiting for them. This invitation the Yaquis accepted and, through this meeting, under that symbol of peace on earth and in Heaven, there came to be a lasting friendship between two peoples who had warred through the many centuries of their savagery.

There presently came to see me some Mayo Christian Indians led by a chief named Tesamo. They protested to me that although so many Yaquis had accepted the Padres and the Christian faith, they persisted in keeping in their possession the scalps of many Mayos whom they had killed during the days of their gentility, still esteeming them as a token of their triumphs in war. This, the Mayos insisted, was not in keeping with the true practice of their new found faith. The Mayos affirmed that they had, upon becoming Christians, burned the scalps captured by them from the Yaquis.

I called the principal Yaqui leaders together to discuss with them this complaint, in which I felt the Mayos had reason. I pointed out to them their obligation to treat each other in friendship and brotherhood, which requires setting aside former hatreds and forgetting and forgiving the past.

After some discussion, the Yaqui leaders agreed to search out those who still kept the scalps of Mayos they had captured. This they did, gathering together these scalps, with other articles pertaining to their heathen rites and burning them in a bonfire in the central plaza of the pueblo where I was then staying. The Mayos, having witnessed this burning, returned to their homes contented in their newly formed bond of friendship with the Yaquis.

Following this course of a Christian people, the Yaquis also made reconciliation with the Guayama, whose Nation lived along the seashore. [*The Guayama or Guaymas Indians are now considered a part of the Yaqui Nation.*]

To prove their good faith, the Yaquis invited these people to come to their river to share their lands with them. Many accepted this offer, coming and becoming Christians. However, some Hechiceros among them continued to practice their diabolical arts in healing by magic or witchcraft. [*Only a few months before completing this translation I called upon a Mayo Indian, Esteban Leyva, who had been a companion of my youth, we having grown up together on my father's farm. I found him still practicing their ancient art of healing. Some Indian patients were living near his home and taking treatment. It is interesting to note how much of their ancient manner of life has been carried forward to this present generation.*]

One of their diabolical methods of healing was to place in the mouth and

123

throat of the victim a long stick, which they carried among the tools of their practice, it being their pretense that this stick penetrated to the stomach and removed the affliction. With such practices they dispossessed their victims of whatever valuables they might have, in compensation for their supposed services.

CHAPTER 56

End of a Mission

IT IS PLEASING to write that our Yaqui Christians, despite repeated invitation by neighboring Nations to join the Tepequane Nation of the Sierras in their great revolt of the year 1616, remained faithful to their promise of alliance with Captain Hurdaide and the Spanish Crown and loyal to those Padres who had assisted in their indoctrination to Christianity. Even the offer of many horses and cattle, and much other loot captured from the Spaniards in the early days of the revolt, failed to divert them from their loyalty.

Two years after the entry of Padre Tomás Basilio and I to the Yaqui, despite the unrest yet remaining in certain areas among them, Captain Hurdaide determined to undertake a journey of peace to Yaqui territory, to further gain their confidence, and to establish the authority of the Spanish Crown.

Whereas two years before they had met in a great battle, now the Captain with his escort of thirty soldiers with armored horses and various camp followers was received with every evidence of good will.

The upper pueblos prepared him a fine reception and, after such a good example, the people of the lower pueblos did likewise.

Captain Hurdaide's visit was extended to the Indian villages lying along the sea and, although the Spanish soldiers on this journey lived on constant guard by night and day, they were everywhere well received. These soldiers marveled at the great numbers of people living in so many pueblos, now without arms; and many of them reciting the prayers of the Church as a practice of their daily lives.

The Captain designated from among the people, Governors and Alcaldes for the pueblos; thus introducing a stronger form of government, which also helps the Padres in their ministrations to their people. The Captain, in his discussions carried on with them, gave them to understand that it was his strong desire that they should continue to listen to and obey the counsels of the Padres, and to revere them as their spiritual fathers, and Ministers of God.

So, despite some efforts on the part of Yaqui Hechiceros to start trouble that might result in war, this visit was significant in affirming peaceful relations between the Yaquis and their Padres.

By the year 1620 we had baptized children to the number of 5,000, and of adults 3,000 and, despite all the efforts by Hechiceros and other restless Indians, the Yaqui Nation continued thereafter to grow in Christianity.

Three years, 1617 to 1620, had now run their course since, by good fortune, I had been ordered to undertake the Mission to the Yaqui.

I was now ordered to leave there for another ministry near the City of Mexico. [*One of various promotions that led to Padre Andrés Pérez de Ribas later becoming "Padre Provincial" of the entire Jesuit Order of New Spain.*]

The Superior now ordered Padre Cristobal de Villalta, who had in his charge the Mission among the Sinaloas, to carry on, together with Padre Tomás Basilio, the work among the Yaquis. Evangelists these, to whom the peoples of Sinaloa are much indebted for their labor there.

Padre Villalta ministered to the Nations of the Province of Sinaloa for twenty years, until his death.

Padre Tomás Basilio has now been laboring among the Yaquis for more than 30 years, having recently been appointed Superior of the Missions of the areas eastward from the Yaqui into the Sierras.

From these two most dedicated Padres I have continued, through the years, to receive a relation of what has occurred, they well knowing how close to my heart has been the welfare of these Missions of the Province of Sinaloa.

It was with much regret that I bade farewell to my brother Padres of the Missions there, and to that great and gallant Captain General don Diego Martinez de Hurdaide, Governor General of the Province of Sinaloa, as well as to my many faithful Indian friends. I departed on the 1,000 mile journey by muleback to the City of Mexico, comforted in the assurance that the work we had pioneered amoung these primitive people would continue to reap an abundant harvest of souls who should be assured of their entry into Paradise.

CHAPTER 57

Continuing the Story of the Yaquis

THESE TWO FERVENT MISSIONARIES from whom I departed were not without problems in the continuance of the Mission to the Yaqui Nation, as their letters to me disclosed.

One evening, while Padre Tomás Basilio was seated at the door of his poor little house, he was struck without warning by a poisoned arrow fired into his chest by an unknown assailant. Fortunately, the arrow penetrated the flesh in a glancing direction and did little harm, except for the infection of the poison it carried.

Had the arrow been freshly poisoned, it would certainly have resulted in the Padre's death. However, report being given at once to the faithful Cacique don Ignacio, he, at the risk of his own life, immediately sucked the wound to lessen the effect of the poison.

Filled with remorse, many friendly Indians formed a guard about the striken Padre. Others hurried to give notice to Padre Villalta, who was then at another pueblo. He came in haste to the assistance of his brother. Fortunately, the effect of the poisoning was little, and the wound soon healed.

Don Ignacio saved the arrow and, through careful diligence, discovered the identity of the owner, although it had since passed through many hands; it being the custom of these Indians to wager arrows, rather than money, in certain of their games such as patoli and cañuelas. Showing the arrow to many persons, don Ignacio finally traced it to the original owner. Such was their skill at identification, that an arrow would be recognized even though it be mingled with a hundred others, although the Padres could not see a sign of difference among them.

The culprit had meanwhile fled to the woods, but don Ignacio had him tracked down and sent to Captain Hurdaide for judgment. It was learned during the investigation that the motive for the attempted murder was that the wounded Padre had previously prohibited the offender from keeping a woman with whom he had become involved.

It was also learned that the man had been further incited by his uncle, a "false brother," who although baptized, was involved in planning a general uprising, to begin with the murder of the Padres.

This second man fled to the Nebome Nation, but he was captured by them and sent with a guard of 40 Nebomes to the Captain at the Villa. This "false brother," finding an opportunity at a stop along the 200 mile trail, wrested a poison arrow from one of his captors, wounding himself in a muscle.

The man being in an agony of death from his self-inflicted wound, the Nebomes sent one of the guards forward in all haste; finding the Padre of the Mayos, they returned with him, that the desperate Indian should have opportunity for confession of his sins before he died.

The Padre arrived while the man still lived, but the latter proved so obstinate and hardened that he would not utter one word to save his soul. Still rebellious, he died within 24 hours, having, like Judas, perished by his own hand.

The nephew who had actually fired the arrow at Padre Basilio was judged guilty by the Captain and sentenced to be hung. God willed that he should confess, thus going to a better death than his stubborn uncle who had actually been the instigator of the crime, as well as a plotter of a larger rebellion.

Soon after the intent against Padre Basilio the Superiors added four Missionaries to the Yaqui Mission: Padres Juan de Ardeñas, Diego Bandersnipe, Pedro Méndez and Angelo Balestra. All these ministers entered upon their assignment with such fervor that during the two years following, 1621-1623, all the Yaqui Nation of more than 30,000 persons were bathed in the holy water of baptism.

In a letter to me, one of these ministers has written: "Many times, in discussions with other Padres, I have contemplated whence comes so much love and devotion to barbarous and often ungrateful people. We live here without escort, surrounded by their witch doctors, in little houses of wood, our lives forfeit to their will, except for the pity of God. . . . of the alms which I have received from the Crown, in food and vestment . . . . during the past two years, not even one-third has been spent on my person. The balance has gone to the purchase of church ornaments and for food and clothing so needed by the Indians in their illness and in their poverty. In fact, these Nations would never have been conquered by arms, of which the men of the Spanish forces have so few, but only by the force of the Divine Word, and the everlasting patience of our Padres."

Reading again from the letter of this Padre:

"I traveled from the Yaqui River to our College of the Villa of Sinaloa, to where I had not returned during my two years in the Yaqui Mission.

"Having taken much consolation from this visit, I returned during the first days of Lent to my charge. In my haste to arrive to be present at confessions and ministries, I took a new route that seemed to be more expeditious. In the darkness, I became separated from my Indian guide and his companions.

"With only a servant, I halted in a most deserted place. Suffering from hunger, we began to dig roots from the earth. At midnight there came in search of us, guided by an intuition no doubt inspired of God, an Indian of our company. He bore with him a little palm basket of broiled fish, and our hunger was soon assuaged.

"On this same journey, the pack mule which carried our supplies, after having traveled two days without water, plunged into a deep bog (cienega) up to his ears. Loaded as it was, our efforts to extricate the poor beast only sank it deeper. Finally, taking a strong pull at its rope, I shouted, 'In the name of my Patron Saint, John the Evangelist, come out of there!' At this, my little mule, old and tired as he was, gave a leap and struggled out of the mire."

This letter, one of many I received descriptive of the lives of my contemporary Padres, was followed by another, from Padre Juan de Ardeñas. He wrote:

"Living as we did night and day among the savages, sleeping in shelters of brush and wood, without doors, guard, nor means of defense except for two or three choir boys who kept a candle burning at the entrance, we marveled to have been left with life.

"Well we knew that numerous witch doctors longed to drink our blood, and others wished to cut us to pieces, to carry away our parts for the celebration of one of their barbaric dances.

"We were altogether at their mercy when called upon, especially at night, to travel through the lonely woods to the aid of an ill person. On many occasions these fierce people could have done away with us, and we found no other reason for the mystery of our continuing to exist, except that God, in his pity, willed that these savage people should be touched by the strength of Divine Faith, to prevent them from tearing us apart and devouring us."

127

With the passing of time, however, the life, customs and laws of Christianity came more and more to be understood and accepted by the Yaqui people. With fervor and punctuality they attended services, hurrying from their little houses at first sound of the church bells. These changes were the marvel of the Spanish soldiers, who would come now and again for the harvest of fruits from the fields of the Yaquis.

There came to pass an event by which the Yaquis were much impressed: In a time of great scarcity of rain, the children of the large Yaqui pueblo of Torim made a procession of blood to a shrine of Our Lady, that had been erected on a little hill near the village.

God honored his Saintly Mother by sending sheets of rain over the fields of these people, without any falling on other nearby places.

At another pueblo, named Vícam, there died the principal Cacique, an excellent Christian of the baptismal name of don Fernando. This man's son had also served in the church and was a young man of a good and gentle nature.

One night, upon passing the cemetery where his father was buried, the spirit of the father appeared to this young man as in the flesh, saying: "Take note, my son, that all pertaining to the world is as chaff, in comparison with this other life."

The son came in fright to the Padre to tell him of this vision; which the Padre took to be a true apparition, as the deceased don Fernando had been a man of great fidelity and devotion.

I have noted, that of the sacrament of extreme unction, these people, as well as others new in the faith, have a certain horror, feeling that its application in effect condemned them to their death. However, after many who had received it were later seen to recover, it was better received.

With some trepidation I treat again of the subject of witchcraft, which so predominated the lives of the Yaquis: A Yaqui woman of those who had been engulfed in such darkness, after becoming enlightened pointed out to a Padre a great range of mountains, peaks and ridges whose skyline could be seen across the Yaqui River, explaining that all these were places of superstition to the Yaquis, which they reverenced and, at the same time, held in dread and fear. She asserted further to this Padre that the devil often appeared in these places, in the form of a dog, coyote, toad or snake.

The principal Yaqui Indians affirmed that at night their Hechiceros held dances in these places, being invited there by demons, and that these Hechiceros returned to their villages through the air.

A certain Padre who dedicated himself to reading the erudite book in which the Padre "Del Rio" explains the diabolic falsehoods of the Magi, found that most of these same falsehoods the devil had introduced as superstitions among the Yaqui Nation.

In a Yaqui pueblo the Padres, through the Indian governor, thought to reprimand various Hechiceros for their practice of witchcraft. These Hechiceros thereupon said to the Padres: "Do not bother yourselves to bring us together to be reprimanded for, not only ourselves, but at least half the pueblo,

"*The Zuaque (Fuerte) River flows across the coastal plains for a distance of 90 miles. It fertilizes beautiful valleys on its way to the sea.*" *View of sunset of the Fuerte River.*

San Miguel Mission Indians. Estaban Leyva and family.

Interior of San Miguel Mission, with central image of San Miguel Archangel.

Carrizo Indians building house of native hardwood timbers on Metate Island in Bahia de San Ignacio. These Indians, called Toroacas by Perez de Ribas, speak the Mayo Language.

Mayo Indian dancers, dressed in their version of the garb of those who crucified Christ, travel about the countryside during the weeks preceding Easter.

"On Sundays the (Tegueco) Indians come from five to ten miles to services. At the hour of their coming it seems that the fields are filled with people."

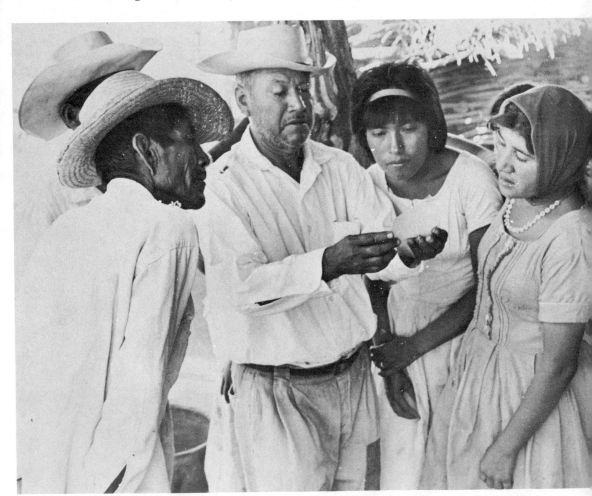

Tegueco Indians examine a polaroid instantaneous picture of themselves.

ng Tegueco couple traveling on a burro, which n import from the Old World, and now an in-uable asset to pioneer living in Mexico.

Tegueco woman showing pots and ollas made for carrying food to the graves of deceased relatives on Halloween (Dia de los Muertos).

Bacabachi Indians, now classified as Mayos. The blanket shown was woven from wool of sheep pastured in nearby woods.

"*A site for a new Presidio was chosen ... on a small hill ... near the abandoned Fort of Carapoa and named the Fuerte de Montesclaros, for the Viceroy of New Spain ...*"

"*The Fuerte de Montesclaros served a very useful purpose in curbing the savage impulses of the Indians of the adjacent plains and Sierras ...*" *View of present Pueblo of El Fuerte, taken from the old Fort.*

Indians living in the woods of Sinaloa and Sonora extract ixtle fiber from the Mescal (sisal) plant, for making ropes, saddle blankets, hammocks and many other useful articles.

"Our fifty soldiers with their armored horses, accompanied by their 1,000 Indian allies, pushed forward, finally making camp in a beautiful valley through which ran the river of the Tepagues."

Doña Librada Valenzuela, of the Tepague (Quiriego) Nation, grinding corn for tortillas.

Quiriego Indian home, with outdoor baking oven at Tepague (Tepahue) Village.

Tepague (Quiriego) Indian group. These Indians are now classified as Mayos.

"At the time of my entry into the land of the Yaquis, in 1617, this Nation lived dispersed along one and another side of their beautiful river . . . some 30,000 people." View of Yaqui River as it flows through the Lower Sierras.

Bronze statue at Cuidad Obregón, Sonora of Yaqui Indian performing the Baile del Venado (Deer Dance). This dance has become a part of the National Folklore of Mexico.

"What these savage Yaquis heard of our Mi: made a deep impression upon them . . ." Y family in cemetery of old Mission at Vicam, on Yaqui River.

"... between the Yaqui and Mayo Rivers, among the lower Sierras, live the Lower Nebomes, the Upper Nebomes and, yet higher, the Mobas, Onabas and Nures." Picture of Movas Mission. No Indians could be found here (in 1967) who spoke their tribal language.

Onabas Indian family. These now call themselves Pimas, and speak the Opata language, although they are neighbors to the Yaquis.

Onabas Indian Mission, still being attended by several of their families.

The Mission pueblos of Batuco, Tepupa and Suaque are now submerged under "El Novillo"
lake, which supplies water and power to the great Valle del Yaqui, Sonora. The Tepupas,
a sub-tribe of the Batucos, have relocated in a little valley. Here they have built the shrine
shown in this picture, and moved their church bells to the new location.

Interior of shrine of the transplanted village, Nueva
Tepupa. The inscription below the painting of the
Virgin of Guadalupe reads, "Indian preserve the
history of your Pueblo."

Mission at Soyopa. This may be one of the Pue
of the Sisibotaris described by Padre Perez de Ri
However, the founding date of 1531 is in erro
Cabeza de Vaca, first explorer, did not appear u
1538.

"There is notice of an exceedingly wild tribe of Indians named Heris (Seris) who live in the barren desert along the seashore . . . on a nearby island (Tiburon) live others of this Nation." Tomás and Dorothy Robertson among the Seris Indians at Punta Chueca, opposite Tiburon Island.

Three Seris braves and two women. The men still wear their hair in long braids. Absence of hair on face is a characteristic of most Indians.

Seris woman offering for sale necklaces made of shark vertebrae, sea shells and seeds of the jojoba (Simondsia) plant common to the deserts of Sonora and Baja California.

including some of your Christians, still believe as we do." The reader may judge if it be not a cause for wonder how the Padres continued to live while preaching against so many and such invisible enemies.

One famous woman witch doctor told a Padre that the Padres had not been killed because they had brought so much good to the people of the Yaqui pueblos, and that they believed that the saying of the prayers at Mass by the Padres did truly keep them from harm.

A principal Hechicero had been baptized, but retrogressed, and being possessed of the gift of oratory, attempted to stir the people to war at a time when Christianity was in flower.

He called councils, revived the savage dances of the days of their gentility, and sought in every manner to recruit followers from among the many Christian Yaquis.

He asserted that Christianity was a pure myth; that there were not in heaven the privileges of which the Indians were told by the Padres. He insisted that the souls of Christians were buried with their bodies in the earth. He counseled his listeners to lead a gay life, for they need have no fear of the hereafter.

He somehow contrived to produce an apparition of the devil, in the figure of a very old Indian, who was seen by many, standing on the bank of the river.

This figure said to the people: "You look upon me now in the figure of an old man, but tomorrow, after having bathed in the river, I shall appear to you as a handsome young man — and it is possible for all of you to become so also."

Upon the day following he did fulfill his promise, appearing to them as a young man of about 20 years.

With such practices of deceit this pernicious Hechicero impressed those who gathered about him at his meetings, and there was kindled a dangerous fire that threatened to spread rebellion throughout the land.

Captain Hurdaide, being apprised of this peril, came with a goodly number of soldiers and a few friendly Indians to visit the Yaqui River, avoiding however, any appearance of or preparation for war.

He well knew that by now he could count on the support of many Christian Yaquis in an emergency, and so felt more free to move among them than in times past.

He was well received in the upper pueblo. However, continuing to some of the others, on the way two arrows were fired at him.

Wise in his judgment of these people, he thought this to be a precipitate act, rather than a part of a general plan for revolt.

Arriving at the nearest pueblo after this incident, he placed his forces in a position of defense. Soon thereafter he took prisoners the Indians who had principally started the trouble, including the Hechicero who had perverted the others.

This man confessed that he had been inspired by the devil, who, in the figure of a crow, talked to him from the branches of a cottonwood tree, urging him to kill the Padres, burn the churches and cast the church bells into the river. He was also told by the devil that the chrisom and oleo with which the Padre had anointed him on the day of his baptism must, by heat and sweat, be removed from his body. Finally, this demon had required of him that he do away with all Christianity in the Valley of the Yaqui, murder the Captain and all the Spaniards, and bring his people to their original state of barbarity.

The motive and acts being proven, the Captain sentenced this man, together with several of his accomplices, to death by hanging.

They were confessed of their sins by a Padre, and received enlightenment before their execution. The Hechicero asked the Padre to accompany him to the foot of the gallows, saying that this Padre had baptized his small son, who had later died, and that by the help of this same Padre, he hoped to meet his son in Heaven.

And so quiet once more reigned in the land of the restless Yaquis.

In the early days of the Mission to the Yaquis there was no time for the construction of permanent places of worship, even for so numerous a people.

When at last came time for the building of the first temples for our new converts, the Padres must be architects, overseers and even laborers, for the purpose of training others. They must supervise the preparation of the daily feeding of perhaps 600 to 800 persons who aided in the various tasks of construction.

Timbers must be hewn from the woods, and carried on the backs of laborers to the building site. Stones must be gathered for the foundations and clay adobes made for the walls.

Each pueblo supplied its labor. The Yaquis, as they had been agressive in war, were diligent in peace, and determined that none should surpass them in the size and beauty of their churches.

The Yaquis of Tórim, the largest pueblo and which had been most unruly, were not content with building one church, but must build in addition, on a little hill, a very attractive shrine. This they dedicated to the Queen of the Angels.

The eight pueblos completed churches that were impressive and of large capacity. Upon the completion of each, there was held a dedication, with great formality, feasting and dancing.

These occasions count for much in the lives of these people, and the Padres saw to the adornment of the newly dedicated churches with appropriate ornaments, images and tapestries of silk, taking for this purpose of the alms given to them by the Spanish Crown.

A Padre who had served in these Missions sent from Mexico, for the shrine at Tórim, a carving in bas-relief depicting the Day of Judgment, showing Christ our Savior and His Saintly Mother side by side in Paradise, together with all else that is symbolic of that great day. It depicted also the gathering of those souls by the angels for entry into heaven, as well as those that were being dragged by demons towards the infernal regions.

This scene, pictured on a tablet, impressed them and at once frightened them. The memory of it was said to have been powerful enough to help keep them from many temptations. [*It seems probable that this carving was a gift of Padre Andrés Pérez de Ribas.*]

Although from the beginning much attention was given to their hearing music of the church, little progress was made until their children were taught to read and write; and then to read the notes of the chants.

There were eventually named choir masters, from among the older and more educated Indians who showed talent in music, and the chapel singers became quite proficient in each of the churches. At present (*1645*) there are celebrated impressive fiestas with organ music, choruses and playing of musical instruments such as bassoons, sackbuts, oboes and flutes.

Their weddings are now celebrated in the manner common in Europe, and their fiestas are no longer carried on with their former savagery, they now preferring more polite dances, including the dances of Spain.

The knowledge of divine law also teaches these people to live a rational life. It is most agreeable to see their pueblos, laid out in good form, with many houses of adobe walls and roofs of brush covered with earth. The Yaquis are now ruled by Governors, Alcaldes, fiscales (elders) of the church, and other persons of authority, these being people of their same Nation. Indian Sacristans take good care of their churches; they are kept scrupulously clean, and are kept decorated with green branches and flowers, always fresh and well arranged.

Many Yaquis now own horses for riding and for packing their loads and their families. This is such a welcome relief, after packing everything on their shoulders, that many have been moved to extend their plantings, so that they may purchase more horses through the money earned from the selling of the produce from their fields to the Spaniards.

This abundant production has done much to insure the Spaniards and people of the Christian Nations of food during years of aridity.

Their plantings of cotton have been increased, and they now have flocks of sheep. From the wool of these the women are making clothing.

Once accustomed to a civilized manner of dress, these Indian women miss it exceedingly. In their new found desire for better clothing, they often travel 50 miles or further to find work in the mines so that they may be enabled to buy wool or cloth.

This search for work to appease their new desires has been one of the causes for a reduction in the numbers of people remaining among all these Nations.

Also there have been many sicknesses among the Yaquis, as among the other Indian Nations. As this is written (*1645*) there remain of the Yaquis in their eight pueblos, numbers varying from 300 to 600 families in each.

[*It would seem evident that the concentration of the Indians of the Province of Sinaloa, from their fields and small rancherias into larger pueblos, for their better indoctrination and discipline, resulted in a greatly increased mortality. From the careful treating of this subject by Padre Pérez de Ribas, this was no doubt a disturbing problem which he has sought to justify in some measure, during the course of this history.*]

CHAPTER 58

Story of Padre Martín Pérez, Co-Founder of the Mission of Sinaloa

PADRE MARTÍN PÉREZ was, with the martyred Padre Gonzalo de Tapia, Co-founder of the Mission of Sinaloa.

Before the death of this illustrious evangelist he was privileged to see Christianity extended for an area of 300 miles northward from the Villa, to the farthest boundaries of the Province of Sinaloa.

Padre Martín was born at San Martín, in the Province of Nueva Vizcaya of New Spain, in the year 1558.

San Martín was well known for its great wealth in silver, and Martín's father, owner of one of the largest mines, sent his son to be educated at Mexico City, where, with the blessing of his parents, he studied for the ministry under the renowned Padre Pedro Ortigoza of our Company. He was received into the Company in June of 1577.

So outstanding was he in scholastic ability that at the age of 21 years he was made Director of the Jesuit College of San Pedro, now San Idelfonso, in the City of Mexico. He spent two years in this position, then became Minister of the College of Puebla.

However, despite his evident ability in administration, God willed his life should be spent in the Mission field. For a period he served among the fierce Chichimeca Indians of the Central Plateau. After this period of preparation, in the year 1590, he was designated, with Padre Tapia, to undertake the conversion of the barbarous Nations of Sinaloa. Of the difficulties that awaited him, I have in much part written.

When the Indians gave death to Padre Gonzalo de Tapia, Padre Martín Pérez remained with the burden of the entire Province, serving an area which is now attended by six missionaries.

He founded pueblos, built the first churches of a permanent nature; in all, laboring there for 26 years, in his later years as Superior of the Missions of the Province. I was privileged to serve with him during those years.

His intensive dedication to his charge, and the little attention to the needs of his own person, eventually caused him to fall so gravely ill that there was no other recourse than to bleed him so many times that he became greatly weakened. He finally lost the use of his limbs, becoming short of sight and halt in speech.

After he retured as Superior, he continued to reside in the College of Sinaloa. For nine years thereafter he held Mass, the last year from a wheel chair. His was a spirit so vigorous that he forced himself even in his weakness to attend to his own needs, including the care of his little cell and the carrying of his water.

He finally reposed in God on the 24th day of April of 1622, at 65 years of age, and 45 years in the Company, 31 of these in the ministry of the Missions.

The Indians called him, "The Padre Who Traveled Greatly," and so he did, incessantly, without regard for sun, rain or foul weather. His fine talents in letters and administration he kept hidden until the pressure of circumstances brought them to light. Silence and brevity were resplendent virtues in this Padre, as may be deduced by a study of his correspondence with his Superiors in the Company.

All the people of Sinaloa came to revere this fine old man as though he were a Saint. There is no doubt that there are great rewards in glory for the venerable Padre Martín Pérez.

CHAPTER 59

Story of Padre Hernando de Villafañe, Superior of the
Mission of Sinaloa

PADRE HERNANDO DE VILLAFAÑE was born in the City of Leon, of Castilla la Vieja, of noble parents. After receiving Christian doctrine he was sent by his parents to Salamanca for the study of law.

He resolved, however, to leave the world of leisure and riches in which he lived, and was admitted to our Company by common approbation.

In his study of philosophy it was his good fortune to have as a teacher Padre Luis de la Puente, a man of saintliness, of great knowledge, and of fame in writing that is well known to the world. This sage left on Padre Hernando an imprint so profound that it carried through all his life.

Requesting to become a Missionary to the Indies, he was sent to New Spain in the company of Padre Francisco Vaez, who was on his way from Rome to become Procurator for the Jesuit Order in Mexico City.

He taught among the Tarascans of the Province of Michoacán, learned their language and became Rector of the College at Pátzcuaro, in Michoacán.

Hearing of the death of his companion Padre Gonzalo de Tapia, who was also from Leon in Castile, he requested to be sent to the dangerous Mission field of Sinaloa, in order to assist in carrying on the work so well begun by his friend.

The Padre Provincial very much wished to send to this new frontier area a person of standing, ability and ample religious preparation, and was happy to designate Padre Villafañe.

Padre Hernando soon was assigned to the Guasave Mission, which served several thousands of Indians. Here he labored untiringly for 30 years, often in peril of death, preaching, founding churches and settling into a republican form of government those savages so foreign to political authority.

He took extraordinary care to learn the languages of the pueblos he administered, and was the first to reduce to rules and writing the language of the Guasaves, which language was used throughout the coastal plains of Sinaloa.

This same zeal for languages evidenced itself again when he became Superior of the Missions of Sinaloa, he mastering them all so well that he could teach them to the other Padres upon their entering into their Missions.

We have told how his first three churches built at Guasave were destroyed by flood, and how by faith and diligence he soon had them rebuilt.

Neither the Governors, nor even the Viceroys of New Spain, could resist his pleading for more funds to increase the work of the Missions. On several occasions he was sent to Mexico City to plead for this assistance.

What the Spaniards of the Province have in cattle on their haciendas, what are constructed in Presidios, and what increased privileges were granted to Captain Diego Martinez de Hurdaide to support him in his notable guidance of the Province in its political authority, all are owed to the diligence of this distinguished Padre, in pleading their needs before the authorities in the City of Mexico.

The renowned Captain Hurdaide always consulted with Padre Villafañe his plans for the government of the Indian Nations of Sinaloa.

For further estimation of the ability of this Padre, there should be mentioned the fact that the gentlemen of the Sainted Inquisition, in respect to matters of our Holy Faith, entrusted to him solely the charge of this holy office in the Provinces of both Sinaloa and Culiacán, until the time of his death.

From the Mission of Sinaloa, Padre Villafañe was called to journey 900 miles to Mexico City to become Rector of our Jesuit College there. He was later chosen Procurator to Rome for the Province of Sinaloa.

Soon thereafter he was ordered by the Padre Provincial to come back to Mexico City to attend the Provincial Congregation of New Spain. This meeting over, despite the fact that he had only recently completed the arduous 1800 mile round trip by mule, with total disregard to his mounting years, he took saddle again to return the 900 miles to enjoy the liberty and peace of the frontier.

With himself he was severe in his penitences, with self-mortifications accompanied by prayer; with others he was most affable and forgiving.

He was ever solicitous of the welfare of those who accompanied him on his travels, including his escort of soldiers who were apt to be sent with him on his long journeys.

Where he most showed his benignity and grace was in his kindness of treatment of the Indians, and he was much loved by them. He helped them with all possible liberality in their temporal needs, distributing among them all he possessed.

The little Indian children would come to gather about him with affection as he ate, he giving them portions from his own plate with a father's loving care. Such kindliness won the Indians to him, and preserved their trust in him through every adversity. The Spaniards marveled to see a man of such age, and of such authority, occupy himself with these services to the poor.

He celebrated Mass daily, without exception, even when traveling aboard ship to and from Rome, and arranged that this should be done on all Spanish ships sailing between the Occident and the Indies. [*Raul Cervantes Ahumada, eminent authority on international maritime law, who caused the 1944 edition of Pérez de Ribas to be printed, comments, at this point in the translation, that the holding of mass either on land or sea is simply symbolic of its being held at the foot of the Holy Cross. He further points out that when Padre Villafañe, unable to secure a decision in the matter from his Superiors in Spain, ordered on his own account that mass be held on board ship, he established a certain precedent of a ship being simply an extension of the territoriality of a Nation, a principle which has been during the centuries incorporated into maritime law, as in the Law of Navigation and Maritime Commerce of Mexico*].

When his infirmities finally prevented him from attending to his church, he witnessed the holding of Mass from a window of his room, with great comfort to his soul.

Forty days before his death, he insisted on returning from the comfort of the College of the Villa to his church at Guasave, preaching with much fervor during those days remaining to him, saying that he never before had felt such overwhelming strength of spirit for the saving of souls.

I content myself with writing of the solid virtues of this virile apostle, rather than of the miracles he accomplished, and of his great tenacity and untiring perseverance in the immense labors of his charge.

It must be told that many times he was condemned to death by his enemies who opposed the doctrine of the church, but he was always saved by his friends, and by Divine Protection.

Seven years Padre Hernando de Villafañe suffered in preparation for death, consuming his life, his force, his talents, in the cultivation of the multitudes whom to him God had commended, before departing this life to enjoy the fruits of his labor and the reward for his services, which we can well believe must have brought abundant glory to himself, and great good fortune to those he assisted to enter into the Kingdom of Heaven.

It was a great privilege, for those of us who labored in the Missions there, to have the benefit of the counsels and companionship of Padre Hernando de Villafañe during those difficult years of pioneering the work of the Missions in Sinaloa.

At this writing, the preaching of evangelism in Sinaloa has continued without interruption for a period of sixty years, the records kept there by the Padres showing that during this period there have been baptized into the Christian Faith some 300,000 adults and children.

CHAPTER 60

Indian Nations of the Northern Frontier of Sinaloa

THE INDIAN NATIONS of whom I shall now tell occupied lands bordering four large arroyos, lying between 32 degrees and 33 degrees north latitude. Some of these arroyos flow eastward, others westward toward the Sea of Californias. Because of the altitude, the climate here is more tempered.

The first of these Indian Nations, the Nebomes Bajos, live between the Yaqui and Mayo Rivers, among the lower Sierras. Next above them live the Nebomes Altos, and yet higher, the Mobas, Ónabas and Nures.

In the lower lands, nearer the western plains, are located the Comoripas, Tecoripas and Zuaques, these latter being no relation to those of the Rio Grande de Zuaque.

Continuing northward and eastward live the Aibinos, Sisibotaris, Batucos, Hures and finally, the Sonoras, who have their rancherias along a river of the same name.

In all the Nations referred to there are twenty principal pueblos, the people of which are now served by six Padres of our Company. Among these Nations there are 3,500 Christian families. Altogether among these Nations there are spoken four distinct languages.

Northward beyond the Sonoras may be found other barbarous peoples, such as the Nacomeras, Nacosuras, and Himeris. [*Imuris is now a small pueblo lying along the Magdalena River, about sixty miles south of the border town of Nogales, Arizona.*]

The Himeris are a particularly ferocious tribe, refusing all overtures of friendship, and are much feared by other Nations. Their lands lie along the margins of a good sized river, which empties into the desert before the Sea of Californias (*Magdalena River*).

There is notice of an exceedingly wild tribe of Indians named Heris (*Seris*) who live in the barren desert and along the seashore. No crops may be grown here; and they subsist from hunting and fishing, drinking water usually from small and sometimes stagnant pools. In time of harvest they may come with deer skins, or salt, to trade for corn or other crops. On a nearby island (*Tiburon*) live others of this Nation. It is said that their language is exceedingly difficult to learn.

Northward beyond the Heris are other Nations, including the Cumapas (*Cumpas*), Buasdabas and Babispes and turning eastward, the Sunas (*Zunis*). Beyond here lies the land of New Mexico.

The Sisibotaris, who reside in a beautiful valley eastward of the Yaqui River, (*Sahuaripa*) are bordered by other tribes, for distances unknown, into the extended Sierras.

There has already been related the mass migrations of the Nebomes, the first when accompanying Cabeza de Vaca in 1536, the second 79 years after, both groups locating on fertile lands at Bamoa, near the Villa of Sinaloa.

As has been said, the Nebomes were almost without exception tillers of the soil, each family possessing a plot of ground which they irrigated with water taken through little canals from their arroyos.

The Upper Nebomes did much hunting of deer, smaller animals and birds.

Their houses were well constructed, of large adobes, with roofs of heavy rafters covered over with brush and a layer of several inches of earth. Some houses were constructed much larger, with turrets at the corners, from which to fire with arrows upon an enemy.

The men, it could be said, went without clothing, although most of them possessed a mantle of cotton which they could throw on or off as they chose.

The women wore neatly designed skirts of buckskin reaching to their ankles. Their upper garment was usually of sisal fiber finely woven, or of cotton of a simple pattern. Their faces they painted with a paste prepared from reddish yellow ochre.

The women were of notable modesty. Once, while on a journey to the Yaqui River with Captain Hurdaide, he and I traveled by way of the lands of the Upper Nebomes. The people formed a line to greet us as we arrived at each of their pueblos and, as was the custom, we placed our hands upon their heads as we passed. The Nebome maidens in their bashfulness shyly covered their faces with their long tresses of hair, that they might not be seen.

The Nebomes Bajos included the rancherias of Comoripa, Tecoripa, Zuaque and Aivino, altogether some 3,000 to 4,000 persons. They were a nomadic sort of people, taking little root anywhere, consequently being difficult to civilize.

Their conversion was eventually undertaken by Padre Martín Burgensis, a missionary of much fervor in the saving of souls. Some of his converts, being of a restless nature, turned against the church. First they gave death to one of the Fiscales, then threatened the Padre, blocking the trails which he accustomed traveling from one of his charges to another.

Upon learning of this disturbance Captain Hurdaide, now an old man, took to the field with forty armored soldiers of horse, enlisting 1,000 Indian allies as he traveled. His trail led for 300 miles from the Villa to the land of the Nebomes Bajos.

The Nebomes had built a large number of camp fires, to lead the Captain to believe that their forces were gathered about them, when in reality the greater number of them were concealed in a dense thicket through which the Spaniards and their allies were expected to pass, and where the armored horses of the soldiers could not be brought into play.

However, the experienced old soldier, veteran of nearly thirty years of Indian wars, was not deceived. Through spies he had already located the main body of the enemy, who were concealed in a well fortified pueblo, where there had been constructed several large towers, from which to shower arrows on their attackers.

Leaving a goodly number of soldiers and Indian allies in his encampment, the Captain proceeded with the main body of his forces by another route, which avoided the ambuscade, to attack the pueblo.

After his departure, many hostile Indians attacked our encampment. The fighting here becoming so severe that the Captain was compelled to return with his forces to the rescue of the men remaining there. In this battle large numbers of enemy Indians, as well as of our allies, were killed. Even the women of the enemy joined in the fighting, firing arrows and hurling stones with as much ferocity as their warriors.

Finally routing the enemy who had fallen upon the encampment, the Captain returned with his forces to continue his attack on the pueblo. Finding that he was unable to take the walls of the pueblo in a frontal assault, he ordered brought large numbers of burning torches, which were thrown over the barricades.

The fumes from these torches were so intense that many of the defenders died suffocated within the walls. Wishing to avoid all bloodshed possible, the Captain rode along the front of the walls, shouting repeatedly that the lives of the besieged would be spared if they should surrender.

Finally the Indians inside sent out messengers carrying gifts of bows, arrows, plumed head dresses and other valuables, in token of their surrender. The walls were then breached and all those inside poured out to cluster around the Captain, begging that he save them from the fury of our Indian allies. This the Captain was able to do, but not to save the most of their provision, which was lost in the burning pueblo.

His strenuous mission accomplished, the veteran Captain remained for a well earned rest of several days with his forces. There came to visit him here the principal Caciques of all the surrounding Nations. By them he was called a Son of the Sun, as had been Cabeza de Vaca by the people of this Nation nearly a century before.

The Nebomes Bajos, now much subdued, solicited, and were granted, a treaty in which they declared their renewed allegiance to the Spanish Crown.

From here Captain Hurdaide departed with his forces for Tecoripa and Comoripa, where he arrested certain Indians known to have been stirring the others to revolt. To other Indian leaders who had remained faithful he distributed gifts, and received renewed assurances of their loyalty, after which he departed on his long return journey to the Villa.

This was the last campaign of this famous champion of civilization and Christianity in the Province of Sinaloa. Not long after his return, the entire Province, Spaniards and Indians alike, was saddened by the news of his death.

For more than thirty years, with a token force of fifty Spanish soldiers, he had, by his great courage and sagacity, ruled the destinies of a hundred thousand people, without the loss during all that time, of the life of a single Spanish soldier in battle.

Through the veins of Captain Diego Martinez de Hurdaide coursed the fiery blood of the Spanish Conquistadores, but tempered with the wisdom and patience of his noble Aztec mother. His was an unusual dedication to the service of the Spanish King, to his Christian God and to the Indian people, of whom multitudes were his devoted friends and followers.

From twenty Nations came their Indian Governors to pay a final tribute to this great man. Of his life and years of service there has been more fully written in another chapter of this history, and more will be learned of him, in recounting the story of other Nations and other places.

CHAPTER 61

The Upper and Lower Nebomes

THE DEATH of Captain Hurdaide left a great uncertainty in the land. Soon restless souls among the Indian Nations were sending pipes of bamboo filled with tobacco, inviting others to join them in rebellion.

There was next appointed, as Captain General of Sinaloa, don Pedro Perea, who had served as Lieutenant under Captain Hurdaide.

During this same period several more priests had been sent from Mexico City to Sinaloa, among them Padre Diego de Bandersnipe, a native of Flanders, who was assigned to the conversion of the distant Nebomes.

From erroneous sources Captain Perea was informed that some of the Nebomes were plotting rebellion, together with Indians of other Nations. He ordered certain ones of the Nebomes to be arrested and sent to the Villa.

Padre Diego wrote Captain Perea that there had been no evidence of guilt on the part of those arrested. However, a month passed without their being released, and a great resentment grew in the Nebome Nation. At this same time, an Indian of a Nation bordering the Nebomes was found guilty of plotting rebellion, and hanged. This action, although justified, caused much concern among the Nebomes, as to the fate of their own friends. Certain ones among them sent word to Padre Diego that if the prisoners were not released within five days, he would be murdered.

As the Padre knelt one evening at the door of his little house, reciting his prayers, two arrows were fired at him; one striking him in the chest, the second lodging in a palm wall of the house. Fortunately, the flight of the arrow that struck the Padre had been diverted by the quick action of a young Indian choir boy who, observing the movements of the assailant, had moved quickly to strike his bow. However, the stone tip, which was poisoned, had remained in the flesh, causing profuse bleeding.

The disciples of Padre Pedro quickly rallied about him. As one who is bidding farewell to life and friends he talked to them, urging that above all they should remain constant in their faith, and maintain peace with the Spaniards. Then, weary from loss of blood and from the effect of the poison, he took the trail, accompanied by some of his faithful followers, toward the Villa, 300 miles away, wishing if possible to end his life among his companions there.

Messengers had sped swiftly to give the tragic news to Captain Perea and the Padres at the Villa. The Captain immediately dispached six mounted soldiers, accompanied by Padre Francisco Olindaño, to assist the wounded man. He was found only thirty miles from where he had started, suffering torments of delirium and pain. Here his friends remained with him for a period of six weeks until he had recovered enough to travel by brief stages to the Villa.

For many years after, the wound remained without healing, but as this is written Padre Diego is still busily engaged in the harvesting of souls for God in the Province of Sinaloa.

Padre Blas de Paredes, recently arrived from the City of Mexico, was next assigned to the Nebome Nation. Feeling, in the meanwhile, had subsided, and he was given a warm welcome. For six years thereafter Padre Blas labored among these people as much as two men should, traveling from one rancheria to another of those Sierras, in the conversion of souls.

God chose to take him quite suddenly, in this place so far away, and quite alone, at only thirty years of age. It is comforting to know that during those brief years he had accomplished much, substituting good for evil in the life of the Nebome Nation, leaving multitudes converted to Christianity, starting a seminary (*at Metape*) for the children of the Indians, and forming choirs who sang at the services in their various churches.

Another Tribe, or Nation, called Nures, were situated on the borders of a large arroyo flowing from the Sierras above the Nebomes. These people had developed the use of water from little canals for irrigation, and were in other ways advanced in their manner of living. They requested indoctrination, and were attended by the Padre ministering to the Nebomes.

Soon after the subjection of the Aibino Tribe of the Lower Nebomes by Captain Hurdaide, Padre Francisco Olindaño was assigned to minister to them, and has continued to do so for twenty years. I shall quote briefly from a letter written by him to his Padre Superior of the Mission of Sinaloa: "Padre Thomas Basilio and I entered Aibino territory on July 1, 1624. As the land is far north, even at this late season nights are still cold. These Aibino Indians live in remote places of the high Sierras in order to better defend themselves from their enemies. We found them well disposed toward us, coming to meet us with crosses outstretched in their hands. . . . Although they show fine humility, they show no fear, but only pleasure in meeting us."

Padre Olindaño quickly learned the two distinct languages of the Upper and Lower Nebomes.

The mountainous area in which the Nebomes lived was subject to severe storms, with lightning, which kept the people in constant fear. They conceived the idea that they could be saved from this danger by making offerings at a tomb in which they had buried a great Cacique of their Nation who had, some years before, been killed by lightning.

They had placed the body of this distinguished Indian in a sitting position in this tomb; building a shelter over it for better protection. To this shrine they brought offerings such as strings of white sea shells with which they adorn themselves, as well as pieces of woven cloth, colored plumes of birds, and other things which they most esteem.

Padre Olindaño, hearing of this, gathered together a group of faithful Christians, went to the place, tore up the tomb and destroyed it, so that this idolatry should not be continued. He made talks to the people, explaining how God alone has power and dominion over the life of man, and over clouds and bolts of lightning which these clouds cause to fall from the sky. With these words, the faithful ones among them were much cheered.

I confess that I write with some hesitation of the case that came to pass soon after this, but I write for the faithful, who know that we must venerate the judgment of God and have belief in the predestination of man, as must believe all Christians who are occult and profound in the extreme.

This most rare case was that on a later occasion when there had been baptized in this same pueblo a goodly number of people; men, women and children, and they were gathered after the service in the courtyard of the church, from an almost clear sky there fell a bolt of lightning among them, killing a woman who held a child in her arms, but leaving the child unharmed.

The witch doctors talked of this event with much discredit to the church and the institution of baptism, counseling others against taking the sacrament, so that the Padre was obligated to again talk to the people, using arguments accomodated to their capacity. He took care to explain that all events come to pass on earth through the exercise of divine judgment, which all men must respect and revere.

Fortunately, shortly after the event related, there came to pass another which helped to restore the faith of the people. A gentile who had steadfastly refused baptism fell extremely ill, and his life being despaired of, the Padre was called in and baptized him. The man immediately came out of his delirium and felt recovered, and the next day arose from his illness. This case was much commented on in all the Christian community, as confirming what the Padres had taught them of the miraculous ways of God.

Some of the same Nebomes who had wounded Padre Diego Bandersnipe once more arose in revolt, burning a church and an entire pueblo. They planned the murder of Padre Olindaño, but his faithful supporters kept constant guard over him and so saved his life. An escort of eight soldiers was sent from the Villa, followed later by a larger company of soldiers, together with some Indian allies. This force held several encounters with the enemy, killing many of them and capturing fourteen prisoners upon whom justice was executed.

The Indian who had wounded Padre Bandersnipe was captured and hung, our Indian allies, in their rage, firing showers of arrows into his body. The companion of this man, captured later by friendly Indians, was beheaded by them and the head sent to the Captain at the Villa, to confirm what they had done. After this last rebellion, which lasted for four months, the tempest subsided, and peace came again to the land of the Nebomes. The Padres again dedicated themselves to the building of permanent churches; and the Captain of the Province was enabled to select Governors and Alcaldes from among the Nebomes for their several pueblos.

CHAPTER 62

The Great Chief Sisibotari

THE COURSE of this history now turns toward the Indian Nations of the Province of Sinaloa who border with barbarous peoples of more remote places.

The next Nations to be told of are the Sisibotaris and Batucos, who populated fertile valleys lying higher into the Sierras, beyond the Yaqui River.

The first of these Nations took its name from a very renowned Indian Chief, Sisibotari, whose fame was much celebrated among the Indian Nations.

I was fortunate enough to meet and visit with this truly great man, on an occasion when I passed near the lands of his people in company with Captain General don Diego Martinez de Hurdaide, in the days before the conversion of the Sisibotaris to Christianity.

Chief Sisibotari came from his lands to greet us. I must say that among the Caciques of the many barbarous Nations I have been privileged to know, no other did I find who in his countenance, his person, his bearing and his dress, showed such distinction, such nobility and dignity as did this Indian.

His courtliness and kindness of manner were as much those of a gentleman as though he had been reared in the courts of Europe. He dressed simply but elegantly. He wore a fine cloth, in the nature of a mantle or a cloak, draped over his shoulders and fastened in the manner of a mantle. In addition, he wore another cloth draped about his waist, as is accustomed by others of his Nation.

On the wrist of his left hand, which supports the bow at the time of drawing the cord to fire the arrow, he had wrapped the very fine fur of a marten, in the manner that other warriors are apt to wrap furs of lesser animals. This, as has been told, is to defend the wrist from the recoil of the cord which speeds the arrow.

The great bow of this Cacique was carried by another Indian, who served as a Page at Arms. These weapons were of their usual style, but of the finest materials and manufacture possible.

He brought in his company a goodly number of troops of bow and arrow, who were his vassals. These followers treated Sisibotari with much respect and even reverence.

I visited with this fine young Cacique through an interpreter, in a tongue with which I was familiar but which was not the tongue of Sisibotari. He gave me a sincere welcome, inviting me to visit his lands and pueblos, which could be discerned in the extreme upper distance from where we stood, although we did not on that occasion reach there.

However, as we conversed he pointed them out to me, and expressed the hope that some day Padres might enter there to teach him and his people the religion of God.

I remained for a good space of time communicating with him, making various inquiries as to his rancherias, pueblos and people, and other matters which they enjoy discussing. He gave me an excellent account of everything about which I inquired. I was indeed impressed with such answers as he gave, coming as they did from an Indian reared among barbarous peoples.

There are, to be sure, among their leaders not few of very good capacity and judgment, their knowledge being more manifest when one is able to converse with them in their own tongue.

I was greatly pleased to have opportunity to meet this fine Cacique Sisibotari, and treated him with all courtesy and affection, giving thanks to God for the door which he had opened for us to return to teach evangelism to his people.

I made presents to him and to his sons (*for so he called his vassals*) of little things which they esteem. We agreed that at times convenient to them he and his subjects should come to visit me at the pueblos (*Ahome, San Miguel and Mochicahui*) where I served, a promise which he later fulfilled.

In due time this distinguished young Cacique, the great Sisibotari, took his leave of the Captain and myself, and returned to his land and people.

The Sisibotaris later made a formal request for a Padre to be sent into their Nation, meanwhile sending eleven of their youths selected from among the most intelligent of their people, to be educated in the College of the Villa. In this act too, they pledged their good faith and fidelity of purpose.

To the Padre Superior of the College, Sisibotari brought a gift of a great royal eagle, a bird seldom captured, in this gift the great Chief seeming to manifest his own royal spirit, not being content to make a gift of less than this symbol of nobility.

At this time the Sisibotaris also petitioned Captain General Hurdaide that he receive them under his direction and protection, as he had other Nations who had become Christians.

I wish to tell now of a signal good deed on the part of the great Sisibotari and his people, which is evidence of their true friendliness and sincerity. In a time of great scarcity of corn among the other Nations of the Province, the Captain was compelled to send envoys to buy corn from as far as the distant land of the Sisibotaris. Upon their arrival, these envoys were asked to remain there, while

Sisbotari sent messengers to the Captain that it was the wish of his people that the great Captain himself should come to pay them a visit.

Upon receiving this message, the Captain comprehended well the feeling of true comradeship it was intended to convey and at once set forth for the lands of the Sisibotaris. Arrived there, he was received with signal honors by his great friend, a sumptuous feast being prepared, at which he was feted with many manifestations of their pleasure at his visit.

After the Captain and his men had been presented of the best of everything they had, their pack mules were loaded with a most welcome gift of corn that was so sorely needed at the Villa.

Before departing, the Captain assured them that he would do what lay in his power to persuade the Padre Superior of the Mission of Sinaloa to hasten the day when they should have a Padre for their Nation. However, before this was accomplished, there occured a great tragedy, which was much felt by the entire Province. This great Cacique, Sisibotari, when returning from a courtesy visit to the Captain and the Padres at the Mission of Sinaloa, had the sickness of death come suddenly upon him, with such rapidity that there was not even time to call the nearest Padre to come to baptize him.

So, for all his desire, this great Indian died without the sacrament which opens the gates to Paradise. It was a misfortune sorely felt by all the Christians of Sinaloa, that this staunch friend of Christians should be lost to us, at only 33 years of age, when his future was so full of promise. There were not lacking those among us who in our grief felt that peradventure God our Father admitted the diligences and desires of this noble man in behalf of himself and his people, and accepted him as baptized in "baptism flaminis." This, in theological terms, is that diligence which one may make to secure the sacrament of holy baptism even though, in fact, it should not be accomplished. We were comforted by the thought that in this manner he may have been saved.

There is to be considered that on many occasions this Indian treated of theological matters with the Padres, taking cognizance of and acknowledging the tenets and mysteries of our Faith and that, from these discussions had come his intense desire to receive the divine sacrament for himself and his people. If all this be not sufficient cause for his eternal salvation, then we must but revere the judgments of God, which are most just in distributing grace and glory.

CHAPTER 63

Mission to Sisibotari and Batuco Nations

To Padre Pedro Méndez, that most venerable missionary of so many years of service in the Missions of Sinaloa, now 70 years of age, was assigned the task of attending to the Missions to be established in the Sisibotari and Batuco Nations.

With an energy as fervent as that of his youth and with as much happiness in his heart, Padre Méndez undertook this new project. I must record here a letter written to his Superiors, telling of his entrance into the lands of these Nations, in the year 1628. He writes as follows:

"After leaving the Villa I first arrived at Ocoroni, which had been my first Mission in Sinaloa. Three miles before coming to the pueblo, I found my path decorated by a succession of green arches formed of boughs of trees. At the entrance to these I was greeted by all the officials of the Mission. Amid music and festivity I entered the church of the pueblo, being given a tumultous welcome.

"After giving my heartfelt blessing to so many friends who manifested such affection for me, we all sat down together, to be regaled all during that day with the various foods that they accustom preparing.

"Later, bidding my friends farewell, I departed for Tegueco, which had been my second charge, and is now under the care of Padre Oton. Here I found a great congregation of Indians awaiting me, all on their knees, with crosses upraised in their hands and chanting the hymns of the church in the manner common to the Indians of Mexico. On the parapet of the church there were musicians playing kettle drums, trumpets and oboes.

"With all this my heart was much comforted; and most particularly with one small child who, elevated on a table, was outdoing himself in shouting a welcome.

"From here we departed for the Mayo River, breaking our journey at Baciroa, a half-way point between the two rivers. Here the Procurator General of the Missions plans to found an Inn for the comfort of travelers between the Missions [*possibly Alamos, Sonora*]. Here I found congregated on a hillside numbers of my Mayo friends, including many warriors. I next continued to the Mayo River, distant 40 miles. As we traveled, men and women came from their little houses to greet me, proffering some gift, of the little they possessed.

"Shelters had been built at intervals for protection against the sun, and crosses placed before them.

"A storm threatening, we were forced to hurry our saddle mules. Our Indian companions ran easily beside us. At the Mayo River, I was given a warm welcome by the Indians and by the Padres attending the Missions there."

Later in his letter, Padre Pedro Méndez tells of his reception by the Sisibotaris:

"I arrived here on the 15th of May (*1628*) with several Indian companions who speak various languages. When they learned of my coming, the Sisibotaris planned for my reception in the manner which they accustom doing. For a distance of three miles they had built a series of arches of green branches, upon each of these having placed large and beautiful crosses. As we traveled through their pueblos, the people knelt, with crosses in their hands; men, women and children, all greeting me with extraordinary evidence of pleasure.

"I was escorted to the church, which was brightly decorated. Their attention was such that it brought tears of happiness to my eyes. So much affection from a people still infidel is most touching.

"Among the people of this Nation there are left no traces of idolatry, nor are there any witch doctors. Although they are a Nation of valor in war, they enjoy living in a spirit of peace.

"I have gathered the greater part of the Sisibotaris into three pueblos, the sites of these being in two fertile little valleys. Through these valleys run arroyos with fine pure water, from which they have learned to irrigate their fields of corn and legumes with notable artifice, so that they never suffer from hunger as do other Nations.

"Withal that they produce ample food, they are modest in their habits of eating, their diet being principally pinole (*corn parched and ground on stones*) mixed with water. Perhaps it is because of this simple diet that they enjoy such good health.

"Whereas the Yaqui and Mayo men wear little covering, the Sisibotaris cover themselves all that is necessary, with a small painted cloth that reaches from the waist to the knees. When the weather turns cold they wear large mantles of cotton or fiber thrown over their shoulders.

"The women wear such ample covering of cotton, fiber or buckskin waists and dresses that when entering church their garments make as much noise as do those of the fine ladies of Spain.

"Their skirts of buckskin, which reach to the ground, are rubbed and burnished until they are soft as silk. On these skirts they may do paintings in several colors.

"For still greater modesty the women wear a sort of apron tied from the waist so that, with this overgarment they present somewhat the appearance of the nuns of Europe.

"The waists of the maidens are apt to be much adorned. When it is cold, women and maidens alike throw over their shoulders a large mantle somewhat in the manner of a Bishop's robe.

"In matrimony the Sisibotari women are exceedingly scrupulous, never being false to their husbands."

With this, concludes the letter of Padre Pedro Méndez.

Padre Bartolomé Castaño succeeded the aged Padre Méndez in his labors among the Sisibotaris and Batucos and was able to bring 300 of this latter Nation into pueblos for indoctrination.

It is cause for pleasure to now see so many pueblos with Missions, in a country so remote and so surrounded by wilderness. There are now in the Province of Sinaloa at least fifty sightly churches, attractively adorned and well preserved, built with as much substance as the poverty of the land may afford. Most important is that these pueblos are now quite at peace with each other, and proceeding to give a good example of Christianity. They are well governed by their Caciques, who are carefully selected by the Spanish authorities from among their most exemplary Christians.

CHAPTER 64

The Sonora Nation

We have now arrived in our story to the last Nation northward in the Province of Sinaloa. The Valley of Sonora, in which is located this Sonora Nation, is located 400 miles distant from the Villa of Sinaloa. The first Mission was established here in 1638, on the Sonora River, the flood waters of which have created broad fertile plains.

The Sonorans are of much the same nature and customs, as well as manner of dress, as the Sisibotaris. Their houses are built of adobe, of very durable construction, as are those of the Sisibotaris.

After the coming of the Padres the Sonoras gathered into several large pueblos of perhaps 1,000 families each. This change from rancherias to pueblos they undertook with singular promptness and good nature.

Padre Bartolomé Castaño was transferred from the Sisibotari Nation to the Sonoras, as they both spoke the same language. The story of the founding of the Mission of Sonora is a felicitous one, with a success comparable to those of the other Nations of which we have told. A letter from Padre Luis de Bonifáz, Provincial of the Company for New Spain, who spent 24 years in the Missions of Sinaloa, and later became Visitador General to these and numerous other Missions, summarizes the state of advancement of the Missions of the Province of Sinaloa. It should be commented in passing that Padre Luis de Bonifáz was eminently versed in the languages of all these Nations. He writes:

"Having just visited the Missions of the Province, I can truthfully say that they are among the most glorious projects in the history of our Company. . . . The Padres in the many Missions preach to their congregations with great fluency in their own language, and the Indians listen with strict attention to the sermons of their Padres. . . . The Indians are being taught good manners. . . . Chants have been translated so that the children, especially, can enjoy singing hymns in their own language. Such was the devotion of the children that on my journey I saw not one child among them who did not wear a rosary.

"Seminaries for the teaching of children have been everywhere established. The seminarists become very adept in learning music, including the choruses sung by the choirs.

"Brush or palm houses have given way to houses of adobe in all these Nations."

To here is quoted the letter from Padre Luis de Bonifáz, Provincial Father to the Missions of the Company of Jesus in New Spain. With this gratifying letter we conclude our narration of the establishment of the Missions of the Province of Sinaloa.

CHAPTER 65

Story of Padre Vicente del Águila

I SHALL CONCLUDE BOOK ONE, which treats of the Indian Nations of the Province of Sinaloa, by telling of the life and virtues of Padre Vicente del Águila, who spent over 40 years in the service of these Missions.

Padre Leonardo Xatini, Visitador to these Missions, as is accustomed upon the passing of a Padre of our Order, gives account of the life of Padre Vicente. He writes:

"Today, March 5th, (*1641*) our Lord was served to take to himself, from the Mission of Sinaloa, Padre Vicente del Águila, 70 years of age, 43 in religion and 26 in the fulfillment of four vows in our Company. . . .

"With preoccupation I undertake this task, knowing well the great estimation, as of a Saint, that this Padre has earned among the natives and Spaniards of this Province. I know that whatever I may write will seem to them insufficient praise.

"Padre Vicente entered the service of the Company in Alcalá de Henares, Province of Toledo in Spain. His brother, doctor Juan del Águila, became Bishop of Lugo. Coming to New Spain at 35 years of age, Padre Vicente spent 36 years here as a missionary, the first two among the savage Chichimecas of San Luis de la Paz, then 34 in Sinaloa. He finally became Visitador, in charge of all these Missions.

"Even in his old age the youngest missionaries could scarce keep pace with him. . . . He arose with the ringing of the first church bell at early dawn, and labored incessantly through the day.

"The poverty of Padre Vicente was almost greater than became his dignity and occupation . . . for many years he wore only the poorest of robes made from the sisal fiber used in the dress of the Indians.

"His modesty was such that after 24 years of association with the women of a church, he scarcely knew one from another.

"Once, although suffering a broken leg, he insisted on being carried on a stretcher for some distance in order to insure the salvation of a soul by baptism.

"Padre Vicente wrote and had printed in Mexico, at his own expense, a brief summary of the mysteries of the Faith, which he later had printed in the Indian languages of the Province, and which he distributed to his Indian disciples.

"He even wrote poetry in the Indian languages, for use in singing in the churches. From all these labors this Padre will continue to harvest souls after his death.

"During all his years of service he was much preoccupied with the adornment of church altars, such as sculptures to be carved on panels in the manner of wreaths, seraphins, and flowers, as well as other designs for church and sacristy.

"At the time of his death he was occupied with the building of two beautiful temples for the last Missions of Sinaloa.

"God willed that death should overtake Padre Vicente in the church of Ahome, and that he should be buried in a spot which he was then in the act of restoring, after its partial destruction by floods in previous years. (*The pueblo of Águila, adjoining Ahome, may well have been named for Padre Vicente del Águila*).

"Throughout his years in these Missions, he was famous for his kindness and his solicitude for the comfort, not only spiritual, but material, of all his people.

"Though his life has left us persuaded of his salvation, still, in order to fulfill my obligation, I plead that there be given for him the orations accustomed for a deceased minister of our Company. . . . dated at the Villa of Sinaloa on March 5, 1641."

To here writes the Padre Visitador of the Missions of Sinaloa. I can in truth add, as one who for some years enjoyed the company of Padre Vicente del Águila in those Missions where it was my privilege to labor in some pueblos with him, that I ever pictured Padre Vicente as an Angel from Heaven in his apostolic virtues.

CHAPTER 66

Expedition to the Californias

THE MISSIONARIES of the Province of Sinaloa, in their zeal for the conversion of souls, became very much interested in the exploration of the land which lies across the arm of the Sea of Californias.

In the year 1642, Captain Luis Cestín de Cañas, Governor of the Province of Sinaloa, made a journey across this Sea, accompanied by Padre Jacinto Cortés of our Company. Of this expedition Padre Cortés writes:

"In obedience to the orders received from Your Excellency, I traveled in the company of our Captain to the Californias. We spent the month of July there, finally being forced back by storms and contrary winds.

"We departed Sinaloa from the Port of Baibachilato, and sailing northward along the coast outward of the Port of San Ignacio, came upon a large Farellon, a rocky island which lies not more than 60 miles distant from this Port. (*Farallon lies approximately 30 miles distant from the northern tip of San Ignacio Island, and 16 miles outside the harbor of Topolobampo*)

"From here we sailed westward, and before losing sight of the mainland of Sinaloa, we sighted the coast of the Californias.

"We disembarked on an island at a port which has been given the name of San Jose, where live some friendly Indians. We then followed a succession of bays southward until arriving at the Bay of La Paz, about 120 miles distant southward.

"The Indians of this place came to greet us in as friendly a manner as do those of Sinaloa. There are said to be, between here and San Bernabé, along this same coast, more than 1,000 Indians. These are all fishermen, as they have no other possible means of sustenance.

"They are friendly people, and of good customs. Among them there is no drunkeness, nor do they have more than one woman. They live in peace, carrying on wars only with some Indians called Guaicuras, who live on the lands opposite these Is-

149

lands. The Guaicuras wish to drive these Indians away from their Islands, coming to attack them from the Port of La Paz, which is near here.

"The weapons of the Indians of the Californias are large bows, and arrows with points of stone, which are however without poison on their tips. Although there grows here the plant from which the poison for arrows is extracted, these Indians neither know of it nor use it, so that war with them would be less dangerous, should it become necessary. They also use some darts of wood with their points charred by fire, which are discharged by use of an instrument which causes the dart to fly like an arrow.

"Spaniards who have arrived on previous expeditions have defended these Indians in their encounters against the Guaicuras, therefore they come from all the nearby bays to greet any expedition of Spaniards that may arrive, bringing them presents of fish, and the fruit of the pitahaya, at the same time begging the Spaniards to fire their arquebuses in the direction of the lands of the Guaicuras, and upon this being done they become much consoled. In a procession which we made along the shore while carrying the Image of the Most Saintly Virgin and singing the litanies, we were accompanied by these friendly Indians, women as well as men, over 200 in number, and all carrying bows and arrows, evidently they concluded we were on our way to attack their enemies the Guaicuras.

"These lands are very scarce of water, nor of any means of securing a living. The only covering of the land is a low form of dry brush, and there are no pools of water from which to drink. If they are to be populated, it will be first necessary to explore to find more fertile soil, and search for streams in the lands populated by the Guaicuras, in order to sustain even the people who now live on the Islands. In the vicinity of the Islands are to be found the underwater feeding grounds of the shells in which grow the pearls.

"On this journey we have secured a few pearls only; these the Captain sends to Your Excellency, that you may see some of the products of these lands. The reason that there are so few is that at the time of our arrival the Indians, who dive for them, had been driven to the shelter of their caves by the heavy rains.

"We returned after having spent only one month there. My impression of this land is that it seems quite distant, and as another world apart, or another New Spain. If God so disposes matters that the Indians of these lands shall be taught our Doctrine, I wish to offer myself to this service, for the purpose of teaching the Indians has brought me here from our College in Mexico, and no other. May Our Señor guard Your Reverence, for the good of all our Province."

When this voyage was undertaken it was not yet known that in the year following, by order of our very Catholic Majesty Felipe Cuarto, Admiral don Pedro Porter de Casanate was to explore this same coast, with the hope of settling Spaniards there, and carrying the light of Evangelism to those peoples. Upon the request of the Viceroy, remitted to us through our Padre Provincial, our Padres in Sinaloa have rendered all possible assistance to this expedition.

CHAPTER 67

Spanish rule in Sinaloa in 1645

GOVERNMENT of the Indian Nations of the Province of Sinaloa at the date of this writing is under direction of the Governor General of the Province of Nueva Vizcaya, with seat of government at Guadiana (*Durango*). To this official pertains the maintainance of Presidios and soldiers; the pacification of the new Indian Nations, and the payment of salaries and expenses of the Militia required for these purposes. This Governor rules through the authority of the Viceroy of New Spain, who has the title of Captain General of all the Provinces of this Kingdom.

Since the inception of the Missions more than 50 years ago, it has been the right of the Governor to dispense civil justice. Usually, this had been done through the Captain General of the Province, who is named directly by the Viceroy.

This manner of government has the convenience that there is one person always in complete authority. When dealing with these primitive Nations, military authority provides added respect, tending to reduce dissention so often attendant upon civil administration. Also, the Captains General of the various provinces, when holding complete authority, can better coordinate their control during times when there are threats of rebellion.

The combined civil and military administration of Captain General don Diego Martinez de Hurdaide was during 30 years notably successful in controlling the destinies of the many Nations of the Province.

Since the death of Captain Hurdaide, there have sometimes been named Chief Justices who were not at the same time Captain General. Not many years since, a gentleman who had served His Majesty as Chief Justice in Sinaloa proposed that there be built another principal Presidio, to be located far northward of those of Sinaloa and Montesclaros, and that the Royal Council of the Indies should grant him quite complete jurisdiction there, with title of Founder. He asked further, to be given title to the lands lying north of the Yaqui River, as a reward for former services to His Majesty in the pacification of certain Indian Nations of the interior of New Spain. In exchange, this gentleman agreed to maintain in this territory a garrison of 25 soldiers, to insure the protection of Spaniards living in the area.

This concession was granted, the gentleman establishing headquarters in the Valley of Sonora. However, there have come to be serious difficulties over the areas of jurisdiction involved.

Many years of experience in this Mission field have, I believe, qualified me to make here some comments that I feel merit consideration. In the first place, I wish to make clear that our Ministers located in the Province, all persons of seasoned experience, are zealous above all else in the imparting of our Christian religion. They desire only to work in harmony with constituted authorities, free from discord or differences. At the same time, they wish to be free to extend ever further their fields of evangelistic endeavor. With this goal in mind, it is our considered judgment that the interests of the Spanish Crown and the Holy Catholic Church may best be served by moving the present Presidios farther northward, that they may on a new frontier serve the same purpose they have so well served in the past; that is, to assure the safety of the Padres, and of their great numbers of Indian disciples who have severed their former bonds with their witch doctors to become Christians and at once vassals of the Spanish Crown. These Presidios are no longer indispensable where they are now located, and cannot at present give protection from 300 miles away.

In conclusion of this chapter, I wish to make clear that the purpose in writing this history has been to make known to persons who should know, the extent of our labors and successes in this remote Province of Sinaloa. There are now established here some 50 Missions, or Teopas (*Houses of God*) in which altogether during these years there have been baptized perhaps 300,000 souls. Thus have we celebrated during these strenuous years the Triumphs of our Saintly Faith, which is the title given to this History.

We shall now turn to the story of the Indian Nations who inhabit the high Sierras eastward of the Province of Sinaloa.

BOOK II

INDIAN NATIONS OF THE SIERRAS OF TOPIA

BOOK II

Indian Nations of the
Sierras of Topia

NEW SPAIN
(MEXICO)

16th and 17th Centuries

TARAHUMARAS

(Chihuahua)

Parral

Santa Barbara

Guanacevi

Zape

SIERRAS

Badiraguato

Santa Catarina

ACAXEES

† Topia

Atotonilco

XIXIMES

Santiago
Papasquiaro

TEPEGUANES

DE

Culiacan

Tenerapa

Santa Maria
de Utais

Otatitlán

TOPIA

San Pedro

HUMIS

Guadiana
(Durango)

San Ignacio

Santa Apolonia

San Javier

Ixtlan

Yamoriba

HINAS

Quelite

San Sebastián
(Concordia)

Mazatlán

Chiametla
(Chametla)

Acaponeta

Zacatecas

Compostela

Guadalajara

Lago de Chapala

Pátzcuaro

Colima

OCEANO PACIFICO

CHAPTER 1

Description of the Sierras of Topia, and of the People Who Inhabit There

THERE HAS first been described the great coastal plain of the Province of Sinaloa; and there has been told of the customs and manner of living of the Indian Nations which inhabit there.

Next have been described the lands, and the Indian Nations who populate the lower westward ranges of the vast Sierras of Topia, northward from the Villa of Sinaloa to the River of Sonora.

Now there will be told of the lofty Sierras of Topia, lying eastward from the Province of Sinaloa for 200 and more miles, until arriving at the broad central plateau of Mexico; and there shall be described the Indian Nations which inhabit those Sierras.

The Sierras of Topia are of extreme height, and of profound depth, altogether the most spectacular of all the Occidental Indies, if not of the entire New World.

They are traversed by numerous large rivers, some of which flow eastward across the vast desert plateau toward the Northern Sea, others westward to empty into the Sea of Californias.

These Sierras are covered in their higher elevations by forests of pines, while oaks and other lesser trees may be found along their lower slopes.

Of these Sierras I write of first hand knowledge, having traversed them by various routes, on journeys from Mexico City to the Province of Sinaloa, a distance of from 900 to 1,200 miles, according to the route taken.

The Sierras of Topia extend from the City of Guadalajara in the south, well over 500 miles until arriving at the unexplored lands of the country called New Mexico.

Politically they are under the jurisdiction of the Province of Nueva Vizcaya.

These Sierras never would have been explored by the Spaniards, had there not existed the ever tantalizing hope of discovering their vast richness in minerals, which draws men irresistibly, even across the far reaches of the unknown seas.

As I traversed those limitless cordilleras, and descended into their deep gorges, I marveled that even savages could penetrate here, much less populate such remote places. I reflected that the Devil must have deliberately led these savages into such hiding places, thinking to thus possess them securely, without fear that the light of Evangelism could reach them there.

In winter, snow may lie two varas (66 inches) in depth along the mountainsides. This snow in melting overflows the rivers, causing them to spread far over the lowlands of the plains, often for a width of several miles.

Fish abound in the larger streams, and are much relished by the Indians living along their borders, being sought after with spear, or bow and arrow, or by seining them from smaller pools left by the receding of the rivers.

During the summer months, June through September, scarce a day passes in the higher Sierras without lightning, thunder and showers. During these storms great pines may be split by lightning, often being devoured by the flame which the lightning causes.

One marvels at the everlasting beauty of those great forests of pines, whose tops rise into the clouds, the trees standing so close one to another that scarcely can the rays of the sun penetrate between.

In contrast to the coolness of the heights, in the vast gorges below them it is so hot that the heat of Africa could not be greater, and the suffering from the plague of mosquitoes can be most exhausting.

In these canyons, and on their lower slopes, grow several varieties of delicious fruits. On the higher slopes is found a variety of pine tree that produces a most tasty little nut, which is much relished by the Indians. These, too, attract great flocks of guacamayas, a large parrot-like bird of brilliant plumage. Also there may be found feeding on these little nuts the smaller parrots, called papagallos.

Among these same trees is to be seen a very industrious bird called a carpintero (*woodpecker*), which drills a series of holes in the trunks of trees for storing nuts, these being inserted into the holes so tightly, by the pounding of the beak of the bird, that they may scarcely be removed by the fingers. One of these industrious birds may drill holes for the storage of as many as 2,000 nuts.

In the higher Sierras there are also some very large birds, black or bronze in color, which the Spaniards term the chickens of New Spain, although they are very much larger than the chickens of Castile.

[*Besides the wild turkeys to which Pérez de Ribas refers here there are, in the forests of Mexico, from the northern lowlands through to Central America, the small glossy bronze black pheasants called quichis, or chachalacas. In the southern rain forests live the faisán griton* (shouting pheasant) *of the same dark color, but about twice the size of a domestic chicken. In these same forests are the faisán real, or curassow bird, of the size of a turkey. This bird is of glossy blueblack plumage, with a brightly colored head. The curassow is extremely difficult to find, as it has the unusual faculty of calling in such manner that it appears to be in a different location from where it is calling.*]

In the high Sierras there are magnificent royal eagles. In the lower areas and on the plains there abound multitudes of birds of many species.

Among the beasts to be found in these mountains are bears, lions and jaguars, as well as two types of wolves. The skins of the bears, lions and jaguars are much sought after by the Indians, to enhance their dress.

Of smaller animals there are a great number, both in the Sierras and on the plains.

The deposits of silver, which are exceedingly rich in many places, were little known to the Indians. Silver was of no interest to them, except for occasionally grinding with bright colored rocks or earth, and mixing into a paste prepared from the bodies of worms, for painting their faces and bodies. It was first discovered by the Spaniards by observing its use by the Indians. It is extracted by the use of azogue (*quicksilver*), or by smelting. God, in his judgment, must have given these savages this dotage of silver that it should be the means of attracting Christians here in peace and friendship.

The first Spaniard to lead an expedition into these Sierras in search of silver was don Francisco de Ibarra, Governor of Nueva Vizcaya, who founded the Reales (*Royal Mines*) of Topia.

The name Topia is derived from a tradition that there once lived among these Indians a beautiful woman named Topia. The name signifies a gourd or large jug made of plaited straw, over which has been rubbed a covering of clay. These jugs, when glazed over, serve for storing water.

There is a myth that, because of her sins, the woman Topia had been converted into an idol of stone. In this form she was much venerated by the Indians.

The Reales of Mines lie nine miles distant from the pueblo of Topia. It is very expensive to pack supplies into such remote places. This fact, coupled with a decrease in the production of silver, has closed many mines in the Sierras.

CHAPTER 2

The Acaxee Indians of the High Sierras

THE ACAXEES are the Indian Nation living in the area surrounding the Valley and Reales of Mines of Topia. Their rancherias are to be found on the more sheltered slopes. Their habitations are usually well concealed in the forests, or among cliffs difficult of ascent, for better defense against their enemies.

Their small houses are apt to be built of rock walls laid with mortar of clay, the roofs being thatched with straw. Some of the Acaxees build cabins of logs, laid together without hewing.

In their several pueblos they have built some larger houses to serve as forts when attacked by enemies. These are built with doors so small that one must bend double to enter, that they may be easier defended. The defenders may fire arrows at the attackers through these small apertures in the walls with little danger to themselves.

In the rancherias and pueblos of the Acaxees at the coming of the Spaniards there were estimated to have been between 12,000 and 16,000 souls. All were tillers of the soil, their principal crops being maiz and beans, together with some smaller seeds that grow in the area. There are pumpkins of several varieties and of different flavor to those of Castile.

They grind maiz to make tortillas to serve as bread. This is solely an occupation of the women; a man would be offended if asked to perform such labor.

[*Tortillas are baked in circular concave clay vessels* (comales) *about 18 inches in diameter. It was interesting to note, on a recent trip to India and Pakistan, cakes being baked in much the same manner except that the baking vessel was placed in reverse form over the fire, with the edges sloping slightly downward, in order to preserve the maximum amount of heat. Fuel is at a premium in those countries. These cakes are apt to be of wheat, rather than corn, and are called chupattis.*]

The diet of the Acaxees is often supplemented by wild fruits, such as ciruelas (*plums*) and zapotes. They also eat the hull surrounding the seed of the guamuchil pod. The guamuchil is somewhat puckery to the taste, but rather sweet.

The rancherias of the Acaxees were located near mountain springs or along the borders of arroyos or rivers, where water was easily accessible.

Another gift of God to all these savage people is the wild honey which, in some areas, they extract from the hollows of trees, in others, from crevices among the rocks. Occasionally hives are formed in branches of trees, as in the Province of Sinaloa. The honeycomb produces a fine wax, which is now used for candles to burn in the altars of the churches.

The dress accustomed by the Indians of the Sierras was sparse and short. The covering of the Acaxees, both men and women, was apt to be of closely woven sisal fiber, as there was little cotton grown in the mountains. The women used skirts made from this fiber, and mantles of the same material thrown over their shoulders. The men also used these mantles, or nothing, as they chose. The Acaxee men accustomed from childhood to wear a small girdle tied about their waist. From this girdle they were apt to suspend a series of tassels, which tended to cover them somewhat. It must be understood that upon their becoming civilized and educated in the Faith, their customs have been greatly improved.

Both men and women grew their hair very long, keeping it with much care. They plaited it into braids, through which were woven strands of bright colors. Both men and women, but especially the men, accustomed adorning their hair with strings of little white seashells, which came to them in trade from the fisher Indians of the Sea of Californias.

Their arms, ears and noses they also liked to adorn with these sea shells. For this purpose their nostrils were perforated in the center cartilage during their infancy.

Their legs and insteps they accustomed wrapping with thongs of buckskin, saying that this practice gave them additional support for traveling over their steep trails. Sometimes, when tired, they would puncture the flesh of their legs to cause bleeding. This they practiced also to relieve headaches, puncturing slightly the flesh of their temples with the thorn of the sisal plant.

The Indians of the Sierras are generally of smaller stature than those of the plains, but more solidly built. They are adept in performing any sort of labor, being especially hardy in climbing their rugged peaks. They move among these as swiftly as do the coastal Indians on the plains. It should be said in passing that the plains Indians do not dare to venture into the higher Sierras, for they are heavy and torpid here and, therefore, are at the mercy of the Indians living here.

The women of the Sierras are most valiant at carrying heavy loads. These they place in baskets to be carried over their shoulders, supported by a broad sash which is placed about their foreheads. In this manner a woman may carry a full fanega (220 *pounds*) of corn in addition to the pottery vessels they use in cooking. Some may also carry a baby and even a papagallo, or some chickens. A little staff carried in their hand assists them much in climbing with these heavy loads.

The nature of these people, barbarous as they will be seen to be, is usually spirited and happy. They converse with Padres and Spaniards in times of peace with much affability. Their good nature is also expressed in their hospitality, for at mealtime their food is placed before the doors of their little houses with invitation to all to share, so long as they be not enemies.

They are without question of good mental capacity, for I have known them to learn in one day, in their own language, both the Ave Maria and the Apostles Creed. So tenacious and determined in nature are they that when coming for baptism they are apt to remain from morning to evening taking part in the services, without pausing to partake of food.

I shall now tell of the wars of their antiquity, which were constantly being carried on against their neighbor Nations, even those of their own language. These conflicts were often of entire communities, one against another, in ambush along their trails, or in their fields. Either in groups, or singly, they would stalk their enemies, for the purpose of devouring them, just as one might stalk a deer for this purpose.

Their offensive weapons were the bow and arrow, the war club (*macana*) and lance, these lances being several feet in length and made of the extremely hard wood of the brazil tree.

For a defensive weapon they used a small shield covered with the skins of wild animals, usually of lion or jaguar.

They would adorn their persons gaudily in time of war. Their head dresses would be either of bright colors of plumage of birds, or brightly dyed head bands of buckskin from which they suspended long tassels, these hanging over their shoulders much in the manner of a tail. Sea shells of bright hues also formed a part of their costume in war, being worn as necklaces or bracelets, or suspended from their ears.

The moment of ultimate triumph for these savages was when arriving at their pueblo with their human flesh for cooking. From a half mile away through the forests they could be heard howling, calling to their children to meet them, as a lioness calls for its cubs to come to participate in its prey. From an early age these savages accustomed their children to the savor of human flesh, that they should later become more interested in its hunting.

159

Their victims they turned over to their older people for cooking. The body was divided at the joints, that it could more easily be contained in their ollas. To the human flesh they usually added frijoles. It was cooked all the night through, that it should be well separated from the bones, for these were preserved as trophies of the hunt.

To this meal of human pottage would be invited all the people of the rancheria or pueblo. There would also be served with this meal large amounts of their home brewed mescal, or other beverages.

The first plate was traditionally given to the hunter who had made the kill. During a ceremony preceding the meal, a small bone of the dead enemy would be inserted into a slit made in the huntsman's lip, this marking him as a warrior of much valor among their people.

Following this barbarous repast, there would be held a wild dance in which both men and women participated. For this dance they formed in a circle. At intervals during the dance their leaders, especially the older ones among them, would deliver orations in a loud voice, during which they exhorted their young warriors to achieve similar triumphs, reminding them at the same time of the vengeance that must be taken against their enemies for the killing of their friends or relatives.

As a part of these hideous ceremonies, a vessel of the human pottage would be poured over the idols which certain of them accustomed keeping before their houses, it being considered this gesture would be pleasing to these idols, which would then bring good fortune to their Nation in future wars against their neighbors.

Before departing for war, they accustomed instituting a symbolic fast, this being undergone by one woman, usually a maiden, in behalf of the whole nation. This fast was rigorous in the extreme, and must be continued for the period of the war. The only food permitted to be taken was a very small amount of parched corn, without the addition of any salt. Salt is an item of diet much cherished by them. They must live apart from all others of their people during this period of fasting, not being permitted even to converse with another person for fear that the sacrificial effect of their fasting might be lessened.

Returning to the matter of their cannibalism: Our Padres found 1,724 human skulls suspended from the rafters of houses in one Acaxee village.

The Padres also gathered, in the Acaxee rancherias or pueblos, great numbers of idols; as many as a dozen large basketfuls from one family.

Some of these idols were purported to bring them victory in war, others to cause the rain to fall more abundantly on their fields; yet others to keep their crops from being destroyed by pests or wild animals, or to bring them better luck while fishing their streams.

These idols varied in form, some being made to represent figures seen in real life, others being of no figure at all, but only of oddly formed stones. Of the stone idols, the principal ones were said to represent a great God named Meyuncame, which interpreted from their language signifies "All Powerful."

In one pueblo the Acaxees gave reverence to a certain large stone which was especially useful to them in making the heads of their stone arrows (*obsidian*), the chips from this stone forming sharp points which were very difficult to extract from a wound.

Some of these idols were sheltered by stone walls laid together with mud and roofed over, in a manner reminiscent of shrines built for travelers in Europe, except that these latter are adorned with figures of the religion of the Saintly Cross. At the base of these shelters the Indians would lay offerings of whatever they most prized.

The ones who interpreted the meaning of these heathen idols were, of course, the Hechiceros, to whom all paid tribute and who, in consequence, were opposed to the coming of Evangelism.

At certain times, at the fall of evening, these Hechiceros would cause the people to assemble, usually at a house before which had been placed an idol. Here they would beat a rhythm on a shallow drum, at the same time calling for the Devil to appear before them. In some strange manner they did cause the Devil to appear, sometimes in human form, at other times in the form of some animal. At these gatherings they were influenced by Satan to commit barbarous atrocities.

It must be said, however, that despite the practices of their savagery, these people had customs much worthy of praise. They did not steal nor lie. Even their children, when questioned, gave honest answers. Married couples lived in much fidelity, and immorality was a cause for banishment from their pueblos.

They were much given to playing games, the favorite of these called Hule, in which a rubber ball is bounced from the shoulder or the hip toward an opposing player. In this game all the Indians of the Sierras were most dexterous, either leaping to meet the ball with their body, or dropping to earth with the great agility to return a ball rolling there. Their playing fields were very well built, usually surrounded by rock fences.

Challenges to games were frequently sent from one rancheria to another, and wagering was customary. After the opening of the mines they wagered silver, as well as personal ornaments, or even their clothing. Each laborer in the mines was permitted to carry away for himself a palm basket of silver ore at the end of the day. This ore, it may be sure, was gathered from the richest available, often having a value of six, eight or even ten pesos of eight reales each, in silver.

Returning to the challenge games of Hule; these were taken so seriously that for at least three days and nights before such a game the men and women of each pueblo would gather on the field where their games were played, dressed in full regalia, as though for war, where they would carry on their savage dances, while extolling in loud voices the valor and swiftness of their players, and exhorting them to carry on to victory.

On the day of the game, the women of the pueblo sending the challenge would prepare an ample banquet. Should the visiting team win, this banquet would be theirs, but should they lose, they would not be permitted to share in any least part.

The numbers of players of the challenging team was usually limited to six or, at most, eight; no limit being placed on the number of challenged who could participate.

For want of other items to wager, the combatants might offer the plucking of one or several of their eye lashes. When this plucking was done, especially if accomplished several at a time, the pain was excruciating. Some would endure the ordeal bravely, but others howled with pain.

Even after the Indians of the Sierras became Christians, these games were permitted to them, as there was no reason to deprive them of any licit entertainment. In this manner they were much more contented.

It may be recalled that in the year 1590 the venerable Padre Gonzalo de Tapia traveled from Sinaloa into those Sierras, where he visited the savage Acaxees. However, it was left to Padre Hernando de Santarén to found the Mission of Topia, in the year 1600. First laboring among the Indians of the mining community of San Andres, he founded a Mission there which came to be attended by over 1,000 Indians. His efforts next turned to the Acaxee Indians of the Valley of Topia. From these places his disciples opened trails from one of their remote villages to another, that the Padre might penetrate their forests and ascend their rocky pinnacles.

The Indians of his charge being so numerous and scattered in places so remote, Padre Santarén appealed to the Provincial Father in the City of Mexico for aid. In the year 1602 there came to his assistance Padre Florean de Aueroe. Padre Florean wrote to his Padre Superior, Padre Santarén, as follows:

"After our parting, I continued on to Colura. While I was visiting a nearby pueblo of the Acaxees, on the 14th day of December (*1602*) there came a rain which, with few interruptions, has lasted until the 12th day of January of 1603, keeping the waters of this mountainous gorge too high for crossing.

"On Christmas Day I went to a small pueblo nearby, where I held Mass once only, as my supply of wafers and wine were nearly exhausted. The Day of Kings (*Dia de los Reyes*) I passed in the narrows of the canyon, isolated from Topia, being limited to a ration of corn and beans. The houses of the pueblo having roofs only of straw, they finally became saturated. In the room where I took shelter I could only keep out of the water by sitting on a little bench with my feet elevated. Regardless of such privations, I am thankful to have been permitted to come among these peoples so far away.

"There has recently come to these Sierras a disease from which few have escaped. From Angostura, in the valley of Topia, I traveled to the village of Aguas Blancas to give consolation to the afflicted. The way was so difficult that we were from six in the morning until two in the afternoon traveling the six miles between pueblos. The terrain was so difficult that I was at times compelled to wrap myself in my cloak and slide down the steep hillsides, through the bushes, after three Indians had gone ahead to help clear the way.

"Several times I expected to drown while crossing these streams, when the water rose over the back of my riding mule. There are more than 360 crossings over the stream which flows from this Valley of Topia, many among steep walls of its canyons.

162

"At one place my guides refused to cross. I then plunged my mule into the flood, which submerged us both. We finally lodged between two large rocks in mid-stream. There, finding more secure footing, the mule again undertook to make its way across the river, finally swimming safely with me to the opposite shore. In this adventure I received a bruised leg which is still healing.

"From here we continued to the pueblo of Atotonilco. There came here to see me twelve barbarous looking Indians carrying bows and arrows, asking that I accompany them to their pueblo to baptize their people. I was told that I could only descend to this pueblo after crossing over two very narrow rocky ledges along the crests of precipices. After crossing these, I was told, I could descend the walls of a canyon to the bottom of the river gorge that flows to join the Humaya River. [*This gorge must have been that of the upper reaches of the Tamazula River, which joins the Humaya just above the ancient Indian pueblo of Culicán, now Capital of the State of Sinaloa, from there flowing into the gulf of California.*]

"This river, the savages told me, was then running so strongly that should we not cross it very soon, we would be unable to do so for three months after.

"However, they did not wish to return to their pueblo without being baptized, so I spent the following week indoctrinating them, finally baptizing them each one with the name of one of the twelve Apostles. With this they departed contented, to advise their people of my coming.

"When I was able to leave, I rode my little mule for two full days upwards into mountains that rise to heaven, then down those precarious ridges to the river. I found the water so deep that it was necessary to cross the stream seated on a little raft of boughs which was carried on the heads of four Indians. Wading ever deeper into the river, the water finally came up so far over their chins that, should one of them have ever so little lowered his head, I would have been finished.

"On the bank opposite fifty Indians were awaiting me. They guided me upstream to an area which lies at the base of two very high peaks, bordering the river. Here I found more than 600 Indians, including women and children. They came forward in four rows, all being adorned with wreathes of green leaves, and each carrying a branch of palm in his hand. They bent to their knees, and to my great astonishment, sang the Creed of God Our Father to me in their own language. I was exceedingly pleased to hear them, to be sure, and asked how it was possible for them to do. They answered that the twelve newly converted Indians who carried the names of the Apostles had taught these verses to all the others.

"Such was their enthusiasm for learning that I soon was able to baptize 480 persons, gathering into one new pueblo all the Indians living in the gorge of this river, and soon they were at work building a substantial church for themselves.

"Leaving this project well begun, I traveled down the river to Culiacán, as your Reverence had ordered me, taking with me numerous Indian disciples, that they might observe how Christians celebrate the Holy Week of our Father Christ Jesus.

"At Culiacán the Alcalde Mayor and the Vicar received them with much courtesy and attention. On Holy Thursday they were reserved places in the church, where I held the service of Communion. On the following day, Holy Friday, it fell to my lot to deliver the sermon. Altogether these disciples who had followed me acquired such a concept of my importance that it seemed necessary that this impression be dispelled, by explaining that such honors were not for me, but for the God of whom I was Minister and servant"

163

Here closes the letter of Padre Florean de Ayeroe, which presents such a bright picture of our labors among these primitive people.

With patience, kindness and attention, the Padres continued to win these people. Gifts such as axes, knives, mantles and other clothing, as well as medicines for those fallen ill, mean much to them, who have so little. Gradually the customs of their gentility are abandoned, their witch doctors ignored, and their idols destroyed.

Before the arrival of the Padres, these Indians accustomed wrapping their dead in a tight bundle, with the body tightly doubled, knees upward toward their faces. They were then placed in certain burial caves of the Sierras, without their being covered with earth. They were left food to accompany them on the journey the dead were supposed to make into another world. Their bows and arrows were placed beside them, in case they should be required on this journey into the unknown. They were then left, after the entrance to the burial cave had been covered with stones and earth. In this practice they indicated some belief that man, though dead, will enjoy another life.

The Padres soon instituted the Christian manner of burial, teaching them also the truth regarding life after death, this instruction being well accepted by them.

At a certain rancheria a mother gave birth to twin babies, herself dying as a result of these births. The father, in his anguish over the loss of his wife, thought to kill the newborn children. However, the Padre took this man severely to task, pointing out that the loss of his wife was in no way the fault of the innocent newborn children. The babies were baptized and given to be reared by a foster mother.

A Padre arrived one day at a pueblo where a game of Pelota was in progress. On one side of the playing field (*batei*) there had been placed an idol resembling the figure of a man. Near it were pottery ollas filled with a drink made from the root named Peyote, which is much accustomed as a beverage among the Indian Nations of New Spain. This drink, although medicinal, has involved in its use so many heathen rituals and superstitions that it is forbidden, and is a matter for punishment by the Tribunals of the Saintly Inquisition. When the Padre saw this idolatry being practiced, he gathered the Indians together, talking to them with such good effect that the idol was on the moment destroyed, and the game interrupted while the people knelt in prayer to the only and true God of all mankind.

Wondrous fruits were these gathered by the Padres. However, the Devil, in desperation at being disposessed of so many souls, raised a most furious tempest; of which we shall tell in the chapter following.

CHAPTER 3

First Revolt of the Acaxee Nation

[ALTHOUGH *the date of this uprising is not given, it must have taken place several years before the general uprising of the Indians of the Sierras in 1616, as Padre Hernando de Santarén survived this first rebellion, to serve as the instrument for returning peace to the Sierras.*]

There lived among the Acaxees an Hechicero of so much authority that he persuaded the Acaxees to make gifts to him of whatever they had. Such a pretentious imposter was he that he even posed as an Indian Bishop, in the manner of a true Catholic Bishop, presuming to baptize children who had already been baptized, and to divorce couples who had been married in the church. This man was known among the Indians as El Obispo.

After committing many atrocities, especially upon Christian Indians, El Obispo and his followers fled to the higher mountains; from there descending at times to attack mines and rancherias of Spaniards, including the Reales of Mines of Topia, San Andrés and Las Virgines.

Las Virgines was the first place razed. Next, their attention was turned to San Andrés. Here there had gathered in the church some forty Spaniards. With them was Padre Alonzo Ruiz, who had come to assist Padre Hernando de Santarén in his labors among these pueblos. For fifteen days San Andres was besieged by some 800 Indians, withstanding one concentrated attack after another. The Spaniards were without sufficient arms to properly defend themselves. Many were sorely wounded. In their desperation they resorted to making sorties into the open area before the church to combat their enemies. Padre Alonzo, with animation no doubt inspired of God, led one of these sorties, a crucifix in his hands, while exposing himself to a multitide of arrows. It seemed a miracle that not an arrow touched him, and that after this sortie the fury of the enemy subsided.

The counter-attack led by Padre Alonzo was in the early morning. The besieged then returned to the church to hold Mass, trusting in God to spare them in time for this preparation for death. They were, in fact, nearing the hour of their liberation, as will be seen. A messenger sent by them 180 miles to Guadiana to plead for aid had successfully avoided the enemy Indians surrounding San Andrés, to deliver his message.

The Governor, don Francisco de Ordiñola, quickly gathered together sixty well armed Spaniards, at the same time dispaching an urgent summons for aid to Indian allies living on the borders of the Laguna de San Pedro, on the desert eastward of the great Sierras. These Laguna Indians were of much fame as fighters of bow and arrow. With this combined force he marched to the rescue of the Spaniards besieged at San Andrés and other communities of Spaniards in the area of Topia.

Upon hearing of the coming of these forces, the rebels lifted the siege of San Andrés and the other places threatened, retiring into the distant peaks which are their fortresses.

At a council of the surviving Spaniards, it was agreed that the most probable manner of securing a return to peace of the rebellious Acaxees was to send as an envoy to them the venerable Padre Hernando de Santarén, whom so many of the Indians loved and respected.

With Padre Hernando on his first journey in search of the rebellious Acaxees went eight Spanish soldiers with armored horses. Although they found many Indians, they were not able to arrange a truce, finally being forced to return to San Andrés.

On a second journey Padre Hernando and his escort encountered a large band of Acaxees who had just assaulted a pack train of mules which was on its way from Culiacán to Topia to carry aid to the people there. The rebels had killed a negro of those laboring in the mines, as well as some Christian Indians; and had wounded a Spaniard. Several of the mules they had slaughtered for meat.

Padre Hernando plead with these savages, many of whom he knew, to return in peace to their homes. In no mood to be conciliated, they forced the Padre to accompany them into a country so rough and mountainous that it seemed a miracle that any human being could make his way through it alive. Padre Santarén was finally permitted to rejoin his escort, which had followed at a distance, not being in sufficient number to attempt his rescue.

His next effort was to dispach into a deep gorge to where many of the rebels had retired, a faithful Indian messenger with a flag of truce, pleading again for them to return in peace to the care of their Padres.

This man relayed to Padre Hernando de Santarén a request that, without soldier escort, he meet the leaders of the rebels, and this the Padre did. There may be imagined the surprise of the Spanish Governor and his forces to behold a few days later, Padre Hernando come marching down from the mountains followed by some 500 of these rebels, all singing the hymns of the church which had been taught to them by Padre Santarén in their own language.

The Sosaibos, a sub-tribe of the Acaxees under the leadership of the false Bishop, continued to refuse offers of peace. The Spanish forces, together with some Laguna Indian allies pursued them into their mountain fastnesses. Coming upon a large group of Sosiabo women and children, they treated these with kindness and returned them to their homes. This action so softened the hearts of the Sosaibo warriors that they sent a messenger to plead for a meeting with Padre Santarén. As a result of this meeting, the good Padre again came marching down from the mountains with large numbers of Indians, to arrange terms of peace.

The Indian witch doctor, El Obispo, was eventually delivered to the Spaniards and sentenced to be hung, together with his principal accomplices. In his last days this fierce savage gave evidence of repentance, and died confessed of his sins.

Peace again reigned in the land of the Acaxees. One restless Indian who attempted to again create unrest among the others was captured by an Indian of much authority among them, who took it upon himself to execute upon this Indian the punishment of dividing his body into two halves, which were suspended in two separate places from trees marking the entrance of trails into their Sierras. After such a measure, the few who had become restless were much subdued, returning to their pueblos and to the influence of their churches.

The Spaniards again returned to the extraction of silver and Padre Santarén, who was then Superior of the Mission of Topia, began to rebuild this Christian community.

I quote from a letter directed by Padre Santarén to the Provincial Father in Mexico City:

". . . We have congregated the Acaxee people into larger pueblos, have built new churches, even though of wood and straw for the present, and now have some 5,000 Indians living in these pueblos."

CHAPTER 4

Continuing the Story of the Nations of the Sierras

A REQUEST of Padre Superior Santarén, supported by Governor Francisco de Ordiñola, brought four new Missionaries to the Sierras of Topia. Alms were at the same time given by the Viceroy of New Spain for the founding of a Seminary for the Indian children. There were now eight Missionaries laboring among the many pueblos and rancherias of the Acaxee, Tepeguane and Sosaibo Nations. In the course of the years many pernament churches were built.

The Indians were instructed by the Padres in many matters, including the need for showing charity toward others. At an Indian pueblo named Otatitlán, in a time of famine, the Padre preached a sermon that so impressed his congregation that of their own reserves of food they gave liberally to other pueblos who were suffering more than themselves. So engrossed did these people become in their works of charity that in the years following they seeded much greater areas in order to distribute from their harvests to other more needy pueblos.

The Padres of the headquarters Mission of Topia soon were undertaking journeys into the most distant recesses of those vast Sierras. In the gorges and on the slopes lying between Topia and the ancient pueblo of Culiacán lived people who, although surrounded on all sides by Christian pueblos, had remained isolated from civilization. In due time the Padres penetrated even this remote area, reducing the Indians to three principal pueblos: Vadiriguato

(*Badiguarato*), Conimeto and Alicamac. Here they built churches and a Seminary for the Indian children.

The Padres also penetrated into the vast craggy Sierras of Carantapa, where the Spaniards had discovered great riches of silver. The silver had long since been exhausted; nevertheless, the Padres continued their ministry to the several thousand Indians of this remote area. The principal pueblo of these people was named Tecuchuapa. Padre Santarén recalls, in a letter, a journey made to this place together with Padre Jose de Lomas, the Minister resident there, in an attempt to calm a furor caused by two Tepeguane Indians who had come from their lands and had forced two Indian maidens from their homes.

The two Padres summoned the culprit Tepeguanes to come before them, but rather than face the Padres, they fled; on their way inducing some Indians from rancherias distant from Tecuchuapa to join them in revolt.

At the request of Padre Santarén, thirty Christian Indians undertook the rescue of the two maidens. Upon overtaking the rebels, there ensued a fierce battle, in which several were killed on both sides, but the maidens were recaptured and returned to their homes.

Incensed at this defeat, the renegade Tepeguanes began to gather companions for the purpose of murdering Padre Santarén. From Tecuchuapa the Padre wrote:

"All through this month of September I have been under constant guard of fifty faithful Christian warriors, who accompany me on my travels from one pueblo to another. It is imperative that I do not desert my followers here, for they need my presence to keep up their courage, even though remaining may cost my own life. May Your Reverence and my Brothers commend me to God in your prayers.

"The Indians of Baimora, a pueblo 90 miles distant from here, desire to embrace Christianity and have sent messengers by the Captain of the Spanish troops stationed at the Real of Mines of Carantapa. The Indians of Carantapa have made the Spaniards rich gifts of silver.

"Finally seeing that I cannot just now abandon my people here, there have come 150 Indians from Carantapa for baptism. Who should see them arrive must shed tears of compassion, knowing that these pilgrims have abandoned entire villages in order to come to a strange land in search of a faith so new to them. The men come carrying their smaller children, the women their few possessions and their food; sometimes the old leading the blind, for a journey of fifteen days over rugged mountains. It is so much more to their credit that they come not in search of riches, but of salvation for their souls.

"Because of such manifestations of faith, I have finally found myself obligated to make a journey of seven days in the direction of their lands, although not without escort of friendly Indians and soldiers. Such is the difficulty of travel that on some days we have not been able to cover more than fifteen miles."

Here concludes the letter of Padre Hernando de Santarén.

There next came to Tecuchuapa to visit Padre Santarén 70 Indians of the Nation of Sicurabas, advising him that 900 more of their Nation were on their way to his Mission for indoctrination. This precise count they gave by delivering to him that number of grains of corn to be counted.

After securing their harvest, these people came to locate on lands near Tecuchuapa so that they and their children could receive instruction from the Padres.

Eventually 1,200 Sicurabas were baptized, and delivered up their idols to be destroyed. Some of these idols were figures of people carved in stone, others were in the form of large hard stones from which could be chipped sharp pieces for heads of arrows. Still others were stones removed from the intestines of deer, which were said to bring them good fortune in hunting.

Some there were who continued in league with Satan. On an occasion when a great pestilence spread through the land, the Hechiceros called meetings of the people, asking them to plead with the Devil to liberate them from this disease.

One faithful Christian concealed himself in some bushes near the house where the others were gathered, to learn what might transpire. All being gathered together, a principal Hechicero began in a loud voice to invoke the presence of the Devil. Presently the figure of a Devil did actually appear before the group, promising them relief from their affliction. The principal Devil was said to have been accompanied by five or six other demons, all of whom conversed with the Hechicero, in sight and hearing of all the others.

At this point the Christian Indian who was concealed could contain himself no longer and began shouting, imploring those assembled not to give heed to these demons, but to have faith in their God Christ Jesus. Providentially, at that very instant there came a great clap of thunder from the heavens. The Infernal Caliphate and his accompanying Demons fled into the night, and all the others made a hasty retreat to their homes.

There are innumerable stories such as these to be recounted of the adventures, hardships and, above all, the spiritual struggles and triumphs of the Padres of our Company among the savages of the Sierras. Some of these we shall recount in succeeding chapters.

CHAPTER 5

The Mission of San Andrés

THE SPANIARDS opened a Real of Mines which they named San Andrés, for a pueblo of that name in Castile. Large amounts of silver ore of high value have been taken from here, although in lesser amounts now than in the first years of its founding.

This Mission, it may be recalled, was founded by the distinguished Padre Hernando de Santarén, later Superior of all the Missions of Topia. It was set upon a firm foundation by Padre Alonzo Ruiz, a man of great virtue, worthy of being well remembered in this history. Among the Indians his name was known and revered even to the farthest places of those great Sierras.

The valor of this Padre was manifest both spiritually and physically. It has already been told how he emerged from the church of San Andrés, crucifix in hand, to lead his congregation in an attack on the savage Acaxees who held them under siege.

From the inception of the rebellion of the Acaxee and Tepeguane Nations, it was planned to give a quick death to Padre Alonzo Ruiz and the other ministers of the Mission pueblos of the Sierras. A faithful Christian Indian had given warning to Padre Alonzo, who was then visiting at the pueblo of San Miguel. The warning came almost at dusk. Padre Alonzo at once took to his mule, to return to warn the Spaniards of the Real of San Andrés.

The rebels divided their forces into two bands, one to march to San Miguel to murder the Padre, the other to close all trails leading to San Andrés, that the Spaniards there should be caught by surprise.

By singular providence the riding mule of Padre Alonzo, leaving the trail in the darkness, avoided the savages guarding the regular pass, the Padre arriving at San Andrés about midnight. He immediately aroused the inhabitants, who fortified themselves as best they could, in the church. The rest of the story of the defense of San Andrés has already been related.

Continuing with the story of the labors of Padre Alonzo Ruiz: even before the days of this first rebellion he had founded the pueblos of San Gregorio, San Pedro, Coapa and Tecaya. After the rebellion passed, he added to these the pueblos of Llexupa, Vegas, Chacala and various others.

In the service of his many parishoners this servant of God took no heed of the greatest obstacles, such as difficult trails nor of inclement weather. His health finally failing, he fell gravely ill at the pueblo of San Gregorio. There were here no medicines, nor any physician who might attend him.

Advised by the Indians of the plight of their Padre, Captain Diego Davila, a great benefactor of the Padres of these Missions, rode at all speed from San Andrés to his aid. The Captain persuaded Padre Alonzo to allow himself to be carried upon a litter, to be treated at the Real of San Andrés. However, the sad procession arrived only as far as an Hacienda along the trail, where the Padre expired. His body was carried onward toward San Andrés. The river was so high in flood that it was necessary to construct a raft on which it might be crossed. His funeral services, held at night, were attended by great numbers of people, who filed in procession to the church, carrying burning torches in their hands, they shedding tears of sorrow over the departure from this life of this great spiritual leader whom they had come to so much respect and love.

Padre Alonzo Ruiz was succeeded in these Missions by Padre Andrés Tutino, who labored here for twenty years, a part of this time as Padre Superior during a time of revolution and strife of which shall later be told.

Padre Tutino writes of the inauguration of a church at San Gregorio:

"Indians gathered from a distance of a hundred miles for the inauguration ceremonies, which lasted for eight days. During this time all were served food by the
people of the New Mission.

"As their part of the entertainment, the visiting Indians performed colorful and
attractive dances.

"Spaniards in the number of fifty gathered from the surrounding Reales of Mines.
All rode well armed, as is the custom in these frontier places.

"Each day there was held a solemn procession, with music. The Spaniards, also
wishing to participate, presented a religious play, all the players being dressed in
fine raiment. The staging of this play was enhanced by the presentation of appropriate accompanying music.

"An exciting feature of the celebration was jousting from on horseback, with
lances.

"Negroes who had come from the south to work in the mines, now being members of the newly built church, also staged a play, presenting attractive dances in
their fashion. During the festivities the Spaniards, at intervals, would deliver salvos
from their arquebuses, using altogether ten arrobas (250 *pounds*) of powder in these
demonstrations."

The pestilences that have already been referred to began with a scourge of
measles of a virulence never before seen, then followed by a small pox often
fatal.

Day and night the Padres traversed the Sierras attending to the physical and
spiritual needs of the stricken Indians. From pueblo to pueblo, from house to
house, they traveled, in one hand the holy unction, in the other what food and
medicine they could secure. To add to their problem, these epidemics chanced
to come at a period of high floods in the Valley of Topia. Two Padres traveling
to attend the sick were carried down stream with their mules, barely escaping
drowning. On another occasion the two were left stranded for eight days on a
small island created between two turbulent streams of the river.

After these floods there came a snowstorm, leaving the Padres marooned for
five days with no other recourse than to roast bitter acorns from the trees
about them, which they mixed with a handful of ground parched corn that
they still carried. God took to their reward during this period of pestilence.
some 800 adults and perhaps an equal number of children.

CHAPTER 6

Story of the Xixime Nation

THE XIXIME NATION was considered by the Spaniards to be the most ferocious of all the great Sierras. In the vast mountains and deep canyons where they lived they carried on their inhuman practice of cannibalism. Skulls and human bones were to be found suspended from the walls and over the doorways of their houses in the same manner as houses are ornamented in civilized countries.

Their constant assaults upon the Acaxees had depleted this latter Nation most seriously. When the Spaniards joined the Acaxees in attempting to curb the ferocity of the Xiximes, Spaniards and Acaxees alike suffered loss of men and reputation.

Matters being in such state, the Acaxees, who were now nearly all converted to Christianity, appealed to Governor don Francisco de Ordiñola of Nueve Vizcaya for aid.

Governor Ordiñola, an astute veteran of frontier wars, had some time before taken care to capture a Xixime warrior; taking him to live among the Spaniards and Christian Acaxees. This man he now sent, well dressed in the manner of civilized people, to serve as an interpreter and counselor in treating of peace with the Xiximes. Accompanying him were a Padre and the Spanish Captain from the Real of Mines of San Hipólito with a goodly escort of soldiers. A meeting was arranged between the principal Caciques of the Xiximes and Governor Ordiñola, at which a truce was declared, and there was celebrated an agreement for mutual protection.

With this understanding the people of the southern border of the Acaxee Nation, where lived the Xiximes, remained at peace for a number of years.

However, the Xiximes were truly a wild and restless people and suddenly, without provocation or warning, fell upon four pueblos, murdering Spaniards and Christian Indians alike, to be carried away to their campfires to be roasted.

The Governor again attempted to conciliate matters without further bloodshed, but failed. He then appealed to the Viceroy and Real Audencia in Mexico City for assistance. It was resolved to make a levy of Spaniards and Indian allies to march against the Xiximes.

This force consisted of two Spanish Companies, each of 100 men in armor, mounted on armored horses, in addition to 1,000 Indian allies. They were accompanied by two Padres of our Company who spoke the Acaxee and Xixime languages.

The Xiximes in revolt numbered perhaps 1,000 warriors; but these held the distinct advantage of knowing their difficult terrain, where Nature has built natural defenses more difficult of penetration than any yet conceived by man. I find no better manner of describing the events of this expedition than to quote a letter of one of the Padres who accompanied it. He writes:

"The rebel Xiximes were divided into two bands, one concentrated at their pueblo of Xocotilma, the other at Guapijuxe. The Governor first marched against Xocotilma, where was reported to be the greatest concentration of the enemy. So steep was the way that we were forced to build a trail as we advanced, moving on foot while leading our animals. The undergrowth was so dense, especially along the streams, that it could only be removed by burning.

"Finally we arrived, in a state of near exhaustion, at the Valley of Xocotilma, where we immediately took possession of some high crags and peaks from whence we could fire upon the stronghold of the enemy.

"When the Xiximes discovered that we had occupied these strategic points, they were much perturbed; and presently sent messengers to discuss terms of peace with Governor Ordiñola. He received them with kindness, proffering them some small gifts. He assured them that we had no wish to harm their people but came only to punish the leaders who had stirred the others to revolt. He asked these messengers to advise the Xiximes that on the day following we would meet them in the pueblo of Xocotilma to discuss terms of peace.

"The following day, the anniversary of San Lucas, was the most pleasant of our journey. Xocotilma is situated on the floor of a lovely valley carpeted with flowers; in an area of refreshing coolness.

"The Spanish soldiers, having donned the armor which they had carried so laboriously over the high precipices, marched in battle formation into the village. In the principal Plaza we were faced by 150 ferocious looking Xixime warriors standing in readiness for battle, their leaders at their head poised with lances and shields, the warriors with bows in hand and quivers of arrows suspended across their shoulders. Others carried the great war clubs they call macanas. Some had tomahawks and knives they had secured in trade from Spaniards. These warriors were of striking appearance. Their long hair was intertwined with bright strands of cloth and wrapped about their heads. Their faces were painted in hideous designs of many colors.

"In this regalia first their leaders, then their warriors stepped forward, one by one, to give greeting to the Governor, who received each in turn in a courteous and kindly manner. This ceremony being concluded the Governor expressed his pleasure at their coming to greet him, but remarked that he could not conclude terms of peace with them until a greater representation was present. He then offered to give those missing two days in which to present themselves.

"For two more days we rested, albeit on guard, in this beautiful valley. Upon the morning of the third day there appeared on the slopes of the nearby Sierras multitudes of Xiximes: warriors, women and children. Of the warriors the Governor required that they first lay down their arms, after which they were all presented before him. He ordered them seated in a circle about him, a cordon of soldiers and Indian allies quietly surrounding this circle.

"The Governor then told them once more that he came seeking to arrange terms for a lasting peace, which should be much preferable to their being forced to wander with their families like wild animals in their forests and mountains. He still insisted that, for a peace to be lasting, it must be pledged by all their warriors, many of whom still had not appeared.

"To this end he required that there remain with the Spanish forces, as hostages, four of the principal Caciques of the Xiximes. The first of those designated was one who exercised great influence over the others and had been responsible for many of the atrocities they had committed. This Cacique was placed under guard without protest on his part.

"The second Cacique named sought to resist the soldiers, whereupon all the other Xiximes also became much excited. An ancient Cacique among them stood shouting in a loud voice, exhorting them all to face death rather than to submit to being imprisoned. Other Xiximes tried desperately to break through the cordon of defense of the Spaniards and allies, even to the point of throwing themselves upon the swords of the Spanish soldiers. Some used knives or hatchets they had concealed upon their persons. In this struggle several Xiximes were killed and many taken prisoners. God willed that my companion priest and I were permitted to catechise and baptize most of those severely wounded before they expired.

"After this council meeting which had resulted in such violence, the Governor ordered camp to be removed from the village of Xocotilma to a location better suited to our defense. Once established here, he proceeded with the questioning of the prisoners, to determine who among them had been most culpable in inciting the others to rebellion. Eleven among those arrested had been among the principal offenders. These boasted, among other matters, that in permitting our troops to enter their village, it had not been with the thought of carrying on negotiations for peace, but only to put us in a position to be attacked by surprise. They asserted also that they still hoped to ambush us from the shelter of their forests and rocky ledges, when our forces should penetrate deeper into their Sierras.

"The investigation completed, the Governor ordered the eleven most culpable to be hanged. God willed they should accept their sentences with good grace. We prepared them for the salvation of their souls. They were baptized at the foot of the trees from which they were hung, nine dying in a manner that left much hope of their being accepted in Heaven. The tenth was the old Indian who had aroused the others to begin the rioting. This fierce man chose to die without the benefit of conversion, and was finally thrown down to hang from the branch of a tree. Some of our Indian allies, angered by his obstinacy, filled his body so full of arrows that it had all the appearance of a porcupine covered with quills.

"The eleventh prisoner, a mere youth, was spared, at the intercession of Padre Francisco de Vera. It had been proven that, although he had accompanied the murderers, he had taken no part in the killings.

"A Xixime Cacique who had come to live among the Acaxees and, at great risk of life offered to act as messenger to his former people, had, together with his wife, accompanied the expedition. They now asked to be baptized, as an example to their Xixime people, and to be married in the Christian manner. The ceremony was performed with much pleasure by Padre Francisco de Vera, with Governor Ordiñola acting as Godfather to the couple. They were given the Christian names of Francisco and Maria.

"At the conclusion of the ceremony, they were saluted with a salvo of shots from the arquebuses of the Spanish soldiers, while their Indian friends beat a rhythm on their great drums in honor of the occasion.

"The Governor dispached this newly married couple back to the land of the

Acaxees, offering pardon to those Xiximes who might choose to accompany them; assuring them that they would be permitted to live peacefully among the Acaxees. As an added inducement for their leaving, the Governor burned their village of Xocotilma. He then departed with his forces for Guapijuxe, where the second contingent of the enemy had gathered.

"In the houses of Xocotilma there had been found the skulls of over 1,000 victims of the cannibalism of these savage Xiximes.

"Our march again lay over rugged mountains. Upon approaching the village of Guapijuxe the Governor sent forward a messenger, this time one of those taken prisoner at Xocotilma, to carry an offer of peace. This man was received with scorn, fleeing back to our lines followed by a shower of arrows.

Our soldiers again took possession of some heights from which the advance of the enemy could be impeded. We first gave their forces a series of volleys from our arquebuses, after which we pushed forward into the village.

"To our horror, we found here several earthen ollas filled with human flesh, still cooking over the fire. The fleeing Xiximes had left a human heart roasting upon a spit over some coals. Several pairs of human eyes, extracted from their sockets, had been placed upon some husks of ears of maiz. A peeled skull and other parts of seletons hung from a pole in the center of the Plaza of the pueblo.

"Despite the rude reception given our first messenger, the Governor decided to send another to their principal Cacique, who ruled his people in the manner of a King. He insisted that this Xixime King should come personally to treat of terms for peace. Upon receiving this request the King, who was in a Council meeting, resolved to dismiss the Council and come to confer with the Governor. In the course of his visit he stated that the seventeen rancherias under his command had not yet broken the peace, although being much perturbed over the events that were taking place.

It was agreed between the Governor and this King that rather than all their people coming down from their Sierras, there should come only their principal Caciques, to discuss terms of peace. This offer on the part of the Governor so allayed the fears of the other Xiximes that presently they all came pouring down the mountainsides: men, women and children.

"A peace was agreed upon, after which all set happily to work building a large enramada of brush under which there could be held church services. Altars were built, crosses erected and all, Indians and Spaniards alike, held Mass here during the several days we remained.

"The Xiximes of the area of Xocotilma had secretly sent people to observe what had been taking place, and soon sent twenty of their principal leaders to negotiate. They offered to locate themselves wherever the Governor should instruct them, to build churches and to become Christians. This offer was accepted in good spirit, and my brother Padre and I agreed to accompany them to where they should form their new pueblos.

"Many of these Indians, some of them former Christians, came to us to kneel and kiss our hands, giving thanks for our intervention on their behalf. In conclusion of this letter, I am happy to say that peace has again been restored to the land of the Xiximes. They are now living contentedly in some sixty-five rancherias, altogether some 5,000 to 6,000 persons. All these people the Governor has left to the care of the Padres of our Company. In this manner was concluded this expedition."

[The Padre who writes this letter, although not identified, is believed to be Hernando de Santarén, then Superior of the Mission of Topia, who took in his charge the resettlement and conversion of the Xiximes, after their return to peace.]

The labor of Padre Hernando Santarén in this regard was favored by a particular event in its very beginning. Among the Xiximes there lived an Hechicero, a giant of a man, over eighty years of age, who was at once greatly feared and greatly respected by his people, being revered only second to the God who is ruler of earth and heaven.

It finally came to pass that this old Hechicero was taken with a very grave illness. Padre Hernando went at once to his bedside, to render whatever assistance were possible. At the same time that he was healing the body of this man, he was also occupied with healing his mind. He quietly recounted to the Indian the mysteries of our faith, telling especially of the one God and Creator of all things. This he discussed with particular emphasis, because he knew that the old man was a worshiper of idols and that, through his example, people of many pueblos continued to worship them also.

God so favored Padre Santarén in his task that, after listening attentively to his teaching, the old Indian destroyed his idols and accepted Christianity. His example was thereupon followed by many others. There were gathered many basketsfull of idols, which were burned in a great bonfire in the center of the Plaza.

Another Indian Hechicero kept an idol formed of a stone that was clear, like a crystal. He insisted that he had been counseled by this idol that, in order to insure a more bountiful harvest, he must undergo a fast, being restricted to a very scant fare of raw herbs and corn, as though he were not a man, but a horse. This practice of fasting as a form of penance was common among them. The Padres finally dissuaded them from carrying on such useless practices.

It was a marvel to see, as the years passed, how the Padres so gained the confidence of these former cannibals that they could travel freely and safely from one mountain village to another, without escort except that necessary to protect them from the bands of marauding timber wolves that are a constant menace to travelers in those Sierras.

In the course of the years the prohibition against cannibalism came to be enforced by the Indian Nations upon themselves, they searching out and delivering to the Spanish authorities for punishment any of their number who should violate their new code of conduct.

With the return of peace, travel was much increased between the Indian pueblos, and along the rivers, including that of the 360 crossings, which flows down through the Valley of Topia to the ancient pueblo of Culiacan. One old Indian who lived along the banks of this river, in his joy over this new freedom in traveling, decided that to provide food for travelers he would seed the borders of the river, which he did for a distance of thirty miles, from his native village of Guejupa to Otatitlán. So many calabazas did he grow that travelers could scarce eat them all.

By order of the Viceroy, a Fort was constructed at San Hipólito, where were garrisoned ten Spanish soldiers with armored horses, under the command of a Captain. This Fort was 180 miles distant from the seat of government at Guadiana.

Churches of a permanent nature were built in all the pueblos, often ornamented with wood carvings beautifully done by the Indians themselves, with only the aid of a small knife. These same Xiximes, in the days of their barbarism had composed in their language a manner of poem, or refrain, which said that the flesh of an Indian was only ordinary, like that of a steer; that the flesh of a Negro was of the taste of pork, but that the flesh of a Spaniard was as truly delicious as that of the wild sheep of their mountains. Yet these same savages, eaters of human flesh, now come regularly to Mass, and there has been introduced among them a faith as strong as that of any of the Indian Nations. Theirs is a faith born of the heart, and there exists a bond of friendship between them and their spiritual fathers such as can scarcely be imagined.

CHAPTER 7

The Tepeguane Nation

THE TEPEGUANE NATION of the great Sierras, although less numerous than some about whom we have written, were fierce and daring enough to perpetrate great cruelties upon the Spaniards and their Indian allies.

In fact, the name "Tepeguane" signifies being of the hardness of rock, and was no doubt derived from the nature of these people. Before the Spaniards and Padres came, they lived in numerous rancherias in the higher Sierras, later most of them being moved to pueblos located along the courses of streams that flowed through the Valleys of San Andrés and Topia.

On their western borders lived the Acaxee and Xixime Nations and, still further westward, other Indian Nations, until arriving at the Province of Sinaloa.

The first Tepeguane pueblo, Santiago Papasquiaro, lies ninety miles westward of Guadiana, and 600 miles in a northwesterly direction from the City of Mexico.

The first motive for entry of the Spaniards into these, as into the other Sierras, was to search for silver, many rich deposits being found here. Besides the much famed Reales of Mines of Guanaceví and Indehe there have recently been discovered the very rich mines of Parral, where there are now (*1644*) many Spaniards working. [*Parral is still one of the richest mining areas of Mexico, in 1967.*]

The land of the Tepeguanes is also attractive to the Spaniards for certain beautiful and spacious pastures suitable for the grazing of cattle, horses and mares.

The settlement of the Reales of Mines and the cattle ranches was without offense to the Tepeguanes living there, rather it was of much benefit to them, for the work it provided and for the opportunity for the Tepeguanes to stock cattle and horses for themselves.

Although the Spaniards entered into this country in peace, they soon found themselves obligated to carry arms and to be always prepared to defend themselves against the savagery of the Indians. They tried by every means possible to avoid war with the Indian Nations, but these were very much inclined to be warlike and savage. The Tepeguanes were particularly inclined to make forays against their neighbors the Acaxees and Tarahumaras, who had finally become so intimidated by them that even a small band of Tepeguanes could, without opposition, enter their pueblos and rob them of their women.

Their manner of making war was with bows, arrows, war clubs and lances, in the same manner as other Nations we have mentioned. However, after securing horses from the Spaniards, they became most dexterous riders, firing their arrows while riding at full speed on their horses, or charging on horseback with long lances.

They even managed to secure some arquebuses from the Spaniards, either by purchase or in raids upon them, but these were of little use to them, because the Spaniards wisely refused to sell them powder.

The Tepeguanes were tillers of the soil, living as did their Indian neighbors, from maiz, beans, pumpkins and other lesser crops. They were persistent hunters of game, especially of deer and peccary, although they also hunted smaller animals, and various kinds of birds.

They dressed much as other Nations we have described, in garments of cotton, or of sisal fiber, which was more common to them.

Their houses are usually of logs from the woods, but some are of rock set with mortar of earth. These houses are built near rivers or springs, of which many run through their lands.

The fierceness of character of these people was such as to discourage even the most hardy from venturing into their lands. However, after much discussion, the Padres in residence in Guadiana resolved that one among their number should risk his life in this precarious undertaking. This good fortune fell to the lot of Padre Gerónimo Ramirez.

Padre Gerónimo entered upon his task without the company of any other Padre, nor escort of soldiers, trusting only in divine protection.

He first visited the Real of Mines of Sauceda, which borders the lands of the Tepeguanes. Here he found some of them laboring in the mines, and became friendly with them. He soon had many people coming to him to study the Christian doctrine.

At Easter season the Padre organized a large celebration, with the participation of both Spaniards and Indians, including many Tarascos who had come from Michoacán to work in the mines. During the celebration of Corpus Christi there were staged dances of the several Christian Indian Nations, in which the Tepeguanes, although not yet Christians, were pleased to take part. In their dances the Tepeguanes covered their bodies with a sort of moss of the woods, which gave them the appearance of being covered with wool. In their hands they carried, elevated, the horns of a stag, simulating its movements while dancing. [*Another version of the famous Baile del Venado of the Yaqui and Mayo Nations.*]

Heartened by the interest of the Tepeguanes of Sauceda, Padre Gerónimo, accompanied by some members of their Tribe, began to visit their nearer rancherias, being everywhere given a warm welcome. One hardened old man did cause him much trouble, shouting indignantly that he would not consider becoming a Christian and insisting that baptism by the Padres would be no more effective for the salvation of his soul than the frequent baths he accustomed taking in the river. The Padre responded most sternly that, despite all his baths in the river, if he refused to become a Christian, he would be devoured in the flames of the infernal regions.

The old savage retorted that he was immortal and would never die, departing with derisive laughter. However, on the very day following, the old man came to the Padre, bleeding badly, his flesh having been torn almost into ribbons, evidently by some wild animal. Now very pentinent, he exclaimed to the crowd that had gathered, "I know now, Padre, that I am as mortal as others. The devil has deceived me, causing me to believe that I shall never die. If God may still choose to save me, I beg that I may soon be baptized, and assured the saving of my soul." At once saddened and overjoyed, the Padre embraced this old man, attended to his physical needs, and later took much pains to teach him our saintly faith.

One Sabbath morning there came to visit the Padre at Sauceda, a young maiden who had that day traveled twenty miles with her parents. She asked of the Padre that she be baptized and, much to his surprise, made no least error in her examination. Accepting the invitation of this family, the Padre traveled to their village, which lay in a beautiful valley through which winds a little river. In the course of time the Padre converted many of the Indians of this valley and finally founded the pueblo that was named Papasquiaro. [*Not to be confused with Santiago Papasquiaro.*] This pueblo soon became a principal cross roads to many mines of the Sierras.

From here Padre Gerónimo, accompanied by twenty friendly Tepeguane warriors of bow and arrow, paid a visit to another rancheria some twenty miles down river, where he founded another Mission, which was named Santa Catarina.

In the course of time Padre Gerónimo Ramirez was given an assistant, and between them they ventured ever further into the land of the Tepeguanes.

For forty years a certain witch doctor had controlled the Tepeguanes through creating in them a great fear of a little idol. This idol he kept always well concealed, saying that death would come to any who should so much as

179

gaze upon it. Padre Gerónimo sought out this old man, spending two full days in his company, while describing to him most painstakingly the mysteries of our faith. On the evening of the day of Saint John the Baptist this famous man, persuaded by Padre Gerónimo, entered the church and, before all the congregation assembled, renounced his idol in favor of the one and only true God. Following the service, the old man, accompanied by Padre Gerónimo and many of the congregation went to his house and, bringing forth the idol, handed it to the Padre.

The Padre unwrapped it, throwing it to the ground and kicking it with his foot, to indicate that it was of no merit nor importance. At this all the Indians, including the old witch doctor, were extremely alarmed, fearing for the fate of themselves as much as that of Padre Gerónimo. When moments passed and nothing hapened, their fears abated and they, too, showed their disdain by taking turns at kicking the idol about.

This idol was of a stone similar to jasper, and only of the size of an apple. It had apparently been covered with several layers of skin from human heads. The old Indian later related to the Padre that one day, when he was yet a young man, and was seated among a group of people, this little stone had come rolling to his feet, a voice that seemed to emanate from it saying that he must preserve this stone, for it would bring him powers such as that of curing diseases, or of protection in times of peril. Later he had found that it seemed also to have the power to prophesy events to come. Before the opening of a war between his people and neighboring tribes, it would become stained with blood. At certain times the stone would disappear, but would always return.

The old Indian had not been altogether happy in the possession of this stone idol, for through exceeding association with it his soul had been tortured by the Devil until he had become exhausted. Although much happier after being relieved of its possession, there yet remained in him a fear that harm from the Devil might come to him. Finally, in order to free him of this fear, Padre Gerónimo placed an image of Saint Toríbio about his neck, after which he was contented. The conversion of this important Indian was only one of many of the fruits of the dedicated labor of Padre Gerónimo Ramirez.

While at Santa Catarina, one of the Padres was invited to visit a place called Zape, which is situated on a river which flows along the base of a high peak. There were found here the ruins of many ancient habitations, showing it to have been a place of much importance in the early history of these people. Many stone idols and other figures are to be found here.

From the relics found, it was concluded by the Padres that this had been one of the places where there had lived the ancient Mexican Nation, during the period of its peregrination from the far north, for these are the same manner of idols as those found in the valley of the Great Lagoon bordering the City of Mexico, which was later peopled by this Nation. On the peak above the river, at the ancient pueblo of Zape, there were found not only idols, but high stone columns and other artifacts of these ancient people.

This valley and river being very conveniently situated and having fertile soil, there was founded here the new pueblo of Zape, its inhabitants being drawn from the nearby mountainous areas.

Not long after the founding of this pueblo there came a great sickness, causing the death of large numbers of the population. The Hechiceros who yet remained among the people preached that in order to save the adult population from this sickness, it was necessary that there should be sacrificed some of their younger children. It took the most persistent effort on the part of the Padres to dissuade the Indians from continuing this horrible practice.

Upon plea of the Padre Rector at Guadiana to Mexico City, there were sent several more ministers, to attend the needs of these people so widely scattered, there coming as Superior of the Mission, Padre Juan Fonte, of whom much is told in this story.

Substantial churches were erected in the Tepeguane pueblos. Many men and women were married in the Christian manner, this being less of a problem than in other Nations, as they seldom had more than one wife, nor were they dissolute in other ways.

Their belief in idolatry and witchcraft was much more firmly rooted and difficult to remove. In one pueblo the Tepeguanes persisted in their worship of a stone idol in the form of a column about four feet in height, with the top carved into the figure of a human face. This idol was located on the crest of a small hill. About it were placed offerings of arrows, bones of animals, pottery ollas, various herbs which they use, strings of beads and other items which they esteem. A smaller idol, made from a sea shell, was placed near the larger one.

Awaiting a day when large numbers of Indians were coming for baptism, the Padre first took them to the hill on which this idol stood, explaining that it must be renounced by them before they could be baptized. Thereupon, the principal Cacique of the pueblo, a baptized Christian, uprooted the idol, rolling it down from its hilltop, to become buried in the waters of the river below.

On that same day, after the church services were over the congregation carried a large cross to be placed on the same prominence that had been occupied by the idol. After adorning this cross with flowers all the Indians marched down the hill while chanting the Apostles Creed in their own language.

I shall here describe the first celebration of Holy Week in Atotonilco, which lies in the same valley. In addition to the Indians, the Padre had invited the Spaniards from all the neighboring estancias. In the evenings many took part in the processions of discipline, the Indian women carrying torches of pine, which give a much brighter illumination than candles.

This pueblo being so near to the borders of other savage Nations, the procession was accompanied by an escort of soldiers with loaded arquebuses, as well as two groups of Christian Indians with bow and arrow. These same escorts divided into watches which guarded the church during each night of Holy Week.

It gave much comfort to see so many Indian warriors arrive, on Holy Friday, to kneel before the Saintly Cross. On the morning of the Resurrection, all attended the procession, some carrying garlands of flowers or wreaths made from green branches, while others carried lighted candles. Marching was to the music of trumpets played by Indian musicians. Later there was dancing by the representatives of the various Indian Tribes that had been invited. Dressed in white, the catechumens who had been prepared for baptism marched in procession. Their heads, however, were adorned with bright feathers, as in the ceremonial dress of the Indians. With their baptism the celebration was concluded.

CHAPTER 8

The Tarahumara Nation

NORTHWARD of the Tepeguanes for a distance of 300 miles the Sierras are populated by the Tarahumaras, a Nation very much more populous than the Tepeguanes. These two Nations were constantly at war with each other.

Soon after the conversion of the Tepeguanes, another such war threatened. The Tepeguanes from Valle del Águila, bordering the Tarahumaras, being in the most imminent peril, sent urgent messages to the other pueblos pleading for assistance.

Ordinarily this appeal would have met with quick response; however, many of the Tepeguanes were now become Christians, and had been indoctrinated in the ways of peace. They concluded that before acting they should send one of their principal Christian Caciques to Padre Juan Fonte, Superior of the Tepeguane Mission, with the suggestion that he attempt to act as mediator in the trouble between the Nations. This office the Padre fulfilled with such success that he won the esteem and respect of both contending factions.

With this auspicious beginning, Padre Juan began to visit among the Tarahumara villages in order to acquaint the people with the fundamental principles of Christianity. His teaching was very generally accepted. He did meet with violent opposition from one witch doctor. This ferocious old man, with a band of ten warriors, murdered a Tarahumara Cacique from the pueblo of San Pablo, who was being indoctrinated for baptism.

The relatives of the murdered Cacique were restless to avenge this murder. However, a promise was secured from them by Padre Fonte to maintain peace while a messenger carried their grievance to the Governor at Guadiana.

The messenger arrived at the very moment that the Governor was departing for the chastisement of the Xiximes. Happily, as the Governor was pondering what action to take, the rebellious old witch doctor came of his own will to surrender and make peace with the Governor. He plead for forgiveness of his impetuosity and begged to be permitted to study to become a Christian. His wish was granted, he became converted, was pardoned, and from that day became a Christian leader of renown among his people.

Among the accomplishments of this reformed rebel was the diversion of water from the streams, under the direction of Padre Juan Fonte, for the irrigation of fertile areas for cultivation of their crops. The pueblo of San Pablo being adjacent to the land of the Tarahumaras, many of these came to visit. Soon Padre Juan Fonte too, was visiting freely among their villages. Padre Fonte writes:

"At the close of the rainy season, which comes in summer, I undertook my first journey into the unknown lands of the Tarahumaras. Accompanying me were four Caciques of their Nation, together with some of their followers. Of all who came with us, only two were Christians.

"From the pueblo of San Pablo we rode fifty miles north through the Sierras, over trails that were not too difficult, although from here the way is said to be so steep that it is impossible to traverse on animals.

"We found many of the Tarahumaras living in caves, some of these being capacious enough for the living of several families. Often they built rock walls within these caves to separate their dwellings.

"Tarahumara women clothe themselves with sisal fiber woven into mantles, which are shaped to cover separately the upper and lower portions of their bodies. They are very modest and withdrawn, and do not accustom sitting among or mingling with their men.

"In the manner of burial of their dead they differ from other Nations. They have places reserved for burial in the same form as in a Christian cemetery. With the dead are buried all the things they are accustomed to use while living and, in addition, food that is supposed to serve them while on their journey into another world. The house of a dead person is burned, or completely torn down, and the timbers removed to another location. As evidence of their grief, the relatives cut their long tresses, which they so much esteem that no greater sacrifice could well be made.

[*This practice of burning the abode of the dead is still practiced by the Cocópah and Kilihua Indian Tribes of the desert and Sierras of the northern area of Baja California. Arthur W. North, in "Camp and Camino in Lower California" (1907) makes the interesting observation that the Kilihuas are the Indians of greatest stature on the North American Continent, commonly being several inches over six feet in height, and often weighing over 250 pounds.*]

"The nature of the Tarahumaras is more docile than that of the Tepeguanes. I was received everywhere among them with affection, they sending runners several miles ahead of us to advise their people of my coming. On arriving at their pueblos, men, women and children would form in lines to meet me. The first greeting in each pueblo would be given by a principal Cacique, who would be dressed for the occasion with all the ornaments which they accustom, highlighted by a head dress of plumage of brilliant colors. One after another the lines of people would approach me, wishing that I should place my hand upon their heads and give them a blessing. After this ceremony, all would accompany me most courteously to the place that they had prepared for my rest.

"At each village I would talk to them in their language, expressing my gratitude at being invited to visit them in their own land, with this acknowledgment of their kindness dismissing myself from them for the time.

"I cannot describe the expressions of wonder, contentment and pleasure which I observed on their faces. Even the women, although at first very retiring, after observing the cordial manner in which I visited with their men, soon came to visit also, and in parting requested that I should soon return to visit them.

"Before departing from their lands I designated four principal Caciques among them to act as stewards for the purpose of inviting the people of the rancherias to assemble in groups large enough to begin to receive instruction in the Christian faith.

"We made a total count of 3,160 persons visited on this first journey.

"So solicitous have the Tarahumaras now become for my safety, that they have insisted on providing me with an escort of thirty of their warriors, who accompany me not only on journeys into their lands, but to more distant places such as the Real of Mines of Santa Barbara, which is peopled principally by Spaniards. I have found such sincerity and fidelity among them that I have now come to Guadiana to treat with the Governor of Nueve Vizcaya for further assistance in the ministry to these people."

Here concludes the letter of Padre Juan Fonte, referring to the very good disposition of the Tarahumara Nation towards the Padres and the Spaniards.

Unfortunately the plans so hopefully made by this fine man were delayed by the conflagration that was even then impending in the Tepeguane Nation, and which spread through other Indian Nations of the Sierras, costing the life of this venerable Padre, as well as that of many others. Of this tragic period we shall treat in the chapters that follow.

CHAPTER 9

The Great Rebellion in the Sierras

PART ONE: THE TEPEGUANES IN REVOLT

IN THE BEGINNING of the year of our Lord 1616 the Christian pueblos of the great Sierras of Topia were living in apparent contentment and peace. In the principal Tepeguane pueblo of Santiago Papasquiaro the people were as compliant in the practice of their faith as any Indian Nation of New Spain. There was a sightly church newly constructed, and a Seminary for the children. Fiestas were celebrated in great solemnity with the participation of the Indians in large numbers.

The new pueblo, well situated in a lovely valley, had become so attractive that several families of Spaniards had located either there or on estancias in nearby areas, where they employed numerous Indians in the cultivation of their fields and the care of their cattle and other livestock.

The Indians of the nearby pueblo of Santa Catarina, who had been of a particularly savage nature, had seemed to lose much of their ferocity.

Despite all this apparent progress, the Padres were from time to time disturbed by small evidences of unrest, finally giving notice to the Governor at Guadiana that all was not well with their congregations of Indians.

This feeling of unrest was very evident to me when, in the early fall of that year of 1616, I passed through the lands of the Tepeguanes on my way to Mexico City to plead before the Padre Provincial and the Viceroy of New Spain the urgency for sending a Mission into the land of the Yaquis. I received a disturbing impression of the aloofness of those savage people, and of the little evidence of their practice of Christianity.

Something of this concern I imparted to my good friend Padre Bernardo de Cisneros, who responded, "I cannot tell what Devil or idol has been raised among these people, that they are so changed and restless." Two months later this Padre, together with seven others, had died at the hands of those apostate Tepeguanes.

The Great Rebellion was stirred in the beginning by a famous Tepeguane witch doctor, who not only went about spreading dissension among his own people, but traveled to the lands of the Acaxees and Xiximes, many of whom already were Christians, inciting them to revolt. This old Hechicero was held in particular awe for being reputed to hold the power to change from one instant to another in the manner of his figure, as from the appearance of an old man to that of a boy. This man worshipped an idol of stone of but sixteen inches in height, which he carried everywhere with him. This idol was said to have the ability to speak to each Nation in its own tongue. The words of the idol the old Hechicero translated to his listeners in a most resplendent oratorical manner, which assisted him much in compelling people to do his will.

He was said to have carried a mirror-like crystal attached to his bare abdomen, this crystal being attributed with the faculty of speaking in any Indian language. It was said that the words spoken by this crystal mirror so resounded upon the ears and so impressed the minds of the listeners that they felt compelled to obey the mandates of this false prophet, whose words were in their main part directed toward opposition to the Church, the Padres and the Spaniards.

Among the Spaniards it was rumored that the demon which worked its evil through the mind and soul of this Indian was the same as one exorcized from the body of an ancient Indian woman who had once led a rebellion among the Guasave Nation of the Province of Sinaloa, as this demon, upon being ex-

185

pelled from the woman's body, had hurled threats of departing for a place from where it could do the Christian people much more harm than before.

With demoniacal intrigues and enchantments this old Hechicero continued to warp the minds and souls of his listeners. Together with his chief advisers, he plotted a simultaneous uprising of all the pueblos of the Sierras, with the plan of attacking at once the estancias, the Reales of Mines, and the churches in each pueblo, doing away with all the Spaniards, the Padres, and their Christian Indian followers.

This attack was planned for the time of the Festival of the Virgin, which in that year of 1616 was to have very special significance, because of there having been sent from Mexico City a beautiful Image of the Virgin, to adorn the church of the pueblo of Zape. The rebels considered that the Spaniards would all be away from their mines and estancias for the purpose of attending this festival, and that most of them would not be carrying arms while participating in this celebration.

The precise date fixed for the attack was the 21st day of November. However, the Indians of the village of Santa Catarina attacked before the date fixed, as shall be related. There had arrived at this pueblo, a trader with a pack train of mules carrying his goods. While resting his animals he had deposited these goods in the house of a friend. Accompanying the trader, for the sake of traveling in company, was Padre Hernando de Tobar, who was returning from the Villa of Culiacán to the Real of Mines of San Andrés, to where he had been directed on some matters intrusted to him by the Superior of the Missions.

The Indians, finding this opportunity to murder and rob the trader and the Padre, resolved to wait no longer. As Padre Hernando was mounting his mule to continue his journey, they fell upon him with savage fury. The Spaniard who accompanied the Padre mounted his horse and fled, shouting to Padre Hernando to follow. It was too late. Surrounded by his attackers, Padre Hernando had only time to exclaim, "If my hour is come, I accept with grace what God has willed." The infuriated Tepeguanes tore the Padre from his animal. The saintly man, with intrepid spirit, still strove to reason with them, but an Indian drove a lance through his chest and he immediately expired.

This tragic scene was witnessed by a Christian Indian who was present and who was, at the same time, captured and bound, but managed later to escape to carry the news of the uprising to the Governor at Guadiana. The Spanish trader fled to the pueblo of Atotonilco, where there soon gathered the Spaniards of the surrounding area. There arrived here, among others, the Friar Pedro Gutierrez, of the Seraphic Order of San Francisco, who chanced to be traveling that way. There soon congregated at Atotonilco altogether some 300 persons. They took refuge in the largest house of the pueblo.

On the day following, the savages who had given death to Padre Hernando de Tovar at Santa Catarina attacked at Atotonilco. Attired in all their gaudy paraphernalia of war, with great shouting and beating of their war drums, they charged repeatedly upon the house where the Spaniards had taken refuge. Soon they opened several holes in its roof and walls, through these openings firing multitudes of burning arrows. These had been smeared with the paste of a fiery red pepper which in Spain is called pimento. The smoke from this chile pepper is excruciatingly painful to the lungs and choked the defenders cruelly, causing many to die from suffocation. With the pitifully few weapons at their disposal, the remaining defenders climbed to the roof of the house to return the fire of the attackers. Finally their ammunition ran out, and they were compelled to surrender. No mercy was given. Even worse, these savages exercised the most extreme cruelties on men, women and children, while murdering them. Of 300 persons, only two escaped.

During the hours while awaiting attack, the good Friar Pedro Gutierrez had prepared the victims for their death. It seemed that God had sent him here for their consolation. When the savages had first arrived this saintly man, with crucifix in hand, went forth alone to plead with them for mercy. He was pierced by an arrow and immediately perished. Upon his death, the crucifix was taken from his hand by a young Spanish youth named Pablo Ignacio, of only fourteen years, who in company of this Padre had traveled all the distance from Mexico City to worship before the new image of the Virgin at Zape, this being an offering made by him for the recovery of his parents from an illness. This brave young man was also pierced with arrows as he stood holding aloft the crucifix over the body of his dead Padre.

One Spaniard, Lucas Benitez, escaped by concealing himself in the hollow of a wall in the building. The only other person who escaped was Cristobal Martinez de Hurdaide, son of the famous Captain General of the Province of Sinaloa, who had come in that same year to reside among the Tepeguane Nation. Observing among the attackers an Indian who had been his good friend, young Hurdaide appealed to him that his life be spared. This Indian, feigning especial indignation in order to deceive his companions, grasped the young man most roughly, exclaiming that this prisoner he intended to personally dispose of by drowning him in the river. In this manner separating Hurdaide from the others, he took him to a place where he could remain safely in hiding until night had fallen.

Through the good offices of this same Indian the two fugitives were brought together afterwards. They traveled, almost naked, in bitter cold, hiding by day, until arriving at Guadiana to give notice of the massacre.

On the same day of the massacre a group of Spaniards who had taken refuge at a rancheria called Guatimape, were attacked by a band of Tepeguanes. The attackers carried bows and arrows, lances of the wood of brazil, war clubs, axes, steel drills taken from the mines, and even a few arquebuses.

There were gathered altogether thirty Spaniards to defend this place. From the roof of the largest building of the estancia they returned the fire of the Indians. However, these attacked with such ferocity that they gained the roof of the building and set it on fire.

The defenders, many of them now wounded, were forced to descend again into the house to flee from the blaze, with steel bars breaking holes in the walls of the rooms of the building as the flames advanced upon them.

These desperate people were apparently doomed, when there occurred a miracle such as scarcely may be believed. There suddenly arose a great cloud of dust upon a road in the direction of Guadiana and the attackers, believing that a troop of Spanish cavalry was coming to the relief of the besieged, turned and fled. To the amazement of the defenders, there soon came galloping into the village a band of colts that had been turned into a nearby pasture and, guided peradventure by an angel, had taken it upon themselves to come galloping down that dusty road to join the horses of the Spaniards gathered there. In any event, these desperate people were spared their lives, and in good time were rescued by the arrival of the forces from Guadiana.

On that same night the principal rebel leaders held a council of war at a village some twelve miles distant from the principal pueblo of Santiago Papasquiaro. Padre Cisneros being advised of this meeting, persuaded a principal Christian Indian, don Francisco Campos, to attend, together with two others, in the hope of dissuading the savages from their plans.

Don Francisco was murdered, one of the others bringing this sad news to Padre Bernardo Cisneros.

That same night there came two friendly Indians, their faces thoroughly concealed, to warn the Lieutenant in charge of the garrison of Spanish soldiers at Santiago of the impending uprising. He at once ordered all the women and children moved into the church, which was substantially built of brick and stone. Soon 200 Tepeguanes, on foot and on horseback, attacked this pueblo. This attack took place on the 16th of November at noon. A message from the besieged reached the Governor at Guadiana on the 17th. He immediately assembled twenty six men, all that could be provided with armored horses, arquebuses and other equipment of war, and traveled by forced marches toward Santiago. At the head of this company rode Captain Martín Olivas, a wealthy mine owner of Topia, and a veteran of many skirmishes with the Indians of the frontier.

The 200 savages were soon joined by many others and their attacks continued. The refugees defended themselves all day Thursday, and that night, although many of their number were wounded.

By Friday more than 500 Indians had gathered from Santa Catarina and other places to join the attackers. They set fire to the entire pueblo, then made a fierce assault upon the church. The house of the Padres they set on fire with burning arrows, also setting fires against the walls of the church.

When the church finally was on the point of going up in flames an Indian named Miguel, whom many of the Spaniards had liked and trusted, shouted to the besieged that there were among the attackers many Christians, and that those wishing to escape could surrender to them with assurance of their lives being spared.

This lead to an exchange of messages, in which the defenders were assured that upon laying down their arms they would be permitted to depart for Guadiana in peace. There being no other recourse, the Spaniards and their families marched out of the church in procession, led by youthful Padre Diego de Orosco, carrying in his arms the reliquary and other ornaments of the church. Behind Padre Diego came Lieutenant Juan de Castilla, carrying an Image of the Saintly Mother, next followed by the women and children. Still simulating friendliness, various Tepeguanes came forward to kneel, in apparent adoration of the Virgin. Meanwhile, others removed the arquebuses from the hands of the few soldiers.

This procession continued to the cemetery, which lies below the church, facing the village Plaza. At this point Padre Diego, holding the Holy Sacrament in his hands, began to speak with kindness to these savages. His words really seemed to be making a favorable impression upon them when suddenly, from the multitude gathered there arose a voice, shouting that the God of the Christians was not their God, and urging them to renounce the Padres and do away with them. This angry tirade put the Indians into a frenzy and they were soon attacking the helpless prisoners. The Images of our Holy Mother and Our Savior they trampled into the earth. All of the Spaniards were murdered, except for three who escaped.

Their fury was turned particularly upon the young Padre Diego de Orosco, who was seized and raised high into the air by some savages while others, in derision, recited words from the Holy Scripture which they had learned from him at Mass. Thus he was held exposed, until an arrow pierced his body. In his dying moments they yet mocked him by holding his body suspended in the form of a cross. Finally, he was felled by a savage blow from an ax.

At the moment of his dying, this brave young man exclaimed to his tormentors, "Do as you will; I am in the hands of my God."

Padre Bernardo de Cisneros, with whom I had so recently visited, they murdered by thrusting him through with a lance, at the same instant striking his head with one of their wicked war clubs, so that he quickly expired. After murdering these Padres and the other Spaniards, this horde of savages stripped them of their clothing, then mutilated their dead bodies, going into a frenzied and barbarous celebration of their triumph.

The three Spaniards who managed to escape this massacre, after hiding in a nearby forest until midnight, agreed that one of them should take the word of the massacre to Guadiana, the other two going to Sauceda. Fortunately, they were all familiar with the terrain and were able to travel by night, through gorges and over mountains distant from the routes used by the savages. The two traveling toward Sauceda met Captain Martín de Olivas and his little force, which had come too late to rescue the people there. Upon hearing the news of the massacre at Santiago Papasquiaro, and learning of the great number of the enemy, the Captain decided to return to Sauceda. Here his troops, and other Spaniards who had gathered, fortified themselves as best they could, gathering water and provision to withstand a siege. The Captain from here dispached a messenger to Governor Albear at Guadiana, pleading for reinforcements.

The Padre Rector of our Company had come from Guadiana with Captain Olivas to determine what he might do to assist under such adverse circumstances. No sooner had all gathered at Sauceda than the enemy was upon them. In order to better protect the families, Captain Olivas and his troops issued at intervals from their barricades, to battle the enemy in the open; the veteran Captain seeking by such tactics to delay the attackers until help should arrive. The enemy, constantly reinforced by savages from other areas, four times attacked the defenses of the Spaniards, but each time were driven off by the stubborn defense of the Spanish soldiers, who made very effective use of their arquebuses.

Another veteran Indian fighter, Captain Gordejuela, owner of a rich estancia near Guadiana, had hurriedly equipped a goodly number of soldiers at his own expense, and it was he who first arrived to relieve Sauceda. Assisted by the soldiers besieged there, he routed the attacking Indians. Other Spaniards from Guadiana soon arrived, there gathering a sufficient force so that they began to make forays against the enemy. For six weeks Captains Olivas and Gordejuela carried out raids with their forces, often attacking in surprise manuevers carried on at dawn, after traveling over mountain trails all during the night. The enemy, finding no easy means of victory, as they had anticipated, became discouraged and began to disperse in groups into the Sierras from whence they had come. Meanwhile, the refugee Spanish families from the area of Sauceda had been sent under escort to Guadiana.

On the same day of the massacre of Santiago Papasquiaro, another band of Tepeguanes undertook the destruction of Zape, a pueblo which now carries the name of San Ignacio. [*In 1967 it carries the original name of Zape.*]

While the people were gathered in the church at Zape for the celebration we have referred to, a great force of Indians suddenly set upon them and, with such cruelties as only Satan could conceive, took the lives of all.

In this attack perished Padres Juan del Valle and Luis de Alvarez.

On the day following the Padre Superior, Juan Fonte, and Padre Gerónimo de Moranta were riding along the trail toward Zape on their mules, innocent of what had taken place, when they were fallen upon and murdered. It seemed incredible to us who knew of the tremendous labor among these people of the venerable Padre Juan Fonte, over a period of sixteen years, and of his warm friendship and loving care of them, that not even his life should have been spared.

Of all the Spaniards gathered at Zape, only one escaped to carry the sad news to Guanaceví. Don Juan de Albear, principal Alcalde of that place, quickly departed for Zape with twelve soldiers to determine what had happened. Entering the ravaged pueblo on a night of bright moonlight, they found themselves surrounded by corpses, all stripped of their clothing and dreadfully mutilated. Within the church they could discern others, although they did not venture to dismount from their horses.

As they rode through the pueblo, they shouted into the night, in the hope that some Spaniards might have escaped and still be hiding, but heard no answer. Being too few in number to resist an attack or to pursue the enemy, they returned toward Guanaceví. Their enemies caught up with them on their return journey. Some of these pursuers were on foot, others were by now riding horses they had captured from the Spaniards. Some of the enemy Indians had committed the blasphemy of wearing the vestments and hoods of the Padres they had murdered.

Although constantly harassed by these hordes of savages, the twelve soldiers on their armored horses retreated in good order, halting at intervals to keep their pursuers out of range by firing volleys into them from their arquebuses.

Although several of the twelve were wounded, they returned to Guanaceví without loss of one of their number. During the retreat the horse of the Alcalde had been shot from under him, his life being saved by a faithful Indian who, dismounting from his own horse, insisted that it be ridden by the Alcalde.

This act of extreme loyalty came near to costing this Indian his life, for he was sorely wounded by arrows of the pursuers, and left for dead. However, he survived, arrived at Guanaceví late the following day and eventually recovered.

Spaniards and faithful Indians to the number of 500 persons gathered at Guanaceví. All who had arms took part in the defense of this Real of Mines. The rebels attacked in force, but were repulsed.

From here the savages turned to other mines and estancias, burning and destroying everything before them. And to such a sad end came the solemn and joyful feast that was to have been celebrated at the picturesque little pueblo of Zape on that tragic day of the 21st of November of 1616.

In conclusion of this chapter I wish to relate some of the circumstances surrounding the death during this rebellion of the very illustrious Padre Hernando de Santarén who, during the later years of his notable labors among the Indians, was minister to the Xixime Nation. The Padres preparing the celebration at Zape, upon learning that this venerable Padre was coming from Culiacán to the Capital City of Guadiana on matters of the Holy Obedience, sent him an urgent invitation to honor them with his presence at Zape. This invitation was gratefully accepted.

His aged friend, the Padre Andrés Tutino, meanwhile had heard such disquieting rumors that he despached messengers to intercept the Padre. None of these succeeded in overtaking him.

Padre Santarén halted at the Tepeguane pueblo of Tenerapa, innocent of what was happening. Wishing to hold Mass, as is accustomed by Padres upon passing through a pueblo where there is no minister in residence, he alighted from his animal, intending to search for the church steward, that the bells might be rung to announce his coming.

Upon looking more closely about, he found that the church had been terribly profaned, the altar destroyed, and the images hauled about and disfigured. Realizing the danger to him in this place, he immediately went outside to mount his horse. At that moment hordes of savages converged upon him from every side. He managed to ride as far as a nearby arroyo, where the savages surrounded him, dragging him from his horse, to tear him to pieces.

The venerable old man spoke to them in their own language, asking what harm he had ever done to them. The savages answered that he had done none, except by being a priest who wished to change them from their ancient manner of living. And in this manner, while invoking the sweet name of his Saviour, the blessed Padre Hernando de Santarén was murdered.

The story of his last moments was later related by some Tepeguane women who had loved and respected him and lamented his death. They, being much less cruel than their husbands, gathered his remains, to be preserved until the Spaniards should come to recover them.

One of the messages intended for Padre Santarén was, most fortunately, received by Padre Andrés Lopez at the moment of his departure for Zape. Padre Andrés rode instead to the Real of Mines of Indehe, where he found gathered some thirty Spaniards, preparing to defend themselves in the strongest house of the place. These Spaniards had twenty arquebuses among them and were successful in resisting attack until Governor Albear came to their rescue.

PART TWO: CAPTAIN BARTOLOMÉ JUAREZ MARCHES AGAINST THE ACAXEES AND XIXIMES

THE SPARK ignited by the rebellion of the Tepeguanes spread so quickly to other Indian Nations that even Guadiana, the Capital of the extended Province of Nueva Vizcaya, was for a time imperiled. The veteran Padre Andrés Tutino, then minister to the Acaxee Nation, in an effort to quiet them, undertook a visit to the rancherias and pueblos under his care.

At a pueblo adjacent to the land of the Tepeguanes he found that two Acaxee Hechiceros, even though they had been baptized, were engaged in sowing seeds of dissension among his previously faithful followers.

These treacherous Indians were known as don Pedro and Juan Gordo. This latter Indian went about preaching of another life which a principal Tepeguane witch doctor had described to him, and which this Tepeguane claimed to already have lived. Among other illusions, was the promise that any warriors that might be killed in fighting against the Spaniards would be returned to life again within a very few days. The Acaxees were being urged to join in the proposed attack of the Tepeguanes on the principal pueblo of Santiago Papasquiaro.

Padre Tutino sent an urgent message to his old friend, the veteran Indian fighter Captain Bartolomé Juarez, in command of the Presidio of San Hipólito, warning him of the peril impending.

Captain Juarez immediately set out with his troops for Coapa, distant 150 miles, where was Padre Tutino, arriving there in a forced march of two long days.

Simultaneously there arrived at Coapa Padre Pedro de Graviña, minister to the Xiximes, with notice of disturbances among his people.

After a brief conference, Captain Juarez rode rapidly to the nearest of the pueblos threatening revolt, accompanied by the Padres. Arriving at midnight

"The Sierras of Topia are of extreme height and of profound depth, altogether the most spectacular of all the Occidental Indies, if not of the entire New World."

"As I traversed their limitless cordilleras, and descended into their deep gorges I marveled that even savages could penetrate here . . . I reflected that the Devil must have deliberately led these people into such hiding places, thinking to thus possess them securely . . ."

From letter of Padre Juan Fonte, written in the early 1600's, "We found many of the Tarahumaras living in caves, some of these being capacious enough for several families."

Tarahumara Indian said to be 103 years of age, with wife of 85 years. This couple lived in the cave shown in previous picture. The wife planted corn on nearby hillsides for their sustenance. This rugged life would appear to be favorable to longevity.

"Northward of the Tepeguane Nation for a distance of 300 miles the Sierras are populated by the Tarahumaras, a Nation much more populous than the Tepeguanes." Tarahumara youth in typical garb, with his mountain pony. The Tarahumaras often wear a white or red band about their foreheads.

". . . there yet remains to tell of other Indian Nations who lived in the shadow and peril of death eternal . . . these Nations lived upon vast arid plains."

Don Anastácio Carreón, of the Chichimeca Indian Nation, with his Tepeguane Indian wife, doña Maria de la Paz. Don Anastácio was in the cavalry of the famous guerrilla chieftain Pancho Villa during the "Mexican Revolution", his wife Maria accompanying him on horseback during several campaigns.

"In the year 1621, King Felipe III instructed the Archbishop of Mexico, don Juan de la Serna, to place the Curate of Tepozotlán in the land of the Otomis near the City of Mexico, into the hands of our Company." Church of San Xavier, of the group of church buildings at Tepozotlán.

View of a portion of the Valley of Mexico, looking toward the legendary Sleeping Beauty, or Ixtlacihuatl.

they caught the inhabitants completely by surprise. Feigning pleasure over this visit, they quickly gathered to form a procession of welcome, carrying lighted torches in their hands.

After seizing the initiative in this move, the Captain sent messengers to all the neighboring pueblos convoking their people to a meeting. When they had gathered together, he spoke to them most forcefully in their own language, ordering them to return quietly to their pueblos and to assist in maintaining peace. Returning then to Coapa with Padres Tutino and Graviña, he requested them to summon all their congregation to Mass. When the Mass was concluded he ordered the people to be gathered together. After delivering a very stern sermon to them all, he arrested the principal agitators among the Indians, including don Pedro and Juan Gordo. These two he hanged, pardoning the others, but with a strict admonition that should they continue their plotting they would share the same fate.

Not many days after the hanging of these two Acaxees, a band of Xiximes, accompanied by some Tepeguanes, fell upon three pueblos of Christian Xiximes, expecting to capture there Padres Pedro de Graviña and Juan de Mallen, who had meanwhile taken refuge in the Presidio of San Hipólito.

Infuriated at not finding the Padres, they set fire to the churches. They were, however, soon routed by faithful Xixime Christians who had gathered. These captured many rebels and, despite their being of the same nation, their heads were severed from their bodies to be taken to Captain Juarez at San Hipólito in proof of the fidelity of the Christian Xiximes. Only the falling of heavy snows at this time prevented the Christian Xiximes from completely defeating the rebel Xiximes and Tepeguanes.

During the desperate days of this great rebellion there were repeated proofs of the constancy in their faith of the Indian disciples of the venerable Padre Hernando de Santarén, who had been the spiritual leader and counselor of both Indians and Spaniards, not only throughout those Sierras, but far beyond, into the Provinces of Culiacán and Sinaloa. Padres and Spaniards alike expressed their gratitude for the steadfastness of faith and the courage in danger of the disciples of the martyred Padre Santarén.

During this critical period the Spanish authorities urged the Padres remaining in the Sierras to temporarily desist from their labors and retire to the security of the larger pueblos. This the Padres of the Company would not do; rather they labored yet more persistently, inspired by the thought that in so doing they were more deeply dedicating their lives to their God.

I have at hand, as I write these many years later, various letters written by friends who were serving in those Missions during those trying days. I shall quote only one, from the pen of the veteran Padre Andrés Tutino, who labored among those primitive people for forty years.

"I give thanks to God to be permitted to serve here at this most trying time. I have never been more fruitfully employed since coming to the Indies. As my own sins have been so many, I doubt being granted the privilege of such a glorious death as my brothers who have been martyred, but at least I live much comforted by the sweet memory of those of our brothers who so gloriously shed their blood here. Blessed are they, and those who may follow them, with such divine favor."

It is merited also to quote from a letter written by the valient Captain Bartolomé Juarez, at a time when, with only a handful of soldiers, he found himself surrounded by hordes of those hostile savages. He writes:

"Padre Andrés Gonzales, Superior to this Mission, and I are, together with a few soldiers, barricaded at the little Indian pueblo of Las Vegas. Although the Indians are quiet here for the moment, we have little hope that peace can be maintained and each night expect that we may be massacred.

"If it be the will of our Lord that we die here, then our lives may be no better employed, and we shall follow the worthy example of our martyred Padres who have died before us."

The Tepeguanes had erected a shrine in a remote spot to which they would come, as to an oracle, to ask for prophesies as to future successes in battle.

As the promises of early success did not come true, nor were their comrades returned to life after being slain in battle, they turned upon this oracle to air their grievances. The only response they received was that they must carry on the war with still greater fury, or else be doomed. No further advice would it give them about their war against the Crown and the Padres.

At the Real of Topia the ministers were Padres Juan Acacio and Juan Alvarez. The Alcalde Mayor, don Sebastián de Albear, upon learning of the rebellion, had fortified the church and the area of the Plaza surrounding it, building here three large towers (torreones) for better defense. The garrison of Topia consisted of sixty soldiers with armor and armored horses, equipped with arquebuses.

Being short of powder, as were the beleaguered forces everywhere, some of the soldiers ventured through the enemy forces surrounding them, to Guadiana; returning with several sacks of powder which they had packed on horses.

Two bands of Acaxees, together with confederates of the Tepeguanes, had been designated to attack the Real of Mines of Topia. The date set for this attack was the 6th of January, the Day of Kings. However, the garrison by this date had been so well reinforced and so well prepared for defense, that the enemy did not dare attack, marching rather in the direction of the newer pueblos of Tecuchuapa and Carantapa, bordering on the Province of Sinaloa.

During these trying days the intrepid Captain General don Diego Martinez de Hurdaide had been most active in insuring that the many Nations of Sinaloa should remain at peace. He had persuaded the Padre Visitador of Missions to induce Padres Diego de Acevedo and Gaspár de Navara, resident ministers in the two border pueblos above mentioned, to retire for a time to the Villa of Sinaloa.

This action was well taken, for the Tepeguanes did persuade many of the Indians along the border of Sinaloa to join in the attack on Papasquiaro. However, the Christian Indians of Techuchuapa and Carantapa did not join in the revolt and presently the two Padres returned to their charges, although accompanied by an escort of six soldiers. There was constructed a small Presidio, to which the people of both pueblos could retire in order to better defend themselves.

Captain Hurdaide arrived soon after and organized a force of 120 well equipped warriors from among the Indians of Tecuchuapa and Carantapa. These fell upon a band of the rebellious Tepeguanes, killing many and bringing their heads to the Captain in proof of their victory. This initiative on the part of Captain Hurdaide discouraged the Tepeguanes from further incursions towards Sinaloa, which, had they been carried out successfully, could easily have incited the entire Province to rebellion, and might have led to the defeat and annihilation of the Spaniards of all the Northwest Provinces of New Spain. Most fortunately the great rebellion in the Sierras had come at a time when a peace had been negotiated between the Captain and the belicose Yaqui Nation, and plans were then being made for the indoctrination of the Yaquis, a project which it fell to my lot to undertake, as has before been written.

PART THREE: GOVERNOR GASPÁR DE ALBEAR CARRIES THE WAR TO THE ENEMY

GUADIANA, the Capital of Nueva Vizcaya, was saved from destruction by the Indians only by a particular providence of God.

The Tepeguanes had invited the Indians of the pueblo of El Tunal, only six miles from Guadiana, to join them in a surprise attack against the city. These agreed and set themselves diligently to gathering arms, even including arquebuses, planning to infiltrate in small numbers, to fall upon the unsuspecting Spaniards.

However, the attack at Santa Catarina, coming several days in advance of the date set for the general uprising, served as a warning to Governor Albear who at once set to work fortifying and provisioning the city.

Ironically, the Indians from the nearby pueblo of El Tunal were requisitioned to assist in these preparations for defense. While passing along a street where some of these Indians were erecting barricades, a priest from the Hospital of San Juan de Dios overheard one of the workers from El Tunal say, "You may hurry us today, but tomorrow will be a different story."

This remark being reported to the Governor, he had these Indians detained and questioned.

The Indians confessed that they had been holding war councils, disguising these by the pretense of their being Indian fiestas. They told that the playing of trumpets at these fiestas was in fact to teach them the trumpet calls that would be used when they should go to war. They further confessed that a certain Chief among them had been selected to be their King. This man kept concealed in his house a crown of feathers of rich and brilliant plumage, to be worn when he should rule the Province of Nueva Vizcaya upon the defeat of the Spaniards. As the plot unfolded, sixty of the principal Indians of El Tunal were proven culpable and were hanged from various trees at the entrances to the city.

Troops of soldiers were placed at the four principal gates. To add to his forces, the Governor issued a pardon to those prisoners of the jail who chose to assist in the defense of the city.

The women and children were gathered into the shelter of the Church of the Company of Jesus or of the Convent of San Francisco.

At the outset of the rebellion the Governor dispached couriers in all haste, to apprise the Viceroy in the City of Mexico. The Viceroy ordered a levy of men to be made from the Real of Mines of Zacatecas, nearest place of any considerable population to Guadiana. He also ordered that money be given from the Royal Coffers there, to defray the expenses of a campaign. It was my privilege to take part in the initial conferences held during those days by the Viceroy, to determine the measures to be taken.

The Tepeguanes that had perpetrated the massacre at Papasquiaro penetrated to within thirty miles of Guadiana. However, their principal leader, the Christian Indian Pablo, who had undertaken to examine the defenses of the City, was captured and hanged, leaving the others so discouraged that they retreated into their mountains.

Leaving the City adequately defended, Governor don Gaspár de Albear set forth with a force of sixty armored Spanish soldiers and twice that number of Indians, to combat the rebels. They took pack mules with flour and other provision and drove before them 800 head of cattle, not only for their own sustenance, but for the succor of Spanish refugees they should find along their way.

Their route first took them to the Reales of Indehe and Guanaceví. Everywhere they found the estancias and mines burned, and the cattle of the Spaniards driven into the Sierras. They had several skirmishes with the enemy, killing some, and routing many. At a point where they were forced to ascend a mountain pass in single file, they were subjected to a most savage attack by the enemy. Stones were rolled down upon them, some so huge that they tore down trees in their path. After a fierce struggle, during which their arquebuses were brought heavily into play, the Spaniards gained the summit of the ridge upon which they had been traveling.

Just below this summit they came upon the dead bodies of Friar Sebastián Montaño, of the Order of Santo Domingo; don Pedro Rendon, of the Royal Council at Guadiana; and many Christian Indians who had been killed in the first days of the uprising. So bitterly cold was the weather that these bodies were perfectly preserved. The bodies of the Christian Indians were given proper burial, and those of the Padre and don Pedro Rendon dispached on the backs of mules to the Real of Guanaceví.

Arriving at Indehe, the Governor routed the forces that had laid siege there, leaving the pueblo well garrisoned and provisioned. Here the Governor divided his forces into two Companies of armored soldiers of horse, each accompanied by a Company of Indian allies. These he placed under the command of Captains Montaño and Ontiveros, both valorous leaders of much knowledge of the Indians and of the Sierras.

Captain Montaño held an encounter with a band of Tepeguanes, killing many and taking prisoner, among others, an Indian named Antonio, whose confession added much to the knowledge of the Spaniards as to the extent of the rebellion.

Traveling by separate routes, the two Companies of Spanish soldiers and their allies converged at the pueblo of Zape. Here the perfidious Antonio was hung from a tree growing in the Plaza, as a warning to other rebels of the fate that awaited them should they continue in revolt.

At Zape were recovered the bodies of Padres Juan Fonte, Juan del Valle, Luis de Álvarez and Gerónimo Moranta, as well as those of some thirty other Spaniards. Here also had died some sixty faithful Christian Indians. Governor Albear ordered that all, Christians, Indians and Spaniards alike, should be buried in the courtyard of the ravaged church of the pueblo.

The two Companies again took separate routes, to meet again at Santiago Papasquiaro. Both Companies were attacked by large bands of Indians, one under the leadership of a most famous Chief, named Canelas, who was of mixed Spanish and Indian blood. [*There is in this area of Durango a pueblo named after this famous chieftain.*]

An Indian who was captured revealed that the main body of women and children of the rebels, together with many of their supplies, were at the pueblo of Tenerapa, near the border of the Province of Sinaloa. Traveling those rugged mountains for a distance of thirty miles during all of one night the Governor, by now accompanied by the celebrated Indian fighter Captain Gordejuela, with a body of fifty soldiers and sixty Indian allies, fell upon Tenerapa at earliest dawn. The defenders of the pueblo, including Chief Canelas, took to flight. However, 20 of them were killed, and 300 captured.

Here were rescued two little daughters of Lieutenant Juan de Castilla, who had been killed in the massacre of Papasquiaro. Also there were rescued some wives of Negroes who had been working in the Reales of Mines, the savages planning to keep these women as servants for themselves when they should become the Lords of these Provinces.

Here the Governor ordered hung some principal rebel leaders, including two old Tepeguane women witch doctors who had been much to blame for inciting the others to rebellion.

Returning toward Papasquiaro, the Spaniards saw everywhere the ravages of these savages. The expedition finally returned to Guadiana, after traversing many mountain ranges and having taken part in numerous battles, bringing with them about 250 prisoners.

ON EACH OF FOUR of his own mules the Governor had ordered placed the body of a Padre, covering them with robes bearing the official insignia of his rank of Knight of the Order of Saint James.

The procession, as it approached Guadiana, was of two lines of soldiers on their armored horses, followed by similar lines of Indian allies. These allies were, in their greater part, warriors of the Nations of the Laguna area, and of the Conchos River. Many of these allies were also mounted on horses. Next in the procession came the pack mules carrying the bodies of the martyred Padres.

Following these came the long pack train of mules, loaded with supplies. So, upon the backs of mules, the dead Padres passed through the gates of the city of Guadiana, to a final resting place in the Convent of Saint Thomas of Aquinas of our Company.

At the request of the Padres of the Convent of San Francisco, the four blessed martyrs were first placed in that Convent, where an impressive service was held. The Padres of their Order led a procession, followed by many other people, all bearing lighted candles and carrying crosses upraised, while chants were sung to the accompaniment of an organ. Our Padre Provincial of New Spain, don Juan Gomez, being in Guadiana at that time, chose to honor the occasion by officiating dressed in a cape of gold. His deep emotion was expressed by a face wet with tears. He would have wished to celebrate a Mass such as is given for the martyrs of Christ, but as a decision in such matters may be made only by the Vicar of Christ in Rome, the distinguished Padre Provincial ordered that there should be held a Mass with a program of solemn music.

From Sunday evening until Tuesday the bodies rested in the main chapel of the Convent of San Francisco. There were kept burning during this time four pillars of fire, while an honor guard of soldiers was maintained by night and day. On Monday there were held here the services for the dead, Mass being recited by our Padre Provincial, with the Padres of the Order of San Francisco also in attendance. This service was accompanied by most solemn music, for these martyred dead were considered to be already in heaven and crowned with glory.

The following day, Tuesday, the Padres of our Company carried the remains of the four martyred Padres to our Convent of Saint Thomas of Aquinas, followed in procession by 150 soldiers of the Citizens Militia, who fired salvos from their arquebuses. After the soldiers came the children of our College at Guadiana. Next came the Spanish Vaqueros in gallant attire, all wearing funeral wreaths above their sombreros.

For this procession the bodies had been draped suitably with fine coverings.
Arrived at our Convent, these martyrs were placed all together in a tomb

around which burned many lights, these being set in large chandeliers, in a most decorous manner. Over the body of each Padre was placed a vestment, a chalice and paten, as is the usage in the burial of priests. There were also placed in the tomb many tributes, written in prose or verse, honoring these valient soldiers of Christ.

After the burial service, there was delivered the sermon left by the Son of God to his Church, for the day on which his physician served the salt that preserved them from the corruption and heresies of the world.

The bodies were buried together in a very fine wooden coffin, in which were placed the names and titles of these blessed men, with a statement of the day, month and year in which they died. The remains of the other four Padres who perished in the massacre of Santiago Papasquiaro could not be recovered, as they were not to be distinguished from the many others who gave their lives that day. No doubt that on the day God has appointed to manifest the glory of his martyred disciples, these four will be taken with all the others into Paradise.

PART FIVE: CONCLUSION OF A DESPERATE CAMPAIGN

WE HERE LEAVE the bodies of these eight ministers resting in the earth, and their souls in heaven, and continue with our story.

Another band of rebellious Tepeguanes had assaulted a pack train crossing over the lower Sierras toward the Coastal plain, on its way to Chiametla, which is an ancient pueblo lying along a river emptying into the Sea of Californias. The assailants killed the soldier escort of this pack train, capturing pack loads of uniforms destined for outfitting soldiers who were taking part in the campaign against these same Indians. The value of this cargo was estimated at three thousand pieces of eight reales each.

At the time that this assault took place, Padre Tomás Basilio and I had arrived on our return trip from Mexico City as far as the pueblo of San Sebastián (*now Concordia*), some twenty five miles eastward into the foothills from Chiametla. Here we found the Spanish residents of the area barricaded in the church, momentarily expecting an attack from the Tepeguanes.

Upon the pleading of the Spaniards of both San Sebastián and Chiametla, the Padre Superior of the Mission of Sinaloa, who rode with us on this part of our journey, asked the two of us to remain here, that there should be Padres to administer the rites of the church if needed. It fell to my lot to remain at the pueblo of San Sebastián, nearest to the Sierras, for fifteen days, preparing the inhabitants with proper talks, hearing confessions, and giving communion. The women and children took refuge in the church each night, while the men did sentinel duty outside, maintaining bonfires all through the night that they might be able to see the attackers before they should breach the walls.

After the period of danger seemed to have passed, we continued on our way.

Later, however, the Tepeguanes did attack the village of San Sebastián, and at the same time the ancient pueblo of Acaponeta, where they set fire to a Convent of Franciscan Friars located there. Notice of these continuing depredations made it imperative that Governor Albear once more take the field against the savages. This expedition was accompanied by Alonzo de Valencia, a Padre of our Company.

The rebels had moved much farther south than their usual places of habitation, so that the route of the pursuing forces followed the great southern cordilleras. They trailed the enemy over rugged mountains and through deep gorges which, in mid-winter, lay deep with snow.

Determined not to return without having finally subjected the enemy forces, the Governor pressed his troops and their Indian allies to the point of exhaustion. Finally their food supplies ran out, and they were forced to slaughter their horses and mules, which were now reduced to mere skeletons of animals. In their greatest extremity they even resorted to boiling the rawhide of the animals they slaughtered; and in a final desperate effort to sustain life they boiled the leather from some of their shoes. By day the desperate little band would conceal themselves in the forests, traveling only by night, in the hope of coming upon the enemy by surprise.

Enemy spies that were captured, even under torture stubbornly refused to reveal the hiding place of their people. Finally, in the depths of a great gorge to where no Spaniard had ever before ventured, they found gathered many Tepeguane women, elderly people and children. In order to descent into this gorge it was necessary to use scaling ladders. Not finding the rebel leaders and warriors here, the Spaniards and their allies continued their search. One day they came by surprise upon a band of some thirty rebel Indians carrying lances, these men being in search of strayed cattle, to keep them from starving. Our Indian allies soon laid an ambush for this band and many of the enemy were killed, among them their very principal leader, who had renounced his Christian name of Francisco for the savage name of Gogoxito. He had been a most clever leader, valiant, sagacious, and daring, being much esteemed for these qualities by the Tepeguanes. His death brought dismay and discouragement to his followers, and from the time of this encounter they sought only to escape being captured. All organized resistance ceased, and the Governor returned toward Guadiana with his weary but victorious forces.

The only Missionary to survive the Great Rebellion of the Sierras was Padre Andrés Lopez. It seemed that God had spared him in order to restore the faith of those Indians who had strayed so far from the fold. From his church at Indehe he not only ministered to those who had remained faithful, but reached out through them to bring back the others.

Authorized by Governor Albear, from his church at Indehe he sent numerous messages to the rebels, assuring them that all who chose to return in peace would be pardoned. In the beginning these messages had little effect. However, among the prisoners taken was an old Tepeguane woman, lame and infirm, who became so impressed by the Spaniards' treatment of the prisoners that she offered to serve as the messenger of peace from the Governor and the Padres to her people.

It was with much misgiving that the Captain in command of the little garrison at Indehe consented to her release, even after the order had been given by the Governor. For two days she remained receiving instruction from Padre Andrés Lopez, as to what assurance she might give those who were fearful to return. Finally, she departed, carrying with her a commission signed by both the Viceroy in Mexico City and the Governor of Nueva Vizcaya and, in addition, a prayer book of the Padres that would be recognized by those rebels who had once been Christians.

After journeying fifteen miles with an escort, this valiant old woman went forward alone, her only credentials being the symbols of good faith referred to, which her people could not read, but only recognize and consider the source from which they came. So ancient was she that it seemed she must have little time left in which to live. However, incredible as it may seem, this woman made her way through that great cordillera of Sierras for a distance of some 500 miles, visiting one village after another, to deliver her offer of peace and pardon. Such was the impression she made upon her people that soon they could be seen, traveling down the steep slopes of the higher Sierras to their old rancherias and pueblos and, very particularly, to the church at Indehe, to receive the forgiveness and blessing of Padre Andrés Lopez, who now alone represented the hope and faith that had been so often pictured to these people by their deceased Padres.

After a little time, except for a very few stubborn ones, those who had taken part in this terrible rebellion were once more busily engaged in cultivating their fields, working in the mines, and rebuilding their pueblos and churches.

The monetary cost of this war to the Royal Coffers of Spain was estimated at 800,000 pesos of eight reales each, without taking into account the lives lost, the mines, estancias, pueblos and churches destroyed, and the many souls lost to Heaven. As I write this, the greater number of characters who have formed the principal part of this story, such as the wise and valorous Captains don Diego Martinez de Hurdaide and don Bartolomé Juarez, and Governor Gaspár de Albear, have gone to their reward, as have many other Spaniards and their Indian allies who lived during the period of this great rebellion. Others who still live have been kind enough to express their approval of the authenticity with which this story has been recorded.

CHAPTER 10

PART ONE: THE TEPEGUANES RETURN TO THEIR LANDS

THE VICEROY of New Spain and the Governor of Nueva Vizcaya were most desirous that peace be restored, that the Spaniards might return to the development of their cattle estancias, and of the many rich Reales of Mines that lay idle throughout the Sierras.

There was also a tremendous task to be faced in rebuilding the churches and restoring the Christian faith. Padre Andrés Lopez wrote an appeal to the Padre Provincial of the Company in the City of Mexico for assistance. Padres from other Missions quickly volunteered to replace their martyred brothers. Padre Jose de Lomas, who had once labored among the Tepeguanes and had knowledge of their language, was selected to lead in this undertaking. Although he had become old, and had retired some years before, this dedicated man returned to his ministry with great heart and spirit.

The news of his coming so gladdened the hearts of many of his old disciples that they came traveling from distant places of the Sierras to greet him, and to offer their services. This story is told in part in a letter from Padre de Lomas to his Provincial Father in Mexico City, from which is quoted as follows:

"I arrived at the pueblo of Santiago Papasquiaro on the 8th day of February (*of 1617*) where I was welcomed by many of my Indian disciples with notable demonstrations of pleasure . . . all the pueblo has been destroyed, and the church torn down and burned.

"We have suffered three snow storms in succession, the wind blowing with such fury that, without shelter, and with little food, my companion priest and I have had little opportunity to acquire merit in the service of our Lord.

"When first we arrived, I gathered my Indian friends at the foot of the cross that still stands in the courtyard of the ruined church. Here we sang the prayers of our Christian faith. We have continued to do so each day thereafter, in this manner aiding these people in rebuilding the faith which they had abandoned. The best judgment that may at present be made of these Indians is that they are now much chastened, but not all are yet completely converted to Christianity.

"They are much disillusioned because the Devil, whom so many of them claimed to have seen visibly, failed to make good his promises. In revenge, they have taken the life of Cuatlatlas, who was the great Hechicero of their religion, and was said to have been on most intimate terms with the Devil. They have also taken the life of one of their principal Caciques, who has attempted to dissuade them from returning to peace. There still remains at large a very principal Hechicero whom they have long held as an oracle. He is hidden somewhere in the forest with some followers. With the help of God, and assisted by the prayers of Your Reverence, I shall endeavour to return these also to the faith.

"Yet another of their rebel leaders, Guixiovita, of the pueblo of Santa Catarina, is in retreat at a place called Boyagame. With him are Indians of the lower areas of the Sierras, such as Tecuchuapa and Tenerapa, who have now taken him for their leader, after the rout of their forces by Captain Hurdaide. Guixiovita it was who stole the Spanish doncellas, daughters of the Lieutenant, who have now been recaptured.

"There can still be little security here among the Tepeguanes without a garrison of soldiers, since their barbaric practices, which we had once persuaded them to discontinue, have been revived. Recently at Santa Catarina there has been held a great drunken feast, at which one young brave, infuriated by drink, killed another, after which the relatives of each have continued killing each other. Another instance of the revival of their former savagery is that, after the river flowing by Santa Catarina had continued in flood for some days, as an act of propitiation to their Gods, those savages wrested a young baby from the arms of her mother, to be thrown into the waters, thinking this to reduce their flow.

"The Spaniards who have returned have advised me that the Tepeguanes still go through a ceremony of greeting upon the rising of the morning star (*Lucero*), and again, upon the rising of the sun, when they go through a manner of prayer of much duration. This form of prayer they also give upon the rising of the moon. All these forms of ceremonies are of course workings of the Devil, as are also such intrigues as causing to fly over our temporary shelter here a form of owl, which makes most distressing cries, as though to frighten us. This manner of menacing will of course avail them nothing." [*Possibly the wierd hooting of an owl was new to the good Padre, or well it could have been a call of some Indian to frighten the two Padres, for the imitation of the calls of animals was a highly developed talent of the Indians.*]

It should be said that some untamed Indians from the Valle de San Pablo did come later, in an attempt to murder the two Padres, being thwarted in a manner that ended most tragically the lives of some faithful Christian Indian women who, while spreading the alarm of the coming of these savages, were killed by their arrows.

In the course of time there were sent four more Padres, accompanied by an escort of soldiers with armored horses, who were garrisoned in a Presidio that was soon constructed at Papasquiaro. Many apostate Indians, wearied of their life as refugees in the forests and mountains, acceded to the pleas of these Padres and returned to their Christian manner of living.

A Captain of the Real of Guanacevi, after the desecration of the Saintly Virgin at Zape, had sworn a vow that he would restore this image, and adorn it with brighter jewels than before. This vow he fulfilled, ordering made one of the most perfect images in all of Gods Kingdom, which was first placed in the church at Guanacevi, until the time should be ripe to restore an image of the Virgin Mother to Zape. The ceremonies of restoration were attended by the Indians of many surrounding pueblos.

At the place where Padres Juan Fonte and Gerónimo de Moranta lost their lives, a shrine was erected to their memory, and all the worshipers walked in bare feet from this shrine to the church nearby, where had been placed the Virgin. Although tragically delayed, the Festival of Zape was held in due time, with much emotion and tenderness of feeling. This church has, during the years, become a shrine where many miracles of healing have taken place.

Because of the performance of these miracles the Virgin has been presented with many rich vestments, jewels and rich ornaments for her altar. An owner of a large pack train, whom the Virgin had protected on his journeys, once from being killed by the lance of an enemy, and again in guiding his pack animals safely through deep snow, dedicated the earnings of his choicest pack mule to the Mother of God. To this mule he gave the name of Maria. Its trappings were richly adorned, even to a lettering that read: "Slave of Maria the Virgin, which works daily in Her service."

All the earnings of this animal were dedicated to the adornment of the altar of the Image of the Saintly Mother at Zape. I could go on at length, telling of the numerous marvelous cures effected through the blessing of this Virgin, which has become more famous through the years.

From the combined efforts of the six Padres now dedicated to the ministry of the Tepeguanes, there has come about not only a spiritual but a temporal resurrection in the land. The reopening of the mines and estancias now gives employment to a large Indian population. Shortly after the return to peace of the Tepeguanes, there was discovered at a place called Parral, one of the richest Reales of Mines in all New Spain, which continues to produce great riches for the community, and for the Crown.

The Christian Indians of the Province of Sinaloa, together with others from the Province of Culiacán, embarked upon an extended pilgrimage, carrying with them an Image of the Virgin Mother, that it should be known to all the pueblos and rancherias of the Sierras. They were well received everywhere, joyous festivities being held in their honor. The illustrious Bishop Fray Gonzalo de Hermosillo, of the Sacred Order of Saint Augustine, made a journey to the land of the Tepeguanes, of which he wrote:

"I offer a thousand congratulations to your Order for the felicitous results of the labors of your Padres on behalf of these Indians . . ."

And truly the Tepeguane Nation, although greatly reduced in numbers, is now much improved in Christianity, and perseveres in peace.

PART TWO: PEACE RETURNS TO THE LANDS OF THE TARAHUMARAS

I HAVE BEFORE TREATED of the conversion to the Christian faith of the great Tarahumara Nation, bordering on the north with the Tepeguanes. This narration I interrupted to tell of the uprising instigated by the Tepeguanes, which spread to so many other Nations.

The Tarahumaras were very much disturbed by the constant persuasion of the Tepeguanes that they should join in the rebellion, although they are by nature a much more gentle and peaceful people. In the years preceding the rebellion, many Tarahumaras had received indoctrination and baptism, although the Padres had not yet penetrated far northward into their extended territory. As a consequence, during the rebellion the Tarahumaras, although they did not go so actively on the warpath as the Tepeguanes, almost all forsook the teachings of the church, returning to the ways of their barbarity.

A principal offender against the church and the rule of the Spaniards during this period was a Cacique named Oñate, a most perverse Indian, who was charged with having given death to Padre Juan Fonte. Governor Albear carried on a diligent search for this savage, both during and after the expedition under his charge which we have previously described. It finally fell to the lot of another Spanish Captain to capture this man, whom he ordered hung from the tree which this same Oñate had designated for hanging a fine Christian Tarahumara leader in the beginning of the revolt. Oñate had ordered the body of this Christian Indian slashed into two pieces.

Upon being catechized before his death the Indian Oñate gave good signs of repentance. It is pleasing to reflect that from Heaven the martyred Padre Juan Fonte may have intervened in favor of saving the soul of this Indian who had once been so perverted. Before his hanging, Oñate preached a fervent sermon to those of his people who stood near, exhorting them to live thereafter in peace and in conformity with the laws of God. This Tarahumara Cacique was the last of the principal leaders of the rebellion to be brought to justice.

Another Tarahumara leader, although he had been at one time cruel and barbarous in the extreme, showed such marked signs of repentance that he was first placed on probation, and later pardoned, becoming one of the principal leaders in bringing the Tarahumara Nation back to reside in their pueblos in peace.

The vast range of mountainous territory in which this numerous Nation lives has made it extremely difficult to bring them into groups sufficiently large for civilization and indoctrination. However, two more Padres are, at this writing, being sent from Mexico City for this purpose.

CHAPTER 11

Brief Account of the Lives of the Martyred Padres

---

1. Padre Juan Fonte

DURING THEIR LIVES the virtues of the martyred Padres were so many, and the examples they set in death were so heroic, as to be worthy of relating. The first of these, Padre Juan Fonte, it was my privilege to know for a brief time. I came to have a great admiration for him. His was a saintly and untiring dedication to the saving of souls. My admiration was doubled, upon traveling through some of the almost inaccessible places where he ventured, for to penetrate such places is to be compared with attempting to enter into the dens of lions or tigers for their subjugation.

Born in Teraza de Barcelona in Spain, Padre Juan Fonte entered the Company at 19 years. In 1599 he came to New Spain with don Diego Diaz, Padre Provincial of the Company, departing immediately for the Mission of the Tepeguanes, succeeding Padre Pedro Ramirez, founder of the Mission.

Alone, with intrepid valor, this young priest newly arrived from Spain entered into those lonely lands peopled by infidels. Confiding only in God, he traversed mountains and valleys, penetrating into unknown country 150 miles further than had any other minister.

His home was a tiny tent of coarse canvas, this serving him too as a manner of altar for the holding of Mass. In the beginning, without knowing their customs or language, he would disappear among those savages for periods extending up to nine or ten months, finally to reappear, accompanied by great numbers of people whom he had searched out and converted, having persuaded them to live either in pueblos with other Christians, or in pueblos which he helped them to build on sites he had beforehand selected for the purpose.

From these pilgrimages he would return emaciated in face and tattered in clothing. His food would be parched corn, as is accustomed by the natives or, for lack of this, herbs gathered from the forests or fields. His drink was apt to be water from little pools left by rains. After returning from one of these journeys, he presented all the appearance of the ancient bearded Padres of Yermo.

In order to domesticate those wild people, he patiently taught them to build dwellings for themselves, using tools which he made for this purpose. He also taught his new disciples to cultivate their fields, using home-made plows which he helped to fashion for them, to be pulled by oxen that he would beg from the Spaniards. In such manner he induced these people to turn from savages to rational human beings.

Their infirmities he treated with his own hands. He cooked food of the little he had for the ill, while nursing them as a mother would nurse her children.

He spent on his disciples all of the little alms sent to him by the King, himself living in the most extreme poverty. For clothing he finally resorted to the use of the woven fiber cloth worn by the poorest of his congregation.

His couch was usually the hard earth, or the robe of a buffalo that someone might have given him, or a plank of rough hewn timber.

Not content to suffer only these hardships, he subjected himself to the most severe disciplines in his daily living, even to such extreme measures as wearing a girdle of hair about his body.

The pagan language of the Tepeguanes he learned with such ease that he not only preached to them with eloquence in their own tongue, but composed it in written form, complete with vocabulary and catechism, so that Padres who followed him could copy it with facility.

His converts numbered into the thousands, and numerous churches and temples are the result of his diligence and devotion. When on occasion his disciples would in their inherent inconstancy abandon their civilized ways, Padre Juan would search them out in their fastnesses, and continue his labors of conversion, until returning them to the fold.

The last Indians to be converted by Padre Juan Fonte were those of the Valle de San Pablo, a band so ferocious and bloodthirsty that they had continuously kept all their neighbors in turmoil, and the Spaniards under the necessity of carrying arms when traveling to the Real of Mines of Santa Barbara, on the eastern slope of the Sierras. Many times the ferocious San Pablo savages threatened Padre Fonte with death for interfering with their wanton manner of living. Twice they held him prisoner for many days. However, he persisted until all these savages had been reduced to Christianity, and gathered from their remote rancherias into a pueblo which he named San Pablo (*Balleza*).

Sixteen years, from twenty to thirty six years of age, this brave man labored, beyond the capacity of mortal man, in his zest for the conversion of souls and attention to their temporal needs, before giving his body to martyrdom and his soul to his God, on that tragic 19th day of December of 1616, at the pueblo of San Ignacio de Zape.

A last pathetic note in the story of this venerable man is that, while lying so many days in death in the great cold, alongside the body of his companion priest Gerónimo de Moranta, their bodies were guarded by their two faithful little Indian dogs, more constant in their loyalty than any of those apostate Christian Indians to whom these Padres had so generously dedicated their lives.

2. PADRE JUAN DEL VALLE

HE WHOM, after Padre Juan Fonte, dedicated the most years to cultivating the friendship of the ferocious Tepeguanes, was Padre Juan del Valle.

Padre Juan was a native of the city of Vitoria, of the Province of Vizcaya in Spain, being of very noble lineage. In the year 1591, at fifteen years of age, he began his studies in the Company, completing them after coming to New Spain in 1594.

As in the case of Padre Juan Fonte, his very first Mission was to the remote land of the Tepeguanes. Here, for twenty two years, he endured all manner of suffering and hardship, ever with high virtue and ability. There was never known any least action on the part of Padre Juan that might detract from his reputation as a religious and saintly man.

Like a peon of the poorest class he labored among his followers, emulating the fine example of Padre Fonte in the building of churches, and in teaching the Indians to plow, cultivate and irrigate their fields. No occupation was too humble for him, even to cooking the food for those Indians who labored with him in the building of churches. All the poor alms he received were dedicated to charitable purposes, leaving him to live in the same poverty as the least of his parishoners.

His Indian disciples he treated with all the affection accorded to ones own brothers. Blessed with an education and a natural capacity such that he might well have become an illustrious leader of the church, he rather chose to remain all his days in the rigorous and confining service of this one Mission.

When by insistence of his superiors he finally consented to become Superior of his Mission, in his humility he persisted in the use of a garb more befitting to the rank of a cook or servant. When the Spaniards with whom he came in contact insisted on making him gifts of silver ample for the purchase of finer clothing, such gifts were apt to go instead to clothe the most needy of his Indian followers.

His bed was reserved for guests, while he slept on a hewn board or a piece of cowhide, even through the cold winters in the Sierras. Most of his time was spent away from his Mission, on the trail, in search of savages to convert to Christianity. Upon uniting various of these new disciples, he would hold services, as had Padre Fonte, in front of the poor little tent which he carried on his travels. When in the little villages, services were apt to be held in huts of straw, through which the bitter winter winds blew freely, as these had only poor palm mats placed before their little doors and windows.

Not content with the suffering caused from such extreme privation, Padre Juan frequently scourged himself, to the point of drawing blood, even when traveling. Often he offered to do penance in behalf of others, so doubling his suffering.

Fasts he observed most rigidly, even though his poor diet could well have been considered one continuous fast. When sometimes invited to the table of other Spaniards, he would eat but sparingly, often being observed to set aside little portions to be taken as a gift to some of the little children who attended Mass.

The numerous churches he founded he took care to adorn attractively with ornaments and images. With great resolution and in the face of danger he destroyed a famous stone idol that had long been adored by those miserable beings whom he so long endeavoured to convert into rational souls. He bravely faced the wrath of numerous Indian leaders, even though the Devil, in his fury over the destruction of this idol, did cause the earth to tremble and fire to be projected into the sky.

The speech of Padre Juan del Valle, although measured and prudent, was filled with expressions of such grace as to fire the hearts of his listeners.

Never did Padre Juan lay his hand to a project that did not succeed. With equanimity he resolved quarrels, dissolved hates, and built friendships where there had before existed only dissention and discord. His coming to a place where discord existed brought assurance of peace, for all willingly placed themselves in his hands for judgment.

The title by which he was commonly known was "Padre Juan de la Paz," and thus is his name now recalled, twenty five years after his death.

Padre Juan was much dedicated to prayer. The fields, the briers of the woods, and the mountain trails, were the scenes of his oratorios.

His deep adoration of the Saintly Virgin Mother had ever been of profound influence on him, in leading a life of perfection and purity. Among the Indians of his mountain churches he founded brotherhoods and sisterhoods dedicated to the adoration of this Virgin, the members all wearing rosaries as a sign of their servitude to her. It can well be believed that as a special premium for such singular devotion, Padre Juan del Valle was selected to wear the crown of martydom in her honor.

Many were the indignities suffered by this Padre at the hands of these savage people during his years of service. In the pueblo of San Ignacio, where he was murdered, an ill-natured Tepeguane had felled him with a blow because of his opposition to the Padre holding Mass. Upon this savage being apprehended by the authorities, the Padre caused him to be freed.

On another occasion, at a paraje called Rio de Ahorcados, he reprehended a band of Indian robbers for abusing the people whom they had robbed, whereupon one of the robbers felled the Padre with a blow. Nothing daunted, the Padre, rising to his knees, humbly prayed to God for the salvation of their souls.

On another occasion the Padre suffered a blow from the bow of an Indian, because of being reprimanded for having three wives. Again he was struck savagely by an immoral woman, for attempting to persuade her to chastity.

Of such indignities he was forced to suffer many, and no doubt these served to better prepare him for the last indignities which he was made to suffer in the hour of his glorious death, on that fateful day of the 18th of November of 1616.

His body was found seventy days later, perfectly preserved in the snow, and was taken, as has been told, to rest with the three other martyred Padres in our Convent at Guadiana. I have not written more fully of other circumstances noteworthy in the life of this blessed Padre, because of my being at this writing in Spain, and so not having access to the material I have collected for this purpose.

3. Padre Luis de Álvarez

Padre Luis de Álvarez, who died in the company of his Padre Superior, Juan Fonte, in the massacre at the pueblo of San Ignacio de Zape, was a native of Oaxaca in the Empire of New Spain, a place which, for being so recently discovered, has produced many illustrious persons.

Padre Luis was born in the year 1589, of very worthy parents. His father was don Melchor de Álvarez, his mother doña Ana de Estrada, both native of the pueblo of Texestitlan.

From our College in Oaxaca he came to Mexico City to receive his degree in our Colegio Real de San Ildelfonso, entering into the service of the Company on May 7th, 1607, being sent to the Mission of Tepeguanes a very few years later.

In this Mission he labored with great zeal and enthusiasm, his first interest being always the physical and spiritual welfare of his poor disciples, himself remaining in singular poverty.

Marvelous indeed were the fruits of his ministry, for despite a rare humility, Padre Luis held a special gift for stirring the hearts of his people.

He had often been heard to refer in his prayers to his future death as a martyr, as though it were a foregone conclusion that his life would be ended in this manner.

There is a curious incident to be related of the final tragedy of the death of Padre Luis. Some little while before, on one of the trips of the Padre to Guadiana, a young Spanish friend there had questioned him as to his easy manner of accepting martyrdom as his fate. Padre Luis had then asked the young man whether he would not be willing to accept martyrdom in the same manner in the service of his God. The youth answered that he would willingly accept such a fate and, upon hearing of the danger to Padre Luis, had ridden to Zape to share his danger, and was murdered with him.

Padre Luis de Álvarez was given the death of a martyr on that same day of 18th of November of 1616, at the early age of twenty seven years. His body was also removed, together with those of his fellow Padres, to be buried in our Convent at Guadiana.

4. Padre Gerónimo de Moranta

Padre Gerónimo de Moranta was born in Mallorca, Spain, in the year 1575. Through persuasion of that outstanding leader of the Company of Jesus, don Alonzo Rodriguez, he came to New Spain in 1605.

Padre Gerónimo came of an illustrious family. His uncle was Padre Geronimo de Nadal, for whom our founding Padre San Ignacio Loyola had held a great estimation. This uncle had also carried on much friendly correspondence with Padre Ricardo Haller, the Father Confessor to the distinguished Queen Margarita of Austria. For many years Padre Gerónimo exchanged letters with those illustrious people.

Sent to the Mission of Tepeguanes, he labored there for ten strenuous years. He was the traveling companion of Padre Juan Fonte on some of his distant perigrinations after lost souls.

The poverty of this Padre was as extreme as that of any of his companions, his vestments finally becoming so patched and shortened that his garb might well be mistaken for that of an Indian.

Even of the simple food of parched ground corn mixed with water which was apt to be his daily ration, he would not partake on days of fasting. Although most severe on himself in the matter of disciplines inflicted, he was most forgiving of the sins of others.

On his journeys through the steepest Sierras he accustomed riding the most humble hack of a horse, an animal of such poor gait that Padre Gerónimo would comment that he felt that he was doing penance while riding it. His Padre Superior recounted that on one occasion, after Padre Gerónimo had disappeared for many months, he came upon him on a trail ninety miles distant from his pueblo where lay his Mission, accompanied by a horde of over 500 Indians whom he was moving en masse to a valley more suitable for their living.

Regardless of rumors of rebellion, Padre Gerónimo would ride alone into the remotest recesses of the mountains, to search out those who were discontent, calm them, and persuade them to remain at peace.

There had come to Padre Gerónimo forewarnings of his martyrdom. In the weeks before this tragic event, while saying Mass at the Indian pueblo of Tizonaco, later named San Jose, upon his attendant offering the Padre the chalice, a dove settled upon it, upsetting it, and pecking the Padre with his bill until drawing blood from his forehead, so much so that it ran down upon his vestment, and upon the altar pedestal. Later, while saying Mass at a rancheria called Las Bocas, the same incident was repeated. Upon the Padre's assistants inquiring what this unusual occurrence might signify, he answered, "My children, what I believe is that my Father desires that my blood shall soon be shed for Him."

So it came to pass. His body was found three months after his death, lying in the snow, stripped of all clothing, in a perfect state of preservation. At his side lay his communion cup, which for some mysterious reason the savages chose to leave beside him, although all of his other effects were taken.

He was taken to be interred with the other Padres in our Convent at Guadiana, from where their blessed souls shall unite with those of other Christians on the day of final resurrection.

5. Padres Bernardo de Cisneros and Diego de Orosco

The Padres Bernardo de Cisneros and Diego de Orosco were companions in attending the spiritual needs of the principal pueblos of the Tepeguane Nation during the years previous to the great rebellion.

Padre Bernardo was a native of Carrión de los Condes, in Castilla la Vieja, Spain, and was only thirty four years of age at the time of his death in 1616. He had arrived in New Spain in 1605, studying theology and otherwise preparing himself before going to the Mission of Tepeguanes.

Padre Bernardo possessed in high degree the virtues desirable for the teaching of the apostolic faith. His extreme zeal won him many converts, as well as some dangerous enemies among the Hechiceros, who led the other Indians to the worship of idols.

This young priest destroyed one of their principal idols, and did so again when it was restored. Inflamed with fury, an Indian assaulted the Padre, thrusting a dagger three times into his chest near the heart. He was left for dead, but God willed he should live to dedicate many more years of faithful service to those same savages who finally turned upon him to bring him the glorious death of a martyr.

It is an interesting note that Padre Diego de Orosco had come to New Spain in 1605 on the same ship with his fellow martyrs Padres Bernardo de Cisneros and Gerónimo de Moranta.

Padre Diego was born in the city of Plasencia, Spain, of noble parents. His father, Doctor don Antonio de Orosco was a Regent of the Council of the city. His mother was the Señora doña Isabel del Toro. One of his uncles, don Rodrigo de Orosco, Marquis de Montara, was Governor of Alejandria de la Valla, in Castile. With this background, Padre Diego could have properly aspired to a very honored position in public life. However, there shone in Padre Diego from his tender years a resplendent inner light which guided him into the priesthood and to journey to the Indies to become a martyr for Christ.

It had ever been his hope to complete his service by becoming a martyr. In this respect I shall write what was told to me by Padre Martín, Rector of our College of the City of Guatemala. There had arrived on a visit to this city the Governor of the nearby Province of Soconusco, accompanied by his wife. With them came a most devout maiden who was a native of the city of Plasencia and who had been reared in the home of Padre Deigo de Orosco. On hearing the sad news of his death at the hands of the ferocious Tepeguanes, this maiden was moved to tears of compassion. She told that, from his childhood Padre Diego had felt that three events must come to pass in his life: first, that he must become a member of the Company of Jesus; second, that he should journey to a foreign land; and last, that he must die the death of a martyr.

Although the years given by this youthful Padre to the ministry of these barbarous people were not many, they were spent most wholeheartedly and generously, to the utmost of his physical and spiritual powers. As I have before written, it was my pleasure to spend several days with these fine young priests, who two months later went to their martyrdom. Together with Padre Bernardo Cisneros I had traveled through the several pueblos he served. The Devil was then already provoking unrest among the Tepeguanes and their allies. On the morning of my departure Padre Bernardo confessed that during the previous night he had been most sorely tempted to ask for my help in pleading with the Padre Provincial that he be transferred to another post, because of his frustration in attempting to cope with the unrest that existed. However, he had finally resolved that his duty required him to remain and face the fate then preparing itself for him and his companions.

The bodies of these two young priests could not be distinguished from those of the many others, Spaniards and Christian Indians, who had been sacrificed, but surely their souls must now rest in heaven as symbols of saintly glory.

Although the lives of all these people might seem to have been sacrificed in vain, yet the many Indians who remained faithful to their teachings in the years that followed influenced most favorably the ministry of those who succeeded them.

We shall now continue with our story of the conversion of other savage Nations of the Sierras.

CHAPTER 12

Land of the Hinas

No Sierras were so extended, nor the savages living there so concealed, but that our evangelical ministers did not finally reach them, although it seemed sometimes that hooves of goats were needed for the task. The people of whom we now relate are called Hinas and Humis, each of notable ferocity, and of large numbers, being scattered over many rancherias.

Various of these rancherias bordered on a river of good size named Piaxtla, which is born in the high Sierras some distance south of Culiacán. Other Indians lived in yet more secluded places, higher into the Sierras.

So fierce were these Indians, and their mountains so inaccessible, that for over sixty years following the establishment of pueblos and Missions in the Sierras, no Spaniard set foot there. Finally, some few years after the end of the great rebellion, the most illustrious Bishop of Guadiana, don Fray Gonzalo de Hermosillo, having notice of those lost souls, requested the veteran minister and Visitador of Missions, Padre Diego Gonzalez de Cueto, to attempt to visit these lost people.

Not only was the conversion of their souls to be desired, but also their conversion from outlaws who constantly harassed the civilized Indians and Spaniards living and working in the mines and on the cattle ranches surrounding those Sierras.

The venture of Padre Cueto into the country of the Hinas and Humis was against the advice of all his fellow workers, for not only were these Indians barbarous and cannibalistic, but they harbored numerous outlaw Indians who had fled from other Nations, or from the Spanish authorities.

On instruction from the Bishop, Padre Cueto began by venturing as far as the first pueblo of the Hinas, named Guaimino [*Now San Ignacio*], where he busied himself with becoming friendly with the people living there. From here he dispached couriers into the higher Sierras, inviting certain of the savage Indian leaders to come to visit with him.

In the beginning those invited excused themselves from participating in this endeavor of the Padre, possibly because they were among those guilty of misdeeds in the past, and were fearful of the consequences of the extension of the authority of Governors into their communities. However, they finally sent word agreeing that if Padre Cueto would go to a pueblo called Ixtlan, twelve miles up the Piaxtla River, they would summon other Indians to join them in meeting the Padre there.

This offer posed a real problem to Padre Cueto, as he had been authorized by the Bishop to go only as far as Guaimino. However, he comprehended that his danger was actually as great where he waited as it would be further into the Sierras; and moreover, that if he should refuse this invitation, he might never receive another, and any opportunity of civilizing these people would be lost.

Weighing these problems, the Padre placed his life in the balance, and continued on to Ixtlan, a place which was later named San Francisco.

Here he found only the residents of the place, because the six Indians who had extended the invitation were still at their rancherias awaiting his answer.

The Padre then tore into three pieces, a cloth of red tapestry which he had used as a background when placing the image of the Saintly Virgin for saying Mass, wrapping in the torn parts three precious objects; his rosary, his reliquary, and a small image of the Virgin which he always carried on his travels. These precious tokens he sent by messengers to the three rancherias where lived the six Caciques, inviting them again to come to talk with him.

Each of the messengers returned with an identical answer, in which Padre Cueto was urged to continue for thirty miles further, to a camping place of the Indians called Oveibos, which is interpreted as Quelitlán, or the land of the quelites, which are weeds much used by them for cooking as greens. This place was later given the glorious name of Santiago (*Saint James*).

A younger Padre accompanying the venerable Padre Cueto at this point was said to have exclaimed, "Oh, by the blessed God, what patience and forbearance of spirit is required for the accomplishment of these missions, and doubly so among these people."

Whom other, after broken appointments in so many places, with such deceits and delays, but would have turned back with no regret whatsoever. Not so Padre Cueto, who, although knowing himself to be caught as between two closed doors, chose the greater risk of continuing forward.

After sending a message back to the Bishop of his decision, he continued the thirty miles farther.

As his party had arrived midway of their journey and were selecting a site for resting at the end of the day, there came pouring out of the hills bordering the two sides of the river a horde of some 300 Indians, robust vagabonds equipped with all the armaments of war. No women nor children accompanied them, which is an ominous indication of evil intention.

Padre Cueto, with a courage born of his faith in God, received them all in the friendliest manner, spending many of the hours of the night pointing out to them the spiritual and temporal benefits that awaited them should the Padres come to teach them the Christian faith and a better manner of living.

At break of dawn of the day following, accompanied by all those savages with whom he had held such saintly converse, and others who continued to arrive, he resumed his journey to Quelitlán. Picture the surprise of this good Padre when, upon arriving there, he found planted in the midst of some spacious fields bordering the River, three staffs, from each of which were suspended one of the three precious tokens he had sent to their leaders. Here in the fields stood these staffs, abandoned and alone, causing much concern indeed to the Padre, that his mission had here come to an inglorious end.

After first recovering his precious possessions, the saintly old man placed himself upon his knees on the earth, and with tears flowing from his eyes, prayed to his God for strength in this hour.

Presently from the woods there began to appear many Indians who had apparently concealed themselves upon the arrival of the Padre, to make sure that he should not be followed later by a company of soldiers. All through the day those wild savages gathered, until by nightfall there were assembled a thousand souls; men, women and children.

All these people rested there that night, along the bank of the river, in the company of the Padres. On the morning following, Padre Cueto assembled them to deliver his message from Bishop Fray Gonzalo de Hermosillo. This message he gave with such grace and persuasion that, upon its conclusion, the entire populace gathered there decided to begin their new form of worship upon this very spot, proceeding immediately with the laying out of a pueblo, under the instruction of the Padres, and to the building of a church.

This first church was a modest building of straw, similar to the poor palace in which our Lord chose to be born into the world. To this church Padre Cueto gave the name of the Iglesia del Espíritu Santo (*Church of the Holy Spirit*). Here he baptized more than 150 children before returning to give report to the Bishop of the success of this manifestly precarious undertaking.

Through a series of circumstances too long to relate here, the work of this Mission was long delayed. However, there finally came a time when the principal Caciques of these people took it upon themselves to make an appeal to the Padre Superior of the Mission of San Andrés of the Sierras of Topia for the services of a Padre. This message was conveyed to the Padre Provincial of New Spain, don Gerónimo Diaz, who chanced to be visiting in the city of Guadiana. Included in this appeal was a stated preference for their beloved minister, Diego Gonzalez de Cueto. This appeal was granted; Padre Cueto returning to the Mission of the Hinas at Quelitlán in the year 1630. He soon had gathered together the Indians whom he had previously converted, as well as many others.

Although Padre Cueto acquired a large following, there were still many rebellious savages among these Nations. An outlaw Indian who had come from the pueblo of El Tunal near Guadiana began plotting with others for the murder of Padre Cueto. Fortunately, this Indian was apprehended, and placed in chains in the Presidio.

This arrest, although effective for the time, provoked other savages to plan a revolt, and the Governor at Guadiana deemed it necessary to dispach his Alcalde Mayor with a levy of men to travel into the lands of the Hinas and Humis to quiet them. As a result of this visit, which was made accompanied by Padre Cueto, these two Nations, to the number of 2,000 persons, were persuaded to come out of their Sierras to places more accomodated to their living, where they constructed pueblos and churches.

There came at this time to assist the aged Padre Cueto a spirited young missionary named Diego Jimenez. In this same year there came a great famine to the lands of the Hinas and Humis. Young Padre Diego undertook a journey to persuade the Governor of Nueva Vizcaya, don Gonzalo Gomez de Cervantes, to send by pack train 100 fanegas of corn (*of 220 pounds each*) for planting, so that the famine should not be continued into another season. This corn was distributed at the proper season, later saving many of these peoples from starving.

Despite such good deeds, there did not lack for depraved souls, stirred by the preachings of their Hechiceros, who planned to take the lives of Padres Cueto and Jimenez. Such threats could not weaken the spirit of the aged Padre Cueto; rather he ventured, with renewed vigor, still farther afield, to found a sixth pueblo among these restless people. To this pueblo he gave the name of Santiago, for the Apostle Saint James.

The disturbances among these people still continuing, the Governor of Nueva Vizcaya found it necessary to order the veteran Captain Bartolomé Juarez de Villalba, who had taken part in the subjugation of the Tepeguanes, and now commanded the Presidio of San Hipólito, to enter into the Sierras where lived the Hinas and Humis, to remain until peace should be restored.

The journey of Captain Juarez with his Spanish soldiers and Christian Indian allies is well told in a letter from Padre Diego Jimenez, who accompanied the expedition. He writes:

"Captain Bartolomé Juarez, Lieutenant General in command of all these Sierras, called together the Cacique leaders of the Hina Nation at a pueblo called Yamoriba. Arriving there on the 18th of November, 1633, we found no Caciques awaiting us. There was a message from Padre Juan de Mallén advising us to proceed cautiously, as the Hinas were reported to be arming themselves to oppose the entry of Captain Juarez' forces into their pueblos and rancherias.

"This was most disturbing news, for most of all, the Captain desired to avoid a clash with these people, so long as it might be possible to deal with them peacefully. Fortunately, there came soon a letter from Padre Cueto saying the Indian leaders would arrive on that same day.

"Moving with caution, Captain Juarez ordered the Indian allies who accompanied him to form themselves into squads at the entrance to the pueblo. These were most reliable Indians who had come from such pueblos as Santa Maria de Utaiz, San Pedro, and Santiago Basio, which were populated by Christian Indians. They came well equipped and maintained good discipline, presenting an impressive appearance.

"The Spanish soldiers, no more than thirty in number, but riding armored horses and armed with arquebuses, were ordered to remain in the center of the pueblo.

"As the Hinas arrived and marched into the pueblo, the Indian allies formed a half-circle about them, keeping this formation until arriving to where the Spanish troops awaited them.

"At their near approach, the thirty Spanish soldiers fired a salvo from their arquebuses and muskets, these being so heavily loaded that the earth trembled.

"After this salvo, the Captain, finely armored and elegantly dressed, came forward to receive his visitors.

"The Hinas were then ordered to stack their arms, after which the veteran Captain addressed them, explaining that he had come with the desire to reaffirm the peace that had now existed for many years between the Hinas and the Spanish authorities.

"Following this meeting, the Hinas made a token gift to the Captain of many of their war arrows, the Captain giving them in return bullets from the guns of the Spaniards, this being the formal manner of giving evidence of confederation and cooperation. While this ceremony was going on, arquebuses were being fired at intervals. The Indians and Spaniards then embraced each other in reaffirmation of peace.

"The Lieutenant General having concluded his part of the ceremonies, I was asked to take charge, and requested that all should march to the church of the pueblo, while singing chants in their own language. This was done, the soldiers still continuing to fire salvos as we marched.

"After all had entered the church, the Captain, in order to manifest before these people his own faith and humility, placed himself before the altar and, to my great confusion, knelt at my feet, brushing them with his shock of venerable gray hair. This act caused in the Spaniards a tender admiration for him, and in the Indians a singular respect for his sincere piety and devotion.

"Following the holding of Mass, the Captain caused to be divided among the Hinas many sacks of dried beef, and much other provision.

"A most spectacular feast was held in the pueblo that evening, with more than 400 Indians partaking. Songs had meanwhile been composed by some of them in honor of the renowned Captain, these being sung in groups, around the campfire, in their own language. [*The custom of composing chants or songs has been carried forward to this century by the Mayo Indians of Sinaloa.*]

"The next day, before continuing his journey deeper into the land of the Hinas, the Captain dispached five of their Caciques ahead to advise of our coming. Two others he retained with us, ostensibly as guides, but in reality as hostages.

"As we traveled towards their larger pueblos, the trail began to widen. On the day of San Pedro Alejandrino we arrived at some broad plains through which flowed a good sized river, very attractive in its many curves and bends, reminding many of us of the Guadiana of Spain.

"To this place we gave the name of San Pedro del Rio. Here I ordered made a large cross and, accompanied by Captain Juarez, raised this cross with befitting ceremony. As this land had not before been seen by Spaniards, we took possession of it in the name of the Province of Vizcaya.

"Following this, for several days we traveled higher into the Sierras. Our Indian guides, who had come from a lower altitude, became faint, refusing to go further, until threatened with hanging.

"Eventually we came to cliffs so steep and rough that we were forced to use picks to make trails for ourselves and our riding and pack animals. In making this crossing several of our pack mules were lost over precipices.

"One day, upon arriving at some fields of the Hinas, our troops, by now in great hunger, began to forage for themselves. The Captain then ordered a blast to be given with a trumpet, after which he gave strict orders that none of the Indians' fields should be disturbed. This act acquired much favor for us with the Hinas, their gratitude being expressed by their sending a gift of twenty pack loads of corn.

"The day following we arrived at the pueblo of Santiago. The people of this pueblo, unsure of our purpose in coming, had fled, but messengers dispached by Padre Cueto soon persuaded them to return. They came to greet us carrying crosses in their hands.

Among these Indians was one who had committed many atrocities during the great rebellion of 1616. In his rage he had set fire to a cross standing before a church, kicking at this cross while it was still burning, and in so doing had damaged his foot so that it had shriveled, causing him a severe limp for all his life thereafter.

"On the day of San Xavier, Mass was held at the pueblo of Santiago. We then traveled down river to a place which was named Pueblo de la Concepción de la Virgen Santisima. Here there had gathered great numbers of people to celebrate Mass with us. This is one of the most pleasing pueblos of all the Sierras, being situated in an agreeable valley, with a fine fertile plain bordering the river on either side.

"The next day, accompanied by two principal Caciques of the Hinas, we continued onward to the Indian pueblo of Santa Apolonia. Here the Lieutenant General ordered a rest of several days for his forces.

"The Indians of that area, upon learning of the arrival of the legendary General Juarez, so much respected and feared on the frontier, came continuously and in large numbers to see us. They were much pleased to find the old soldier so humane and friendly.

"We were sent a special invitation to visit the pueblo of San Ignacio, where, upon arriving, we found gathered a great many people from the neighboring native pueblos of San Xavier, Ixtlán, and San Gerónimo de Ahoya. There people had constructed a large shed of green branches in our honor, and met us carrying crosses in their hands while wearing other crosses made of plaited straw suspended about their shoulders. These same people brought us a fine offering of food for our forces.

"It gave particular pleasure to Captain Juarez to be received at San Ignacio by his old friend Padre Diego de Cueto, for whom the Captain held particular reverence and affection. It pierced our hearts to see these fine old men now so tired and worn. Nevertheless, they continuously sought to outdo each other in their consideration, both ending with their faces covered with tears of happiness and compassion for the other.

"To all the people assembled, the old Captain delivered an excellent Christian lecture, charging them to maintain respect for their church and their ministers, and very particularly for their venerable Padre Cueto, who had so faithfully served them through every adversity. Padre Cueto was so moved that he could only respond to this eulogy with tears.

"The Spanish troops and their Indian allies remained at San Ignacio for thirty seven days, during which time several impressive services were held, attended by the Captain and his soldiers.

"In the Sierras above Santiago there remained rancherias that had never softened to the pleading of the Padres. The Captain sent some friendly Indians to them with an invitation to come to make peace and be baptized, praying that he should not have need to send troops for them. Soon there appeared many families, who agreed to live in a pueblo together. Seventy five couples were married during Easter week, the men having discarded their several wives in favor of one, leaving the others to search for new husbands. The new pueblo was named San Luis, in honor of don Luis de Bonifáz, then Governor of Nueva Vizcaya, and to the principal Cacique was given the name of don Luis.

In conclusion of this letter, I wish to state that the coming of Captain Bartolomé Juarez, Lieutenant General of the forces located in the Sierras, has been very beneficial in settling the natives to live in peace. They are now so quiet that with only two young Indian assistants I travel as securely from pueblo to pueblo in attending to the duties of my ministry, as though I were traveling in Castile."

Here concludes the letter of the young Padre Diego Jimenez, in which he tells of his eventful journey with Captain Bartolomé Juarez into the upper reaches of the Piaxtla River, an area which lies between the land of the Tepeguanes and the Province of Culiacán, but somewhat southward, into the Sierras.

CHAPTER 13

Land of the Humis

THIRTY MILES above the Hina pueblo of Quelitlán, traveling eastward, lie the rancherias of the Humis, so named because of two large and jagged peaks which extend upward above the lands surrounding their dwelling places. Fifty years previously Spaniards had come through this country in search of metals for mining, and had mined there briefly, but the ores were soon depleted, and they had long since departed.

Some of the Humi Indians had occasionally come down to the Christian pueblos to visit the Padres that ministered to the Tepeguanes nearest their borders. However, the remoteness of the area and the occupation of the Padres in nearer places had precluded their entering into the land of the Humis, until the Bishop Fray Gonzalo de Hermosillo, happy with the success in conversion of the Hinas, requested the Padres nearest the Humis to communicate with them in anticipation of their indoctrination.

Padre Pedro Gravina began this formidable task in the year 1633, after having served many years in the ministry of savage Nations, and ended his life here. In the year 1634 Padre Pedro Jimenez also undertook the ministry of the Humi Nation. I shall here quote from a letter written to his Superior in the Missions:

"The Humis live in an area extending about thirty miles, in which are included two principal pueblos, in addition to several rancherias. There are altogether about 300 persons. During more than a year I have traversed their rugged and lofty peaks, the highest of all these mountains, in ministering to them.

"Into these recessed had retreated the principal Tepeguane Cacique Gogoxito after the great rebellion, driving before him multitudes of cattle, sheep, goats, horses, mares and mules, many of which still roam wild among those Sierras. From the offspring of these animals there have grown many other herds of animals, some wild, others domesticated by the Indians. The sheep furnish much wool, which is carded and used for weaving warm clothing.

"It is said that so many of the cattle were slaughtered by the Tepeguanes during their flight, that their remains may still be seen along one mountain pass for a distance of six miles.

"Despite the general pardon issued by the King of Spain to the members of the great Tepeguane Nation, many of them chose to remain hidden among those remote peaks, some even settling down to marry maidens of the Humis' and to rear families there.

"The Humis themselves were much attached to their lofty peaks, and found among them some plots of land so fertile that corn grew to a height of ten feet.

"After having spent six months with a band of these Indians opening a trail into their heights, one which, after all this effort, could only be traversed on foot, I persuaded a part of the Humi Nation to congregate and build a pueblo on some fertile lands in a lower valley. This valley is traversed by a river which eventually flows into the sea near Mazatlán. Here were located 500 persons. This pueblo we named San Pablo.

"It has been an arduous task to separate these men from their numerous wives, and as difficult to remove their vice of drunkeness.

"This new pueblo is putting down firm roots, although the proximity to the land of the Tepeguanes causes us some concern, and we think that a visit from the Cap tain would be beneficial in curbing the restless ones among them. Most of these restless spirits live at a rancheria called Rincon de Zamora."

Here concludes the letter from Padre Diego Jimenez, who, in 1645, yet perseveres in his labors among the Hinas and Humis.

CHAPTER 14

Padre Pedro Graviña

IN CONCLUDING BOOK Two of this History, which treats of the Indian Nations of the vast Sierras of Topia, and their civilization and conversion to Christianity, I wish to tell of the life and saintly virtues of the venerable Padre Pedro Graviña, whom God willed should come from his native Italy to this far and forgotten land, where he labored for over thirty years, principally in the Mission of the Xixime Nation, of whose savagery and cannibalistic practices we have already written.

It fell to his lot to follow the blessed and renowned Padre Hernando de Santarén in ministering to these wild and restless people. His ministry is written of by Padre Francisco Ibarra, his Superior in the Missions, in a letter directed to the Padre Provincial of the Jesuit Order in the City of Mexico, which reads as follows:

"On this 15th day of January of 1635, our Father has chosen to take into His Kingdom the reverend Padre Pedro Graviña, at seventy years of age, and thirty in the service of these Missions. Padre Pedro was first placed as a companion priest to the Padre who ministered to the Indians of San Gregorio de la Sierra . . . this period of proving having passed, he was assigned by his Superior to the care of the Xixime Nation, whose lands, forests, rivers and mountains are notoriously difficult of access. Here he became a pilgrim traveler, visiting among the savage Xiximes, with great persistence and fervor conquering every difficulty of terrain, climate, and human weakness.

"He learned several Indian languages, as well as Castilian, which he did not know upon coming to this remote land. Padre Pedro put into written form the vocabularies of these Indian languages, for the benefit of those who should follow him.

"He was severe in his self-discipline. He slept always on a hard surface such as a board, a steer hide, or a bare earth floor, even when he was at times invited to use a bed. His ordinary food while living in the Sierras was ezquite (*parched corn*) and sometimes a pottage of herbs gathered from the woods, as is accustomed by the Indians . . .

"Such was his consideration, even for the beasts and animals of the field, that he would walk long distances on foot over those steep mountain trails, rather than tire his mule. When riding, he was apt to carry his face raised in contemplation of Heaven, permitting his mule to go where it willed, as a consequence of this custom often receiving cuts and bruises on his face and shoulders.

"Padre Pedro was a secure refuge for all who were afflicted. So exhausted was he by the end of each day, from his attention to the needs of others, that he was wont to sink to the earth, to lie until morning. This extreme dedication to his task gave him the name among the Indians of Santo Padre Pedro.

"The valiant Captain Bartolomé Juarez for many years maintained his headquarters at the Presidio of San Hipólito, not many miles from the Mission of Padre

Graviña, and the two maintained a lose friendship. This Captain, and many others who knew Padre Pedro, felt that the light of the Holy Spirit resided very especially in the heart of this good man. The venerable Padre Hernando de Santarén confided in a friend, señor Gerónimo Acosta, that on an occasion he had seen a light glow in the room of Padre Pedro Graviña, and thinking it to be a candle, had sent his Indian servant, Juan Gamuza, to take a light from it, but was told by the servant that there was no real light, but only the reflection that shone from the figure of Padre Graviña.

"No less miraculous was the manner in which God chose to protect this reverend man while riding those mountain trails. It was told that one day, while riding from a village called Bahome to the pueblo of San Gregorio, traversing a sharp ridge above a precipice, his mule reared violently into the air, and swinging in a cirle, threw the Padre from the saddle, but leaving one foot suspended from a stirrup. It truly seemed a miracle that the stirrup leather parted in a break as smooth as though being cut with a knife, so freeing the Padre from imminent peril of death.

"While riding another mountain trail to Coapa, the mule of Padre Pedro threw him to the earth, at the same time giving him two such violent kicks that those who accompanied him thought he must be dead. However, the Padre arose unhurt, exclaiming, 'Thanks be to God, it is nothing.'

"Once, upon his being called late at night to ride to hear the confession of an ill person, his servant by mistake saddled for him a young mule that had never before been ridden. Behaving like a well trained animal while the Padre was on its back, after he dismounted, it pitched mightily with the empty saddle.

"Another mule, upon being ridden by a soldier named Francisco de la Bria, had pitched lustily, throwing the soldier to the ground. The Padre in his gentle manner approached the animal, exclaiming, 'Hold, I can ride this mule,' and so he did, the animal behaving gently as a lamb.

"These particular cases are selected from the many told of the life of Padre Pedro Gravina, as being evidence of the particular care of God in protecting this except ional servant.

"The death of Padre Gravina was caused by a severe pain in his side, occasioned by his exposure during his continuous travels. The climax of his sickness came when, upon crossing a river one day upon his mule, his clothes were completely immersed in water. Continuing in this cold damp clothing, he arrived only as far as the pueblo of Yamoriba, where his final sickness overcame him.

"Comprehending that the day of his blessed transition to Heaven had arrived, he requested one of his assistants to bring him a crucifix. Holding this crucifix in his hands, in phrases filled with devotion he delivered his soul to his God.

"Complying with a request of Padre Gravina made during the hours of his illness, his body was carried on a journey of two and a half days for burial at his favorite Mission of Santa Maria de Utais, which he had himself constructed . . ."

Here end the quotations from the letter of the Padre Superior of the Mission to the Padre Provincial in the city of Mexico, in which he advised that another dutiful servant of God had been taken into Paradise.

With this story of the life of the venerable Padre Pedro Gravina ends the history of the Missions of the Sierras of Topia.

BOOK III

MISSIONS OF THE CENTRAL PLATEAU OF MEXICO

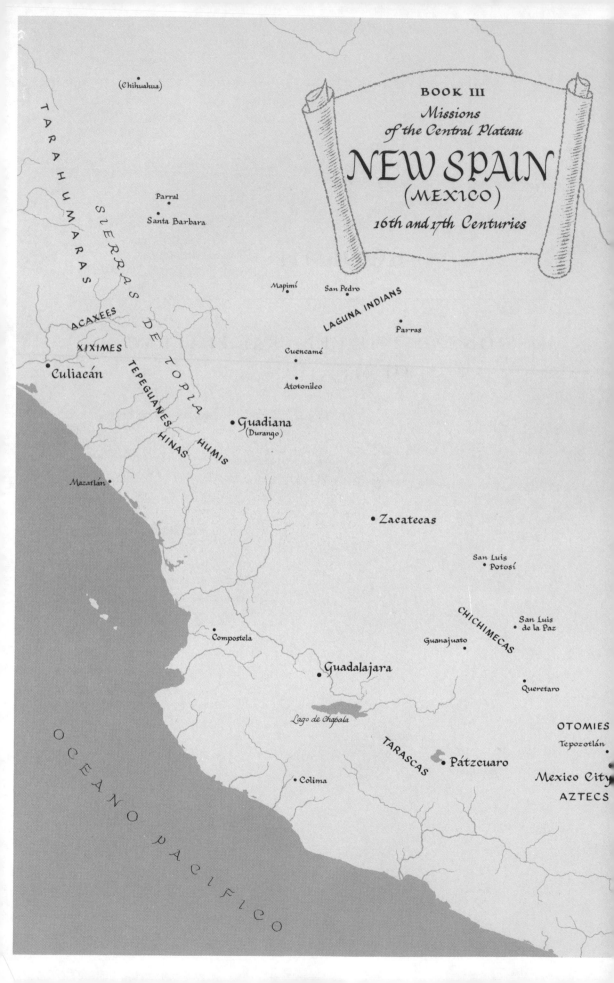

CHAPTER 1

Parras and the Great Lagoon of San Pedro (Coahuila)

AFTER WRITING of the Nations of the Province of Sinaloa and those of the great Sierras of Topia, there yet remains to tell of other Indian Nations who lived in the shadow and peril of death eternal, until the coming of the Padres to insure their spiritual salvation. These Nations, residing eastward and southward of the great Sierras we have so often referred to, did not live as those we have just described, among high peaks nor in deep gorges, but rather upon vast arid plains.

Penetrating their lonely deserts, the Soldiers of the Militia of Jesus with imminent risk of their lives implanted among them the doctrine of our Holy Faith. To the principal of these desert Missions there was given the name of Parras, because of the abundance in that place of wild grapes similar to those grown in Castile.

It is interesting to note in passing, that the grapes of Castile grow in the soil of Parras as in no other place in new Spain. Grapes are planted only around the area of the great Lake of San Pedro which lies near Parras, for the dryness elsewhere is such that no trees can survie.

This great Laguna de San Pedro lies some ninety miles northeastward of Guadiana. To arrive there one must travel over trails so scarce of water that at certain seasons its must be carried in barrels for travelers and their riding and pack animals. [*Probably in leather water bags as well.*] From the Real of Mines of Zacatecas there is a less formidable approach, but over a much longer distance.

The Laguna Grande de San Pedro, as it is called, has in dry season a circumference of some 125 miles, and in flood season of perhaps 200 miles. Its floods come from a large river called De Las Nazas, whose flood waters, after filling the Lagoon, often extend over vast areas of plain. This river, as do those that flow westward to the Seas of Californias, has its source in the great Sierras of Topia.

The Laguna de San Pedro is sheltered on one side by woods and mountains, on the others is surrounded by plain.

In the summer the climate of the plains is stifling hot. The soil about the lake is mellow, capable of producing any crop in great abundance, especially during the warmer seasons of the year.

Rises in the Rio Nazas bring great numbers of fish to the Lagoon, providing much food for the Indians who live about its borders, or on the numerous Islets of the Lagoon. As the water lowers, these fish are apt to be concentrated into estuaries or large pools, and then are more easily caught. Among the fish caught are some called matalotes, which are much esteemed for eating by the Indians.

The Indians also capture wild ducks from the Lagoon. Many of these are taken with arrows. However, others are captured in a most unique manner, by huntsmen who, placing over their heads a half of a hollowed out pumpkin or gourd, with slots for the eyes, swim quietly through the water and, drifting among the ducks, upon approaching pull them quickly under water, then wringing their necks to prevent other ducks from learning what has happened to their companions. This unusual manner of capturing ducks is known also to the Indians living about the great lake of the Valley of Mexico.

With the receding of the waters each season, the exposed lands are seeded to maiz, beans, pumpkins, chilis, cotton and other crops. The Laguna Indians, from all these sources have an abundant food supply, except during exceptionally dry seasons.

When the conversion of the Laguna Indians was begun, and they were advised of the precept of the church of abstaining from the eating of meat on certain days, it was not easy to persuade them that ducks should be included in the flesh restricted. They argued that ducks should be considered as fish, as they swam under water, laid their eggs in the damp marshes, and took their food from the water of the Lagoon. However, they eventually submitted to the teachings of their ministers in this matter, as they did in others of greater consideration.

Continuing to describe the sustenance provided by God for these people, one of these very peculiar to the Great Lagoon is the espadaña (*cattail or tule*), like those called anea in Spain, from which the roots are taken to be eaten. These roots they treat and grind into a form of flour, from which they make a food good to taste, either as a beverage mixed in water, or in the form of cakes made from the paste obtained by dampening the flour with water. These cakes, when dried, may last them for several days without becoming too hardened. With so many sources of food available, the Indians of the Laguna are not as diligent in the sowing of maiz and other crops, as are those of many other Nations.

The mesquite pod they also grind into a flour for bread. It has already been told that these mesquite pods, pounded and fermented, also serve for the brewing of wine.

These Indians spend much time in the hunting of game, such as birds, rabbits and deer, all of which there are in abundance about the Lagoon. In some of the deer are found the healing stones (*piedras bezares*) well known in other parts of the world for their use in medication.

I shall now tell of some of the barbarous customs peculiar to these people. One is that, upon a mother giving birth to a child, the father abstains for a week from tasting meat or fish, believing that should he fail to do so, the deer and other wild game would depart beyond the reach of his arrows, and the fish would depart from the shallower pools into the deeper areas of the Lagoon.

The desert Indians preserved the heads and horns of the deer they captured, feeling that keeping them would bring good luck in future hunting. In this custom they might be said to practice a form of belief in the supernatural. Others of their superstitions were those common to the Indian Nations of which have been written, and need not be repeated.

These Indians did have a particular name for the Devil in their language, and gave voluble and innumerable testimonies of his appearances before them, always describing him as a horrible figure, sometimes dressed in black, often with jets of flame pouring forth from his eyes. At other times he appeared to be spouting blood from his mouth and ears. Yet others saw him as a fiend who brought such terror that they felt compelled to follow him in his diabolical intrigues, so becoming slaves to his cruel tyranny.

This tyranny might sometimes even take the form of requiring that they take the lives of others, at times even of their own children, and particularly that of a first born child. They were sometimes required to take the life of some person elderly on infirm, that the Devil might claim the victim to further populate his infernal-regions.

At other times the Devil threatened them with illnesses, trying to lead them to believe that he is the author of life and death.

These people often indulged in barbarous dances, which they celebrated with great numbers of people, all forming a circle, attired in gaudy head dress and trappings, moving and swaying in perfect rhythm and unison with each other. Such dances were held·while circling about a great bonfire, and lasted usually from the beginning of night until the rising of the sun on the day following.

In these barbarous dances there was some separation of men and women; nevertheless such celebrations were not apt to be wholly free of the immoralities which the Devil provokes on such occasions. To all of these orgies must be added their habit of drinking, which was much practiced by them during their long period of spiritual darkness.

Into this drinking they had introduced the use of the herb called peyote, before referred to, which is very celebrated among the Indians of the Nations of New Spain and which, although considered to hold certain medicinal properties when taken in moderation, when taken in excess causes derangement of the mind, bringing diabolical fantasies to the imagination. To the use of this herb are leagued the practice of many of their superstitions inspired by the Devil.

Also they believed that the Devil caused the great whirlwinds which frequently rose high above the desert. Upon seeing these, the Indians would prostrate themselves in fear, shouting to each other the word "Cachinipa," which is the name of the particular Devil which they believe causes these whirlwinds.

The Padres, with patience, explained the true cause for such phenomena. They also made clear how certain angels had fallen from Heaven to become Devils and were, therefore, enemies of all people who aspire to Heaven.

It is well to recount to them the original sin of Eve and Adam, for the remedy of which God has instituted the ceremony of baptism. This explanation is easily accepted by the Indians, who have a facile concept of the malicious intent of the Devil in such matters. They soon acquire an abhorrence of the ways of the Devil equal to that of the most devout Christians.

Their practices and superstitions at the time of death and burial, with long lamentations for the dead, were very similar to those described earlier in this history.

With this description of the Indians of the Laguna Grande de San Pedro and their ancient manner of living, we shall now turn to the period of the coming of the Padres.

CHAPTER 2

The Coming of the Padres

IN THE YEAR 1594 two Padres traversed the desert from the rich Real of Mines of Zacatecas to begin the indoctrination of the Indians of the Laguna Grande de San Pedro. They were Gerónimo Ramirez, of whom is made mention in the story of the Tepeguane Mission, where he later served, and Juan Augustín, who ended his life in the service of the Indians of the desert.

Padre Gerónimo wrote of his first months of the service, in a letter to his Superior in the City of Mexico, which letter was in turn passed on to the Viceroy. Quoting from Padre Gerónimo:

"Our Father has guided me across the great desert to the Indian pueblo of Cuencamé, in a valley of the same name, which lies surrounded by distant mountains. Cuencamé is distant still twenty five miles from the Rio Nazas, which flows into the Laguna de San Pedro.

"The people of this desert speak the same language as those of the Real of Zacatecas, and many have gone there to work in the mines.

"There have come Indians from as far as the Rio Nazas to welcome me. Several were riding horses which, from their earnings in the mines, they have purchased from Spaniards.

"These people are decently, if somewhat scantily, clad; and appear genuinely friendly. I was able to give words of greeting to them in their own tongue, which I had been studying in preparation for this Mission.

"I have been lodged in the small adobe house of a Tarascan Indian, the only such one in the village. To this I have now added a porch, and am using this for holding services.

"My teaching has begun with reciting biblical stories to them, and they seem much content with this manner of learning. I am confident that if the Governor of the Province and the Viceroy will lend us some assistance, we shall be able to reach many more people, even of those who now live in isolated places on the desert. May God move those gentlemen to feel pity for those poor souls."

A letter from Padre Juan Agustín describes his journey, which finally terminated in meeting with the Indians of the Great Lagoon, as follows:

"The first pueblo where I paused to give doctrine, on my journey across the desert to the Great Lagoon, is called Cerro Gordo, for a nearby mountain of much height and grandeur which carries that same name. Some distance before arriving I was met by the principal Cacique and numerous other Indians, all proudly riding horses.

"These people expressed much reverence for me, and pleasure at my coming. That first night after meeting we camped together on the desert. The day following, our trail passed through various little pueblos and rancherias, at each of these places there being gathered many persons to greet me. Finally we arrived at a pueblo where many people had formed into two long lines, to await my coming.

"We proceeded all together to a little building that is to serve, for the time, as a church. Here, before all the people who had assembled, I invoked the blessing of God in favor of our undertaking. Before the building we erected a framework and suspended a church bell which I had brought, after which some of the group sang some oratorios they had learned in their own language while laboring in the Real of Mines of Zacatecas. After this, the first Mass was held.

"There soon came Indians from the Great Lagoon to plead with me to accompany them there, to give spiritual consolation to many people gravely ill from small pox. One of them said to me, 'We have come to you, Padre, for we know that you do not come selfishly, in search of gold and silver, as do many other Spaniards, but only to insure that our souls shall be taken into Heaven. This being your motive, we know you will not look down upon us because of our poverty.'

"We departed at once for this Great Lagoon. Here I quickly baptized eighteen children and heard confession and gave baptism to large numbers of older persons, all of whom were ill.

"I have found much affection and loyalty among these people. It is pleasing to them for me to be able to converse with them in the Zacatecan language. This is a good beginning, and I do not doubt that our Mission shall carry on to greater glory."

It was found by the Padres that there lived a total of perhaps 12,000 Indians around the borders of this Great Lagoon.

In the desert areas the Indians make much use of the mescal plant, of the same family as that growing on the plains of the Province of Sinaloa, which after roasting is full of moisture and sweetness.

Their women commonly wore hides of wild animals, rubbed and treated to make them pliable, adding attractive fringes to the borders of their dresses. This leather clothing they often dyed in bright colors.

The Indians braided their hair with much care. They commonly wore collars of little sea shells of bright colors, or larger conches, which they felt added much to the gaiety of their appearance.

The desert Indians are of large stature, well muscled, and extremely dextrous in the use of weapons. The men are clever in the making of bows, which they fashion much longer than those of Indians living in the forests. These longer bows have greater carrying power, for shooting game at longer distances.

The Indians of the Laguna are of a generous nature, sharing with largess of

229

whatever they have. Their houses are left open, and visitors are welcome. To the Spaniards generally, they are very friendly, cheerfully becoming their allies in war, as during the period of the Great Rebellion of the Tepeguanes and other Nations in the Sierras of Topia. The alliance of the Spaniards with the Laguna Indians was also of much assistance in keeping in check the neighboring Chicimecas.

As the Company of Jesus receives no pittances nor donations for their labors in the conversion of these savage peoples, it has been necessary to depend upon the officials of the Spanish Crown for assistance, which, to the glory of their Catholic Majesties, has been provided.

Padre Francisco Arista, from the Mission of Guadiana, founded the principal Mission at the pueblo of Parras. I here quote from a letter to his Superior:

"With the assistance of the Caciques from the surrounding rancherias I have now gathered here many hundreds of families, all of whom are receiving religious training. In addition to these, there are groups constantly coming and going. I invite the Caciques now and then to dine with me, and on holidays people assemble from near and distant places to attend services. On these occasions there is much feasting afterwards. Christian songs are sung in their own language. The children hold their little feasts apart, after attending Mass. All these activities have been a fine medium for enlisting the interest of these people.

"Many groups who have made pilgrimages to our Mission have returned to erect crosses at their rancherias, before which they worship.

"For those families who settle here in the pueblo, there is measured a parcel of land for a home, a garden and a small field . . . I advise them in the planning of their houses . . . also I attend those who are ill . . . all are asking now to be baptized, there remaining none now who dare act as they accustomed in the days of their paganism.

"When a Christian Indian child is buried, the other children follow in the funeral procession, their heads properly covered with garlands of flowers, all singing the proper prayers in their own language. May God preserve them in their present good disposition, and may He send us other companions to assist in this effort . . ."

The Indians of the area surrounding the Laguna de San Pedro were finally concentrated into only five pueblos, containing many hundreds of persons in each. Others lived on little Islets on the Lake. Even here they were frequently visited by the Padres who, in order to reach these places, often must ride long distances in water up to the shoulders of their animals.

The Spanish authorities designated Governors from among the principal Caciques, presenting them with swords to denote their positions of authority.

In the course of time, the Viceroy financed the sending of additional Padres for setting up parochial schools, assigning 300 pesos annually for the education of each Indian youngster of promise, with the intention that they should later return to their places or origin, for the purpose of educating their own people.

The rich production of silver, especially in the Real of Zacatecas, has more than justified the expense and effort that has been made to enlighten the neighboring Indian Nations, and to keep them in peace.

However, one of the richest rewards of ministering to these humble savages has been the enthusiastic cooperation of the little Indian children and younger people. Many little fiestas have been planned especially for them. Some of these children arise before dawn, to go shouting through the streets, that their young companions shall awaken, and follow them to Mass.

On the Dia de los Santos Inocentes a meal was served to all the children in the patio of the church. To add importance to the occasion, a trumpet was played between each course of the meal. Everyone was excited and impressed by this ceremony, including the carnal fathers of these little barbarians so recently converted.

A most cruel superstition of these Indians was that the sacrificing of a child might lead to the healing of older people in times of epidemics of sickness. Another unnatural belief was that one should not be present at the death of another person, else they might follow the other in death. To avoid this supposed calamity, the person ill was apt to be carried away from the dwelling, to die alone in the desert.

Friends and relatives of the deceased would gather for several evenings after the burial, their faces smeared with black soot, to carry on a loud and prolonged lamentation for their dead. In the course of their wailing they would recite the virtues of the deceased, such as his valor in war, his skill as a hunter, and his ability to provide for his family, sadly lamenting his death. Had these sad mourners only realized to where the souls of their unbaptized friends had departed, their wailing would have been much greater.

On a certain day of the year there was held a tribal dance in honor of the deceased hunters and warriors of their Nation. At the climax of this dance, the heads and horns of all the deer that had been killed by the deceased during his lifetime would be cast into the flames, the additional brilliance resulting being said to be the spirit of the deceased rising into the air.

At a time when a Padre had stopped for the night at an Indian village, there was heard a great calling, as of a person in agony. Thinking some faithful Indian was being carried away by the Devil, the Padre gathered some disciples, and all followed the sound of the voice, discovering that it issued from the entrance of a large cave, from which there extended several smaller caves. The Indians told the Padre that the Devil often appeared here, at times in the form of a serpent, at others in a human form that was fierce and terrifying.

Entering this cave, the Padre found a graveyard filled with human skulls, over which had been piled some stones, in the belief that by so doing these skulls could be kept from rising to frighten the living.

He further found that the walls of this large cave had been marked with characters somewhat in the form of writing, having been drawn apparently in human blood. Some were located at such height that it seemed impossible that a human hand could have executed them. These paintings were so securely encrusted on the stones that neither winds nor rains had blurred or marred them.

The Padre and his companions presently found the man who had been clamoring so loudly. He was lying unconscious, appearing to be dead. However, having been carried out of the cave to a home, by the following morning he recovered consciousness.

After some exhortation by the Padre, he agreed to have no further dealings with the Devil, and was eventually confessed and baptized.

The Padre asked a group of Christian Indians to re-enter the cave with him, carrying a high cross, which they placed on an elevation at its center, after which there were carried out the exorcisms and benedictions accustomed by the church in such extreme cases. This place was thereafter called the Cueva de Santiago, for the day the cross raising ceremony was held, and the disturbances of the Devil have ceased.

The Indians of the community have continued very much relieved and grateful, as well as being properly impressed with the potence of the Ministers of God in dealing with such matters.

By the year 1607 all the children and most of the adults of the area of the Laguna Grande de San Pedro had been converted and baptized, although even to this late date (*1645*) there still come wandering from out of the wilderness occasional Indian families to join others in their practice of Christianity.

Feasts of the Nativity through the years have become memorable occasions among these Indians. In these they are joined by many Spaniards. The Indians now celebrate their dances more in conformity to Christian usage. Great bonfires are lighted before the church and about the Plaza. Dances are performed by groups from the several surrounding villages. Later, after entering the church for adoration of the Christ Child and His Saintly Mother, the Indians all gather outside in the courtyard of the church, which also serves as a cemetary. Here they present a combined dance of all the villages. This dance is called a Mitote, and in it there may take part as many as 2,000 to 3,000 persons, all with heads and bodies gaily adorned with tufts of brilliant feathers. The greatest leader of these dances was an Indian Cacique named Iritles. This multitude of dancers, under his direction, would perform in a rhythm with as much perfection as though only a few were performing. At intervals, around the great circle there were placed small groups of these same dancers, carrying little drums built of a special wood with which they carried the rhythm and compass of the dance.

All carried spears in their hands as they danced, and sang chants much in their ancient barbarian manner, except that now the words were those of the Christian faith. Translated from their native language, the words to one of their chants ran in this wise:

> "Worthy is God of being praised;
> Happy are we while celebrating this feast
> In honor of our Holy Mother;
> All people praise our Holy Mother;
> Worship we the place wherein resides
> Our Holy Mother,
> The Mother of God;
> He who is our true Father."

232

This song and rhythm they also repeat to the accompaniament of an organ, while attending church services.

At the hour of cocks-crow, and again at daybreak, appropriate Masses are held. Following this, a fine breakfast of barbecued beef is prepared by the Spaniards of all the areas near enough for them to attend the feasting.

Much credit should be given to a blind Indian of the Laguna Nation who, having learned the chants by rote, trained the choir of the principal church from one year to another.

Padre Francisco de Arista, at the Lenten season, accustomed singing a Miserere, accompanied by this fine choir.

Into these lands there came a terrible scourge of cocolitzle [*Small pox, called Tomtíahuame in the Yaqui-Mayo language*]. Indians perished by the thousands.

Taking with them what they could secure of corn and flour to prepare gruels, the Padres traveled night and day to the physical and spiritual aid of the stricken. Of medicaments there were few, and none of these greatly effective. The Indians had no other remedy than to apply little coals from fagots to the sores, or to bleed themselves with the points of their arrows.

When the great sickness came, the witch doctors still remaining called gatherings of the people, which were said to be for the purpose of placating the Devil, and inducing him to remove the disease. They insisted that the Devil did really appear to them at these gatherings, sometimes in the form of a pillar of fire, again as a stag or a serpent, and yet again as a figure of fierce countenance robed in white, which told them they were thus threatened with death because of having become Christians.

These same witch doctors caused them to dance before a heathen idol night after night until they became exhausted. They also advised the Indians to suspend their long stone knives on a thong from the doorways of their houses, as a manner of propitiation of the Devil. Some Hechiceros advised their followers to suspend instead, bodies of falcons, which they hung by their talons.

Another absurd argument used against the Padres was that they had brought the sickness in order to decimate the numbers of Indians, so that the Spaniards could possess their lands.

Stirred by such falsehoods, one group came from a distant rancheria to tear down a Christian cross that stood in a pueblo. On their return journey many were afflicted by the pox. A Padre who had heard of their sacrilege followed after them, and remained as their Minister until they had either died or recovered.

Concurrently with the coming of this pestilence there had appeared a great comet in the sky. At the desert pueblo of Mapimí, the inhabitants held a ceremonial dance for the purpose of propitiating the Devil, whom they felt had caused the sickness.

Before joining in this dance the people made a procession, men with men, women with women, and children with children, all carrying baskets in their right hands and in their left a lance, with its head of stone pointed at their hearts. These baskets were filled with offerings of the food of the land, such as the fruit of the yucca; the nopal cactus; roasted mescal heads, and pods of the mesquite trees. Other baskets contained dead rats, gophers, rabbits or snakes.

Because the comet appeared to have a tail, many wore tails of animals, such as foxes or lions, at the same time imitating the calls of these animals, as they traveled in the procession.

In the center of the Plaza there was built a great bonfire, into which each person, as they walked past, would throw their basket with whatever it contained. It was felt that this flame must reach into the sky until touching the comet, in the belief that this would appease its supposed hunger for their bodies. As the smoke arose, the old men among them flailed it with whips which they carried, seemingly believing that this action would release the smoke to arise further into the sky.

On the first attempt, a wind arose, scattering the smoke. This the four principal witch doctors took as a bad omen. In a further attempt to propitiate the comet, they cut the hair from the heads of six of their maidens; then using some sort of combs, they cruelly scratched the scalps of the maidens, causing them to bleed so profusely that the blood could be gathered into gourds. Into this blood was dipped the hair of the maidens, which was then shaken into the air. While this ceremony was going forward, the four Hechiceros continued dancing and howling most horribly.

Finally the smoke arose in a tall straight column, and the dancers were content, feeling they would now be freed from the terrible malady. With this ended their diabolical dancing.

However, despite all these superstitious antics, the sickness eventually came to Mapimí. One of those most gravely ill was a principal Cacique, and in their desperation to save him, his relatives planned the sacrifice of a new born child. They went to the child's mother, offering in exchange for her baby, many deerskins, gourds, pottery, strings of beads, and bones which are used by the Indians in their heathen rituals.

Desperately frightened, the mother fled with her child into the darkness, traveling ten miles over the desert to the home of some relatives. The savages followed her, but were confronted by a group of the relatives. A bloody battle took place in which many on both sides were severely beaten.

While her relatives battled in her behalf, the mother fled once more through the night until arriving at Mapimí, where she sought the protection of the Padre. Here the pursuers dared not intrude, but in their rage they set fire to a hut in which lived an old man, relative of the fleeing woman, this poor man being literally burned alive.

As time passed, and the sickness continued, the Indians who had at first followed the suggestions of the witch doctors, now became disenchanted, and turned to the Padres to be indoctrinated and baptized, so that should they perish, at least their souls should be saved from perdition. The terrible scourge finally passed, leaving the population of the mountains and deserts much decimated.

Those who survived seemed more than ever to feel the need for spiritual guidance and consolation. They continued diligently with the building of churches, which were inaugurated with great fiestas, to which came large numbers of people, both barbarian and Christian, and from among the barbarians many were won to Christianity.

Not many years after the pestilence of small pox there came a second great calamity to add to the desolation of the inhabitants of the Laguna area. The Rio Nazas rose to a height not seen in thirty years, overflowing all the surrounding plain. The pueblos of San Gerónimo, San Ignacio and San Pedro were threatened with extinction, as the river left its normal course to cut deep new channels near these pueblos.

At San Pedro the two Padres were warned that they must flee immediately. Gathering some clothing and the most precious treasures of the church, they departed into the night, in a tempest of wind and rain.

Guided by two faithful Indians, they traversed fearful thickets of brush filled with thorns, and crossed swollen streams, until they arrived at water so deep they could go no further, being saved from drowning by some Indians who found them and swam them across a river, to where other refugees from the storm were gathered about some camp fires. For two days the group was kept imprisoned in a mesquite thicket that stood slightly above the waters. The refugees finally were forced to still higher ground, a strip of land so narrow that there was scarcely room to erect a brush shelter upon it.

The flood finally subsiding, they returned to the pueblo, rejoicing at finding the walls of the church and dwelling of the Padres still standing, although they had been deep in the flood waters.

Fortunate indeed were the Padres and their Indian companions to have come through this adventure without having been bitten by the scores of venomous vipers which had also sought relief from the flood in the higher areas. At times these had crawled over their bodies when they were attempting to secure some rest by lying on the earth. After the great flood, in one pueblo over fifty poisonous snakes were killed, some of them five feet in length.

One happy result of this flood was that it cut a great canal through the land at precisely the point where it was needed to irrigate more crops with which to feed the people. Many people from more distant places were, for this same reason, enabled to find lands for planting, and came to live among the Indians surrounding the Great Lagoon.

In years of great drought, Indians from other areas had come in search of food to save themselves from starving, but had been driven away by the Laguna Indians. Now, in their new found Christianity, they invited their former enemies to share of what they had, including lands for planting. To symbolize this newly established friendship, the Indians of the Laguna held a ceremony in which they cut the strings of their bows and handed them, together with their quivers of arrows, to the strangers they now welcomed to their lands. Thus they demonstrated their newly discovered faith, although in a manner reminiscent of their ancient days.

235

CHAPTER 3

The Tepeguanes Bring Unrest to the Desert

THE TEPEGUANES made special diligence to induce the Indians of Parras and the Laguna to join them in the great revolt of 1616. Tepeguanes living near the Rio Nazas and the desert Missions assaulted Reales of Mines, pueblos and rancherias, killing numerous Spaniards and driving off great numbers of livestock.

The Spaniards living in and near Guadiana believed the desert Indians culpable together with the Tepeguanes, and executed those of one and another Indian Nation as they came upon them. This hasty and unpremeditated action caused much fear, as well as indignation, among the Indians from the Rio Nazas and the Laguna, leading many of them to join the uprising of the mountain Nations. The desert Indians being of such renown as warriors, the leaders among the Tepeguanes, and other Indians who led the revolt, made every effort to secure their assistance. War councils were called, and Hechiceros busied themselves once more with stirring the feelings of their people against the Spaniards and Padres.

At the Mission of Parras the situation became so threatening that the Padres called a council of their oldest and most trusted Christian Indians. After the Holy Sacrament had been administered to them, these faithful ones followed the Padres to the principal Plaza of the pueblo, where a large crowd had gathered. A principal Christian Indian leader who accompanied the Padres made a most inspired talk to all the people assembled, reprimanding the disturbers, and inviting all to join their Christian leaders in the defense of their pueblo and their Padres. The people reacted favorably to this exhortation and gathered in the church, mounting guard outside. It was a fearful night, stormy, with torrents of rain falling. Fortunately, the next day the crisis had passed.

Much the same action was taken at the pueblos of Las Nazas and Mapimí, there being at each place Christian Indian leaders who with calm reasoning persuaded their followers to remain at peace.

It was these evidences of faithfulness that inspired Governor don Gaspár de Albear to invite them to accompany the Spaniards as allies on their expedition into the Sierras in 1616 against the Indians in revolt there. Many hundreds of them volunteered, a Mass being held for them in the church of Parras before they departed.

This excellent relationship between the Laguna Indians, the Spaniards, the Spanish authorities, and the Padres, has continued through the years.

CHAPTER 4

Padre Juan Augustín, Founder of the Mission of Parras

IT HAS BEEN MY PURPOSE to write at the conclusion of the story of each principal Indian Nation or groups of Nations, something of the lives of the outstanding Missionaries who served these people in the beginning of their conversion from savagery. I wish to tell here of Padre Juan Augustín, founder of the Mission of Parras, which is the largest of the desert area of which we have just written. In order that the reader may judge the character of this dedicated young man, and the trials which he faced, I now quote from a letter written by him:

". . . In addition to continuous teaching of these people, I am constantly busy with confessions, baptisms and marriages. It is also my frequent lot to act as an arbiter of peace, not only among my Indian disciples, but even among Spaniards, when occasion requires.

"All this I do with sincere pleasure, yet at the same time with wonder that God has given so much responsibility into my hands, who am so little qualified to serve as the instrument of his Divine Majesty in these matters.

"What patience, and what confidence in the divine, is required to minister to these primitive souls. In what solitude do these Indians live, in such a wilderness, with such perilous desert trails, and so little water, and such scarcity of food for their travels.

"There is so much solitude in the nights spent alone on the desert, and so much suffering from heat during the day. There is such unbearable torture from the hordes of mosquitoes near the places where there is water.

"It is so difficult to cope with their witch doctors, and to keep the people from joining them in their war councils.

"Yet withal, I console myself with the thought that if all were a bed of flowers here on earth, there would be little left to appreciate upon arriving in Heaven. In this isolated place each day I await death, and continually pray that I may accept it with a contrite and humble heart, hoping only that my soul may find acceptance in God."

This brief and poignant letter from Padre Juan Augustín summarizes and epitomizes his worthy and virtuous life. In the lonely and isolated Mission of Parras he died at scarce thirty years of age, of which the last four were spent here, virtually alone, in the service of our God and our Company.

CHAPTER 5

Story of Padre Gerónimo Ramirez

IT IS ALTOGETHER FITTING that there be told here also of the virtuous life and great labors of Padre Gerónimo Ramirez, whose name has first appeared in the story of the conversion of the great Tepeguane Nation, then later in describing his efforts in behalf of the Indians of the Great Laguna of San Pedro.

I have before me a memorandum from the pen of his boyhood friend, Padre Andrés Cozorla, one of the oldest living members of our Company, and highly esteemed in Andalucía. It states that Padre Gerónimo was born in Seville, of honorable parents, in the year 1557, was reared in the home of the Duchess of Alcalá, then placed at the proper age under the tutorship of don Garcia de Haro, Bishop of Cadíz. His teaching was continued at our very excellent College at Córdoba.

He traveled to Mexico in the year 1584 in the company of our Padre Provincial don Antonio de Mendoza. (*who was later Viceroy*). Sent to the College at Pátzcuaro, in the Province of Michoacán, he quickly became proficient in the Tarascan language.

Soon he had multitudes of Indians coming to the central market place to listen to his sermons, which included frequent references to the life of Our Lord and of the Saints. From here he extended his field of endeavour to the far countryside; from the highlands often covered with snow to the lowland jungles of Colima and Zacatula.

After three years he was transferred to Zacatecas, from whence he undertook the adventurous journeys into the lands of the Tepeguanes and to the desert regions already described.

From here he was selected for a most delicate mission 2,500 miles southward, to the City of Guatemala. Bishop Juan Ramirez of the Order of Santo Domingo, who presided there, was so opposed to the coming of a Jesuit Missionary into his territory that, in order to avoid meeting Padre Gerónimo, he absented himself for a long period from the city. However, our Padre followed him, and upon their finally meeting, engaged the Bishop in such profound and learned discussions that the latter forgave his coming. For many years thereafter he preached to multitudes of Indians in Guatemala.

He was recalled to Mexico City to become a teacher in our school for Indian boys at San Ildefonso. At 60 years of age, because of the death of Padre Juan Ferro, he cheerfully returned to his old charge at Pátzcuaro, traversing again the rugged highlands and torrid jungles to minister to his many disciples.

Finally, in the year 1621, old and wearied from his immense labors, he fell ill while at a lonely lowland mission, living only long enough to receive the blessed sacrament from the hands of his friend Padre Gerónimo de Santiago, who had come hurriedly from Pátzcuaro to his aid. His body, against the wishes of his Indian disciples, was later transferred to our College at Pátzcuaro, to await that glorious day when, united with his soul, it should enjoy glory through eternity.

I had the privelege of knowing Padre Gerónimo but a brief time, yet long enough to acquire a concept of him well worthy of the description written by his old boyhood friend.

CHAPTER 6

Mission of San Luis de la Paz

I SHALL NOW TELL BRIEFLY of the founding and location of the Jesuit Colleges of New Spain, beginning with that of San Luis de la Paz, which although distant only 120 miles from the City of Mexico northward, lies in the territory of the fierce Chichimeca Indians.

The Chichimecas are an ancient Nation, as is proven by the fact that when the Mexican (*Toltec-Aztec*) Nation came to found the City of Tenochtitlán (*City of Mexico*) the Chichimecas already populated the desert areas where they still live.

So valiant and warlike were the Chichimecas that not even the great Aztec Emperor Moctezuma, with all the legions at his command, and who subjected many other Kings and Nations, was ever able to conquer the Chichimecas. If, in any of the numerous encounters between Aztecs and Chichimecas through the centuries, the former were able to earn any least advantage in battle, this was held a feat so outstanding as to be celebrated with much feasting and dancing in the councils of the Aztecs.

The Spaniards also were forced into frequent warfare against this Nation, long after other Nations had become civilized.

Through the land of the Chichimecas runs the principal road (*Camino Real*) from the City of Mexico to the northern Provinces of Nueva Vizcaya and Galicia, where were located so many fabulously rich Reales of Mines. Wagons loaded with merchandise for these Reales of Mines, or returning towards Mexico City with silver bullion, were frequently assaulted and robbed by outlaw Chichimecas.

I once passed along this Camino Real on my way to the Province of Sinaloa, and saw with surprise and pity the great number of crosses that lined its borders, as it passed through the lands of these primitive savages. They were not so many in number as many other Nations, but their daring was great, and their manner of making war, scattered in roving bands as they were, made it extremely difficult to locate and subdue them. Like the Alarabes of Africa, they lived as wanderers on the great desert, without a fixed location, nor houses, nor lands which they cultivated.

They moved with the ripening of each of the desert fruits in its season. The principal of these fruits were the tuna (*nopal cactus*), and a poorly flavored fruit called the date of the desert, which grows on a species of wild palm. They also toasted the heads of mescales for food, and made wine from it by fermenting the juice. All the products mentioned they fermented, living to a large extent from drinking their juices, which kept them more or less in a state of constant intoxication.

Succeeding Viceroys of New Spain had ordered Presidios to be constructed, one day's travel apart, across the desert, along the route of this Camino Real. Groups of fifteen to twenty wagons traveled in convoys over this road, escorted by detachments of soldiers. In each convoy was a wagon on which had been constructed a tall tower (*torreon*) of heavy timber, so that arrows could not penetrate it. Here the women and children took shelter when attacked. However, at times the wild Chichimecas fell upon the convoys without the least warning, capturing and murdering men, women and children.

Chichimeca warriors accustomed carrying a human leg bone suspended from their belt, on which they would place a notch for every Spaniard they had killed, some warriors having recorded from twenty to thirty notches.

In the year 1594, soon after the first Padres had ventured as far as the Province of Sinaloa, the Chichimecas were making it almost impossible to travel across the desert toward the northern Provinces. The Viceroy and Captain General of the Spanish forces at that time was don Luis de Velasco the First, a gentleman of much ability and zeal in serving their divine and Catholic Majesties of Spain. Finding that the measures until then taken to subdue the fiery Chichimecas had been almost fruitless, as well as excessively expensive, this Viceroy resolved to avail himself of the strength of the Divine, rather than that of soldiers and fortifications, in attempting their submission.

In truth, the subjection of the savage Nations of the New World has always been less costly and more effective, when accomplished peacefully, by Ministers of the church through Divine assistance.

In this instance, the Viceroy arranged that our Company should undertake the founding of a pueblo on the border of the Chichimeca Nation, the site selected being on the banks of a small river, where there were some lands for cultivation. To this pueblo was given the name of San Luis de la Paz, in honor of the Viceroy don Luis de Velasco.

As a first measure, there were moved to this place a goodly number of families of the Otomí Nation who had become Christians, that their example might prove exemplary to their savage neighbors.

In order to induce the Otomís to take root here, they received exemption from payment of the ordinary tribute paid by the Indian Nations to the Kings of Spain, and in addition were given free land with water for the growing of crops.

To all the Chichimecas who should agree to settle here in peace, the Viceroy ordered given a weekly ration of meat and corn. To the Caciques among them who chose to take the path of peace, they gave official duties as Governors of their people, making an annual distribution of gifts and clothing to these leaders.

Funds were provided from the Royal Treasury for the building and maintaining of an adequate church, and for the support of ministers who should attend these people. To begin their formidable task there were at first sent three Padres.

A few of the Chichimecas came in the beginning to greet them, and in due time, seeing with what kindness and affection they were treated, many others followed their example. With great patience, and enduring many hardships in their stewardship, these Padres finally gathered into the pueblo of San Luis de la Paz, 300 families of Chichimecas. From the beginning the Padres had dedicated themselves assiduously to learning the language of these savage people, which is generally considered to be the most difficult of all the native languages of New Spain.

A notable occasion at San Luis de la Paz was the baptism, and marriage in the church, of the first twenty couples of the Chichimecas. On the day previous, those that were to be baptized, together with many of their friends, had gone into the desert to search for honey from wild bees. Others had gone along the shore of the little stream, to capture wild fowl for the celebration.

The large brush enramada that served in the beginning as a church was gaily decorated with green branches and flowers. Under this enramada, after the ceremonies of baptism and marriage had been concluded, the Indian women served a delicious repast of wild fowl, tortillas and honey.

As the night fell, the Plaza of the little pueblo was lighted with torches. The men among the Indians each took their woman by the hand to form a great circle, performing a native dance after their own fashion, this dance being accompanied by singing their chants, and beating the great drums that once had called them to war against the Spaniards. The words of the chants were by now in praise of God our Lord.

A Seminary was instituted for the education of the children, that these might later return to the deserts of their ancestors to assist others in the learning of Christianity. A group of children from the Seminary of Tepotzotlán, near Mexico City, came to assist the Chichimeca children in learning the songs of the church, and also a civilized manner of living. As though in a story of romance, the voices of these Indian children could be heard singing in the Refectory before their meals were served. The children soon became so content that when their parents would come to take them for a visit to their old places of habitation, they would conceal themselves in order to remain with the Padres and the other children.

It cannot be truthfully said that all of these young savages were equally content with their new mode of living, for a few among them continued to be as wild as goats, rather than as gentle as proverbial lambs.

Among those baptized was a famous outlaw, who was known to have given death to well over thirty Spaniards, and to many times that number of Christian Indians, and of servants of people who traveled these lonely lands. This Cacique, baptized with the name of don Juan, held the title of Governor, and worked for many years to dissuade his people from drinking and other vices. It is sad to relate that on an evil day, he himself succumbed to this vice. Finally, in great remorse, he went to the Padres to plead for their pardon. For the time, however, they judged best to keep their doors closed to him. He next went to the Captain of the Presidio to beg his intercession with the Padres. The Padres then agreed to forgive him, but on condition that he must apologize for his conduct before all the Christian Indians in a public meeting.

241

To this the old Chief consented, with tears flowing down his face telling of his repentance. He continued thereafter to be an outstanding example of virtue, persuading many of his people to abstain from drinking and other vices.

In the years following the conversion of the fiery Chichimecas there were founded many rich Reales of Mines, such as Pozos and Sichu, and a most renowned Real named San Luis Potosí. The smelting of the ores at this time was done with charcoal, at estancias which were called carboneras.

There also came to be many cattle estancias on the great desert. To all these places the Padres now journeyed in safety, ministering to their disciples.

The original church at San Luis de la Paz is rich in ornaments, such as lamps and goblets of silver. Today it serves as a shrine for travelers through that once forbidden land. Many Spaniards, descendants of the original Conquistadores who came from Spain, now make their homes in this pueblo along the little river. In the years following the spiritual conquest of the once savage Chichimecas, it has truly lived up to its name of San Luis de la Paz.

,CHAPTER 7

The Curate of Tepotzotlan

IN THE YEAR 1621 King Felipe III instructed the Archbishop of Mexico, don Juan de la Serna, to place the Curate of Tepotzotlán, in the land of the Otomís near the City of Mexico, in the hands of our Company. At the same time His Highness instructed the Viceroy of New Spain, then don Diego Fernandez de Córdoba, Marquez de Guadalcazar, to attend to carrying out this order.

This Curate, which is for the training of Jesuit Missionaries, is the only one of its kind in New Spain. It was first requested by the Otomí Nation, whose people held a very special regard for the Jesuit Padres, for the reason that these had gone to much effort to learn the language of the Otomís, and reduce it to writing. By reason of its extreme complexity, it has not yet been printed.

In addition to the Curate, there is a Seminary where some fifty sons of the most prominent leaders of the Otomí and Aztec Nations are being educated. Here they are reared in all virtue, learning to read, write and sing, and to play all manner of instruments that may serve for the music of ecclesiastical services and celebrations. In the learning of these arts they have proved most dextrous, and are now being sought by churches, and even the larger cathedrals, with offers of good salaries. Other students of this Seminary have returned to become Governors of their pueblos. Yet others have continued on to places of higher learning, some graduating from Colleges with distinction in languages and other courses.

Don Francisco Manzo, Archbishop of Mexico, chose to honor an Indian student, don Gerónimo, by admitting him into the priesthood, a case most rare in the Indies. This young Indian Padre was further honored by having as his Godfather at his first Mass, don Diego de Guevara, Archbishop of Santo Domingo and Primate of the Indies.

Another young Indian, don Fernando, was graduated from the same College in 1642, and is now completing his studies for the priesthood.

I must explain here the reasons why so few Indian students of Theology have graduated to the priesthood. One is that the Indians as a whole are still neophytes, new in the faith. Another reason is that there are so many and so worthy Spanish clergymen, who are much advanced in learning, with profound knowledge of our ancient Catholic faith. The Indians ordained were sons of great Caciques, besides being of exceptional character and ability in their own right. They also had the distinct advantage of having perfect knowledge of their Indian language.

The principal church of Tepotzotlán is most beautiful, being surmounted by a great dome, which is newly adorned underneath with fine paintings. Its altars contain precious images. Its ornaments and vases are rich in appearance. The organ is considered to have a value of six thousand ducats.

The choir of Tepotzotlán is considered to be the finest of New Spain, being frequently taken to perform in the churches of other principal cities. People come from the most remote places, as to a shrine, to hear the services and choir music of Tepotzotlán.

Two days of very particular devotion here are Holy Thursday, and the Dia de los Inocentes (*Day of the Innocents*). Holy Thursday is celebrated by the Rector of the College bathing the feet of twelve poor Indians, being assisted in this office by the Indian Governor and other principal Caciques. Clothing is distributed to the poor, and afterwards a great feast is held, during which food is served generously to all who attend.

The climate of Tepotzotlán is so cool and refreshing that many persons of authority come here from other places to rest, and to enjoy the church services and fine music.

Too much stress cannot be given to the desirability of perfecting oneself in learning the Indian languages, which must be used not only in church services for the Indians, but by persons of authority everywhere. That great master of Theology, Padre Juan de Ledesma, who dedicated his high theological wisdom to the material and spiritual assistance of the poor and humble Indians of the Valley of Mexico, has described the language of the Aztecs who reigned at the coming of the Spaniards, as being most reverential in its manner of expression, resembling much the languages of the Courtiers of Europe.

It is most important to learn the fine distinctions in speech, in addressing their Princes and Caciques, as contrasted with addressing their common people. If a Padre, in preaching to a distinguished Indian congregation, misuses one word or phrase, he is apt to be subjected to ridicule.

Withal, the formation of nouns and verbs in their reverential manner of speaking is simple enough, as the terms of reverence are incorporated into the nouns and verbs themselves. For this reason, even a very young child of their Nation, accustomed to using the simpler language, knows how to address a Padre, or any other person of authority.

The people of the laboring class are, among the Indians, called mazeuales.

A Padre of noble lineage, don Antonio del Rincón, has reduced the language of the Aztecs, in both its elegant and simple forms, to writing.

Returning to the matter of teaching the Indians, in connection with the principal Jesuit College of San Pedro and San Pablo in Mexico City, there is a Seminary for Indian children to which has been given the name of San Gregorio El Magno, where there are also some fifty sons of Caciques in training.

Before the services opening the Lenten Season, these children, accompanied by their Padres, form a procession, with a Standard and a Cross, traveling through the principal streets and the large Plaza, followed by a great concourse of Indians, all joining the children's chorus in singing as they march. The services which follow at the beautiful Cathedral of San Gregorio are attended by all this multitude, and many families of Spaniards besides.

On one day of the Easter Season, all the poor of the community are especially invited to attend services, following which the Indian women serve them a repast of whatever they are able to provide, which usually includes a chicken (turkey) which the Spaniards call fowl of the Indies.

The congregation of the church then makes gifts to the poor, such as rebozos for their women, and other items of clothing. These gifts also include coins of a real (*one-eighth peso*) each, or beans of cacao, which still pass for money among these people.

After these gifts are distributed, a sermon is delivered in the Indian language, directed as much to the donors as to the poor who receive the gifts. Afterwards all return to their homes consoled, especially so the Indian women who prepare such delectable food for the poor in the name of Christ our Lord. I must confess that on occasions when I have been present at these so Christian festivals, it has been motive for yet deeper devotion in me to witness the devotion of these women, who include the very principal ones of their Nation, when so happily distributing of their choicest possessions to the blind, the leperous, the crippled and the aged, all of whom attend this festival in great numbers.

There remains to write of the celebration of communion which is frequently held in this same church of San Gregorio, to which church His Saintliness has conceded special permission to celebrate certain unusual festivals which help to win the interest of the poorer Indians, who are those most restless during these days. By the mercy of God, the pagan festivals formerly held in the City of Mexico have been discontinued; however, that the Indians may join with greater pleasure in our own spiritual celebrations, our students of the College of San Gregorio during the Easter season present talks on religious themes, in the Aztec language, as well as Indian dances accompanied by instrumental music and vocal chorus, for all of which the students have been carefully trained.

I shall tell here of a particular festival which is most attractive, as well as novel for persons coming from Spain or other countries, which is called the Dance of the Emperor Moctezuma. This (*mitote*) dance, once performed for their pagan people, now is dedicated to the King of Kings, Christ our Lord.

The most singular feature of this festival is the manner of dress and adornment of the dancers, this dress being in the style worn by the ancient Aztec Princes. This includes a mantle thrown over the right shoulder, and tied in a rosette at the top of the shoulder. This mantle consists of an outer fold of fine transparent cloth which covers another underneath, this latter embroidered with beautiful and colorful flowers and other designs. On the heads of the dancers are placed pyramid shaped diadems covered with gold and precious stones, in the manner of those worn by their Emperors. On their left upper arms the dancers wear bracelets, from which are fastened large clusters of bright green feathers, of those much esteemed by the Indians. In the same hand is carried another cluster of these bright plumes, which are waved to the compass of the dance. In the right hand they carry what is called by them an *ayacaztli,* which is a small brightly painted gourd filled with pebbles, which when shaken produces an agreeable sound. The body is further adorned with a highly embellished doublet worn about the waist, together with trousers of two coverings of the same material as the mantle. To complete their attire they wear sandals which are richly adorned, to further enhance the gaiety and gallantry of their costume.

The area in which the dance is held is strewn with flowers, at one end their being placed the throne of Moctezuma. This seat or throne is in the manner of a low stool or taboret, and is painted red in color. To one side of this theater area is located a table, upon which is placed a small drum which in their language is called (*Teponoztli*). This drum guides all the music and dance. Their music is to be sure very different from that of Europe.

This drum is of the finest hardwood, apt to be red in color, and is built with two little boards at its opposite ends, these forming a hollow space underneath. The drum is beaten with two sticks covered with rubber.

To the instruments above described the Spaniards have added some of their own, including harp, trumpet and bassoon.

About the table where rests the drum are gathered the oldest and most distinguished of the Mexicans (*Aztecs*), who intone the chant or song which always accompanies their dances. These older Indians dance with slow and dignified step, but with little movement of the body.

Those participating in the central dance are usually fourteen in number, besides the dancer who impersonates the Emperor Moctezuma. This latter figure appears towards the close of the dance, moving with every demonstration of modesty. His dress is similar to that of the others, but more rich in material and more highly ornamented. Following the Emperor closely comes a child bearing a great cluster of bright plumage, which while the Emperor is dancing is held over the latters head in the manner of a canopy. Two other children accompany the Emperor, one on either side and a step forward, sweeping a path before him, and now and again strewing flowers in this path.

The appearance of the Emperor is heralded by music and singing. The song translated runs somewhat like this: "Appear, Mexicans; dance Tocontin, for we now have with us the King of Glory."

The three syllables of the word To-con-tin are sung to the rhythm of the beating of the drum. For this reason the entire dance is sometimes given the name of Tocontin.

The remaining dancers appear in two rows, as in the Spanish hacha. The movement of their dance is always slow and dignified, including not only the feet, but arms and hands, always waving in the same motion the long clusters of plumes and shaking their ceremonial gourds with rattles.

The object which they wave may be either of feathers, or of branches covered with aromatic flowers.

At the end of this group dance each dancer takes his position to await the coming of the Emperor. The person representing the Emperor then advances with majestic dignity to take his place on the bias or throne, while all others maintain the rhythm of the dance. Upon the Emperor being seated, the others dance before him, giving such demonstrations of obeisance and humility that it seems they might sink through the earth at his feet.

This formality concluded, the dancers change to a more lively tempo, still performing before their Emperor. It should be noted that these dancers now render reverence instead before the most Sacred Sacrament at the altar.

After the dancers have performed for a little time, the Emperor arises to perform a dance, always accompanied by the three children, the one maintaining the gay canopy overhead, while the other two continue to sweep his path and cover it with flowers. As the Emperor dances, the others too move their bodies gently in such perfect rhythm that they all appear to move as one. During the dance of the Emperor, all other persons in attendance are standing at their proper stations, bowing deeply before him.

Finally the Emperor passes, still dancing, between the two rows of dancers, with an instrument which he carries touching the feet of each, to illustrate their submission before him. His dance finished, the Emperor again takes his seat, and the group of dancers continue performing much as they had before, in a fashion which although repeated never seems tiring to witness.

This Dance of the Emperor, with its accompaning music and vocal chorus, and its participants so gaily adorned, is of a novelty that has given pleasure to many persons of high degree, including Nobles and Archbishops who have come from Spain to see it performed. There are other dances performed by Indian vassals and slaves, but these are more vulgar (*common*) in nature. That which has just been described is now often imitated by sons of the principal Spanish families living in Mexico.

CHAPTER 8

The Story of the Indian Lorenzo

THE STORY OF THE MINISTRY of the church to the Spaniards living in this great and noble Republic of New Spain is material for a pen more elegant and erudite than mine. My story has been of the Indian Nations, begun with the most remote Nations of this great land, approaching with each chapter nearer to the center of the Empire, which is the City of Mexico, where the great Emporer Moctezuma reigned. This city the Spaniards found populated by immense numbers of Indians. It is still, despite great depreciation in population, a city of many people.

The City of Los Angeles (*San Angel*) near Mexico City, is the home of many of the most distinguished Spanish families of New Spain. Here has been built a very beautiful Cathedral, and a residence for the presiding Bishop. There are located here also two Colleges of the Company, both of which offer extensive courses to the young men of Spanish families.

There is a separate church for the Indian families of the community, in which preach Padres who must be well versed in the Indian language. In this place, as in others over the world, the Padres are most zealous in attending to the welfare of the native people, omitting no effort in serving them. As I have previously written of the lives of many distinguished Spanish Padres, so now I wish to write in the concluding chapters of this history, of an Indian Padre, who might well be considered to be a perfect product of such a church environment as we have just described, and an example for the Christian Indians of other Nations to follow.

Lorenzo, for so he was called, was born in the great City of Mexico, of a very noble family of the Aztec Nation. At a tender age he entered the Seminary of our College at Tepotzotlán, that he might learn to read and write, and serve in the church there.

So outstanding was his talent in letters, that he became a master teacher, serving in this capacity for more than forty years in the Seminaries of Tepotzotlán, San Gregorio and Mexico City. Such was his renown, that the most distinguished Indian families, as much Aztecs as Otomíes, placed their children under his care, to be taught not only reading and writing, but all the virtues of living known to the highest Spanish families.

Don Lorenzo was an eminent teacher of the courtly and reverential form of the Aztec language. Being himself of noble lineage, his knowledge of their elegant forms of expression was of the highest, so much so that many Padres studied under him to achieve perfection in its use.

He was a man renowned for his moral virtue. So satisfied was he with his services and teaching that he never married, although there were ample opportunities for him to do so, and with women of high standing and ample resources.

Don Lorenzo seemed to find his greatest happiness in the service of his church, dedicating himself especially to the beautification and perfection of church grounds and buildings. In Tepotzotlán he took particular pleasure in growing an extensive flower garden for the decoration of several nearby churches. When flowers were not in season in the Valley of Mexico, he would send fifty or sixty miles away, into the more temperate lands, for flowers to be brought by carriers to Mexico City.

He took particular care to see that the church of Tepotzotlán was gaily decorated for the Mass said in honor of the Conception of Our Lady the Virgin. So that his Indian disciples should form the highest possible concept of this celebration, he would add certain of his own reflections to the sermon, in the elegant form of the Aztec language.

He also caused the pupils of the Seminary to act out the principal biblical scenes, the children being richly adorned in what don Lorenzo conceived to be the manner of dress of those ancient days. These pageants became so famous that Spaniards, as well as Indians, came from afar to enjoy them.

Into these pageants he incorporated the mitote dances made famous by the great Emperor Moctezuma, employing in them the dancers of the Aztec peoples. In these dances, however, he took care to express the abomination felt for the cruel sacrifices of so many thousands of people before the coming of the Padres.

The devotion of the good Lorenzo was not limited to oratory, flowers and pageantry. His labors began with his arising at three in the morning, and ended far after dark.

His confessions manifested such a perfect conscience that his confessors were amazed, and sometimes even disturbed, as to how to respond to them.

Without being ordained a priest, he practiced all the virtues of priesthood. I can serve as a witness to this fact, as he was for some years under my direction in the College of the Company in Mexico City.

Although of Indian nobility, his vestment was ever of the most simple. He steadfastly refused gifts from grateful parents of his many disciples. If ever he requested material aid from his own Indian Nation, it was for such purposes as the celebration of feasts in the church, or for its improvement and decoration.

A virtue unusual in this Indian was that he steadfastly refused the use of liquor. He even refused the chocolate drink so commonly used in his country.

In his attitude toward the mothers of his pupils, as well as other women, he maintained always a dignified and unfailing courtesy and composure, being much respected by them for his exceeding virtue.

This same nobility and dignity he maintained in his relations with the outside world, as when marketing in the Tianguis for the food supplies for his pupils.

So admired and respected was he by his own people, that when some emergency arose in relations between them and the Spanish rulers, don Lorenzo was immediately dispached to mediate the problem.

It was a great source of comfort to this fine Indian, that before his death, which came at sixty years, he was ordained to the priesthood by the Padre Provincial of New Spain, the highest honor to which this venerable man could have aspired.

Forty years had don Lorenzo, now Padre Lorenzo, labored in the service of the Company. At his burial he was given the burial ceremony ordained for priests, there being present multitudes of his Indian and Spanish friends, as well as his many disciples, all of whom rejoiced in the rare honor which he had received, and which he so richly deserved.

CHAPTER 9

Jesuit Padres Martyred in Florida

ALL OF THIS HISTORY has to do with the employment of Padres of our Company among the savage Nations of New Spain. Although there has been told principally of the period of early colonization and Christianization of the Indians of the Province of Sinaloa, the Sierras of Topia, and the great desert Plateau, to complete our story there must be told of the first ventures of our Padres into the land of Florida, which resulted in the martyrdom of nine members of our Company.

It should be known that Florida is a remote part of the continent bordering on New Spain. It was discovered, and even explored to a limited extent, soon after the conquest of New Spain, beginning in 1519.

There has been told of the remarkable journey of Cabeza de Vaca and his three companions, over a period of ten years, in which, being sole survivors of an expedition of Pánfilo de Narvaez in 1527, they found their way across the entire continent, until encountering other Spaniards in the unexplored Province of Sinaloa.

The story of the nine Padres martyred in Florida was recorded by Padre Juan Rogel of our Company.

In the year 1566 don Pedro Menendez, Governor of Havana, requested that some of our Padres accompany an expedition to Florida, where there had been opened a few small ports, and some Presidios erected.

It was agreed between Felipe II, King of Spain, and Padre Francisco Borja, Director General of the Company at that time, that twenty four Padres would be assigned to this undertaking. The first of these, Padres Pedro Martinez, Juan Rogel, and Brother Francisco de Villareal, sailed to Florida in a Flemish ship, in a squadron which included several other vessels. They first landed on the east coast of Mexico, then sailed for a port named Saint Augustine in Florida.

The pilot of the sloop in which the Padres sailed became lost, searching the coastline for thirty days, without finding Saint Augustine. Finally Padre Martinez requested to be set ashore, to ascertain the language and tribe of Indians seen there. The Indians proved hostile, and setting upon this well-meaning Padre, they murdered him. These savages were worshippers of idols, which they kept in a manner of temple in a little pueblo which had been named Carlos by the Spaniards.

The Flemish sloop returned to Havana to give an account to the Governor of the misfortune which had befallen them. The Governor then requested Padre Juan Rogel to return to Florida, but to limit his labors to the vicinity of a small Presidio that had been erected near the pueblo of Carlos.

The Governor, on a voyage to New Spain, had met an Indian Cacique who had gone to Mexico City in the company of some Dominical Friars. While there he had requested to become a Christian, a request so pleasing to the Viceroy, don Luis Velasco the First, that he had served as Godfather at the baptism. The Indian, in honor of the Viceroy, was christened with the name of Luis.

After various adventures, this Indian Luis arrived in Spain, where, filled with zeal for the conversion of the people of this man, Padre General Francisco Borja recommended that he be returned with the second expedition, now of eight Padres, which was under the direction of Padre Juan Bautista de Segura. Departing from San Lucar in Spain, they arrived safely this time at Saint Augustine on the coast of Florida.

The Padres were soon deserted by the Indian Luis, on a pretext of going to visit relatives in a nearby village. Desperately short of provisions, the Padres were finally forced to wander through the swamps and forests in search of fruits and herbs.

In this manner they sustained themselves for a period of six months. The Padre Luis de Quirós finally went to the pueblo of the Indian Luis, who had given himself up to a life of drunkeness and licentiousness, to plead for help in this extremity in which they found themselves. The treacherous Luis pretended friendship, asking Padre Quirós to return to the others with a message that help would be sent them.

That same night this Indian, accompanied by several others, overtook the Padre where he was sleeping and murdered him. They then continued to where the other Padres were encamped along the seashore, at first pretending friendliness, until well in their midst, when they fell upon and murdered them also, beating them to death with their war clubs.

So were sacrificed those eight Padres who had spent precious years in preparation for laboring in behalf of those brutal savages, with no other satisfaction than that of having perished as martyrs for their God. The names of those who died, in addition to Padre Luis de Quirós, were Gabriel Gomez,

Sancho de Ceballos, Juan Bautista Méndez, Pedro de Linares, Cristobal Redondo and Gabriel Solís.

Only a young boy named Alonsico, son of a Spanish father and an Indian mother, was spared, he being the one who later gave account of the tragedy.

Many months later a ship came in search of the lost Padres. Upon approaching land, seeing no sign of them, they became suspicious. The traitor Luis, who was then living at the former camp of the missionaries, caused some of his companions among the Indians to parade along the shore in the garb of the murdered Padres. The Spaniards still did not disembark, whereupon two of the Indians swam out to the ship. Here they were seized by the Spaniards, who soon secured from them a confession of what had happened.

Taking the two Indian prisoners with them, the ship sailed for Havana. Upon approaching the harbor, one of the Indians sought to escape by leaping from the vessel, and was drowned. The other Indian was confessed and hanged.

Incensed at what had happened, the Governor of Havana led an expedition with some soldiers, accompanied by the Padres Juan Rogel and Francisco de Villareal, to search out the traitors. They did not find the Indian Luis, but captured ten others, including the half-Indian boy Alonsico. He having described what had happened, was cleared of culpability, but the others were hung from the yard-arm of the ship, after having been confessed.

It is to be hoped that the martyred Padres at least had the satisfaction of seeing their murders confessed, that they might perhaps be sent to join the Padres in Heaven.

This divine harvest of martyrs of our Company in Florida was to be followed later by those of whom we have told in the Province of Sinaloa and the Sierras of Topia.

CHAPTER 10

The End Cannot Yet be Written

THE VALUE OF HISTORY lies in presenting the exact truth, and this I have endeavored to do in this writing. What I must now write in conclusion, is that this history is neither perfect nor complete; not perfect because I doubt my ability to have made it so; not complete because the story continues to unfold, and the end cannot yet be written.

The fervor which fires the hearts of the sons of the Company of Jesus burns unabated, and they more and more busy themselves in the salvation of the souls of countless thousands of humble Indians who still remain in a state of spiritual darkness. It is the destiny of our Ministers to search them out and bring to them the Evangelism of Jesus, even though it may be at the cost of our own lives. In the sacrifice of life, the Redeemer of the World has set us a glorious example.

I do not cease to ponder at the immensity of the task that lies before us, in the conversion of yet unnown multitudes of people still savage, fierce, and uncultured, as were those of whom this history relates. God has preserved this glorious task for the Catholic Spaniards of the civilized world. Our blessed monarch, Felipe Cuarto, has in this year of 1644, ordered populated the remote land of the Californias. To the north of the great Province of Sinaloa there remain endless Indian Nations to be discovered and converted to our faith. Each day we are bringing out of spiritual darkness native Indians from the wilds of Peru and Paraguay. In just the past two years our Company has discovered hosts of unknown savages along the borders of the River Paraná in South America.

Turning from the continents of the Americas: In the Islands of the Filipinas, which are, in a manner of speaking, another colony of New Spain, we are constantly bringing evangelism to more savage people. Not only in the New World of the Americas, but in the great Nations of the Orient; Japan and the Great Kingdom of China, there are hordes of people still to be reached.

And who has given life to and multiplied these millions of people but our own God and Creator. He it was who declared that He had multiplied the Nations of the Earth, and to what purpose, and it is now worthy of note that the promises of God are being fulfilled.

I have told in this history of the abundant harvest of souls that has been made in the Nations of which have been written. It becomes the task of others to continue the relation of this glorious undertaking as it unfolds into the future.

What I have written, the enterprises I have referred to, together with he who writes them, are placed as an offering at the feet of Our Divine Lord, pleading that the defects of my telling may be forgiven, and their substance be accepted as an humble offering of the least of His servants. Under the banner and protection of our Divine Captain, Jesus, by happy fate we may be permitted to continue to more glorious endeavors, it being our hope to finally reside with God in Heaven through eternity.

PADRE ANDRÉS PÉREZ DE RIBAS
Provincial of the Company of
Jesus in New Spain
Año Domino 1644

ACKNOWLEDGMENTS

I wish here to express my gratitude to Licenciado Raul Cervantes Ahumada for introducing me to this history.

Thanks also to my wife, Dorothy, for her encouragement and assistance in typing the original draft; to Terry Sullivan for many of the photographs that appear in the book; and to our friend, Mrs. Helen Melrose Niemann, for the final editing and typing.

Tomás A. Robertson
San Miguel Village
Ensenada, Baja California
Mexico
1967

INDEX